# THE
# GOSPEL
# KINGDOM

*John Taylor*

1852

# THE
# GOSPEL
# KINGDOM

Selections from the Writings
and Discourses of

## JOHN TAYLOR

*Third President of The Church of
Jesus Christ of Latter-day Saints*

Selected, Arranged, and Edited,
with an Introduction
by
G. HOMER DURHAM

BOOKCRAFT
Salt Lake City, Utah

# NOTES ON SOURCES AND ABBREVIATIONS

The materials appearing in this work have been taken from the sources listed below, using throughout the abbreviations noted, unless otherwise shown. The sermons of John Taylor appearing in the *Journal of Discourses* (1851-1886) were reported by G. D. Watt, J. V. Long, David W. Evans, John Irvine, James Taylor, J. Q. Cannon, Julia Young, and George F. Gibbs. We owe much to these pioneer stenographers, as the preface to volume nineteen says: "Years shall enhance the interest of these volumes as a library of reference and repository of truth." The authorship of editorials attributed to John Taylor has been verified by the practice of the Church Historian's Office, as well as by internal evidences.

Key to Abbreviations:

*D. & C.*—Doctrine & Covenants.

*DHC—The Documentary History of the Church*, Period 1 —Joseph Smith (6 vols.) ; Apostolic Interregnum (vol. 7).

*DN—The Deseret News* (Salt Lake City: 1850-............).

*GG*—John Taylor, *The Government of God* (Liverpool; Published by S. W. Richards, 15 Walton Street, 1852; 118 pp.)

*IP*—John Taylor, *Items on Priesthood* (Salt Lake City: n. d., 43 pp.)

*JD—Journal of Discourses* (26 vols., 1851-1886).

*JH*—Journal History of the Church (mss., Historian's Office, Salt Lake City, 1830-............).

*M—On Marriage* (Salt Lake City: Official Declaration by John Taylor, President of the Church of Jesus Christ of Latter-day Saints, n. d., 8 pp.)

*MA*—John Taylor, *The Mediation and Atonement of Our Lord and Savior Jesus Christ* (Salt Lake City: The Deseret News Publishing Co., 1892, 205 pp.)

*MS—The Latter-day Saints' Millennial Star* (Liverpool: 1840-............).

*PD—Three Nights' Public Discussion Between the Reverends C. W. Cleeve, James Robertson and Philip Carter, and John Taylor of the Church of Jesus Christ of Latter-day Saints, at Boulogne-Sur-Mer, France* (Liverpool: published by John Taylor, 1850, 49 pp.)

*TS—The Times and Seasons* (Nauvoo, Illinois: edited by
John Taylor, November 15, 1842, February 15,
1846).

References to *The Wasp* (weekly newspaper, Nauvoo, edited
by John Taylor, December 10, 1842, until May 3, 1843, when
it became the *Neighbor*) ; *The Nauvoo Neighbor* (founded and
edited by John Taylor and Wilford Woodruff, May 3, 1843;
ceased publication on October 4, 1845) ; and *The Mormon* (New
York City, a weekly newspaper founded by John Taylor and
edited by him from February 17, 1855 to May 30, 1857), are
shown by name, with the page and date of issue.   This volume is
not the place for compiling historical utterances on the plural
marriage question, hence the historian and other students will note
the absence of the "Taylor-Colfax Discussion" from the above
list, as well as some notable discourses to be found in the *Journal
of Discourses.*   Such material must wait for suitable historical
treatment in another work.—*GHD.*

# HIGHLIGHTS

## IN THE OFFICIAL MINISTRY

### of

## JOHN TAYLOR

1808—November 1: Born at Milnthorpe, Westmoreland County, England, the son of James and Agnes Taylor.

1832—Emigrated from England first to Brooklyn and Albany, New York, finally taking up residence in Toronto, Canada.

1836—May 9: Baptized a member of the Church of Jesus Christ of Latter-day Saints.

1838—July 8: Called to the apostleship by revelation to the Prophet Joseph Smith (D. & C. section 118).

1838—December 19: Ordained an apostle by Brigham Young and Heber C. Kimball.

1839—August 8: Left Nauvoo, Illinois, for a mission to England.

1840—January 11: Arrived in Liverpool.
He introduced the gospel into Ireland and the Isle of Man, extending his labors into Scotland.

1841—July 1: Arrived in Nauvoo, Illinois, from his completed mission in England.

1841—October: Appointed with Elias Higbee as a committee to petition Congress for a redress of wrongs in Missouri. He was appointed by the Prophet Joseph Smith to present the petition.

1842—November 15, 1842, to February 15, 1846: Editor of the *Times and Seasons*.
Nauvoo city councilman.
Regent of the University of Nauvoo.
Judge Advocate of the Nauvoo Legion.

1843—May 3, 1843, to October 29, 1845: Editor of the *Nauvoo Neighbor*.

1844—June 27: Seriously wounded by the same mob which killed the Prophet Joseph and his brother, the Patriarch Hyrum Smith, at Carthage, Illinois.

1846—Assisted in organizing the Mormon Batallion at Winter Quarters.

1846—October 3: Arrived in England for a second mission.

1847—Returned with a number of British emigrating Saints, and arrived in the Salt Lake valley in late fall.

1849—March 12: Chosen one of the associate judges of the Supreme Court of the Provisional State of Deseret.

1849—October: Called on a mission to France.

1851—Published in the papers *Etoile Du Deseret* and *Zion's Panier* in Paris and Hamburg, respectively.

1851—Completed manuscript of *The Government of God.*

1852—Book of Mormon translated into French and German under his direction and published in Paris and Hamburg.

1852—August 20: Arrived in Salt Lake City after completing European mission.

1854—Elected a member of the Territorial Legislature, but subsequently resigned to fill a mission in New York and preside over the Eastern States Mission.

1855—February 17, 1855, to September 19, 1857: Published the *Mormon* in New York City.

1857—Called home at the coming of Johnston's army.
Speaker of the House of Representatives, Utah Territorial Legislature, for five successive sessions after 1857, member until 1876.

1877—Elected Territorial Superintendent of Schools, an office later abolished by Act of Congress in 1887.

1880—October 10: Sustained as President of the Church.

1882—Completed manuscript of *The Mediation and Atonement of Our Lord and Savior Jesus Christ.*

1884—May 17: Offered the dedicatory prayer at the Logan Temple.

1885—February 1: Made last public appearance and withdrew to voluntary exile in view of anti-polygamy laws and persecutions thereunder.

1887—July 25: Died at Kaysville, Davis County, Utah, aged 78 years, 8 months, 25 days.

# CONTENTS

## BOOK ONE

### SOME LATTER-DAY SAINT PHILOSOPHY

*Chapter*                                                                 *Page*

## BOOK THREE

### PRIESTHOOD: THE GOVERNMENT OF GOD

BOOK FIVE

THE KINGDOM OF GOD AND THE KINGDOMS OF MEN

## BOOK SIX

### SOME PERSONAL REFLECTIONS AND FOOTNOTES
### TO HISTORY

# FOREWORD

The family of the late Elder G. Homer Durham (1911-1985) of the Presidency of the First Quorum of the Seventy (1981-1985) of The Church of Jesus Christ of Latter-day Saints is pleased that Bookcraft has selected *The Gospel Kingdom* to inaugurate a distinguished series of republications of significant Latter-day Saint works that will thereby be made available anew to readers interested in the doctrines and history of the Restoration. Elder Durham's association with Bookcraft extended over forty years and included an ongoing friendship and deep respect for Bookcraft's founder, the late John Kenneth Orton. These feelings of respect and affection continue to this day between our two families and extend to many others of the Bookcraft "family."

Elder Durham's purpose was "to collect and arrange within a single volume the representative substance of John Taylor's thought." Published initially in 1943, *The Gospel Kingdom* is the product of a skilled thirty-two-year-old compiler and arranger who had worked with his remarkable father-in-law, Elder John A. Widtsoe of the Council of the Twelve, in preparing *Gospel Standards* (1941), a collection of the teachings and discourses of President Heber J. Grant. Elder Richard L. Evans, then of the First Council of the Seventy and subsequently of the Council of the Twelve, had also directed Elder Durham in the production of *Gospel Standards*. The introduction to *The Gospel Kingdom* includes a beautiful tribute to Elder Evans as well as a sincere acknowledgment of the contribution of our mother and Elder Durham's life's love and companion—Eudora Widtsoe Durham. Elders Widtsoe, Evans, and Durham would subsequently collaborate on *Gospel Ideals* (1953), a selection from the writings and discourses of President David O. McKay. Bookcraft would also publish another Durham compilation, *The Discourses of Wilford Woodruff* (1946).

A student of government, Elder Durham earned the first Ph.D. in political science awarded by the University of California, Los Angeles (1939). In 1943 he was a faculty member in political science at the Utah State Agriculture College (now Utah State University). The years during which *The Gospel Kingdom* was being prepared were years of war, upheaval, and extraordinary challenge. President John Taylor's teachings—whether about the

gospel of Christ, priesthood, the kingdom of God and the kingdoms of men, or other topics—are the thoughts of a prophet of
God whose own life spanned most of the nineteenth century. This
compilation, produced during the threatening years of World
War II when many despaired of civilization as it had been, is now
republished and presented to a generation meeting our own
human challenges as we enter the fifth decade of the nuclear age.
In young Homer Durham's words from the Introduction:

> The "dynamite" in these pages, if any, is of the constructive
> variety, producing better homes, communities, factories,
> hospitals, schools, social stability; not the destructive, war-
> ring type, bent on wrecking the institutions and hopes of
> others.

Our task is unchanged from President John Taylor's counsel
(*Journal of Discourses* 23:324):

> We are here to do the will of God, to build up the kingdom of
> God, and to establish the Zion of God.

GEORGE HOMER DURHAM II

November 1986

# INTRODUCTION

The purpose of this book has been to collect and arrange within a single volume the representative substance of John Taylor's thought. As the note on sources indicates, materials have been compiled from his own written works as well as from the mass of extemporaneous sermons printed in the *Journal of Discourses*. Of the men who have, in turn, been president of the Church of Jesus Christ of Latter-day Saints, such books now appear for five: Joseph Smith, Brigham Young, Joseph F. Smith, Heber J. Grant, and now, John Taylor. As the gap between Joseph Smith and the present is slowly filled, Mormonism will become better understood, both by its adherents and its outside observers. The messages of the men who have been presidents, to date, overlap, in point of time, to considerable degree. This volume, for example, draws on the entire published record of John Taylor's works, embracing Mormon history from the Nauvoo period until 1887. It contains materials, accordingly, which ante- and post-date the utterances in *The Discourses of Brigham Young* by ten years, illuminates that volume, and serves as a connecting link between the past and the present in unique fashion, primarily because John Taylor was a writer as well as a speaker.

In this present compilation, so far as possible, materials have been allowed to fall into the categories their subject matter appears to dictate. Throughout, sincere effort has been made to achieve some systematic arrangement without violating the essential meaning intended. Chapters have been divided into sections and paragraphs, all titles and sub-titles having been added by the compiler. For convenience, chapters have been grouped to compose "books," six of which appear as shown in the table of contents.

Whatever path-breaking ideas the work may convey to the present generation of readers will undoubtedly begin to appear in Book III, "Priesthood—The Government of God," rising to climactic proportions in Book IV, "The Kingdom of God," and Book V, "The Kingdom of God and the Kingdoms of Men." In this, the heart of the volume, may be found the application of the Latter-day Saint philosophy embraced in the earlier portion of the work, to the stirring questions of social organization and political and economic life. These were fields of favorite interest with John Taylor, it seems, both by choice and because these questions were thrust upon him for answer and treatment not only by Joseph and Brigham, but also by events of his lifetime. He served as a missionary in continental Europe at the time its nations were convulsed and beset with the revolutions of 1848 and the question of "legitimacy." He responded with his notable work, *The Government of God*, and later, the discourse on "Legitimacy" (the Mormon theory thereof) as found in this work. Five months before John Taylor's death, the Church of Jesus Christ of Latter-day Saints, as a corporate entity, was abolished, dissolved by Act of the Congress of the United States! The third president of the church had ample cause, foreign and domestic, to contemplate the meaning and role of government in the good society!

With the Manifesto of 1890 and the subsequent restoration of properties (by Joint Resolution of Congress, 1893) and corporate status to the church it was natural to expect new and different emphases. In an advancing age of technology such would be the normal expectation from any institution or society, let alone one professing to be guided by modern revelation. Such emphases continually appear. Yet, the student who scans these pages, line by line, will find that the essential principles upon which older practices and new developments have been reconciled are essentially as much a part of John Taylor's thought, John Taylor who died July 25, 1887, as they are of those who have since succeeded him. The same could be said of Joseph Smith or Brigham Young.

This does not change the fact that John Taylor viewed his church and the priesthood he held as the kingdom and government of God on earth, respectively. *If* this book has a contribution to make to Mormon literature, it will have been in clarifying and defining those concepts for a generation who may have largely forgotten their unique content and development.

It is clear to anyone who makes a deep-rooted study of Mormon history that the key to understanding lies in thoroughly understanding the idea of the Restoration of the gospel in relation to the concept of the kingdom of God, and in understanding the relationship of the church as a society of believers to the social and political institutions neighbor to it, particularly those of the United States. A long line of documents punctuates this relationship and the Mormon effort at reconciliation: Section 134 of the Doctrine and Covenants (1835); "The Political Motto of the Church" (1838); a series of U. S. Supreme Court decisions from Reynolds v. U. S. (1878) to U. S. v. Late Corporation of the Church of Jesus Christ of Latter-day Saints (1893); the Reed Smoot investigation (4 volumes) before the United States Senate; the official *Address To The World* (1907); recent circulars, in war time, of the First Presidency; as well as a century's string of statements about "the inspired Constitution" and the Twelfth Article of Faith.

*The Gospel Kingdom* will add some illumination to this

history for many, as a by-product of its doctrinal teachings. For example "Did the Mormons seek to overthrow the United States government?" What a question! If nothing else, these sermons and writings of John Taylor give the lie to that ancient controversy, long since happily settled. At the same time, these pages will demonstrate the thinking by means of which a freedom-loving group strived to be loyal—even to a government that dissolved their corporation—while yet advancing the purposes and ideals of a "more perfect" society as they conceived it. The "dynamite" in these pages, if any, is of the constructive variety, producing better homes, communities, factories, hospitals, schools, social stability; not the destructive warring type, bent on wrecking the institutions and hopes of others.

John Taylor helped drive sturdy stakes in the settlement of the American west. The Mormons had been forced into isolation for their own safety. Called to the leadership of the group after 1877, John Taylor *might* be said to represent the apogee of Mormon isolation in America—although his world and domestic views belie this! Even so, he laid forth the bases for future adjustments of Mormon society with the American and the world community, as well as showing forth the line and plummet for "the gospel kingdom." He was a great man, a great leader; a political as well as a religious philosopher, well worthy of the American tradition. As he was titled in Nauvoo, he might well remain known as "The Champion of Liberty."

\* \* \*

Certain freedoms have been taken with punctuation and spellings appearing in the original sources. Portions of some selections have been deleted, some of great length, others of only a word. All omissions are shown uniformly by a line of three dots (. . .). No effort has been made to "edit" the work for accuracy of statement or to "bring it up to date." Where reference is made to controversial theories, strict honesty has been observed in letting the mind of John Taylor make and take its own course. Anyone may verify any statement by the mere process of looking up the reference supplied at the conclusion of every selection. It may be noted in passing that John Taylor seems to have been blessed with one of those minds that would not balk at testing and accepting new ideas, provided their "truth" could be established. Other details of the compilation may be gathered from the note on sources.

In the preparation of this volume I have had access to the libraries of the L. D. S. Institute at Logan, Utah, the Utah State Agricultural College, and the Church Historian's Office at Salt

Lake City.  Items concerning John Taylor were also checked at the libraries of Columbia University, and the University of Pennsylvania, during a year's resident teaching at Swarthmore College, Swarthmore, Pennsylvania.

The collaborative experience and techniques developed in the compilation of *Gospel Standards* (1941) led quite naturally to the present volume.  The personal library, experience, and constant assistance of Dr. John A. Widtsoe must again be acknowledged, as detailed in the introduction to the former volume.  For its appearance now, this work is most heavily indebted to Richard L. Evans, of the First Council of the Seventy, and managing editor of *The Improvement Era.*  Like Brigham Young in referring to John Taylor, "I will use a term to suit myself" and state that President Evans is the most careful and painstaking editor that ever edited, as printers from Liverpool to New York to Salt Lake City will testify.  A committee of the Council of Twelve, headed by Joseph Fielding Smith, the Church Historian, also read and criticized the manuscript or galleys, contributing invaluably to the present length and style, as did Dr. Widtsoe, President Evans, and Marba C. Josephson.  Marvin E. Smith and Albert L. Zobell, Jr., and others checked references and assisted in the gathering of fugitive materials at the Historian's Office and at the Widtsoe library.  Eudora Durham assisted notably at all stages of the work and suggested the title, *The Gospel Kingdom.*  Thanks are also due President E. G. Peterson and the administration of Utah State Agricultural College for many courtesies which made the volume and its appearance a possibility. Alten B. Davis, Ethel Nelson, and Ivean Hansen assisted in typing the manuscript.

Finally, John K. Orton deserves the commendation and gratitude of those who will appreciate the addition of these pages to the library of Mormon literature.  Sincere thanks to him and to the Bookcraft Company, for assuming, under most trying circumstances, the responsibility for producing this book.

—G. Homer Durham.

— SECOND EDITION —

The second edition of *The Gospel Kingdom* is identical with the first with the exception of corrections in style and doctrinal items which replace some things of purely historic interest.  Pagination and organization have been maintained uniformly inasmuch as the work has been adopted as a text for the quorums of the Melchizedek priesthood of the Church of Jesus Christ of Latter-day Saints. —G. H. D.

"*With regard to Brother John Taylor, I will say that he has one of the strongest intellects that can be found. He is a powerful man, and we may say that he is a powerful editor. But I will use a term to suit myself and say that he is one of the strongest editors that ever wrote.*"

BRIGHAM YOUNG
*August 31, 1856.*

# BOOK ONE

## SOME LATTER-DAY SAINT PHILOSOPHY

> "... We must be philosophers too, and make it appear that our philosophy is better than theirs and then show them that religion is at the bottom of it."
>
> —JOHN TAYLOR
> *August 22, 1852.*

CHAPTER I

# WHAT IS MORMONISM

## THE MEANING OF MORMONISM

SIGNIFICANCE OF THE TERM.—Mormonism is . . . a revelation from the heavens to man, introducing a new dispensation to the human family, viz.: the *everlasting gospel,* which has been corrupted, transformed and changed. It is the religion that Adam, Enoch, Noah, Melchizedek, Abraham, Lot, Isaac, Jacob, Moses, Jesus, and the apostles had . . . and that Lehi, Nephi, Alma, Moroni, Mormon, and a host of others had. . . . It has its origin from God, and is merely, at present, introductory to the fruition of the hopes of those men of God, who though believing, died "in faith," without the possession, "having seen the promise afar off." It is the living, breathing, energetic, intelligent power; instead of the dead, withered, lifeless, inaminate body or form. It introduces man to a knowledge of himself, shows him his relationship to his fellow man, to the world, to saints, angels, spirits, and to God. It unfolds his origin and destiny, and unlocks the dark, impenetrable future; the heavens are unveiled, and eternity is laid open.

THE ETERNAL VISTA.—Standing upon its broad platform, encircled by the mantle of truth, the man of God, by faith, peers into the future, withdraws the curtains of eternity, unveils the mystery of the heavens, and through the dark vista of unnumbered years, beholds the purposes of the great Elohim, as they roll forth in all their majesty and power and glory. Thus standing upon a narrow neck of space, and beholding the past, present, and the future, he sees himself an eternal being claiming an affinity with God, a son of God, a spark of Deity struck from the fire of his eternal blaze. He looks upon the world and man, in all their various phases, knows his true interests, and with intelligence imparted by his Father Celestial, he comprehends their origin and destiny. Such was the religion of the aforesaid worthies; it was not an idle fable; they knew in whom they believed, and knowing, filled with the spirit of prophecy and revelation, "they spake as they were moved upon by the Holy Ghost." Such also is Mormonism. It is no vain faith, no trite, hackneyed shavelings or priestly, canting creed, that would hang man's destiny over a yawning gulf with a fragile, brittle thread, and threaten him with fiery, liquid flames, pitchforks, gridirons, serpents, and eternal

fires, to frighten him to fear a God whom they describe, the
which he cannot love.

THE MOTIVATION OF THE MORMON.—His intelligence, lit
up by God and followed out, will be expansive as the world and
spread through space; his law is the law of love; his rule, the rule
of right to all. He loves his neighbor, and he does him good; he
loves his God and therefore worships him; he sees the power of
truth, which, like the light of God, spreads through all space,
illuminates all worlds, and penetrates where men or angels, God
or spheres are known; he clings to it. Truth is his helmet,
buckler, shield, his rock, defense; his all in time and in eternity.
Men call him a fool because he cannot be directed by their folly,
nor follow in their erratic, truculent wake. But while they are
grasping at shadows, he lays hold of the substance. While they
are content with a rickety, sprawling religion, fashionable for a
time, but having nothing to do with eternity, and smother the
highest, noblest principles of man, he dare acknowledge God; and
acknowledging him, he dare obey him and confess that faith
which God has given to him. He grasps at all truths, human and
divine. He has no darling dogma to sustain or favorite creed to
uphold. He has nothing to lose but error, and nothing to gain but
truth. He digs, labors, and searches for it as for hidden treasure;
and while others are content with chaff and husks of straw, he
seizes on the kernel, substance, the gist of all that's good, and
clings to all that will ennoble and exalt the human family.

RESTITUTION OF ALL THINGS: SOME CONCRETE MEAN-
INGS.—Such was the religion of the ancients, both upon the continents of Asia and America. The everlasting gospel made known
in the last days is nothing more nor less than the ancient religion
restored. It is the commencement of the "restitution of all things,
spoken of by all the holy prophets since the world was." It is
the bringing back of ancient, eternal principles, whereby men can
know God as they knew him formerly; not a vague fantasy, not
a simple form, but a living reality. Its doctrines, its ordinances,
its principles, its priesthood are from above, revealed from the
heavens, and yet strictly in conformity with all former revelations.
It has not been, it cannot be successfully controverted, either in its
divine authenticity, its doctrines, ordinances, or priesthood. It
is adapted to the wants of the human family, to the world morally,
socially, religiously and politically. It is not a sickly, sentimental,
effeminate plaything; not a ghostly, spiritual, sing-song, ethereal
dream, but a living, sober, matter-of-fact reality adapted to body
and spirit, to earth and heaven, to time and eternity. It enters
into all the ramifications of life. It does not adapt itself to the
philosophy, politics, creeds, and opinions of men, but fashions
them in its divine mold. It cannot be twisted into the multi-

tudinous latitudinarian principles of a degenerate world; but lifts all that are in the world, who will be subject to its precepts, to its own ennobling, exalted and dignified standard. It searches all truth, and grasps at all intelligence. It is the revealed living and abiding will of God to man; a connection between the heavens and the earth. It is nature, philosophy, heavens and earth, time and eternity united. It is the philosophy of the heavens and the earth, of God, and angels, and saints.

Did ancient men of God revel in the truth? So do we. Did they have revelations and visions? So do we. Did they prophesy? So do we. Did God communicate with them? He does with us. Did they prophesy of "the restitution of all things?" We say it is at our doors. Did they prophesy of a kingdom of God? We are helping to build it up. Had they the ministering of angels? So have we. Had they prophets, apostles, pastors, teachers, and evangelists? So have we. Had they the spirit of prophecy and revelation? So have we. Did they look for the second advent and glorious appearance of our Lord and Savior Jesus Christ? So do we. Did they expect that God would purge the wicked out of the earth and introduce a reign of righteousness? So do we. Did they look for Jesus and the saints to reign on the earth? So do we. We are, in fact, looking for all things that they did; seeking to know all things that they knew, and to bring to pass all things that they prophesied of, the great consummation of which is the restitution of all things; and men may lie and rant and rave; they cannot frustrate the designs of God, nor stop the progress of eternal truth one moment—its course is *onward*, ONWARD, ONWARD, and it defies opposition. . . .

The omnipotent power of eternal truth will stand unscathed in the view of gathering hosts, and the nations will know that God rules in the heavens, that Mormonism is not a vague phantasy and wild chimera, but the greatest boon that could be conferred upon man; the offspring of heaven, the gift of the Gods, a celestial treasure, an earthly, heavenly inheritance, a living, abiding, and eternal reality.—*The Mormon*, Vol. 1, No. 23, July 28, 1855.

## TRUE PHILOSOPHY

RELATES MAN AND TRUTH.—What is true philosophy? It seems to me to be a true principle for men to try and find out who they are. I like to examine myself a little, and I sometimes ask who am I? where did I come from? what am I doing here? and what will be the condition of things when I leave here?

If there is anybody who can tell me anything about these things, I want to know. If I had an existence before I came here, I want to know something about it; and if I shall have an 6:823-825, March 1, 1845.

existence hereafter, I want to know what kind of existence it will be. I do not want to be frightened about hell-fire, pitchforks, and serpents, nor to be scared to death with hobgoblins and ghosts, nor anything of the kind that is got up to scare the ignorant. But I want truth, intelligence, and something that will bear investigation. I want to probe things to the bottom and to find out the truth, if there is any way to find it out.—*JD*, 11:317, February 24, 1867.

IS MORMONISM PHILOSOPHICALLY TRUE?—It may be asked: Are all Mormons, then, philosophers?

To this we answer: Not in the general acceptation of the term. Mormonism is philosophically true, but all Mormons are not philosophers—neither do we consider it necessary. A man may understand first principles, without knowing the mysteries. He may also enjoy certain influences and powers and priesthood without being able to define the cause of those operations or their scientific bearings. We have taken the pains to investigate this subject, but the Mormons arrive at conclusions by a much shorter route. The above may be necessary to some. The Mormons know by obedience. They may not all be philosophers, but they know it by inspiration through obedience. A blacksmith can heat iron in a fire, as well as a philosopher; a lady . . . can make bread, without understanding how wheat is raised, dressed, or ground into flour. Nor is it necessary for an elder, who "baptizes for the remission of sins," or "lays on hands for the gift of the Holy Ghost," to understand the philosophy of its operations. They are God's ordinances, and he bestows the blessings promised through obedience to his commands. The blind man might not know much about Jesus nor, be acquainted with the mysticisms and intricacies of Jewish theology; but one thing he knew as well as any theologian, that he "was once blind, but he then could see." The ancient apostles were not all philosophers, but Jesus told them that they should heal the sick and cast out devils in his name. They simply believed him, tried the experiment, and found it effectual; and, when they returned from a mission, reported that even "devils were subject to them in his name," or by his power. This was all they understood about it at that time. They could not tell how the Spirit operated, nor by what invisible agency the devils were subjected or banished; they simply knew it by its effects—just the same as a boy would know that a ball would rebound if struck against a wall or the ground, without knowing the properties of matter or the nature either of resistance, elasticity, or projectile force. A man, under the direction of another, may be able to make an electrical machine and not understand its properties nor the nature and force of electricity. So a man may receive the gospel through faith in testimony. By yielding obedience, by baptism administered by an authorized agent, and having hands laid upon him for the gift of the Holy Ghost by an elder legally qualified, the blessing will follow the administration, whether the person to whom it is administered or the administrator be a philosopher or not. Furthermore, God imparts his philosophy frequently to men of limited abilities. They follow his teachings —the result is, they confound the wise. It is not their philosophy, but God's; but being true to law, it is always obedient thereto. A boat with a hole in it will sink with a good man in it—a sound boat will bear up a wicked man. Telegraphic wires will operate as they are operated upon, and might convey either a revelation of God or of the devil. So, when the apostles were put into communion with God, although illiterate, "they spake as they were moved by the Holy Ghost." Hence they became intelligent and "a mouth and wisdom was given to them that all their adversaries were not able to gainsay nor resist." They had the gift of the Holy Ghost, that brought things past to their remembrance, led them into all truth, and showed them things to come. They had a principle of living revelation, or a living fountain of true eternal principles. Those principles would always overturn the puerile principles of a corrupt philosophy and the ridiculous fantasies of a false religion and vanquish them; they might not always understand why—it was the gift of God to them; but it was philosophical. Such is Mormonism.—*The Mormon,* Vol. 2, No. 3, March 8, 1856.

THE COMPREHENSIVE NATURE OF MORMONISM.—Is there a true principle of science in the world? It is ours. Are there true principles of music, of mechanism, or of philosophy? If there are, they are all ours. Is there a true principle of government that exists in the world anywhere? It is ours, it is God's; for every good and perfect gift that does exist in the world among men proceeds from the "Father of lights with whom there is no variableness, neither shadow of turning." It is God that has given every good gift that the world ever did possess. He is the giver of all good principles,—principles of law, of government, and of everything else, and he is now gathering them together into one place, and withdrawing them from the world, and hence the misery and darkness that begin to prevail among the nations; and hence the light, life, and intelligence that begin to manifest themselves among us.—*JD,* 10:57, May 18, 1862.

THE ENIGMA OF MORMONISM.—Mormonism is an enigma to the world. . . . Philosophy can not comprehend it; it is beyond the reach of natural philosophy. It is the philosophy of heaven; it is the revelation of God to man. It is philosophical, but it is heavenly philosophy, and beyond the ken of human judgment, beyond the reach of human intelligence. They cannot grasp it;

it is as high as heaven; what can they know about it? It is deeper than hell; they cannot fathom it. It is as wide as the universe; it extends over all creation. It goes back into eternity and forward into eternity. It is associated with the past, present, and future. It is connected with time and eternity, with men, angels, and Gods, with beings that were, that are, and that are to come.—*JD*, 15:25, April 7, 1872.

THE STRENGTH OF MORMON DOCTRINE.—I have traveled to preach these doctrines in most of the United States and in the Canadas; I have preached them in England, in Scotland, in Wales, in the Isle of Man and the Jerseys, in France, Germany, in the principal cities of America and Europe, and to many prominent men in the world; and I have not yet found a man that could controvert one principle of Mormonism upon scriptural grounds. —*JD*, 5:239, September 13, 1857.

There is a spirit in man, possessed of so much "divinity," that it will discover truth by its own light; no matter whether it is covered with a "sectarian cloak," or thrown among the rubbish of scoffers.—*TS*, 6:855, April 1, 1845.

## THE ORIGIN OF MORMONISM

COMMITTED FROM THE HEAVENS.—How did this state of things called Mormonism originate? We read that an angel came down and revealed himself to Joseph Smith and manifested unto him in vision the true position of the world in a religious point of view. He was surrounded with light and glory while the heavenly messenger communicated these things unto him, after a series of visitations and communications from the Apostle Peter and others who held the authority of the holy priesthood, not only on the earth formerly but in the heavens afterwards.

That they hold it in the heavens we know from the scriptures. In them there are certain principles revealed in relation to that matter that nobody could reveal unless they were acquainted with the principle of revelation. Moses and Elias were seen with Jesus on the mount, when Peter and his brethren saw them, who said, "Master, it is good for us to be here, let us build three tabernacles, one for thee, one for Moses, and one for Elias." Who was this Moses? He was a man who had officiated before on the earth, had held the holy priesthood, had been a teacher of righteousness, and who, with the elders of Israel, had talked with God, and had received revelations from him, holding the priesthood that administered in time and eternity. When he got through with this world, his official duties were not ended, for he appeared to Jesus, Peter, James, and John upon the mount, to confer on them certain principles, authorities, and priesthood, that they might also be enabled to administer in the ordinances of salvation, and officiate as the representatives of God upon the earth.

And hence, when Joseph Smith came, those who had held the keys before came to him, so he told me and others, and revealed unto him certain things pertaining to the kingdom of God upon the earth, and ordained him and set him apart to the ministry and apostleship unto which he was called.

He presented himself before the world and informed the people that God had spoken, and that he had spoken to him. He told them that the heavens had been opened and that angels clothed in light and glory had appeared to him and revealed unto him certain things. Then we have Oliver Cowdery, who tells us something about these things, and gives his testimony as a living witness. Again, there were eleven witnesses in relation to the Book of Mormon, who testify that the Book of Mormon was a divine revelation from God. And some of these witnesses tell us that an angel of God came and laid before them the plates from which the Book of Mormon was translated, and they knew that their testimony was true and faithful. Others saw and handled the plates from which the record was taken. I have conversed with several of those men who say they have seen the plates that Joseph Smith took out of the Hill Cumorah; I have also conversed with Joseph Smith, who has told me of these things and many more. . . . Here, then, is an abundance of testimony that assumes a supernatural agency—an interposition of the Almighty—an opening and an unfolding of something to the human family with which they have been unacquainted.—*JD*, 10:127-128, March 1, 1863.

NOT THE PRODUCT OF MEN.—Neither Joseph Smith, nor Hyrum Smith, nor Sidney Rigdon, nor Brigham Young, nor myself, nor anybody associated with the Church at the present time, has had anything to do with the origination of these things. This work was commenced by the Almighty; it has been carried on by him, and sustained by his power, and if it is ever consummated it will be by the power and direction and sustenance of the Lord Jehovah, of Jesus, the mediator of the new covenant, and then through the medium of the priesthood here upon the earth. These things originated in the heavens, in the councils of the Gods; and the organization of the priesthood and the power thereof, and everything pertaining thereto, have been committed from the heavens through Joseph Smith, principally, and through others who have been associated with him in this great work.—*JD*, 24:227, 1884.

## THE POSITION OF THE LATTER-DAY SAINTS

THE FUNDAMENTAL QUESTION.—There is one of two things true. We are either laboring under one of the greatest delusions that ever afflicted the human race, or we are under the direction of the great God. There is no half-way business about it. I have said to men where I have been preaching, when they professed to believe me to be honest but deceived, I did not want them to set me down so for I was either right or I was a hypocrite and a deceiver. We know that we have embraced the principles of eternal truth, and we also know that we cannot get rid of them. I tested them thoroughly at the commencement. If I could have overthrown them by truth, I would; but I could not. I had either to embrace Mormonism or acknowledge myself dishonest. I believed, obeyed, and rejoiced in the gospel. Since I received and obeyed the truth, I have never seen anything to cause me to waver. I have examined our religion closely and have found nothing to doubt. Neither has anything crossed my mind in regard to the saints' accomplishing the purposes of the Almighty upon the earth nor that has caused me to fear and tremble, but I have ever felt strong in the Lord God of Israel, and I feel today, as I have felt for the last twenty years.—*JD*, 9:342-343, April 13, 1862.

A STATEMENT OF THE MORMON POSITION.—I am aware of the position that we occupy today. I feel that I am surrounded by a large number of intelligent men and women, and while I am addressing you, I am also addressing the world, for the remarks I make will be reported and published to the world. Therefore, I am desirous to advance such sentiments as will be in accord with the enlightenment of the Latter-day Saints, with the intelligence of the . . . century, and with the principles that have emanated from God.

Any intelligence which we may possess and which we may be able to impart, is not of ourselves, but of God. It did not originate with us; it did not originate with Joseph Smith, with Brigham Young, with the Twelve Apostles, nor was it received from any institution of learning, nor of science, either religious, political, or social. Our philosophy is not the philosophy of the world; but of the earth and the heavens, of time and eternity, and proceeds from God.—*JD*, 23:48, April 9, 1882.

AIMS AND OBJECTS.—Do we expect to immortalize our fame by demolishing cities, wasting countries, and destroying their inhabitants? No. Do we expect to have our name perpetuated by being embalmed and laid by, as the Egyptians were after they died? No. Do we expect to perpetuate our fame by building cities and monuments? No. What then? We expect to perpetuate our fame and our name by living and propagating correct principles—by the establishment of correct laws—by the building up of the kingdom of God—by imbibing and receiving light and intelligence from the living God—by living in the enjoyment of all the blessings that God has in reserve for his saints—by driving back the dark cloud of error and superstition that has overspread the moral horizon of the world—by establishing a nucleus of truth, intelligence, light, morality, philosophy, religion, government, and everything else that is calculated to promote and exalt the human family in time and in all eternity; and then, like some of the ancient patriarchs—like Abraham, Isaac, and Jacob, and many of the ancient saints—enter into the New Jerusalem, and there live with our posterity, our friends, and relations; and then pass on by the eternal laws of progression to associate with the Gods, worlds without end, in all intelligence and perfection, and in promoting the happiness of all beings pertaining to this world and the world that is to come.—*JD*, 8:5-6, February 19, 1860.

"FOR HEAVEN AND HAPPINESS."—So far as I am personally concerned, I am here as a candidate for eternity——for heaven and for happiness. I want to secure by my acts a peace in another world that will impart that happiness and bliss for which I am seeking. If I am driven with my brethren as I have been, I ask myself what is the meaning of it. If I have to pass through afflictions, I wish them to be sanctified to my good.—*JD*, 7:197, November, 1859.

"WE ARE . . . CITIZENS OF THE WORLD."—Some people will say, "You are harsh; you are exclusive; you do not wish to associate and to mix with others." To a certain extent we do, and to a certain extent we do not. To a very great extent we feel very much interested in the welfare and happiness of the human family. I very much question whether greater philanthropy has been developed among any other people under the face of the heavens than among this people. I am at the defiance of anybody, or class of men, or nation, to show that greater sacrifices, so to speak, have been made anywhere than have been made among the elders of this church to promulgate among the people that dwell upon all the earth the things that God has revealed unto them. Can you point out another people who have exhibited the same degree of intelligence, earnestness, and zeal in traveling from nation to nation, from city to city, by land and sea, over mighty oceans and desert wastes, even to the ends of the earth in order to promote the happiness and well being of their fellow men? There are no philanthropical societies existing in the world that have done what the elders of this church have done.

Are we misanthropists? No. We are cosmopolitans, citizens of the world, and have implanted in our bosoms the spirit of the living God, which prompts us to seek for the welfare and happiness of all the human family. All this, and more, we have done, and I very much question whether you can find anybody that would dispute it. They would say we are in error. That they have a right to say, and to think, if they please. But there is not one who can say in truth that we have not done all we claim to have done.—*JD*, 11:55, January 18, 1865.

CHAPTER II

# ETERNALISM

## AN INTERPRETATION OF LIFE

THE VITAL PROBLEMS.—We frequently talk of the advancements made in society and the progression of the world generally in intelligence, in science, in literature. But what is all that to a man when he is about to leave his earthly tenement, to go hence? Of what moment is it to him how bright his genius, or how expansive and varied his learning may be? It makes no difference; he is gone and is apparently helpless and inanimate, at least so far as the body is concerned. We struggle sometimes while we are occupants of these mortal bodies, for riches and position, for fame and honor. We jostle one against another, entertaining various conflicting sentiments, ideas, and theories, but they are all leveled with the balance in the grave. Such has been, and such is the position of the human family.

PURPOSE IN LIFE.—There is a scripture which reads, "And as it is appointed unto men once to die, but after this the judgment" (Hebrews 9:27). If we are to be associated only with this world, if, when this vital spark expires, we end our entire existence, it would be scarcely worth while to pay that attention to its affairs that we do, merely for so short a time. But when we reflect, we are reminded that man is a dual being, possessing a body and a spirit, and that he is associated with this world and the next, that he is connected with time and eternity. It then becomes a matter of more grave and serious importance. These are things which we cannot ignore, even if we would. According to our ideas of things as they have been revealed to us, we had an existence before we came here. We came here to accomplish a certain purpose which was decreed by the Almighty before the world was. We came to receive bodies or tabernacles, and in them to pass through a certain amount of trial in what is termed a probationary state of existence, preparatory to something to be developed hereafter. Hence this world is the state of our probation, and we look forward to the future as something with which we are as much connected as we are with anything pertaining to time. We look forward to another state of existence with that degree of certainty and confidence that we do when we go to bed in the evening expecting to see the light of the sun in the morning, or that we do with anything else that is associated with any of the affairs of this world upon which we place any degree of certainty. Were it not so, it would be, as I have already stated, of very little importance what our struggles were, or what we had to do with in this world.— *JD,* 18:306-307, December 31, 1876.

ETERNITY OF THE GOSPEL.—It has been remarked frequently that we are in eternity, and that we have now begun to live for ever. A great many are at a loss to understand the nature of this eternal life, and how we are connected with eternity. The remarks are certainly novel; and in order to get at the subject, it will be necessary for us to investigate in some measure the meaning of the word eternity. In entering upon this subject, I shall necessarily have to refer to certain remarks which I advanced last Sabbath in relation to the everlasting, unchangeable principles of the gospel; but as every principle pertaining to the gospel of Jesus Christ is eternal, it is all relevant to the subject about which we are now speaking.

The same principles that now exist, in relation to the gospel, existed in the various dispensations that have been in being in the different ages of the world. They existed in the days of Moses, in Enoch's day, and in the days of Adam; and they existed in eternity in the mind of God, before this world rolled into existence, the morning stars sang together, or the sons of God shouted for joy. When we speak of these things we have reference not so much to our existence here on the earth, as we have with regard to principle; principles relative to our coming into existence in this time, to live upon the face of the world a few years. For although we came into corporal existence here, we existed thousands of ages before we came here. We only came here to live on this stage of action, whereon we are to work out our probation, and to prepare ourselves for the eternal courts of glory and a celestial kingdom of God. Time is a short space between, or in, eternity. Eternity existed before time was, and will exist when time will cease; and so did we.—MS, 8:84-85, July 6, 1845.

THE GOSPEL IS EVERLASTING.—What is meant by the everlasting gospel? I know that some people think there was no gospel until Jesus came; but it is a great mistake. Adam, Noah, Abraham, and Moses had the gospel; and when Jesus came he came to offer himself a sacrifice for the sins of the world, and to bring back the gospel which the people had lost. "Well," says one, "do you mean to affirm that the men you have just named had the gospel? I do, and hence it is called the everlasting gospel. "How do you know?" Why, the Scriptures say the gospel held the keys to the mysteries of the revelation of God. Now, Adam was in possession of these things; he was in possession of the spirit of prophecy and revelation. He talked with

God, and it was through the medium of the gospel he was enabled to do it. Enoch also conversed with and had revelations from God, and finally he was not, for God took him. Noah conversed with God, and God told him to build an ark, and gave him revelations about the size of it and the kind of animals he was to introduce into it. And wherever the gospel existed there was a knowledge of God. Moses had the gospel and so had Abraham, and they communicated with Him from time to time. And by what medium was this done? It was through the medium of the Gospel. "Do you mean to affirm," says the objector, "that Moses had the gospel?" Yes, let us take the Bible for it, we all believe in that. In that book we read that "unto us was the gospel preached as well as unto them." We are also told that the gospel was preached to them, but it did not profit them, not being mixed with faith in those who heard it. Therefore the law was added because of transgression. Added to what? Why, the gospel, which the Scriptures say Moses preached to the children of Israel. In the New Testament we read, Galatians, 3rd chapter and 8th verse. "And the Scripture foreseeing that God would justify the heathen through faith, preached before the gospel unto Abraham, saying, in thee shall all nations be blessed." It was through the medium of the gospel that Abraham obtained these promises. Now, some people think the law of Moses, as it is called, was given to the children of Israel as a peculiar kind of a blessing; but it was a peculiar kind of a curse, added because of transgression. It was as Peter said—neither they nor their fathers were able to bear it.

We read also that Jesus came and was a priest for ever after the order of Melchizedek. Who was Melchizedek? He was the man who blessed Abraham, the father of the faithful, yet Melchizedek was greater than Abraham, for verily the lesser is blessed of the greater. For wherever and whenever the gospel has existed there has been the opening of the heavens, revelations and visions given to men; and wherever the gospel has not existed there has been no vision, no revelation, no communication between the heavens and the earth. Hence that which is called the Gospel in the Christian world is not the gospel, but a perversion of it.

When Jesus came he came to do away with the law and to introduce the gospel that their fathers had lost because of transgression. After its restoration by Jesus the same results followed: the heavens were opened, the purposes of God unfolded, and His power made manifest among the people.—*JD*, 13:17-19, March 14, 1869.

ETERNALISM IN HUMAN RELATIONS—Others make their marital relations to end in death; their covenants last only till death does them part. Ours take hold of eternity, they enter into the eternal state of existence, and contemplate an eternal union of the sexes worlds without end.

We believe in the resurrection of the dead and in the life in the world to come; and not only in the resurrection of the male, but also of the female. We believe also in eternal unions, union on earth and in heaven. And as the heavens declare the glory of God, and the stellar universes roll on according to eternal laws implanted in them by the Deity, and perform their revolutions through successive ages, so will man progress and increase—himself, his wives, his children—through the eternities to come.—*JD* 23:65, April 9, 1882.

## ETERNALISM AND EARTH LIFE

THE DOCTRINE OF ETERNALISM.—We are not connected with a something that will exist only for a few years, some of the peculiar ideas and dogmas of men, some nice theory of their forming. The principles that we believe in reach back into eternity. They originated with the Gods in the eternal worlds, and they reach forward to the eternities that are to come. We feel that we are operating with God in connection with those who were, with those who are, and with those who are to come. —*JD,* 17:206, October 7, 1874.

As eternal beings, we existed with our Father in the eternal worlds. We came on this earth, and obtained tabernacles, that, through taking possession of them, and passing through a scene of trial, and tribulation, and suffering, we might be exalted to more glory, dignity, and power than would have been possible for us to obtain had we not been placed in our present position.—*JD,* 1:230-231, April 8, 1853.

EARTH LIFE—ONE STAGE OF EXISTENCE.—We are here for a short time only. Our spirits dwelt with our Father before we came to the earth. In coming here we took upon ourselves bodies according to the decree of the Almighty, and if our bodies are required, it would not be for me or for you to say when or how these things shall be. It is the Lord who directs in all these matters, both in regard to us individually and also in regard to the whole human family.

The present is only one stage of our existence. We existed before we came here; we exist here for a time; and when we depart from this mortal life, we shall have a spiritual existence, an existence without the body, and then again with the body.

And it is for those who manage and manipulate these matters to do as seemeth good in their sight, and it is for us to yield a willing and an obedient submission to the will of our Heavenly Father, feeling always that whatever he does is perfect and right. —*JD*, 22:354-355, January 29, 1882.

We came forth from our Father in heaven, having the privilege of taking bodies in this world. What for? That our bodies and spirits together might accomplish the will of our Heavenly Father, and find their way back again into his presence; that while we are upon the earth, we might be governed by his wisdom, by the intelligence and revelations that flow from him; that he might be a guide and dictator of our steps while we sojourn here; and that we might fill up the measure of our creation in honor to ourselves, in honor to our progenitors, and in honor to our posterity; and finally, find our way back into the presence of God, having accomplished the object for which we came into the world.—*JD*, 1:368, April 19, 1854.

GOD'S INTEREST IN EARTH LIFE.—God has always felt interested in the welfare of the human family. But there are certain eternal laws associated with his economy that have to be carried out, whether in his Church or out of his Church. From the members of his Church he expects a higher state of morality than he does from those that are outside. All men will be judged according to the deeds done in the body, whether they be good or evil. The gospel has been sent to them from time to time. The old disciples were told to go to every nation, kindred, tongue, and people, and proclaim its glad tidings, and the people on this continent had the same testimony delivered among them. In the last days there was another angel to fly in the midst of heaven, having the everlasting gospel to preach to them that dwell on the earth. What gospel? The same gospel that Adam had, the same gospel that Enoch had, the same gospel that Seth and Mahalaleel and Noah had, the same gospel that Abraham, Isaac, and Jacob had, and that Moses and the prophets had, the same gospel that Jesus had, the same gospel that was taught on the Asiatic continent and on the American continent, and proclaimed to the various peoples of the earth.

As Latter-day Saints we believe this gospel has been restored, and further, we know that we are in possession of it. . . . Through obedience to its principles, and the reception of the Holy Ghost, you Latter-day Saints do know that this is the work of God; and if you don't know it, it is because you are not living your religion, and keeping the commandments of God.—*JD*, 25:94-95, February 10, 1884.

God is interested in the welfare of all humanity that has ever lived, that now lives, or that ever will live. He is, we are

told, the God of the spirits of all flesh, and he has introduced
principles which have been made known to us for the benefit
of all. The principles that we are associated with reach back
into eternity and forward into eternity.—*JD*, 23:23-24, December 11, 1881.

SOME PRINCIPLES OF EARTH LIFE.—We believe in the
restoration of all things. We believe that God has spoken from
the heavens. If I did not believe he had, I would not be here.
We believe that angels have appeared, that the heavens have been
opened. We believe in eternal principles, in an eternal gospel,
and eternal priesthood, in eternal communications and associations. Everything associated with the gospel that we believe
in is eternal. If it were not so, I would want nothing to do
with it. I do not want to make a profession, and worship
a god because this one, that one, or the other one does it, and
I not know whether I am right, and those whom I imitate not
know, any more than myself, whether they are right or wrong.

I profess to know for myself, and if I did not know for
myself, I would have nothing to do with it. Acting upon this
principle, I associated myself with the Latter-day Saints. I preach
that doctrine which I verily believe with my whole soul. I
believe in its principles, because there is something intelligent
about it. For instance—if I am an eternal being, I want something that is calculated to satisfy the capacious desires of that
eternal mind. If I am a being that came into the world yesterday, and leaves it again tomorrow, I might as well have one
religion as another, or none at all; "let us eat, drink and be
merry; for tomorrow we die." If I am an eternal being, I want
to know something about that eternity with which I am associated. I want to know something about God, the devil,
heaven, and hell. If hell is a place of misery, and heaven a place
of happiness, I want to know how to escape the one, and obtain
the other. If I cannot know something about these things which
are to come in the eternal world, I have no religion; I would not
give a straw for it. It would be too low and grovelling a
consideration for a man of intelligence, in the absence of this
knowledge. If there is a God, I want a religion that supplies
some means of certain and tangible communication with him. If
there is a heaven, I want to know what sort of place it is. If
there are angels, I want to know their nature, and their occupation,
and of what they are composed. If I am an eternal being, I
want to know what I am to do when I get through with time;
whether I shall plant corn and hoe it, or be engaged in some
other employment. I do not want any person to tell me about
a heaven that is "beyond the bounds of time and space," a place
that no person can possibly know anything about, or ever reach,

if he did. I do not wish any person to frighten me . . . by telling me about a hell where sinners are roasted upon gridirons, and tossed up by devils upon pitchforks and other sharp-pointed instruments. . . . I want nothing to do with such things, I care nothing about them. But as an intelligent being, if I have a mind capable of reflection, I wish to contemplate the works of nature, and to know something of nature's God, and my destiny.

NATURE AND BELIEF IN GOD.—I love to view the things around me; to gaze upon the sun, moon, and stars; to study the planetary system, and the world we inhabit; to behold their beauty, order, harmony, and the operations of existence around me. I can see something more than that mean jargon, those childish quibbles, this heaven beyond the bounds of time and space, where they have nothing to do but sit and sing themselves away to everlasting bliss or go and roast on gridirons. There is nothing like that to be found in nature—everything is beautifully harmonious, and perfectly adapted to the position it occupies in the world. Whether you look at birds, beasts, or the human system, you see something exquisitely beautiful and harmonious, and worthy of the contemplation of all intelligence. What is man's wisdom in comparison to it? I could not help but believe there is a God, if there were no such things as religion in the world.—*JD*, 1:151, 152, June 12, 1853.

## SOME PROBLEMS OF ETERNITY

ETERNAL CONFLICT.—There has been a conflict in the world ever since the creation of man to the present time. And that spirit of antagonism to the truth that existed in former ages exists in this age, and we have reason to know it.—*JD*, 24:36, January 21, 1883.

THE ROLE OF EXPERIENCE.—What is eternity? It is duration. It had no beginning, and it will have no end. What is the priesthood? It is everlasting; it had no beginning and will have no end. What is matter? It is eternal. What is spirit? It is eternal. God did not make this world out of nothing— that would be impossible. But the Christians say nothing is impossible with God. He made the world out of matter that existed before he framed it. He spake, chaos heard, and the world rolled into existence. There is no end to the works of the Almighty, and we may soar amidst the knowledge of God forever. . . .

It is also necessary that we should learn the principles of order and government, but we must first learn how to govern ourselves, then how to govern our families, and lastly, learn how to be governed, which is the most difficult lesson that can be set us—it is infinitely worse than governing others. Jesus was not prepared to govern till he was placed in circumstances that gave him experience. The scriptures say it was necessary to the bringing of many souls to glory that the captain of our salvation should be made perfect through sufferings; so he was not perfect before, but had to come here to be made perfect. He had to come here to pass through a multitude of sufferings, and be tempted and tried in all points like unto us, because it was necessary. Had it not been necessary, he would not have been placed in those circumstances, and this is the reason why we are here, and kicked and cuffed round, and hated and despised by the world. The reason why we do not live in peace is because we are not prepared for it.—*MS*, 8:87, July 6, 1845.

We are engaged in a work of importance. We are immortal beings. We are dual beings associated with time and eternity; I might say associated with the past, the present, and the future. We have a work to perform here upon the earth, and with the help of Israel's God we expect to do that work.—*JD*, 25:93, February 10, 1884.

ETERNAL MARRIAGE.[1]—What man has a claim upon his wife in eternity? It is true that some of the writers of the yellow-backed literature have a philosophy a little in advance of the priests of the day. Some of them do tell us about eternal unions. They expect to be married here and hereafter. They know nothing about it, still they are in advance of the clergy. They follow the instincts of Nature, and Nature unperverted looks forward to a reunion. We are not governed by opinion in these matters. God has revealed the principle, and our wives are sealed to us for time and eternity. When we get through with this life, we expect to be associated in the next, and therefore we pursue the course that we do, and no power this side of hell, nor there either, can stop it.—*JD*, 13:230, May 6, 1870.

LAW AND JUSTICE.—We enter into obligations here as young men or young women, or as old men or old women, as the case may be, no matter what or how we enter into covenants before God, holy angels, and witnesses, and pledge ourselves in the most solemn manner to be true to these covenants. If we violate these covenants, and trample under foot the ordinances of God, we ought to be dealt with by the church and either repent of our sins or be cut off from the church, so that by purging the church from iniquity, we may be acceptable before God; for the Gods spoken of are not going to associate with every scalawag in existence; scalawags are not going where they

---

[1]See Chapter 26, "The Law of Marriage" for complete discussion.

are; and if men do not live according to the laws of a celestial kingdom, they are not going into a celestial glory; they cannot pass by the angels and the Gods, who are set to guard the way of life. Straight is the gate, and narrow is the way that leads to life, and few there be that find it.

Is God merciful? Yes. Will he treat his children well? Yes. He will do the very best he can for all. But there are certain eternal laws by which the Gods in the eternal worlds are governed and which they cannot violate, and do not want to violate. These eternal principles must be kept, and one principle is that no unclean thing can enter into the kingdom of God. What, then, will be the result? Why, the people I have referred to— people who do not keep the celestial law—will have to go into a lesser kingdom, into a terrestrial, or perhaps a telestial, as the case may be. Is that according to the law of God? Yes, for if they are not prepared for the celestial kingdom, they must go to such a one as they are prepared to endure. Certain principles have been developed, and a great many have not. But we are here in a school to learn, and it is for the elders of Israel who are desirous to do the will of God, and keep his commandments, to put themselves in the way of doing so, to seek to the Lord for his guidance and direction, to repent of their follies, their nonsense, and wickedness of every kind, and to come out for God and his kingdom, and to seek to build up the Zion of God and the kingdom of God upon the earth, and if we do this, God will bless us and exalt us in time and throughout the eternities that are to come.—*JD,* 25:165, 166, June 15, 1884.

LAWS AND KINGDOMS OF GLORY.—We ought to observe the laws of God. The Lord has taken a great deal of pain to bring us where we are and to give us the information we have. He came himself, accompanied by his Son Jesus, to the Prophet Joseph Smith. He didn't send anybody, but came himself, and introducing his Son, said: "This is my beloved Son, hear him." And he permitted the ancient prophets, apostles, and men of God that existed in different ages to come and confer the keys of their several dispensations upon the prophet of the Lord, in order that he should be endowed and imbued with the power and Spirit of God, with the light of revelation and the eternal principles of the everlasting gospel, and that the keys committed to him, might, through him, be conferred upon others, and that the principles of eternal truth as they exist in the heavens, might extend to the nations of the earth, that these degrading, loathsome, damning principles might cease, that his people might be gathered to Zion from the four corners of the earth, and learn his laws.—*JD,* 21:116-117, November 28, 1879.

We are told that if we cannot abide the law of the celestial kingdom we cannot inherit a celestial glory. Is not that doctrine? Yes. "But," says one, "are not we all going into the celestial kingdom?" I think not, unless we turn round and mend our ways very materially. It is only those who can abide a celestial glory and obey a celestial law that will be prepared to enter a celestial kingdom. "Well," says another, "are the others going to be burned up?" No. "Do you expect everybody to walk according to this higher law?" No, I do not. And do I expect those that do not are going into the celestial kingdom? No, I do not. "Well, where will they go?" If they are tolerably good men and do not do anything very bad, they will get into a terrestrial kingdom, and if there are some that cannot abide a terrestrial law, they may get into a telestial kingdom, or otherwise, as the case may be.—*JD*, 26:133, October 6, 1883.

CONFORMITY.—We are living in a very important day and age of the world, in a time which is pregnant with greater events than in any other period that we know of, or in any other dispensation that has existed upon the earth. It is called "the dispensation of the fulness of times," when God "will gather together in one all things in Christ, both which are in heaven, and which are on earth"; for the heavens, the Gods in the eternal worlds, the holy priesthood that has existed upon the earth, the living that live upon the face of the earth, and the dead that have departed this life, are all interested in the work in which we are engaged. Consequently, it is of the greatest importance that everything we do, that every ordinance we administer, that every principle we believe in, should be strictly in accordance with the mind and word, the will and law of God.—*JD*, 25:177, May 18, 1884.

THE ESSENTIAL EQUALITY OF MEN.—Looking upon ourselves as eternal beings, connected with heaven as well as earth, with eternity as well as time, what difference is it to us what our lot may be, whether we abound in wealth, or whether we have to struggle with grim poverty; whether we possess the good things of this world, or have to crawl around as Lazarus did, and be glad to eat of the crumbs that fell from the rich man's table? It will soon be with the rich as if they were not rich, and with the poor as if they had not to struggle—all will find a level in the grave.—*JD*, 18:311, December 31, 1876.

DEATH AND RESURRECTION.—We believe in a religion that will make a man go down to the grave with a clear conscience, and an unfaltering step, and meet his God as a father and friend without fear. . . . We have no craven fear of death; we are looking for life eternal, and an association with the Gods in celestial mansions. We are not ashamed of our religion, and we believe God is not ashamed of us.—*The Mormon*, March 31, 1855.

"IT IS APPOINTED FOR MEN ONCE TO DIE."—When we reflect upon the position of the world that we live in and of humanity in general, look back through the dark lapse of ages that have transpired, and contemplate the millions upon millions, and hundreds of thousands of millions who have inhabited this earth, and that they have all of them gone, we see that there is no staying of these things, no arresting the course of destiny, no stopping the hand of fate, or the power of the destroyer. An eternal decree has gone forth, and it is appointed for all men once to die. It is impossible for us to evade this, and with the exception of the very few to whom I have before referred,[1] all men have paid the great debt of Nature. The human body may be propped up through the ingenuity, nursing, and care of man for some time, but, like a sweeping flood, although you may dam up the water from its natural course and arrest it in its progress and keep it back, back, back, for a while, yet by and by it will rush over its barriers, seek its natural channel, pursue its own course, and find its own resting place. So it is with the human family. We come into the world; we exist for a short time; then we are taken away, no matter what our feelings, ideas, or faith may be; they have nothing to do with this great universal law which pervades all Nature. . . .

Who is there that can stay the hand of death? What talent, what ingenuity, what philosophy, religion, science, or power of any kind? Who possesses that power, individually, in this assembly, or combined, to say to the great monster death, stand back, thou shalt not take thy victims? There is no such person, there is no such power, no such influence; such a principle does not exist, and it never will exist until the last enemy is destroyed, which the scriptures tell us is death. But death shall be destroyed, and all then, even all the human family, shall burst the barriers of the tomb and come forth—those who have done good to the resurrection of the just. Then and not until then will that influence, that fell tyrant, be destroyed.—*JD*, 15:347-348, February 23, 1873.

A SOLILOQUY ON DEATH.—A few days ago I attended the funeral of one of my wives; and while doing so I looked upon the great city of the dead. I thought to myself, here are thousands of honorable men and women who are sleeping the sleep of

---

[1]Reference was made in the original discourse to the three Nephite disciples and others who apparently were blessed not to "taste of death" but to undergo the necessary change as in the "twinkling of an eye."

peace, who have served their God, and who have got through with the affairs of this world; and while their bodies are decaying here, their spirits are soaring in the heavens. Do I feel sorry for them? No, they have gone to rest, and all is peace with them, according to the mind and will of God in relation to those matters, he having appointed unto man that he must die.

Since the organization of the world, myriads have come and have taken upon themselves bodies, and they have passed away, generation after generation, into another state of existence. And it is so today. And I suppose while we are mourning the loss of our friend, others are rejoicing to meet him behind the veil; and while he has left us, others are coming into the world at the same time, and probably in this our territory. There is a continuous change, an ingress of beings into the world and an egress out of it. As near as my memory serves me, from one-third to one-fourth of our population today are children under eight years of age. There are thousands of men upon the earth today, among the Saints of God, of whom it was decreed before they came that they should occupy the positions they have occupied and do occupy, and many of them have performed their part and gone home; others are left still to fulfil the duties and responsibilities devolving upon them.—*JD*, 23:177, July 24, 1882.

FUNERAL CUSTOMS.—It is proper to sorrow; it is proper to show respect for the departed. It is proper that our sympathies should be drawn out; it is proper that we should assemble together to attend to appropriate funeral services, as we are now doing, that we may reflect upon our lives and upon the uncertainty thereof, and upon death and the results that may follow after; and that we consider the gospel of the Son of God, and reflect upon our position. But I have thought, and indeed President Young thought, and so did Brother George A. Smith and others with whom I have conversed upon this subject, that we pay too much attention to these outward forms. We, above all other people upon the face of the earth, ought to be free from outward show, and from the appearance of sorrow, and mourning, having had planted within us the germs of immortality and eternal life; inasmuch as when we get through with the affairs of this world, we not only expect, but we know that we will inherit eternal lives in the celestial kingdom of God. And knowing this, it would not be for us to mourn as people without any hope.—*JD*, 22:355, January 29, 1882.

PRIESTHOOD AND THE FUTURE STATE.—When men leave this earth, they leave it to occupy another sphere in another state of existence. And if . . . they hold the priesthood that administers in time and in eternity . . . they hold that priesthood in the eternal worlds, and operate in it there. It is an everlasting priesthood, that administers in time and in eternity. And the gospel that we have received unfolds to us principles of which we were heretofore entirely ignorant. It shows us the relationship that exists between God and man, and it shows us the relationship that exists between men who have dwelt upon the earth before and those who exist today. It shows that while God has revealed the priesthood to us upon the earth and conferred upon us those privileges, that in former generations he revealed the same priesthood to other men, and that those men holding that priesthood ministered to others here upon the earth; and that we are operating with them and they with us in our interests and in the interests of the church and kingdom of God, in assisting to build up the Zion of God, and in seeking to establish truth and righteousness upon the earth; and that there is a connecting link between the priesthood in the heavens and the priesthood upon the earth.

God, our Heavenly Father, has gathered unto himself, through the atonement of Jesus Christ, very many great and honorable men who have lived upon the earth, and who have been clothed with the powers of the priesthood. Those men having held that priesthood and administered in it upon the earth are now in the heavens operating with the priesthood in the heavens in connection with the priesthood that exists now upon the earth.—*JD*, 23:176, July 24, 1882.

NATURE OF THE RESURRECTION.—What, will everybody be resurrected? Yes, every living being. "But every man in his own order, Christ the first fruits; afterward they that are Christ's at his coming. Then cometh the end." That is, the saints shall live and reign with Christ a thousand years. One of the apostles says, "But the rest of the dead live not again until the thousand years are expired." But all must come forth from the grave, some time or other, in the selfsame tabernacles that they possessed while living on the earth. It will be just as Ezekiel has described it— bone will come to its bone, and flesh and sinew will cover the skeleton, and at the Lord's bidding breath will enter the body, and we shall appear, many of us, a marvel to ourselves.

I heard Joseph Smith say, at the time he was making a tomb at Nauvoo, that he expected, when the time came when the grave would be rent asunder, that he would arise and embrace his father and mother, and shake hands with his friends. It was his written request that when he died, some kind friends would see that he was buried near his bosom friends, so that when he and they arose in the morning of the first resurrection, he could embrace them, saying, "My father! My mother!"

How consoling it is to those who are called upon to mourn the loss of dear friends in death, to know that we will again be associated with them! How encouraging to all who live according to the revealed principles of truth, perhaps more especially to those whose lives are pretty well spent, who have borne the heat and burden of the day, to know that ere long we shall burst the barriers of the tomb, and come forth living and immortal souls, to enjoy the society of our tried and trusted friends, no more to be afflicted with the seeds of death, and to finish the work the Father has given us to do!

I know that some people of very limited comprehension will say that all the parts of the body cannot be brought together, for, say they, the fish probably have eaten them up, or the whole may have been blown to the four winds of heaven. It is true the body, or the organization, may be destroyed in various ways, but it is not true that the particles out of which it was created can be destroyed. They are eternal; they never were created. This is not only a principle associated with our religion, or in other words, with the great science of life, but also it is in accordance with acknowledged science. You may take, for instance, a handful of fine gold, and scatter it in the street among the dust; again, gather together the materials among which you have thrown the gold, and you can separate one from the other so thoroughly, that your handful of gold can be returned to you; yes, every grain of it. You may take particles of silver, iron, copper, lead, and mix them together with any other ingredients, and there are certain principles connected with them by which these different materials can be eliminated, every particle cleaving to that of its own element.—JD, 18:333-334, December 31, 1876.

Says John, when wrapt in prophetic vision, and clothed upon with the Spirit and power of God and the revelations of Jehovah, "And I saw the dead, small and great, stand before God; . . . And the sea gave up the dead which were in it; and death and hell delivered up the dead which were in them: and they were judged every man according to their works" (Revelation 20: 12, 13).

I want a part in the resurrection. The angel said, "Blessed and holy is he who has part in the first resurrection." I want to have part in the first resurrection. It is that which leads me to hope. It is that hope which buoys me up under difficulties and sustains me while passing through tribulation, for I know as well as Job knew that my "Redeemer lives, and that he shall stand in the latter day upon the earth," and I know that I shall stand upon it with him. I therefore bear this testimony.—JD, 13:231, May 6, 1870.

ETERNAL JUDGMENT.—President Young remarked . . . that "God sees and knows the acts of all men." We read something like this, "But I say unto you, that every idle word that men shall speak, they shall give account thereof in the day of judgment." Now, this is a remarkable declaration. Look at the millions of human beings that inhabit this earth, and that have inhabited it from the creation up to the present time. It is supposed, generally, by the best authorities, that from eight hundred to a thousand millions of people live upon this earth at the same time, that is, this has been the case for a great many generations at least; they are coming and going continually; they pass into the world by thousands and tens of thousands, and go out of it in the same way daily; a daily stream of this kind is coming and going. Then, if we could discover the thoughts and reflections of these numerous millions of human beings, look at the wisdom, the intelligence, the folly, the nonsense, the good and the evil that are connected with every one of them! It is so vast and complicated that the human mind could not receive it, and it seems as if it would be almost a thing impossible for God to gaze upon the whole of them—to comprehend the whole, and judge of the whole correctly. How shall this be done? My understanding of the thing is, that God has made each man a register within himself, and each man can read his own register, so far as he enjoys his perfect faculties. This can be easily comprehended.

Let your memories run back, and you can remember the time when you did a good action; you can remember the time when you did a bad action; the thing is printed there; and you can bring it out and gaze upon it whenever you please. As I stated before, if you have studied language, you can call that out at pleasure; you can show the distinction between the different parts of speech very readily. If you have studied mechanism, your mind will go to the place where you saw a certain machine, and you will go to work and make one like it. If you have traveled in cities, you can tell what kind of houses and streets composed the different cities you passed through, and the character of the people you associated with; and you can ruminate upon them, and reflect upon them by day or by night whenever you think proper, and call the things up which you did and saw. Where do you read all this? In your own book. You do not go to somebody else's book or library. It is written in your own record and you there read it. Your eyes and ears have taken it in, and your hands have touched it; and then your judgment, as it is called, has acted upon it—your reflective powers. Now, if you are in possession of a spirit or intellectuality of that kind, whereby you are enabled to read your own acts, do you not think that

that being who has placed that spirit and that intelligence within you holds the keys of that intelligence, and can read it whenever he pleases? Is not that philosophical, reasonable, and scriptural? I think it is. Where did I derive my intelligence from that I possess? From the Lord God of Hosts, and you derived your intelligence from the same source. Where did any man that exists or breathes the breath of life throughout this whole universe get any intelligence he has? He got it from the same source. Then it would be a very great curiosity if I should be able to teach you something and not know that something myself. How could I teach you A, B, C, if I did not know the alphabet, or the rudiments of the English grammar, or anything else, if I did not know it myself? I could not do it. Well, then, upon this principle we can readily perceive how the Lord will bring into judgment the actions of men when he shall call them forth at the last day. —JD, 11:77-78, February 5, 1865.

# Chapter III

# THE CONCEPT OF GODHOOD

## "THE LIVING GOD"[1]

PLURALITY OF GODS.—It will . . . be necessary to treat the subject of the "Living God," in contra-distinction to a *dead God,* or, one that has, "no body, parts, or passions," and perhaps it may be well enough to say at the outset that Mormonism embraces a plurality of Gods—as the Apostle Paul said, there were "gods many, and lords many," (I Corinthians 8:5.) in doing which, we shall not deny the scripture that has been set apart for this world, and allows one God; even Jesus Christ, the very eternal Father of this earth; and if Paul tells the truth,—"by whom also he made the worlds." (Hebrews 1:2.)

It was probably alluded to by Moses, when the children of Israel were working out their salvation with fear and trembling in the wilderness, at the time that he spake these words:

> And it came to pass, when ye heard the voice out of the midst of the darkness, (for the mountain did burn with fire,) that ye came near unto me, even all the heads of your tribes, and your elders;
> And ye said, Behold, the Lord our God hath shewed us his glory and his greatness, and we have heard his voice out of the midst of the fire: we have seen this day that God doth talk with man, and he liveth.
> Now therefore why should we die? for this great fire will consume us: if we hear the voice of the Lord our God any more, then we shall die.
> For who is there of all flesh, that hath heard the voice of the living God speaking out of the midst of the fire, as we have, and lived? (Deuteronomy 5:23-26.)

Again, Moses in the before-mentioned quotation uses our text, the "Living God"; and who will undertake to say that he meant any other person than Jesus Christ, the Holy One of Israel? "Before Abraham was, I am." In all probability that meant Christ[2] for there is but one God. . . . In Matthew we learn:

> When Jesus came into the coasts of Caesarea Philippi, he asked his disciples, saying, Whom do men say that I the Son of man am?
> And they said, Some say that thou art John the Baptist: some, Elias; and others, Jeremias, or one of the prophets.
> He saith unto them, But whom say ye that I am?
> And Simon Peter answered and said, Thou art the Christ, the son of the living God. (Matthew 16:13-16.)

---

[1]This is the title of Elder Taylor's editorial in the *Times and Seasons* from which the following selection has been taken.

[2]Jesus himself makes the statement in response to questioning Pharisees. See John 8:58 and *passim.*

Now, two facts, making two worldly mysteries, meet the mind in the foregoing passages. Jesus says he is the "son of man," and Peter says, he is the "son of the living God." This makes two "living Gods," because the Savior never once said that he begat himself, or came into the world of his own accord, or upon his own business; but upon the contrary, he came to do the will of his father *who sent him.*

What shall we say then, to make Moses', Jesus', and Peter's words true? We will say that Jesus Christ had a father and mother of his spirit, and a father and mother of his flesh; and so have all of his brethren and sisters: and that is one reason why he said, "*ye are Gods*"; or that Isaiah prophesied: "Shew the things that are to come hereafter, that we may know that ye are gods: yea, do good, or do evil, that we may be dismayed, and behold it together." (Isaiah 41:23.) In fact, "the gods," in old times, was common intelligence. Satan, in his first sectarian sermon to Adam and Eve, told them, if they would eat of the forbidden fruit, they should become as "gods," knowing good and evil. (Genesis 3:5.)

This is not all: the first line of Genesis, purely translated from the original, excluding the first *Baith* (which was added by the Jews) would read:*Rosheit* (the head) *baurau,* (brought forth) *Elohim* (the Gods) *ate* (with) *hah-shau-mahyiem* (the heavens) *ueh-ate,* (and with) *hauaurates,* (the earth.) In simple English, the Head brought forth the Gods, with the heavens and with the earth. The "Head" must have meant the "living God," or Head God: Christ is our head. The term *Elohim,* plural of *Elohah,* or *ale,* is used alike in the first chapter of Genesis, for the creation, and the quotation of Satan. In the second chapter, and fourth verse, we have this remarkable history: "*These are the generations of the heavens and of the earth, when they were brought forth; in the day that the Lord of the Gods made earth and heavens.*" The Hebrew reads so.[1]

THE PRESIDENCY OF THE TRINITY.—Truly Jesus Christ created the worlds, and is Lord of Lords, and, as the Psalmist said: "judgeth among the gods." (Psalm 82:1.) Then Moses might have said with propriety, he is the "living God," and Christ, speaking of the flesh could say: I am the son of man; and Peter, enlightened by the Holy Ghost: Thou art the son of the living God—meaning our Father in heaven, who is the Father of all spirits, and who, with Jesus Christ, his first begotten Son, and the Holy Ghost, are one in power, one in dominion, and one in glory, constituting the first presidency of this system, and this

---

[1]Compare Genesis 2:4.

eternity. But they are as much three distinct persons as the sun, moon, and earth are three different bodies.

THE NOBLE RACE IN THE HEAVENS.—Without going into the full investigation of the history and excellency of God, the Father of our Lord Jesus Christ . . . let us reflect that Jesus Christ, as Lord of lords, and King of kings, must have a noble race in the heavens, or upon the earth, or else he can never be as great in power, dominion, might, and authority as the scriptures declare. But here, the mystery is solved. John says: "And I looked, and, lo, a Lamb stood on the mount Sion, and with him an hundred forty and four thousand, having his Father's name written in their foreheads." (Revelation 14:1.)

Their "Father's name," bless me! that is GOD! Well done for Mormonism; *one hundred and forty four thousand* GODS, among the tribes of Israel, and, two living Gods and the Holy Ghost, for this world! Such knowledge is too wonderful for men, unless they possess the spirit of Gods. It unravels the little mysteries, which, like a fog, hide the serene atmosphere of heaven, and looks from world to world, from system to system, from universe to universe, and from eternity to eternity, where, in each, and all, there is a presidency of Gods, and Gods many, and lords many; and from time to time, or from eternity to eternity, Jesus Christ shall bring in another world regulated and saved as this will be when he delivers it up to the Father; and God becomes *all in all*. As John the Revelator said: "And there shall be no more curse: but the throne of God and of the Lamb shall be in it; and his servants shall serve him.

"And they shall see his face; and his name shall be in their foreheads." (Revelation 22:3, 4.)

"His name in their foreheads," undoubtedly means *"God"* on the front of their crowns; for, when all things are created new, in the celestial kingdom, the servants of God, the innumerable multitude, are crowned, and are perfect men and women in the Lord, one in glory, one in knowledge, and one in image: they are like Christ, and he is like God: then, O, then, they are all "living Gods," having passed from death unto life, and possessing the power of eternal lives!—*TS*, 6:806-807, February 15, 1845.

THE FATHERHOOD OF GOD.—God is our Father; we are his children. He has brought us into his covenant, and it is our privilege to go on from wisdom to wisdom, from intelligence to intelligence, from understanding of one principle to that of another, to go forward and progress in the development of truth until we can comprehend God, for we are his children; we are his sons and daughters; and he is our Father.—*JD*, 21:93, April 13, 1879.

No matter what words are used, it is the principles we are after, and our religion interests and affects us in all the ramifications of life. It does not set up God as some austere being that we cannot approach, but it tells us he is our Father, and that we are his children, and that he cherishes in his bosom a paternal regard for us; and we have experienced something of the feelings that exist between father and son, mother and daughter, parents and children. But we could not apply that unto our God and consider that he was our Father before we embraced the gospel.—*JD*, 5:262, September 20, 1857.

The object that God has in view is to benefit mankind as much as lies in His power. We talk sometimes about moving heaven and earth but God has moved heaven and earth for the accomplishment of that object. . . . God desires our welfare, and He has instituted laws for that purpose. He has introduced the everlasting Gospel for that purpose; and He has restored the Holy Priesthood that existed anciently, together with all the principles, blessings, powers, rites, ordinances, and privileges that have graced the earth from the commencement of time.—*JD*, 26:105-106, October 20, 1881.

THE JUSTICE OF GOD.—What would you think of the conduct of a God who would let the human family continue forever to transgress his law without interfering? You would think he was getting foolish and in his dotage—that he did not understand himself nor correct principles in allowing a lot of bad boys to rise up and increase around him, letting evil principles exist instead of righteous ones, and the wicked afflict and persecute the good with impunity.—*JD*, 6:25, November 1, 1857.

GOD LIVES.—We have learned this, that God lives; we have learned that when we call upon him he hears our prayers; we have learned that it is the height of human happiness to fear God and observe his laws and keep his commandments; we have learned that it is a duty devolving upon us to try and make all men happy and intelligent, which happiness and intelligence can only be obtained through obedience to the laws of God. It is in him that we trust. We are not so much concerned about the destiny of this kingdom[1] as some people think we are. God is interested in it; the holy angels are interested in it; the ancient patriarchs and prophets and men of God who have lived in other ages are interested in it; and in the councils of heaven it was agreed that this kingdom should be established; it is according to the word and will and eternal designs of Jehovah. And, as he called men in other days, he has called them in these days, and this priesthood administers in the earth and in the heavens.—*JD*, 22:292, October 9, 1881.

[1]See Book IV, "The Kingdom of God."

## THE ANGELS

ANGELS AS WATCHMEN AND MESSENGERS.—The angels are our watchmen, for Satan said to Jesus: "He shall give his angels charge concerning thee: and in their hands they shall bear thee up, lest at any time thou dash thy foot against a stone." (Matthew 4:6.) It would seem from a careful perusal of the scriptures, that the angels, while God has saints upon the earth, stay in this lower world to ward off evil: for the prophet Isaiah has left this testimony on the subject:

I will mention the lovingkindnesses of the Lord, and the praises of the Lord, according to all that the Lord hath bestowed on us, and the great goodness toward the house of Israel, which he hath bestowed on them according to his mercies, and according to the multitude of his lovingkindnesses.

For he said, Surely they are my people, children that will not lie: so he was their Saviour.

In all their affliction he was afflicted, and the angel of his presence saved them: in his love and in his pity he redeemed them; and he bare them, and carried them all the days of old. (Isaiah 63:7-9.)

The angels that have gone forth at sundry times to execute the decrees of God, fully substantiate this fact: Abraham, Hagar, Jacob, Balaam, Joshua, Gideon, together with the enemies of the Lord, are the witnesses who knew the power and offices of angels on earth.

But lest we take up too much time on the resurrected bodies, who go and come at the bidding of him who was, and is, and is to come, we will change the theme to the thoughts and witnesses of the heart.

The action of the angels, or messengers of God, upon our minds, so that the heart can conceive things past, present, and to come, and revelations from the eternal world, is, among a majority of mankind, a greater mystery than all the secrets of philosophy, literature, superstition, and bigotry, put together. Though some men try to deny it, and some try to explain away the meaning, still there is so much testimony in the Bible, and among a respectable portion of the world, that one might as well undertake to throw the water out of this world into the moon with a teaspoon, as to do away with the supervision of angels upon the human mind. . . .

POLICE OF HEAVEN.—But, without going into a particular detail of the offices and duties of the different grades of angels, let us close by saying that the angels gather the elect, and pluck out all that offends. They are the police of heaven and report whatever transpires on earth, and carry the petitions and supplications of men, women, and children to the mansions of remembrance, where they are kept as tokens of obedience by the sanctified, in "golden vials" labelled "the prayers of the saints."—TS,

# CHAPTER IV

# REVELATION

## COMMUNICATION BETWEEN GOD AND MAN

BELIEF IN REVELATION.—Very few men upon the face of the earth believe in revelation from God. They believe in their own theories and notions and ideas and principles, but they know nothing about "Thus saith the Lord," as men used to do when they had the gospel; and wherever the gospel exists, there exists with it a knowledge of God and of the laws of life.—*JD*, 22:291-292, October 9, 1881.

There is a feeling generally extant in the world that God is a great and august personage who is elevated so high above the world, and is so far separated from humanity that it is impossible to approach him. And although the Christian religion, under whatever form it may be practised, teaches mankind to pray unto God in the name of the Lord Jesus Christ, yet it is very few who suppose that their prayers amount to anything, that God will listen to their supplications, or that they will prove of any special benefit. A feeling of this kind tends more or less to unbelief instead of faith in God, and hence we find very few men in our day who act as men of God did in former days, that is, seek unto him for guidance and direction in the affairs of life. If we examine what is termed the sacred history of the Bible, we shall find that in the various ages of the world, until soon after Christianity was introduced, there was a feeling among men to call upon God and to have their prayers answered—a feeling that if they would approach the Most High and call upon his name in faith, he would answer their supplications and give unto them wisdom, intelligence, and revelation for the guidance of their feet in the pathway of life; and it was not based as it is now, generally, upon some old theories, or upon communications made unto others. But if we trace the records of scripture through, we shall find that men generally sought for themselves guidance and direction and revelation adapted to the peculiar circumstances in which they were placed.—*JD*, 14:357, March 17, 1872.

THE HOLY SPIRIT AND REVELATION.—Nothing but the Holy Spirit proceeding from the Father and the Son can impart unto us that intelligence which is necessary to place the Church and kingdom of God upon a sure and firm basis.—*JD*, 11:23, December 11, 1864.

Without revelation from God the world is but a wilderness. —*TS*, 5:748, December 15, 1844.

## NECESSITY OF MODERN REVELATION

REVELATION NEEDED TO AMELIORATE THE WORLD.—
We are living in a world in which the spirits who have dwelt in
the bosom of God are coming into and leaving this state of existence at the rate of about a thousand millions in every thirty-three
years; and here are thousands of so-called ministers of religion with
an inefficient gospel, that God never ordained, trying to ameliorate
the condition of mankind, and sending what they call the gospel
to the heathen, and they are continually calling for the pecuniary
aid of their fellow Christians to assist them in this enterprise. But
if they have not the truth themselves how can they impart it to
others? How can blind leaders lead people in the way of life and
salvation? Was it not necessary, in view of the ignorance and
blindness of the people everywhere, in regard to the principles of
salvation, that something should be done to ameliorate the condition of a fallen world? The Christian world, by their unbelief,
have made the heavens as brass, and wherever they go to declare
what they call the gospel they make confusion worse confounded.
But who shall debar God from taking care of his own creation,
and saving his creatures? Yet this is the position that many men
have taken.

TESTIMONY OF THE PROPHET'S REVELATIONS.—But notwithstanding the unbelief so prevalent throughout Christendom,
God restored his ancient gospel to Joseph Smith, giving him revelation, opening the heavens to him, and making him acquainted
with the plan of salvation and exaltation of the children of men.
I was well acquainted with him, and have carefully examined the
revelations given through him, and notwithstanding all the asper-
sions that have been cast upon him, I believe that, with the exception of Jesus Christ, there never was a greater prophet upon this
wide earth than he. To the revelations he made known are we
indebted for the glorious principles that God has communicated to
the world in these last days. We were as much in the dark as
other people were about the principles of salvation, and the relationship we hold to God and each other, until these things were
made known to us by Joseph Smith. A great deal is said at the
present time about the relation of husband and wife; but where
is there a man outside of this church who understands anything
about this relationship, as well as that of parents to children?
There is not one, and the Latter-day Saints knew nothing about
it until it was revealed by Joseph Smith, through the gospel. It
is the gospel that teaches a woman that she has a claim upon a
man, and a man that he has a claim upon a woman in the resurrection. It is the gospel that teaches them that, when they rise
from the tombs in the resurrection, they will again clasp hands,

be reunited, and again participate in that glory for which God designed them before the world was.—*JD*, 16:373-376, February 1, 1874.

## NECESSITY FOR CONTINUOUS REVELATION

THE SCRIPTURES ARE AN INSUFFICIENT GUIDE.—The Bible is good; and Paul told Timothy to study it, that he might be a workman that need not be ashamed, and that he might be able to conduct himself aright before the living church, the pillar and ground of truth. The church-mark, with Paul, was the foundation, the pillar, the ground of truth, the living church, not the dead letter. The Book of Mormon is good, and the Doctrine and Covenants, as land-marks. But a mariner who launches into the ocean requires a more certain criterion. He must be acquainted with heavenly bodies, and take his observations from them, in order to steer his barque aright. Those books are good for example, precedent, and investigation, and for developing certain laws and principles. But they do not, they cannot, touch every case required to be adjudicated and set in order.

REVELATION NEEDED FOR TIME AND CIRCUMSTANCE.— We require a living tree—a living fountain—living intelligence, proceeding from the living priesthood in heaven, through the living priesthood on earth. . . . And from the time that Adam first received a communication from God, to the time that John, on the Isle of Patmos, received his communication, or Joseph Smith had the heavens opened to him, it always required new revelations, adapted to the peculiar circumstances in which the churches or individuals were placed. Adam's revelation did not instruct Noah to build his ark; nor did Noah's revelation tell Lot to forsake Sodom; nor did either of these speak of the departure of the children of Israel from Egypt. These all had revelations for themselves, and so had Isaiah, Jeremiah, Ezekiel, Jesus, Peter, Paul, John, and Joseph. And so must we, or we shall make a shipwreck.

FAITH THE GUIDE.—Then, while we examine our books, and search them diligently, don't let us put those before the priesthood, but seek to support it in all its branches, that life, and health, and salvation may flow to us through the various branches or channels. I do not wish to be understood as despising those books, for they are good, and there are a great many useful revelations in them; and God will not deny himself, or contradict, without cause, his former revelations; and every principle of truth is eternal and cannot be changed. But I speak of them as I would of children's schoolbooks, which a child studies to learn to read; but when it has learned to read, if its memory is good, it can dispense with. But I would here remark, that we are most of us children as yet, and, therefore, require to study our books. If there are any, however, who think themselves men, let them show it, not by vain glory or empty boast, but by virtue, meekness, purity, faith, wisdom, intelligence, and knowledge, both of earthly and heavenly things.—*MS, 9:323-324, November 1, 1847.*

"PRESENT AND IMMEDIATE REVELATION."—We believe that it is necessary for man to be placed in communication with God; that he should have revelation from him, and that unless he is placed under the influences of the inspiration of the Holy Spirit, he can know nothing about the things of God. I do not care how learned a man may be, or how extensively he may have traveled. I do not care what his talent, intellect, or genius may be, at what college he may have studied, how comprehensive his views or what his judgment may be on other matters, he cannot understand certain things without the Spirit of God, and that necessarily introduces the principle I before referred to—the necessity of revelation. Not revelation in former times, but present and immediate revelation, which shall lead and guide those who possess it in all the paths of life here, and to eternal life hereafter. A good many people, and those professing Christians, will sneer a good deal at the idea of present revelation. Whoever heard of true religion without communication with God? To me the thing is the most absurd that the human mind could conceive. I do not wonder, when the people generally reject the principle of present revelation, that skepticism and infidelity prevail to such an alarming extent. I do not wonder that so many men treat religion with contempt, and regard it as something not worth the attention of intelligent beings, for without revelation religion is a mockery and a farce. If I can not have a religion that will lead me to God, and place me *en rapport* with him, and unfold to my mind the principles of immortality and eternal life, I want nothing to do with it.

The principle of present revelation, then, is the very foundation of our religion. The Christian world rejects that, and says the Bible is all-sufficient. I can remember in my younger days searching its contents very diligently. It is a glorious book to study, and I earnestly recommend it to the attention of our young men and young women, and of our old men and old women. "Search the scriptures," was the command of Jesus, "for in them ye think ye have eternal life: and they are they that testify of me." (John 5:39.) I would not only search the scriptures that we now have, but I would search also every revelation that God has given, does give, or will give for the guidance and direction of his people, and then I would reverence the Giver, and those also whom he makes use of as his honored instruments to promulgate and make known those principles; and I would seek to be governed by the principles that are contained in that sacred word.—*JD*, 16:369-371, February 1, 1874.

## THE REALITY OF REVELATION FROM GOD

OUR PRINCIPLES EMANATED FROM GOD.—As regards our religious principles, we are not indebted to any men who live upon the earth for them. These principles emanated from God. They were given by revelation, and if we have a First Presidency, if we have high priests, if we have seventies, if we have bishops, elders, priests, and teachers, if we have stake and other organizations, we have received them all from God. If we have temples, if we administer in them, it is because we have received instruction in relation thereto from the Lord. If we know anything pertaining to the future, it comes from him, and in fact we live in God, we move in God, and from him we derive our being. Men generally will not acknowledge this, but we as Latter-day Saints believe in these truths. . . .

In the organization of man, in the organization of this earth, and in the organization of the heavens, there were certain things designed by the Almighty to be carried out, and that will be carried out according to the purposes of the Most High, which things were known to him from the beginning. There exists all manner of curious opinions about God, and many people think it impossible for him to take cognizance of all men, but that is very easily done. If I had time to enter into this subject alone, I could show you upon scientific principles that man himself is a self-registering machine, his eyes, his ears, his nose, the touch, the taste, and all the various senses of the body are so many media whereby man lays up for himself a record which perhaps nobody else is acquainted with but himself; and when the time comes for that record to be unfolded, all men that have eyes to see, and ears to hear, will be able to read all things as God himself reads them and comprehends them, and all things, we are told, are naked and open before him. . . . We are told in relation to these matters that the hairs of our heads are numbered; that even a sparrow cannot fall to the ground without our Heavenly Father's notice; and predicated upon some of these principles are some things taught by Jesus, where he tells men to ask and they shall receive. What! the millions that live upon the earth? Yes, the millions of people, no matter how many there are. Can he hear and answer all? Can he attend to all these things? Yes. "Ask, and it shall be given you; seek, and ye shall find; knock, and it shall be opened unto you:

"For every one that asketh receiveth; and he that seeketh findeth; and to him that knocketh it shall be opened." (Matthew 7:7, 8.)

It is difficult for men to comprehend some of these things, and, as they cannot comprehend them, they begin to think they are all nonsense—that is, many do—and, hence, infidelity and skepticism prevail to a great extent. A great many strange notions are entertained in regard to God and his dealings with humanity. This is because men do not understand the things of God. I read in one of our papers a short time ago that there was some kind of commission going to meet—some two or three professors or scientists, men who are supposed to possess superior intelligence— to examine the manuscript of the Book of Mormon, to find out whether it was true or not. I suppose if these people—especially if they should be pious men, possessing a little learning and science —should come out and say the Book of Mormon was not true, we all of us should have to lay it aside, should we not? This to me is the veriest nonsense. It would not make one hair's difference with us whether such a commission should decide that the Book of Mormon is right or wrong. If they decide that it is true, it will not increase our faith in it. If they decide that it is not true, it will not decrease our faith in it. Yet these are ideas that men entertain.

AN INCIDENT IN EUROPE.—Speaking upon this point I am reminded of an incident that took place a number of years ago. Several prominent European scientists called upon me, and they talked a little upon our religious principles. Then they asked me if I was acquainted with the advanced ideas in regard to geology. I told them I knew a little about them from what I had read. "What do you think," said one of them to me, "of these views as compared with the scriptural account of the creation of the world?" "Well," said I, "the great difficulty is that men do not understand the scriptures." They could not see any difficulty on that ground, for they all had their eyes to see, and they had an understanding of words, languages, etc. "Well," said I, "we won't go through the whole Bible, for that is quite a large book; but I will take one or two of the first lines in the Bible. In the beginning God created the heaven and the earth. Will you please tell me when the beginning was?"

"We don't know."

"When you find that out," said I, "then I will tell you when the world was created."

A good many other things transpired associated with this interview that I do not wish now to repeat. Suffice it to say that before they got through, one of them said: "I have read a good deal; I have studied a good deal; I find I have a good deal more to read and study yet." I thought so too. I thought if men could not understand the first two lines of the Bible, it would be quite a task to teach them the whole of it.

REVELATION AND THE BUILDING OF ZION.—In regard to the work in which we are engaged, as I said before and as you have heard over and over again, it emanated from God, and all the principles pertaining to it came from him. We talk sometimes about this work, and how it is going to be accomplished. The work we are engaged in is the work of God. If it is accomplished, it will be accomplished by the power of God, by the wisdom of God, by the intelligence of God, and by the priesthood that dwells with the Gods in the eternal worlds, together with that which he has conferred upon his people here upon the earth, and not by any other power or influence in existence. We talk of a Zion that is to be built up. If a Zion is ever built up on this earth, it will have to be under the guidance and direction of the Almighty.

REVELATION AND THE CHURCH.—We talk about a Church that is to be built up and purified. If it is ever built up and purified, it will be under the influence of the gift of the Holy Ghost, the power of God manifested among his people, whereby iniquity will be rooted out, righteousness sustained, the principles of truth advanced, honor, integrity, truth, and virtue maintained, and hypocrisy, evil, crime, and corruption of every kind be rooted out. That will have to be done by the aid and under the guidance of the Almighty. There is no man living in and of himself, can guide the ship of Zion or regulate the affairs of the Church and kingdom of God unaided by the Spirit of God, and hence he has organized the Church as he has with all the various quorums and organizations as they exist today.—JD, 26:30-32, December 14, 1884.

THE BIBLE CAME BY REVELATION.—To whom are we indebted for this book called the Bible? We are told that holy men of old spake as they were moved upon by the Holy Ghost. And whence did they receive that Holy Ghost? Not of man, nor by man, but by the revelations of God, through our Lord and Savior Jesus Christ. . . .

REVELATIONS OF THE HOLY GHOST.—By obedience to the gospel we have received the Holy Ghost, and that Spirit takes of the things of God, and shows them to us. We have received this and hence have been baptized into one baptism, and have all partaken of the selfsame Spirit, as Paul expressed it, "dividing to every man severally as he will." (I Corinthians 12:11.) The question arises, What is the object of this? It is that the world should be visited from time to time and communications made to the human family.

Because light cleaves to light, truth cleaves to truth, intelligence cleaves to intelligence; and as we are all made in the image of God, and as God is the God and Father of the spirits of all flesh, it is his right, it is his prerogative to communicate with the human family. We are told that there is a spirit in man and the inspiration of the Almighty giveth it understanding. God having made the earth, made the people to inhabit it, and made all things that exist therein, has a right to dictate, has a right to make known his will, has a right to communicate with whom he will and control matters as he sees proper: it belongs to him by right; and he has seen proper in these last days to restore his gospel to the earth, and, as I said before, intelligence cleaves to intelligence.—*JD,* 23:259-260, October 8, 1882.

REVELATION AND REALITY.—I presume as we obtain more of the Spirit of God—as we receive faith and intelligence that flow from him and the revelations that he imparts and will continue to impart to those who are faithful, we shall begin to understand things in a very different light from what many of us at the present time understand them. Even in temporal things there is a great difference among men in regard to their judgment, capacities, reasoning powers, and their comprehension of justice, equity, the rights of man, the duties that we owe to each other, and the various responsibilities that devolve upon us. But when we come to contemplate the things of God, the end of our existence, our origin, the position that we occupy in relation to our families, to each other, and to the church and kingdom of God, it is very difficult sometimes for us to understand things correctly in relation to the position of the world, to the things that have been, to the things that are, and to the things that are to come— to the purposes of God in relation to the human family, and how these purposes will be best advanced. We shall find, in reflecting upon all these matters, that there is a very great difference between the reasoning of the human family upon these matters and the plan that God would adopt for the accomplishment of his purposes and for the bringing to pass the things that have been spoken of by the holy prophets since the world began.—*JD,* 6:105-106, December 6, 1857.

Associated as we are with the kingdom of God, we may reasonably expect, so long as we do our duty before the Lord, to have continual developments of light, truth, and intelligence that emanate from the great God, for the guidance, direction, salvation, and exaltation of this people, whether it relates to time or to eternity. For everything we have to do with is eternal; and when we speak of time and eternity, they are only relative terms which we attach to things that are present, and things that are to come, and things that are past. But in relation to ourselves as individuals, we are eternal beings, although we occupy a certain space of eternity called time. In relation to the gospel we preach, it is eternal. In relation to our covenants and obligations, they are eternal. In relation to our promises, prospects, and hopes, they are eternal. And while we are acting upon this stage of being, we are merely commencing a state of things that will exist while countless ages shall roll along; and if we have right views and right feelings, and entertain correct principles as eternal beings, all our thoughts, our actions, our prospects—all our energies and our lives, will be engaged in laying a foundation upon which to build a superstructure that will be permanent, lasting, and enduring as the throne of the great Jehovah. If anything is short of this, it is short of the mark of the high calling whereunto we may or ought to arrive; and many of the little incidents and occurrences of life that we have to pass through are transient in comparison to the things that are to come; and yet all these little things are so many links in the great chain of our existence, of our hopes and prospects.—JD, 1:366, April 19, 1854.

FOREKNOWLEDGE AND ITS USE.—The gospel reveals many things to us which others are unacquainted with. I knew of those terrible events which were coming upon this nation previous to the breaking out of our great fratricidal war, just as well as I now know that they transpired, and I have spoken of them to many. What of that? Do I not know that a nation like that in which we live, a nation which is blessed with the freest, the most enlightened and magnificent government in the world today, with privileges which would exalt people to heaven if lived up to—do I not know that if they do not live up to them, but violate them and trample them under their feet, and discard the sacred principles of liberty by which we ought to be governed—do I not know that their punishment will be commensurate with the enlightenment which they possess? I do. And I know—I cannot help knowing that there are a great many more afflictions yet awaiting this nation. But would I put forth my hand to help bring them on? God forbid! And you, you Latter-day Saints, would you exercise your influence to the accomplishment of an object of that kind? God forbid! But we cannot help knowing these things. But our foreknowledge of these matters does not make us the agents in bringing them to pass. We are told that the wicked will slay the wicked. We are told in sacred writ that, "Vengeance is mine; and I will repay, saith the Lord." (Romans 12:19.) And in speaking of ourselves we need not be under any apprehensions pertaining to the acts of men, for the Lord has said, "And it is my purpose to provide for my saints." (Doctrine & Covenants 104: 15.) But it is our business to be saints. And to be worthy of that character it is our duty to live by the principles of virtue, truth, integrity, holiness, purity, and honor, that we may at all times secure the favor of Almighty God; that his blessings may be with us and dwell in our bosoms; that the peace of God may abide in our habitations; that our fields, our flocks, and our herds may be blessed of the Lord; and that we, as a people, may be under his divine protection.—*JD*, 22:141-142, July 3, 1881.

## THE SPIRIT OF GOD AND THE GIFT OF THE
## HOLY GHOST

ALL MEN HAVE CLAIMS ON GOD FOR GUIDANCE.—Now outside the gospel, outside of revelation, outside of any special communication from the Lord, all men, more or less, everywhere, have certain claims upon their Heavenly Father, who is said to be the God and Father of the spirits of all flesh. Then we are told, when Jesus spake to his disciples, they asked him how they were to pray. He said, say, Our Father who art in heaven, hallowed be thy name. Who? Our Father—the God and the Father of the spirits of all flesh. When you approach him, say, Our Father who art in heaven. Then, they belong to our Father, as well as we.

THE SPIRIT AVAILABLE TO ALL MEN.—In regard to the operation of the Spirit upon man, let me draw your attention to a fact that is generally understood by all reflecting men, and that is, no matter how wicked a man may be, how far he may have departed from the right, such a man will generally admire and respect a good man, an honorable man, and a virtuous man; and such a man will frequently say; "I wish I could do as that man does, but I cannot: I wish I could pursue a correct course, but I am overcome of evil." They cannot help respecting the good and the honorable, although they may not be governed by principles of honor and virtue themselves. This same spirit which is given to every man outside of the gospel has been manifested in the different ages of the world. When I say outside of it, the Latter-day Saints will understand me. When I speak of the gospel, I speak of the gospel revealed by our Lord and Savior Jesus Christ, and which has existed at times through the different ages, and which, wherever it did exist brought men into close communion with the Lord; hence the gospel is called the everlasting gospel. The scriptures unequivocally state that our Savior brought life and immortality to light through the gospel, and wherever a knowledge of life and immortality existed, it was through the gospel; and whenever and wherever there was no knowledge of life and immortality, there was no gospel.

etc. And what shall we say of such men? Shall we say that they were wicked? No. It is lawful to do good always, and anyone who seeks to promote the welfare of the human family is a benefactor of mankind and ought to be sustained.—*JD*, 23:370-372, February 11, 1883.

THE SPIRIT OF GOD AND THE GIFT OF THE HOLY GHOST.— There is and always has been a spirit abroad in the world which is really a portion of the Spirit of God, which leads mankind, in many instances, to discriminate between good and evil, and between right and wrong. They have a conscience that accuses or excuses them for their acts; and although the world of mankind is very wicked and very corrupt, yet it will be found that almost all men, though they may not do good themselves, appreciate good actions in others.

The scriptures say that God "hath made of one blood all nations of men for to dwell on all the face of the earth, and hath determined the times before appointed, and the bounds of their habitation.

"That they should seek the Lord, if haply they might feel after him, and find him, though he be not far from every one of us." (Acts 17:26-27.) The scripture further says, he has given unto them a portion of his spirit to profit withal. But there is quite a distinction between the position that these people occupy and the one which we occupy. We have something more than that portion of the Spirit of God which is given to every man, and it is called the gift of the Holy Ghost, which is received through obedience to the first principles of the gospel of Christ, by the laying on of hands of the servants of God. . . . It is this Spirit that brings us into relationship with God, and it differs very materially from the portion of Spirit that is given to all men to profit withal. The special gift of the Holy Ghost is obtained, as I have said, through obedience to the first principles of the gospel. Its province is to lead us into all truth, and to bring to our remembrance things past, present, and to come. It contemplates the future and unfolds things we had not thought of heretofore, and these things are very distinctly described in the Bible, in the Book of Mormon, and in the Doctrine and Covenants. Herein lies the difference between us and others, and it was so in former times.—*JD*, 23:320-321, November 23, 1882.

JOSEPH SMITH'S ADVICE ON THE GIFT OF THE HOLY GHOST.—Joseph Smith, upwards of forty years ago, said to me: "Brother Taylor, you have received the Holy Ghost. Now follow the influence of that Spirit, and it will lead you into all truth, until by and by, it will become in you a principle of revelation." Then he told me never to arise in the morning without bowing before the Lord, and dedicating myself to him during that day. Some people treat these things lightly. I do not, because I know that we derive our food, our raiment, and all earthly as well as spiritual blessings from the goodness of God our Heavenly Father. I know, furthermore, that as president of this church I should not know how to dictate if the Lord did not help me. Should I desire people to yield to my ideas? I have no ideas only as God gives them to me; neither should you. Some people are very persistent in having their own way and carrying out their own peculiar theories. I have no thoughts of that kind, but I have a desire, when anything comes along, to learn the will of God, and then to do it, and to teach my brethren to do it, that we may all grow up unto Christ our living head, that we may be acquainted with correct principles and govern ourselves accordingly.—*JD*, 22:314, October 19, 1881.

THE COMFORTER.—This same Comforter has been given, in connection with the gospel in these days, for our enlightenment, for our instruction, for our guidance, that we may have a knowledge of things that are past, of the dealings of God with the human family, of the principles of truth that have been developed in the different ages, of the position of the world and its relationship to God in those different ages, of its position in years that are past and gone, and of its present status. It is also given for our enlightenment, that we may be enabled to conduct all things according to the mind and will of God, and in accordance with his eternal laws and those principles which exist in the heavens, and which have been provided by God for the salvation and exaltation of a fallen world; also for the manifestation of principles which have been and will be developed in the interest of man, not only pertaining to this world, but also to that which is to come, through which medium the Lord will make known his plans and designs to his priesthood and his people in his own due time.—*JD*, 25: 178-179, May 18, 1884.

THE NEED FOR WISDOM AND TRUST IN GOD.—There is not a position that we can occupy in life, either as fathers, mothers, children, masters, servants, or as elders of Israel holding the holy priesthood in all its ramifications, but what we need continually is wisdom flowing from the Lord and intelligence communicated by him, that we may know how to perform correctly the various duties and avocations of life, and to fulfil the various responsibilities that rest upon us. And hence the necessity all the day long, and every day and every week, month, and year, and under all circumstances, of men leaning upon the Lord and being guided by that Spirit that flows from him, that we may not fall into error—that we may neither do anything wrong, say anything wrong, nor think anything wrong, and all the time retain that Spirit, which can only be kept by observing purity, holiness, and virtue, and living continually in obedience to the laws and commandments of God.—*JD*, 6:106, December 6, 1857.

There is not a man upon the earth that has put his trust in God, I do not care what part of the world he has been in, but what can say that he delivered him. I know that has been the case with me, emphatically so. I have been satisfied, when in foreign lands and in strange countries, where I had no access but to the Almighty, that he was on my side, and I know that he has answered my prayers.—*JD*, 8:96, June 17, 1860.

THE TESTIMONY OF THE SPIRIT.—When the light that is in heaven communicates with the light within us, when the Spirit that dwells in the bosom of the Almighty dwells in ours, and an intercourse is opened between heaven and us, we are then placed in a position to understand that which it would be impossible to comprehend upon any natural principle known to us, and hence it is written, "For what man knoweth the things of a man, save the spirit of man which is in him? even so the things of God knoweth no man, but the Spirit of God." (1 Corinthians 2:11.) In order that men may indeed become the children of God, he has introduced in the first principles of the gospel the means of their becoming possessed of his Spirit through baptism and laying on of hands by those having authority, being sent and ordained and authorized by him that they may receive the Holy Ghost. What can be a stronger evidence to any man than an evidence of this kind? It is not something that affects the outward ear alone; it is not something that affects simply his judgment, but it affects his inner man; it affects the spirit that dwells within him; it is a part of God imparted unto man, if you please, giving him an assurance that God lives. This is a thing of very great importance, more so, perhaps, than many people imagine. A man receives an assurance that God lives, and not only that God lives, but that he is a son of God, because he feels that he has partaken of his Spirit, the Spirit of adoption; and hence it was said concerning the saints of old, "For ye have not received the spirit of bondage again to fear; but ye have received the Spirit of adoption, whereby we cry, Abba, Father.

"The Spirit itself beareth witness with our spirit, that we are the children of God." (Romans 8:15, 16).—*JD*, 11:22-23, December 11, 1864.

THE SPIRIT OF UNDERSTANDING.—I do not know of any way whereby we can be taught, instructed, and be made to comprehend our true position, only by being under the influence of the Spirit of the living God. A man may speak by the Spirit of God, but it requires a portion of that Spirit also in those who hear, to enable them to comprehend correctly the importance of the things that are delivered to them, and hence the difficulty the Lord and his saints have always had in making the people comprehend the things that are especially for their interests. We all consider that if we could be taught of God it would be very well. I suppose the world generally would consider it to be a great blessing. Then the question arises in their minds, whether the teachings they receive come from God or not. How are they to know that? I know of no other way than that which is spoken in the scriptures, "But there is a spirit in man: and the inspiration of the Almighty giveth them understanding." (Job 32:8) And, again, we are told in the New Testament, that "No man knoweth the things of God but by the Spirit of God."[1] Hence all the wisdom, all the intelligence, all the reasoning, all the philosophy and all the arguments that could be brought to bear on the human mind would be of no avail unless the mind of man is prepared to receive this teaching—prepared by the Spirit of the Lord, the same Spirit which conveys the intelligence.—*JD*, 10:145, April 6, 1863.

THE PRAYER OF FAITH.—Through some remarks already made I am reminded of my boyhood. At that early period of my life I learned to approach God. Many a time I have gone into the fields, and, concealing myself behind some bush, would bow before the Lord and call upon him to guide and direct me. And he heard my prayer. At times I would get other boys to accompany me. It would not hurt you, boys and girls, to call upon the Lord in your secret places, as I did. That was the spirit which I had when a little boy. And God has led me from one thing to another. But I did not have the privilege that you have. There was nobody to teach me, while you have access to good men at any time who can direct you in the way of life and salvation. But my spirit was drawn out after God then; and I feel the same yet.—*JD*, 22:314-315, October 19, 1881.

---

[1]Compare 1 Corinthians 2:11.

CHAPTER V

# TRUTH

## THE QUEST FOR TRUTH

THE CONSTANT SEARCH.—We are after the truth. We commenced searching for it, and we are constantly in search of it, and so fast as we find any true principle revealed by any man, by God, or by holy angels, we embrace it and make it part of our religious creed.—*JD*, 14:341-342, March 3, 1872.

One great reason why men have stumbled so frequently in many of their researches after philosophical truth is that they have sought them with their own wisdom, and gloried in their own intelligence, and have not sought unto God for that wisdom that fills and governs the universe and regulates all things. That is one great difficulty with the philosophers of the world, as it now exists, that man claims to himself to be the inventor of everything he discovers. Any new law and principle which he happens to discover he claims to himself instead of giving glory to God.— *JD*, 11:74, February 5, 1865.

THE POWER OF TRUTH.—If the saints could understand things correctly; if they could see themselves as God sees them; if they could know and understand and appreciate the principles of eternal truth as they emanate from God, and as they dwell in his bosom; if they could know their high calling's glorious hope, and the future destiny that awaits them, inasmuch as they are faithful, there is not a saint of God, there is not one in these valleys of the mountains, but would prostrate himself before him. He would dedicate his heart, and his mind, and his soul, and his strength to God, and his body, and spirit, and property, and everything he possesses of earth, and esteem it one of the greatest privileges that could be conferred upon mortal man. If there are those who do not see these things aright, it is because they see in part and know in part. It is because their hearts are not devoted to God, as they ought to be. It is because their spirits are not entirely under the influence of the Spirit of the Most High. It is because they have not so lived up to their privileges, as to put themselves in possession of that light and truth that emanate from God to his people. It is because the god of this world [Satan] has blinded their minds that they cannot fully understand, that they cannot be made fully acquainted with the great and glorious principles of eternal truth.—*JD*, 1:367, April 19, 1854.

THE VALUE OF TRUTH.—There is nothing of more value to me than the principles of eternal truth; than the principles of eternal lives; eternal salvation, and eternal exaltations in the kingdom of God. But then it is for us to comprehend them, for if we do not comprehend them, no matter how great the truths, they cannot benefit us. We frequently think a little more of a nice span of horses, or a nice wagon, or a favorite cow, and such things, than we do of God's work, as our boys sometimes get attached to a few marbles thinking that they are everything. They do not like to leave their marbles to obey father or mother, and God finds us about the same. We get a few dollars, or a farm, and a little stock, and a few other things, and we cannot afford to neglect these. We cannot afford to take time to pray, nor to listen to the voice of Father, we are so busy playing marbles. And occasionally when we play marbles among the dollars, we try to cheat one another, as boys sometimes do at marbles, and try to take advantage one of another. I never like to see boys cheat and never like to see men cheat at their kind of marbles. Our feelings and affections get placed on wrong things.

We are here to build up Zion, and to establish the kingdom of God.—*JD*, 22:219-220, June 27, 1881.

THE ROLE OF TRUTH.—We are not satisfied, as many men are, with simple theories, because this, that, or the other man or bodies of men have told us they are true. We are governed by no man's *ipse dixit*. We have not any particular dogmas to sustain, or any special theory to establish. Living in the world of mankind, surrounded by the works of Nature, walking, as it were, in the presence of the Great Elohim, we wish to comprehend and embrace all truth and seek for and obtain everything that is calculated to exalt, ennoble, and dignify the human family. And wherever we find truth, no matter where, or from what source it may come, it becomes part and parcel of our religious creed, or our moral creed, or our philosophy, as the case may be, or whatever you may please to term it.

"WE ARE OPEN FOR THE RECEPTION OF ALL TRUTH. . . ." —We are open for the reception of all truth, of whatever nature it may be, and are desirous to obtain and possess it, to search after it as we would for hidden treasures; and to use all the knowledge God gives to us to possess ourselves of all the intelligence that he has given to others; and to ask at his hands to reveal unto us his will, in regard to things that are the best calculated to promote the happiness and well-being of human society. If there are any good principles, any moral philosophy that we have not yet attained to, we are desirous to learn them. If there is anything in the scientific world that we do not yet comprehend,

we desire to become acquainted with it. If there is any branch
of philosophy calculated to promote the well-being of humanity,
that we have not yet grasped, we wish to possess ourselves of it.
If there is anything pertaining to the rule and government of
nations, or politics, if you please, that we are not acquainted with,
we desire to possess it. If there are any religious ideas, any
theological truths, any principles pertaining to God, that we
have not learned, we ask mankind, and we pray God, our
Heavenly Father, to enlighten our minds that we may comprehend, realize, embrace, and live up to them as part of our religious
faith. Thus our ideas and thoughts would extend as far as the
wide world spreads, embracing everything pertaining to light, life,
or existence pertaining to this world or the world that is to
come. They would dig into the bowels of the earth, or go to
the depth of hell, if you please. They would soar after the
intelligence of the Gods that dwell in the eternal worlds. They
would grasp everything that is good and noble and excellent and
happifying and calculated to promote the well-being of the human
family.
There is no man nor set of men who have pointed out the
pathway for our feet to travel in, in relation to these matters.
There are no dogmas nor theories extant in the world that we
profess to listen to, unless they can be verified by the principles
of eternal truth. We carefully scan, investigate, criticize, and
examine everything that presents itself to our view, and so far as
we are enabled to comprehend any truths in existence, we gladly
hail them as part and portion of the system with which we are
associated.—*JD*, 14:337-338, March 3, 1872.

## TRUTH: THE LATTER-DAY SAINT ATTITUDE

TRUTH, ERROR, AND TOLERANCE.—I believe God has a
great design in view, in the creation of the human family. I do
not believe that an all-wise Being would ever make a beautiful
earth like this, and people it with man, and a multiplicity of
other kinds of beings designed to exist upon it, and all for no
purpose. I do not believe that three-hundred-fifty millions of
people that live in China in a state of heathen darkness are created
to live in this state, and be damned because they have not the
right religion. I do not believe that all the nations that worship
various kinds of idols, in different parts of the earth, and know
nothing about the true God, will be consigned to be burned in
fire hereafter, because they know no better than worship as they
do. I cannot receive any such ideas into my mind. Although
I was going to say I am not a Universalist, but I am, and I
am also a Presbyterian, and a Roman Catholic, and a Methodist.

In short, I believe in every true principle that is embodied in any person or sect, and reject the false. If there is any truth in heaven, earth, or hell, I want to embrace it, I care not what shape it comes in to me, who brings it, or who believes in it, whether it is popular or unpopular. Truth, eternal truth, I wish to float in and enjoy.

Now I come to us, Mormons. We are the only true Church, so we say. We have the only true faith, so we say and believe. I believe we have many great and true principles revealed from the heavens. I will tell you how I feel about it, and what I have said many times when I have been abroad among the priests, people, and philosophers. If any man under the heavens can show me one principle of error that I have entertained, I will lay it aside forthwith, and be thankful for the information. On the other hand if any man has any principle of truth, whether moral, religious, philosophical, or of any other kind, that is calculated to benefit mankind, I promise him I will embrace it, but I will not partake of his errors along with it. If a man should say, I am in possession of one piece of truth, and, because I have got that, I must be right, am I to believe him? Certainly not. It does not follow that he has not many errors.

The Catholics have many pieces of truth. So have the Protestants, the Mohammedans, and heathens. And am I to embrace one of these systems because it has certain things that are right? No. Suppose a person should tell me that two multiplied by two makes four. Well, that is right. I believe it with all my heart. But suppose he believes and teaches also, that six and four make twenty, and exhorts me to believe it, saying—I was right in the other calculation, did I not prove the other to you? O yes, but you did not prove that six and four make twenty. I will take out the truth and leave the error. . . .

On the other hand, am I to think it is right, because I am right, to send everybody else to hell? No, I will leave them in the hands of God. He has told me to preach the gospel to every creature, saying, "He that believeth and is baptized shall be saved; but he that believeth not shall be damned."[1] He has told me to do this. And how many millions of mankind are there who have never heard the gospel? And are they going to be damned for not believing in a thing they have not heard, and that never came within their range, and that they have not the slightest knowledge of? No. What is it we have to do? We must spread forth the light of the gospel. Why? Because God has communicated a system of religion which is calculated to ennoble and exalt the human family.—JD, 1:154-156, June 12, 1853.

---

[1] See Mark 16:16.

TRUTH AND INTELLIGENT JUDGMENT.—The heavens and the earth are full of intelligence, and God rules over and directs the affairs of nations as well as those of individuals and people. Whatever may be our peculiar notions or ideas of other men and their profession, the time will come, and is not far distant when the secrets of all hearts will be revealed, and when all of us, Latter-day Saints and others, Jews and gentiles, peoples who now live, those that shall live and those who have lived, will be judged, not according to their peculiar theories, ideas, or notions, but according to the principles of eternal truth as it exists in the bosom of God, or is manifested by his eternal laws.—*JD*, 19:363, June 16, 1878.

# CHAPTER VI

# MAN

## THE NATURE OF MAN

Man stands at the head of creation. God gave unto him dominion over the fish of the sea, the fowls of the air, the beasts of the field, and every creeping thing that creepeth upon the face of the earth. He is lord of all.—*M*, 2.

THE ORIGIN OF MAN.—If we take man, he is said to have been made in the image of God, for the simple reason that he is a son of God, and being his son, he is, of course, his offspring, an emanation from God, in whose likeness, we are told, he is made. He did not originate from a chaotic mass of matter, moving or inert, but came forth possessing, in an embryonic state, all the faculties and powers of a God. And when he shall be perfected, and have progressed to maturity, he will be like his Father—a God, being indeed his offspring. As the horse, the ox, the sheep, and every living creature, including man, propagates its own species and perpetuates its own kind, so does God perpetuate his.—*MA*, 164-165.

A man, as a man, could arrive at all the dignity that a man was capable of obtaining or receiving; but it needed a God to raise him to the dignity of a God.—*MA*, 145.

A GOD IN EMBRYO.—Man is a dual being, possessed of body and spirit, made in the image of God, and connected with him and with eternity. He is a God in embryo and will live and progress throughout the eternal ages, if obedient to the laws of the Godhead, as the Gods progress throughout the eternal ages.—*JD*, 23:65, April 9, 1882.

SOME POINTS OF VIEW.—"What is man, that thou art mindful of him? and the son of man, that thou visitest him?" (Psalm 8:4.)

In one point of view, man appears very poor, weak, and imbecile, and very insignificant: in another point of view, he appears wise, intelligent, strong, honorable, and exalted. It is just in the way that you look at a man that you are led to form your opinions concerning him. In one respect, he appears, as it were, as the grass of the field, which today is, and tomorrow is cast into the oven. He is changeable in his opinions, in his thoughts, reflections, and actions. He is idle, vain, and visionary, without being governed by any correct principle. He comes into existence, as it were, like a butterfly, flutters around for a little while, dies, and is no more. In another point of view, we look at him as emanating from the Gods—as a God in embryo—as an eternal being who had an existence before he came here, and who will exist after his mortal remains are mingled and associated with dust, from whence he came, and from whence he will be resurrected and partake of that happiness for which he is destined, or receive the reward of his evil deeds, according to circumstances.

If we look at the position of man as he has been and as he is, what is he, whether we regard the most powerful and mighty, or the most humble—whether as emperors, warriors, statesmen, philosophers, as rich or poor, we find he has passed away, and to us is sleeping in oblivion. Where are some of those great and mighty men that made the earth tremble—at whose nod and beck, and at the crook of whose finger nations quaked with fear? They have returned to dust and ashes, and worms prey upon their systems. They have waned away, and many of the great and hororable are as much despised since they died as they were honored while they lived and were in the possession of their earthly glory. What is man?

In some points of view, the human race are feeble indeed. They are feeble in their bodies, minds, and spirits, and need some sustaining influence to uphold them both in body and mind before they can occupy their true position in society, whether in relation to this world or in relation to the world which is to come. For instance, a man may study for years, and perhaps some faint affliction of his body will overturn his intellect; he loses his senses, his reason is fled, and he becomes a raving maniac. We are indeed poor creatures. Think what a number of infirmities the human system is subject to, until finally death closes its mortal career, and it is laid among the silent dead. . . .

MEN IN SOCIETY.—Look at him in a social capacity. Are we much better off now socially than the people were several thousand years ago, with all the teachings of our philosophers and moralists, and with all the essays there have been written, combined with all the influence of the priesthood of the present day? Men are paid in our age for doing a great deal, and they ought to accomplish, at least, something. . . . When we contemplate all these things, how weak and inefficient and poor and feeble and contemptible man appears!—how little he has accomplished for the benefit of his fellow man, or for succeeding generations!

"What is man, that thou art mindful of him?" (Psalm 8:4.)

MAN AS AN ETERNAL BEING.—What is he? Let us look again and view him in another aspect. Why, he is an eternal being, and possesses within him a principle that is destined to exist

"while life and thought and being last, or immortality endures."
What is he? He had his being in the eternal worlds; he existed
before he came here. He is not only the son of man, but he is
the son of God also. He is a God in embryo, and possesses within
him a spark of that eternal flame which was struck from the blaze
of God's eternal fire in the eternal world, and is placed here
upon the earth that he may possess true intelligence, true light,
true knowledge,—that he may know himself—that he may know
God—that he may know something about what he was before
he came here—that he may know something about what he is
destined to enjoy in the eternal worlds—that he may be fully
acquainted with his origin, with his present existence, and with
his future destiny—that he may know something about the
strength and weakness of human nature—that he may understand
the divine law, and learn to conquer his passions, and bring into
subjection every principle that is at variance with the law of God
—that he may understand his true relationship to God; and
finally, that he may learn how to subdue, to conquer, subject all
wrong, seek after, obtain, and possess every true, holy, virtuous,
and heavenly principle; and, as he is only a sojourner, that he may
fulfil the measure of his creation, help himself and family, be a
benefit to the present and future generations, and go back to God,
having accomplished the work he came here to perform. . . .

MAN'S PURPOSE AND DESTINY.—What is man? He is an
immortal being. He is a part of the Deity. . . . and he has come
here to work out his salvation and accomplish the thing he came
into existence for. We have come here to build up the kingdom
of God, to establish correct principles, to teach the world righteousness, and to make millions of the human family happy—even all
who will listen to the principles of eternal truth. We are here to
introduce correct doctrine, to introduce correct morals, to introduce
correct philosophy, to introduce correct government, and to teach
men how to live and how to die—how to be happy in this world
and in the world which is to come, and to lay the foundation for
eternal lives in the eternal worlds.

MAN, A SON OF GOD.—What is man? A God, even the son
of God, possessing noble aspirations, holy feelings, that may be
governed by virtuous principles, possessing elevated ideas, wishing
to realize everything that God has destined to submit to all his
laws, to endure every kind of privation and affliction and suffering, as seeing him that is invisible, looking for a city that hath
foundations, whose builder and maker is God—feeling to live
for that purpose, and that alone.

This is what man is, if he lives the religion of heaven, and
performs faithfully those things God has appointed him to do,

that he may increase from intelligence to intelligence, and go on with that eternal progression, not only in this world, but in worlds without end.—*JD*, 8:1-2, 3-4, 5, February 19, 1860.

## THE MIND OF MAN

There is something peculiar in the organization of man, particularly in regard to his mind. We can think, we can reflect, we can conceive of things, we can form our judgment of events that are transpiring around, but it is difficult for us to perceive or to comprehend how those things are accomplished, and by what process they are brought about. A man, for instance, can store up in his memory thousands and tens of thousands of things. A good linguist, for example, can retain in his memory thousands of words in his own language, and thousands and tens of thousands in other languages, and he can draw upon these when he pleases, and remember their significations. I can remember the time, some years ago, when no person could tell me a passage in the Bible but what I could turn to it. I could not remember every passage, but I knew their connections and could tell others where they could find them.

BRIGHAM YOUNG'S MIND.—President Young's memory is remarkable in regard to names and persons. I have traveled with him throughout the length and breadth of this Territory, and I do not know that I have ever yet seen him come in contact with a man whose name he did not remember and the circumstances connected with him. There is something remarkable in this.

THE MIND'S STOREHOUSE.—Again, on theological subjects, a man will remember not only all the doctrines which he himself believes, but also the doctrines of various systems of religion that exist in the world, and be enabled to separate, to describe, or define them. Now, the question is, where are all these things stowed away? What book are they written in; where are they recorded? A man may travel over the earth, he may visit towns, cities, and villages, and gaze upon oceans, seas, rivers, streams, mountains, valleys, and plains; upon landscapes and different kinds of scenery, and make himself acquainted with all the vegetable world, and these pictures and this intelligence are carefully laid away somewhere. He may study chemistry, botany, geology, astronomy, geography, natural history, mechanics, the arts and sciences, and everything in creation which man is capacitated to receive, and store it away in his memory from the time of his youth up to old age.

There is something very remarkable in that. And then the question arises, how do we judge of those things? If a man sees a thing, how does he see it? There is something very remarkable in the construction of the human eye; it is something like these photographic instruments that receive impressions, only he gazes upon them and his eye takes them in, and the scene he gazes upon is actually imprinted upon what is called the retina of the eye; and one thing after another is recorded, until thousands, and tens of thousands, and millions of things are laid away through that medium, and he is enabled to see any of these things whenever he pleases; his will can call them forth, and they pass in panoramic form before his vision from some source, where they are deposited and registered; all those things that he has gazed upon, that he has handled with his hands, or felt by the sense of touch, he can call up at his pleasure. There is something remarkable in this when we reflect upon it. Men talk about this registry being in the brain, but men's heads do not get any larger. When men get what is called the "big head," it is because there is nothing in their heads. The heart gets no bigger, the body no larger, and yet all these records are laid away somewhere.

UNDERSTANDING.—Let us examine the scriptures in relation to some things, and see what they say concerning man. "But there is a spirit in man; and the inspiration of the Almighty giveth them understanding."[1] We learn from this that there is a spirit in man in addition to this outward frame, to these hands, these eyes, this body, with all its powers, and appliances, and members; there is a spirit, an essence—a principle of the Almighty, if you please—a peculiar essence that dwells in this body, that seems to be inseparably connected therewith. . . .

THE IMAGE OF GOD.—We are made in the image of God, we were designed by the intelligence of God, and the organs we have are the same kind of organs that the Gods themselves possess. I consider that the body and the spirit are connected together in some inscrutable, indefinable, and intelligent manner; that, if we comprehended, would be a greater wonder and mystery to us than anything that we have already referred to.—*JD*, 11:74-77, February 5, 1865.

## MAN AS MAN

THE OPPORTUNITIES AND POSSIBILITIES.—Man, as man, can only make use of the powers which are possessed by man. Made, indeed, as represented in the scriptures in the image of God, as monarch of the universe, he stands erect on the earth

---

[1]Compare Job 32:8.

in the likeness of his great Creator; beautifully constructed in all his parts, with a body possessing all the functions necessary for the wants of humanity; standing, not only by right, but by adaptability, beauty, symmetry and glory, at the head of all creation; possessing also mental powers and the capacity of reflecting upon the past, with capabilities to reason upon cause and effect, and by the inductive powers of his mind, through the inspiration of the Almighty, to comprehend the magnificent laws of nature as exhibited in the works of creation; with the capacity also of using the elements and forces of nature, and of adapting them to his own special benefit; and by his powers penetrating into the deep, ascending into the heavens, rushing with mighty velocity across the earth, making use of the separate or combined forces of nature with which he is surrounded and subjugating them to his will; as, likewise, by his intelligence, he has dominion over the fishes of the sea, over the fowls of the air, and over the cattle. He can girdle the earth with the electric fluid and convey his thoughts to any land or zone; by the same subtle influence he can talk with his fellows, and be heard when hundreds of miles apart. He can apply the forces of earth, air, fire and water to make them subservient to his will, and stands proudly erect as the head of all creation and the representative of God upon the earth. But while he occupies this exalted position, and is in the image of God, yet he possesses simply, as a man, only the powers which belong to man; and is subject to weakness, infirmity, disease and death. And when he dies, without some superior aid pertaining to the future, that noble structure lies silent and helpless, its organs, that heretofore were active, lively and energetic, are now dormant, inactive and powerless. And what of the mind, that before went back into eternity and reached forward into eternity? And what of its powers? Or what of that spirit, which, with its Godlike energies, its prescience and power, could grasp infinity? What of it, and where is it? . . . If . . . there is a spirit in man which reaches into futurity, that would grasp eternal progress, eternal enjoyments, and eternal exaltations; then those glories, those exaltations, those capabilities and those powers must be the gift of some superior being, power, or authority to that which exists in man; for the foregoing is a brief exhibition of the powers and capabilities of humanity. It is of this gift that we now speak. . . . It is for the exaltation of man to this state of superior intelligence and Godhood that the mediation and atonement of Jesus Christ is instituted; and that noble being, man, made in the image of God, is rendered capable not only of being a son of man, but also a son of God, through adoption, and is rendered capable of becoming a God, possessing the power, the majesty, the exaltation and the position of a God. . . .

CHRIST'S SERVICE PLACES GODHOOD WITHIN MAN'S REACH.—As a man through the powers of his body he could attain to the dignity and completeness of manhood, but could go no further. As a man he is born, as a man he lives, and as a man he dies. But through the essence and power of the Godhead, which is in him, which descended to him as the gift of God from his Heavenly Father, he is capable of rising from the contracted limits of manhood to the dignity of a God, and thus through the atonement of Jesus Christ and the adoption he is capable of eternal exaltation, eternal lives, and eternal progression. —MA, 139-141.

## THE PROBATION AND DESTINY OF MAN

THE PROBLEM AND THE OUTLOOK.—Now, this earth was formed for a certain purpose, and man was also formed for a certain purpose. And there are certain principles laid down—you will find them in the Bible, in the Book of Mormon, in the Doctrine and Covenants, and in the various revelations that God has made through his servants. There are certain principles laid down indicating that there are different grades of men possessing varied powers and privileges, and that these men have to pass through a certain ordeal, called by man a probation. That is, we are here in a probationary state, in a state of trial. As men live and act according to the intelligence they are in possession of—the privileges which they enjoy, and the deeds that they perform, whether for good or evil—there will be a time of judgment, and there will be a separation of these various peoples according to the way in which they have lived and acted upon the earth. Hence Paul tells that there are bodies celestial and bodies terrestrial, that there is one glory of the sun, another of the moon, and another of the stars, and as one star differeth from another star in glory, so shall it also be in the resurrection.[1] Joseph Smith, in speaking on the same subject,[2] tells us that there are bodies celestial, bodies terrestrial, and bodies telestial, which agrees precisely with the remarks made by Paul, only in other language. Thus there are many curious things associated with our existence here upon the earth, which the natural man does not and cannot comprehend. No man can know the things of God, but by the Spirit of God.—JD, 26:33-34, December 14, 1884.

ON BECOMING LIKE GOD.—We talk of becoming like God. What does he do? He governs this and other worlds, regulates

---

[1]See 1 Corinthians 15:40-42.
[2]Doctrine and Covenants, Section 76.

all the systems, and gives them their motions and revolutions. He preserves them in their various orbits, and governs them by unerring, unchangeable laws, as they traverse the immensity of space. In our world he gives day and night, summer and winter, seedtime and harvest. He adapts man, the beasts of the field, the fowls of the air, and the fishes of the sea to their various climates and elements. He takes care of and provides for, not only the hundreds of millions of the human family, but the myriads of beasts, fowls, and fishes. He feeds and provides for them day by day, giving them their breakfast, dinner and supper. He takes care of the reptiles and other creeping things, and feeds the myriads of animalculae, which crowd earth, air, and water. His hand is over all and his providence sustains all. The hairs of our head are numbered, and a sparrow cannot fall to the ground without our Heavenly Father's notice; he clothes the lilies of the valleys and feeds the ravens when they cry.

> His wisdom's vast and knows no bound,
> A deep where all our thoughts are drowned.

We would be like him! Be kings and priests unto God and rule with him, and yet we are obliged to have guardians placed over us to teach us how to take care of a bushel of wheat. We are far behind, but we have time for improvement; and I think we shall have to make some important changes for the better in our proceedings, before we become like our Father who dwells in the heavens.—*JD*, 10:260, October 10, 1863.

## FREE WILL

AN ETERNAL PRINCIPLE.—We talk sometimes about free will. Is that a correct principle? Yes. And it is a principle that has always existed, and proceeded from God, our Heavenly Father. When God revealed himself to Joseph Smith, it was optional whether he obeyed his counsel or not. I suppose, however, looking at things as they exist, and as they are in truth, God understood that he would do it, he having been selected for that purpose a long, long time ago. And [I suppose] that the Lord knew that he would adhere to those principles and would carry out the designs of heaven as they should be communicated unto and required of him.

NO COERCION IN THE GOSPEL PLAN.—We received the gospel. Was any one forced to obey it? Was there any coercion in any possible way manifested toward us? Not that I know of. Was Oliver Cowdery, who was the second elder in the church, obliged to receive this gospel? No, he was not. Was Hyrum

Smith obliged to received it? No, he was not. Were any of the witnesses to the Book of Mormon—the Whitmers and others? No. And after they did identify themselves with this church, were they compelled to stay in it? No. Have any of the members of the quorum of the twelve, the seventies, the high priests, or the members of the high councils, or the presidents of the seventies, or any class of men in this church, been compelled to occupy the position to which they have been called? I do not know of any, do you? I know there was no coercion used with me further than the force of truth recommending itself to my mind; neither was there with you, further than the power of truth operating upon your minds. And after you received the gospel, were you compelled to leave your homes to come here? No, you were not. In fact, it was your desire to come here, and you could not be kept back from coming because you were impelled by the spirit which the Latter-day gospel inspires to come to the land of Zion. If this is called compulsion, it is not the compulsion of man, but the operation of the Spirit of God which you received through obedience to the gospel.

THE FREEDOM OF FAITH.—We may here ask, in acting under the dominion or control of the priesthood are any of you forced to do anything you do not want to? If you think you are in any possible way, I absolve you from it today, every one of you. These are my ideas about the rights of men. It is "all free grace and all free will," as the poet has it. We have not been coerced to come into the church; we are not coerced to remain in it. But we have taken upon ourselves a profession of faith in God, and as Latter-day Saints we believe that God has spoken, that the heavens have been opened, that the everlasting gospel has been restored to man, and we believe that God has organized his church by revelation, through his servant Joseph Smith in the form that we now have it. This is our faith. We cannot help that faith. I cannot help my faith, neither can you help yours. There was from the first, scriptural evidence adduced and a certain kind of reasoning used to enlighten our minds. We believed, after hearing the preaching of the gospel, that it was our duty to be baptized in the name of Jesus for the remission of our sins, and to have hands laid upon our heads for the reception of the Holy Ghost. And when we received that Holy Ghost, which takes of the things of God, it showed them unto us. And then we were placed upon another footing from what we were before. And that Spirit has enlightened our minds in regard to those things of which I have spoken, as well as in regard to many others. If God has revealed unto us certain things, can we help our faith in them, and can we help knowing this to be the church and kingdom of God? No. Can I? No. Can you? No. What

THE HUMANE INFLUENCE.—But outside of that there have
been many good influences abroad in the world. Many men in
the different ages, who, in the midst of wickedness and corruption,
have tried to stop the current of evil, have placed themselves in the
catalogue of reformers. Some of those have been what are called
heathen, others what are termed Christian, and others have been
scientific and philanthropic—lovers and benefactors of the human
race. The many reformers that existed in former ages have been
men many of whom have been sincerely desirous to do the will
of God, and to carry out his purposes, so far as they knew them.
And then there are thousands and tens of thousands of honorable
men living today in this nation, and other nations, who are honest
and upright and virtuous, and who esteem correct principles and
seek to be governed by them, so far as they know them.

DIFFERENCE BETWEEN UNIVERSAL GUIDANCE AND THE
GIFT OF THE HOLY GHOST.—But there is a very great difference
between this spirit and feeling that leads men to do right, which
is emphatically denominated a portion of the Spirit of God, which
is given to every man to profit withal, and what is termed in the
scriptures the gift of the Holy Ghost. Men may be desirous to do
right; they may be good, honorable, and conscientious; and then
when we come to the judgment pertaining to these things, we are
told that all men will be judged according to the deeds done in
the body, and according to the light and intelligence which they
possessed.

I will take, for instance, the position of the reformers, going
no further back than Luther and Melancthon; and then you may
come to Calvin, Knox, Whitfield, Wesley, Fletcher, and many
others; men who have been desirous in their day to benefit their
fellow men; who have proclaimed against vice, and advocated the
practice of virtue, uprightness, and the fear of God. But we all,
who have contemplated these subjects, know that those men never
did restore the gospel as it was taught by our Lord and Savior
Jesus Christ; neither did they see nor comprehend alike in biblical
matters. They groped, as it were, in the dark, with a portion of
the Spirit of God. They sought to benefit their fellow man; but
not having that union with God that the gospel imparts, they were
unable to arrive at just conclusions pertaining to those matters.
Hence, one introduced and taught one principle, and another introduced and taught another; and they were split up and divided, and
the spirit of antagonism was found at times among them; and with
all their desires to do good, they did not and could not restore
the gospel of the Son of God. None among them was able to
say, Thus saith the Lord. And that is the condition of the religious
world today. It is Babylon or confusion—confusion in ideas, confusion in regard to doctrine, confusion in regard to ordinances,

would men have to do to deprive me of this faith? They would have to cut off my head, or in some other way to kill me and then they could not change my faith. That would be impossible. If a man knows a thing, he knows it, and he cannot un-know it. There is one way whereby we can un-know these things, and that is by giving way to evil influences, to the powers of darkness, and by departing from the light of God; and then the light within us becomes darkness, and then "how great is that darkness."

A MAN'S FAITH CAN NOT BE CONTROLLED.—But when you talk about controlling a man's faith, it cannot be done; and I would say to people who are bent upon having me change my faith, all you have to do is to cut off my head, and even that would not do it, because I would still be myself, entertaining the same faith in the next world. And therefore, all that men could do toward accomplishing this object would be to destroy the body. But that principle which God has implanted in our hearts, it would be impossible to destroy. Hence says Jesus, "And fear not them which kill the body, but are not able to kill the soul: but rather fear him which is able to destroy both soul and body in hell."[1]—*JD*, 22:7-9, January 9, 1881.

## HUMAN NATURE AND HUMAN ENJOYMENT

ASSOCIATION OF THE SEXES.—We have a great many principles innate in our natures that are correct, but they want sanctifying. God said to man, "Be fruitful, and multiply, and replenish the earth, and subdue it: and have dominion over the fish of the sea, and over the fowl of the air, and over every living thing that moveth upon the earth." (Genesis 1:28.) Well, he has planted, in accordance with this, a natural desire in woman towards man, and in man towards woman and a feeling of affection, regard, and sympathy exists between the sexes. We bring it into the world with us, but that, like everything else, has to be sanctified. An unlawful gratification of these feelings and sympathies is wrong in the sight of God, and leads down to death, while a proper exercise of our functions leads to life, happiness, and exaltation in this world and the world to come. And so it is in regard to a thousand other things.

NURTURE, DO NOT PERVERT, THE EMOTIONS.—We like enjoyment here. That is right. God designs that we should enjoy ourselves. I do not believe in a religion that makes people gloomy, melancholy, miserable, and ascetic. I would not want

---

[1]See Matthew 10:28.

to spend my life in a nunnery if I were a woman, or in a monastery if I were a man; and I would not think it very exalting to be a hermit and to live by myself in a poor miserable way. I should not think there was anything great or good associated with that. . . . While everything else enjoyed life, why should not we? But we want to do it correctly and not pervert any of these principles that God has planted in the human family.

MUSIC AND THE THEATER.—Why, there are some people who think that the fiddle, for instance, is an instrument of the devil and it is quite wrong to use it. I do not think so, I think it is a splendid thing to dance by. But some folks think that we should not dance. Yes, we should enjoy life in any way we can. Some people object to music. Why, music prevails in the heavens, and among the birds! God has filled them with it. There is nothing more pleasing and delightful than it is to go into the woods or among the bushes early in the morning and listen to the warbling and rich melody of the birds, and it is strictly in accordance with the sympathies of our nature. We have no idea of the excellence of the music we shall have in heaven. It may be said of that, as the apostle Paul has said in relation to something else—"Eye hath not seen, nor ear heard, neither have entered into the heart of man, the things which God hath prepared for them that love him." (I Corinthians 2:9.) We have no idea of the excellency, beauty, harmony and symphony of the music in the heavens.

Our object is to get and to cleave to everything that is good, and to reject everything that is bad. One reason why religious people in the world are opposed to music and theaters is because of the corruption that is mixed up with them. Wicked and corrupt men associate themselves with these things, and degrade them; but is this any reason that the saints should not enjoy the gifts of God? Is that a correct principle? Certainly not. It is for them to grasp at everything that is good, and calculated to promote the happiness of the human family.

SOCIAL STANDARDS.—I remember the time very well, and many of you do, when we used to commence our theatrical amusements here by prayer. We do not do so much of it now. This practice is put to one side. I suppose one was right and the other is right. I merely speak of these things. All our acts should be sanctified to God. You know that we are in the habit of having parties occasionally. I will give you my ideas about some of them. I have attended one or two lately, and I think we are running rather wild, and we do not act as much like gentlemen and ladies as we should, nor quite as much like saints as we ought to do. I think there is a great deal of impudence and pertness, a great amount of interfering with other people's rights in these places, and I think that we need correcting, that is, in our ward. I do not know how it is here in yours. Perhaps you do better here. I am speaking of things as I see them. I think we ought to elevate everything of this kind to its proper standard. We ought not to intrude upon or take advantage of anybody, even in amusements. When this is not observed, I will tell you what it leads to; it leads to a separation in society, inducing men and women who desire to be polite, refined, and courteous, to keep out of the company of those who do not take this course, and produces, if you please, something like an aristocracy, which is very repugnant to the wishes of good-feeling men and women. But they have either to do this or to be run over in many instances.—*JD*, 15:270-272, January 5, 1873.

THE NATURE OF HUMAN NATURE.—The principles of justice, righteousness, and truth, which have an endless duration, can alone satisfy the capacious desires of the immortal soul. We may amuse ourselves like children do at play, or engage in the frivolities of the dance. We may take our little enjoyments in our social assemblies. But when the *man* comes to reflect, when the saint of God considers, and the visions of eternity are open to his view and the unalterable purposes of God are developed to his mind—when he contemplates his true position before God, angels, and men, then he soars above the things of time and sense and bursts the cords that bind him to earthly objects. He contemplates God and his own destiny in the economy of heaven and rejoices in a blooming hope of an immortal glory.—*JD*, 1:221, April 8, 1853.

## THE BROTHERHOOD OF THE HUMAN RACE

ALL ARE GOD'S CHILDREN.—How does God feel towards the human family? He feels that they are his children. What, all? Yes, the white, the black, the red, the Jew, the gentile, the heathen, the Christian, and all classes and grades of men. He feels interested in all. He has done so from the beginning and will continue to do so to the end. He will do all that lies in his power for the benefit, blessing, and exaltation of the human family, both in time and eternity, consonant with those laws and those eternal principals that I have referred to, from which he himself cannot deviate.—*JD*, 21:16, February 8, 1880.

A MORMON ETHIC.—Because one man is more talented than another, he should not use that talent to take advantage of his brother and then expect that God will approve of his actions, for he will not do it. He never did, nor ever will. We should operate for one another's interest, having sympathetic feelings for each other.   We are supposed to be brethren in the church and kingdom of God, knit together by the indissoluble ties of the everlasting gospel; not for time only but for eternity.   Hence all our operations should be for that end, founded on the principles of righteousness and friendship.—*JD*, 18:284, November 5, 1876.

CHAPTER VII

# THE NATURE OF THE UNIVERSE

## GOD AND NATURE

EARTH, PLANETS, SEASONS.—The earth, and all the planetary systems, are governed by the Lord; they are upheld by his power, and are sustained, directed, and controlled by his will. . . .

If the planets move beautifully and harmoniously in their several spheres, that beauty and harmony are the result of the intelligence and wisdom that exist in his mind. If on this earth we have day and night, summer and winter, seedtime and harvest, with the various changes of the seasons, this regularity, beauty, order, and harmony, are the effects of the wisdom of God.—GG, 1, 1852.

The power that causes this earth to roll on its axis, and regulates the planets in their diurnal and annual motions, is beyond man's control. Their revolutions and spheres are fixed by Nature's God, and they are so beautifully arranged, and nicely balanced, that an astronomer can calculate the return of a planet scores of years beforehand, with the greatest precision and accuracy. And who can contemplate, without admiration, those stupendous worlds, rolling through the immensity of space at such an amazing velocity, moving regularly in their given spheres without coming into collision, and reflect that they have done so for thousands of years.—GG, 3-4, 1852.

## THE PRINCIPLE OF LIFE IN THE UNIVERSE

INTELLIGENT ORGANIZATION.—We see men who are considered very talented, whose names are handed down to posterity as great sculptors or painters. Their works are among the ancient ruins, and are exhibited as specimens of artistic skill, that men may see how intelligent their forefathers were. And what is it which they had wisdom to make? Something like a man, or a beast. But break off an arm or a leg, and you discover that it is but a lifeless piece of matter, though the outlines may be true to nature; and in this alone consist the beauty and skill of the artist. But there is no life in them, and they fall far short of perfection, beauty, and symmetry, as it is seen in the human system, or that of any other animal. Look upon a man, he is a perfect being; he is perfect inside and outside. If you remove the skin, the perfect covering of the human form, the nerves, muscles, arteries, veins, and everything necessary for this peculiar system, are there found in perfect harmony, and in every way adapted to make complete a living, moving machine. Not only so, but he is an intelligent being, capable of reflecting and acting. We profess to know a great deal, but what of our philosophy? Who is there can tell me by what power I lift my right arm? If that cannot be told, what do we know? How far short, then, are we of that intelligence that governs the universe and regulates all the works of nature. I look at the bones of the mammoth, and they tell me of something that was. I can gaze upon an elephant as it now is, a mighty, ponderous, moving machine, with strength and energy. Who planned and contrived these mighty beings? I look again at the animalcula, a thousand of which can float in a drop of water, and I see, by means of a powerful glass, the veins, muscles, and everything that is perfect to constitute a living, moving creature, invisible to the naked eye. He who organized the one, regulates the other. Man is an intelligent being, but how far does his intelligence fall short of that which regulates the world! He cannot even govern himself; he never was able to do it, and never will be able until he receives that wisdom and intelligence of that kind, and from that source, which governs the world, and keeps in order all the planetary systems, and adapts every fish, fowl, and insect to its own peculiar position in the world, and supplies all its wants. If he can receive it from God, as his instructor, he is then able to govern himself, possessing intelligence which he now knows nothing about, an intelligence which indeed is worthy of God and man. If I cannot have a portion of that intelligence and that wisdom, if the great Elohim cannot impart a portion of that spirit to me, and teach me the same lessons that he understands, I want nothing to do with a system of theology at all.—*JD*, 1:153, June 12, 1853.

THE VITALITY OF NATURE.—There is a principle of life associated with the gospel—life temporal, life spiritual, and life eternal. Hence men are called to be fathers of lives, and women are called to be mothers of lives. We are fathers and mothers of lives. And there is something different associated with the order of God from any order of men that exists upon the earth.

When God created the earth and placed man upon it, and the fishes of the sea and the fowls of the air, and the grasses and plants and trees, etc., he placed in them the principle of life, or, in other words, the power of propagating their own species. And if it were not for that, what would you farmers do? Men can accomplish a great many things. They can build houses, railroads, and steamboats, and can do a great many clever things whereby they can command, to a certain extent, the forces of

Nature; but they cannot give vitality to any of them. They cannot even furnish material to make a grain of sand, the wisest of them. But God has ordained that this principle of vitality exists within themselves. You take a single grain of wheat, for instance, and put it into the earth and you will see the principle of life begin to manifest itself; it is very small apparently, but contains within itself the power of increase. The same is also true with regard to the grasses, shrubs, plants, and flowers, and the various things that exist in creation. They spread, they extend, and they have spread over the face of the earth as man has spread, and the rain descends and the sun shines and Nature, as we term it, operates; but I would call it the power of God which operates according to eternal laws and principles that he has ordained. He gives vitality to all creation and sets life into motion and controls it, in the heavens as well as in the earth; not only among men, but among the beasts of the field, the fowls of the air, the fishes of the sea, and all the grasses, plants and flowers and herbs etc., everything possessing the principle of life within itself. . . .

This principle of life is the origin of our world, not only of this world, but of others; and this propagating and multiplying is ordained of the Almighty for the peopling of these worlds. And this production of life that I have briefly alluded·to is another principle that exists to supply the want of another kind of life that exists here upon the earth. And without this there could be no world; all would be chaos, all would be darkness, all would be death, and the works of God would amount to nothing if it were not for this life and vitality.—*JD*, 21:112-113, November 28, 1879.

## A UNIVERSE OF LAW

LAWS PLACED IN ORDER BY THE ALMIGHTY.—All things are under the influence, control and government of law, just as much as the planetary system with which we are connected is governed by law. It makes no difference what a few of us may do, or how the world may act, the sun rises and sets regularly, the earth revolves upon its axis, and so it is with all the planetary systems. There is no confusion, no disorder in any of the movements of the heavenly bodies. They are governed by a science and intelligence that is beyond the reach of men in mortality. Yet they move strictly according to certain laws by which all of them have been, are, and will be governed. And these laws are under the surveillance and control of the great Law-giver, who manages, controls, and directs all these worlds. If it were not the case, they would move through space in wild confusion, and system would rush against system, and worlds upon worlds would be destroyed, together with their inhabitants. But they are governed by a superhuman Power, by a Spirit and Intelligence that dwells in the bosom of the Gods, about which mankind knows but very little. It is so with regard to all the forces of Nature—the earth on which we stand, the elements of which it is composed, the air we breathe, the water we drink, and everything in Nature is governed strictly according to immutable, eternal, unchangeable laws, practical, philosophical, and strictly scientific, if these terms are preferred; but they are, nevertheless, placed there by the Almighty.—*JD*, 20:111-112, January 6, 1879.

The laws of matter and of mechanism are unchangeable, and so are the laws pertaining to life, and also the medium of communication between God and man.—*JD*, 19:366, June 16, 1878.

ETERNAL LAW CHANGES ACCORDING TO LAW.—There are eternal, unchangeable laws associated with God, and with all his plans, his works and ways, the requirements of which must be met. Nor can they be evaded or changed, except on certain principles provided for and contained in the laws themselves. When man had transgressed, an atonement had to be made commensurate with the act, and fully adequate to meet the inexorable demands of justice; so that, as stated, justice might be satisfied, which, if it had not been, the law pertaining to this matter could not have been carried out, and must necessarily have been violated.—*MA*, 163.

APPARENT DEVIATIONS FROM GENERAL LAW.—There are some apparent deviations from general laws. But these apparent deviations are merely appendages to the great general law, in order that creation may be perfect in all its parts. For instance, there is a general law of what is termed gravitation which causes bodies to fall to the earth from a given height. . . . But there are other local laws which disturb the normal conditions, so far as they extend, of what may be termed the general law. As, for example, the magnet in its limited sphere is more powerful than the general law of gravity, it attracting certain matter to itself in opposition to the general law, while the magnet itself is subject to the general law. . . . Take away these local agencies and everything resumes its normal condition. A bird, through the use of its wings, possesses the power of locomotion through the air; let that bird, however, lose its mechanism and power by being maimed or killed, and it is governed by the same law of gravitation and drops to the earth. Balloons will ascend and carry a specified weight with them to great altitudes, but this is owing to a modification of one part of the law of gravitation which causes denser bodies to cling with greater tenacity to the earth, and the gas that enters the balloons is more rarified than the atmosphere immediately contiguous to the earth, which dense atmosphere forces the lighter gases to their proper place, causing them to bound upwards. This being done and the equilibrium obtained, if the gas is permitted to escape, the materials of which the balloon is composed, together with its occupants, are precipitated, according to the general laws of gravitation, to the earth.

God is unchangeable, so are also his laws, in all their forms, and in all their applications, and being himself the essence of law, the giver of law, the sustainer of law, all of those laws are eternal in all their operations, in all bodies and matter, and throughout all space. It would be impossible for him to violate law, because in so doing he would strike at his own dignity, power, principles, glory, exaltation and existence.—*MA, 167-168.*

## APPLICATIONS OF THE CONCEPT
## OF UNIVERSAL LAW

APPLIED SCIENCE.—Today we can talk of railroads and steamboats. I remember the time, and many of you old people also remember, when there were no such things in existence. Well, but did not steam possess the same properties five thousand years ago as it does today? Yes, it did. The properties were precisely the same, but we did not understand it, that's all. The principles were the same, and there is an eternal law by which all these things are governed. The same thing applies to electricity. You remember very well when it took several months to send a message to Washington and receive an answer. Now we can do it in as many minutes. But did not that principle always exist? Yes; but man did not know how to avail himself of it. I remember the time too, very well, when there was no such thing as gas, when whale oil was used which produced a light that just about made darkness visible. We knew nothing about kerosene, or gasoline, or gas or any of these superior artificial lights. But the principles existed then as they do now, but we did not understand them. We did not comprehend the position of things and it is only quite recently that some of these discoveries have been brought into operation. The art of photography has not been long known. When I was a boy people would have laughed at you if you had talked of taking a man's likeness in a minute's time; yet it is done. Did not light always possess the same properties? Yes, but man did not understand it. The same thing applies to the mineral world, the vegetable kingdom, the animal creation, and all the works of God. They are all governed by certain laws. The vegetables which you grow here, how were they organized? God organized them and placed them upon the earth, and gave them power to propagate their species. So also with regard to the animal creation, as well as birds, fishes, insects, etc.

UNITY OF MAN WITH NATURE.—We talk sometimes about our temporal things. If we could understand things as God does, we should not be much troubled about them. If for a moment we reflect upon all creation that live upon this little globe—those that move in the air, the waters, and on the land, we find there is a wisdom, an intelligence that provides for all. There is a prescient and an omnipotent power that governs, controls and shapes the affairs of this world according to the counsel of his will, and especially so in all matters pertaining to the human family. As one nation rises up and another falls, it is by his power that it is done. Nations and peoples may be in prosperity for a short time, but one touch of the finger of the Almighty and they wither, crumble, and decay. Change succeeds change in human affairs, but the laws of God in everything are correct and true, in every stage and phase of nature, everything on the earth, in the waters and in the atmosphere is governed by unchangeable, eternal laws. There are some bodies that will unite. There are others that will not unite. You cannot, for instance, mix oil and water. You may shake them up together, but soon each one adheres to its own element. The sisters sometimes say they have good or bad luck, as the case may be, in the making of soap. But in reality there is no luck about it, for you would find that if you have the same properties equal in strength and quantity, using the same process, that the same results would be reached ninety-nine times out of every hundred, and you would find that you could afford to throw the other one in too—the conditions being the same. And so it is with the various minerals in all their organizations and conditions. They assume certain forms and they are known by geologists by their shapes, etc., and they are always true to them. And so it is with all the elements with which we are surrounded in the atmosphere, in the earth, and in the water. We think we have learned a great deal, but if we did but know it we are only at the foot of the hill. When we are able to comprehend things as God does, we shall comprehend a great many principles that have never entered into our hearts to conceive of, although we are surrounded with those materials and are even treading them under our feet.

MORMON "SOCIAL SCIENCE": THE BASIS FOR A HAPPY HUMAN SOCIETY.—What next? Are we mortal? Yes. Are we immortal? Yes. Have we to do with time? Yes. We have also to do with eternity. We are the offspring of God, and God in these last days has seen fit to place us in communication with himself. He has, through the revelations of himself and of his Son Jesus Christ, by the ministry of holy angels and by the restoration of the holy priesthood which emanates from God, and by which he himself is governed, placed us in a position whereby we can fulfil the object of our creation. . . .

There are certain eternal laws that have existed from before the foundation of the world. There has been a priesthood also in existence always, and hence it is called the everlasting priesthood, and it administers in time and in eternity. That priesthood has been conferred upon man together with the right of the gospel. And we are told how man can get into possession of the Holy Spirit of God, and how he can be placed in communication with God, just the same as you would place one town in communication with another by means of the electric wire. . . . What for? For the building up of something that is called Zion or the pure in heart. What for? For my aggrandizement? For yours? For my individual interests or for yours? No. But in the interest of God and of Jesus the Mediator of the New Covenant, of Adam and of all the ancient patriarchs and apostles and men of God who have lived before, both on the Asiatic and American continent. . . .

APPLICATION OF THE MORMON "SOCIAL SCIENCE" IN SOCIETY.—And what next? Can we make them believe? No. Can we make them obey the gospel? No. We would not if we could, because if there was any force made use of for the accomplishment of that object, it would only result in evil instead of good. We are told by Joseph Smith that "No power or influence can or ought to be maintained by virtue of the priesthood, only by persuasion, by long-suffering, by gentleness and meekness, and by love unfeigned; by kindness and pure knowledge."[1] They are not to be exercised by force. This is the way I look at these things, and I take the same view of our temporal affairs. . . . Should I wish to control any man? No, I would show him the right way. . . .

THE FRUITS OF THE MORMON "SOCIAL SCIENCE."—Well. now, a little further in relation to these things. Shall we benefit? Yes, we will do all the good we can. But if men lie and become fraudulent, and delight in abominations and are void of principle, then we will say, with him of old, "my soul, enter thou not into their secret, and mine honor with him be not thou united. . . ."[2] We are gathered here for the express purpose of carrying out the purposes of God. The world, however, do not understand it. But I tell you what they will do, by and by. You will see them

[1] See Doctrine & Covenants 121:41-42.
[2] Compare Genesis 49:6.

flocking to Zion by thousands and tens of thousands. And they will say, "We don't know anything about your religion, we don't care much about religious matters, but you are honest and honorable, and upright and just, and you have a good, just and secure government, and we want to put ourselves under your protection, for we cannot feel safe anywhere else."

THE TASK OF THE SAINTS.—There is a scripture which says, the time will come when he that will not take up his sword to fight against his neighbor, must needs flee to Zion for safety. And they will come. But we must prepare ourselves. We have got to have the invigorating influence of the Spirit of God to permeate all of our organizations, all feeling that we are under the guidance and protection of the Almighty, every man in his place, and every man according to the order of the priesthood in which God has placed him. . . . This is the kind of feeling we should have and be governed by. As for these other matters of a temporal nature before referred to,[1] if we cannot co-operate together and do it honestly and in good faith, as this is one of the very best things that can be required of us, it is very little that we can do. We should cultivate the Spirit of God ourselves; we ought to drink freely of that water which the Savior told the woman of Samaria that he was able to give to her, even that water that would "be in her as a well springing up to everlasting life." We have drunk already at that well. It remains now for us to permit it to bubble and burst forth, to flow and spread its revivifying influence all around. We ought to have a heaven upon earth—to be really the Zion of our God, the pure in heart, each one seeking another's welfare. "Thou shalt love the Lord thy God with all thy heart, with all thy might, with all thy soul, with all thy strength, and thy neighbor as thyself." We have hardly got to that yet. But supposing Paul were to come along and say a little further—each one preferring his neighbor. That part of it we will let alone awhile. But if we could feel we are the children of God, all animated by that same Holy Spirit, producing peace and joy, and all welded together in one common brotherhood, in the bonds of the everlasting gospel, all operating with God and the holy priesthood who have lived in other ages, we could carry out his purposes upon the earth and establish his kingdom, never more to be thrown down. If we could feel like this, we should drop our individuality and self-esteem a little, we should seek to do not our own will, but the will of him who sent us.—JD, 20:130-137, December 1, 1878.

---

[1]See the chapter on The United Order and Cooperation.

# CHAPTER VIII

# PHILOSOPHY, SCIENCE, AND RELIGION

## THE SEARCH FOR KNOWLEDGE

THE LIMITATIONS OF SECULAR HYPOTHESES.—Man, by philosophy and the exercise of his natural intelligence, may gain an understanding, to some extent, of the laws of Nature. But to comprehend God, heavenly wisdom and intelligence are necessary. Earthly and heavenly philosophy are two different things, and it is folly for men to base their arguments upon earthly philosophy in trying to unravel the mysteries of the kingdom of God. —JD, 14:191, March 20, 1870.

THE LIMITATIONS OF DEDUCTION.—There are men, it is true, who profess from the little knowledge they have of earthly things, by a series of deductions, to be able to find out heavenly things. But there is a very material difference between the two. There is a philosophy of the earth and a philosophy of the heavens. The latter can unravel all mysteries pertaining to earth. But the philosophy of the earth cannot enter into the mysteries of the kingdom of God, or the purposes of the Most High. But because of the advancement to which I have alluded, men set themselves up as teachers of things pertaining to spiritual matters, of which they know nothing. But the moment they do that, they exhibit their folly, vanity, imbecility, and shortsightedness, for, as I have stated, they never did comprehend the things of God without the Spirit of God, and they never will. . . . Who can draw aside the veil and tell how or why we came here, and what awaits us when we lay aside this mortal coil? None can do this, unless God reveals it. There never was a man, neither is there a man now, nor ever will be, that can comprehend these things upon the principle of natural or human philosophy, and nothing short of the philosophy of heaven—the intelligence that flows from God, can unravel these mysteries.—JD, 13:222-223, May 6, 1870.

FACT, THEORY, AND INFERENCE.—We have a great many ignorant, learned fools. But when you meet sensible, intelligent men . . . they will acknowledge principle when it is presented to them. But many men have not the understanding to do it. Talking about saving themselves, who among the philosophers can save themselves? . . . What do they do when they have to grapple with the sting of death, and when it stares them in the face? Why,

they take a leap in the dark. And this darkness is the end of all
their philosophy and all their science. And the little they do know
in divining the laws of God is only with regard to some very
few of the fundamental principles of those laws that God has
planted everywhere throughout the universe, and I do not therefore have that reverence for their theories, notions, and vagaries,
nor do I attach that importance to their intelligence that some
people do. . . .

If we have to submit to their theories, we should really
be in a sorry condition.—*JD*, 20:119-120, January 6, 1879.

THE RELIGIOUS NATURE OF MANKIND.—There is and
always has been a feeling of reverence existing among the human
family for a Divine Being of some kind and of some form, even
amongst the most low and debased people of the earth.—*JD*, 21:
155, December 7, 1879.

## PHILOSOPHY, SCIENCE, AND RELIGION

APPROACH TO DEITY.—We think we are very superior in
intelligence and in religion. Men, everywhere, are egotistical;
they always think they are the smartest and most intelligent that
ever lived; and it must be confessed that in many respects the
generation in which we live are very far in advance of many
others in regard to the arts and sciences, and certain branches of
literature and mechanism. But how vague and uncertain are
the ideas entertained by men in general, about the Deity! Are we
intellectual in this? I think not. We have our bodies of divinity,
our schools of theology, our religious seminaries, and places where
ministers are manufactured and prepared to perform certain work
which they call preaching the gospel, and these ministers, as
well as the people, have different ideas about the Deity and the
proper modes of worshiping him. Does the incongruity of this
state of things ever strike the minds of reflecting men, men of
science, who are accustomed to weigh the force of an argument
and to solve knotty problems? . . .

THE ABSURDITY OF SOME RELIGIOUS NOTIONS.—Now,
what can God think of a people, placed here on the earth, the
most intelligent of his creations, possessed of reasoning faculties,
who, in many instances, have investigated and understand the
laws of Nature, I say, what can he think of men who set up
every form, notion, and theory, every species of absurdity that
can be imagined, and call it the worship of God? Suppose we
were to put ourselves in his place for a little while, we should
think there was something a little strange in relation to these
matters. He might reasonably say, these men exhibit wisdom

and intelligence in many respects. So far as discovering the operations of Nature, and examining and testing the laws thereof, they all agree; but in religious matters they exhibit imbecility and weakness, in that there is no union. . . .

THE NECESSITY OF SUBJECTING BELIEF TO TESTS AND CRITICISM.—In regard to Nature and its laws, the world and the elements with which we are surrounded, and the laws operating in the world with which we are acquainted, all men arrive at the same conclusions, and there is no difference, unless we come to theorizing, and then there is always difficulty. Well, in regard to all these things we all think alike, because our thoughts are based on correct principles. But when we come to religious matters, we discover that, though men are naturally intelligent, they act like fools. They do not use their common judgment, reason, or intelligence. "Well," say they, "you know we are governed by the Bible." Now that is exactly what we do not know, and therefore I doubt it. "But our divines tell us we are." Oh, do they? Well, suppose somebody was to tell you the result of some scientific analysis; you would be very likely to say—"I believe you in part, but I would like to test it for myself. When I have done that I shall know it. Yet strange as it is, you are willing to take anybody's *ipse dixit* in relation to things of the most vital importance. In things pertaining to the immortal part of man, we act like the veriest babies or consummate fools, while in regard to the affairs of this life we act intelligently.

Is there a way of arriving at a knowledge of the things which pertain to man's eternal welfare? Why, yes, we are inclined to think there is. . . .

CHRISTIANITY WILL BEAR HONEST INVESTIGATION.—We call ourselves Christians, that is, we Methodists, Baptists, Presbyterians, Congregationalists, Episcopalians and Mormons, we all call ourselves Christians. Well, perhaps we are, and then, perhaps we are not. It is a matter that would bear investigation, I think. And then I think . . . we should be honest with ourselves about all things, and especially in religion and the service and worship of God. "Well, but my father was a Methodist, and I am one." "My father was a Presbyterian, and I am one." "My father was a 'jumper,' and I am one." "My father was a Mohammedan, and I am one." "My father was a worshipper of Buddha, and I am one." And among us Christians we are Episcopalians, Wesleyans, Presbyterians, and members of the various professional phases descended from that remarkable man, Martin Luther, or Catholics or Greeks. Let us examine these things for a little while; or, at least, try to go to the foundation. Believing in the Bible, we will not go at once into these outside systems, but examine our own for a little while, and see how it stands, and how we stand in relation to it.

THE PRINCIPLES OF JESUS.—Jesus, we are told, "brought life and immortality to light by the gospel." (II Timothy 1:10.) There was something peculiar about it—it gave men who lived up to and honored its principles in their lives and actions, a knowledge of life and immortality. They were not dependent upon the sayings or doings of Adam, Noah, Abraham, Lot, Moses, Isaiah, Jeremiah, Malachi, or any of the prophets. But the gospel brought a knowledge of life and immortality to all who obeyed it and lived according to its precepts. It informed all such that they were immortal beings; that they would exist after they had got through with time; if they died they should live again; if they were buried they should burst the barriers of the tomb and come forth to immortality.

Seeing that man is both a mortal and an immortal being, having to do with eternity as well as time, it is proper that he should become acquainted with those principles that are so nearly concerned with his happiness and well-being in time and in eternity. We will let John Wesley, Luther, Calvin, Melancthon, Henry the Eighth, and any other organizer of religion go, and we will come to the scriptures of truth and see what they say about it. Christ, we are told, brought life and immortality to light, and he did it through the medium of the gospel. And what course did he pursue in doing this? The scriptures inform us that when Jesus commenced to preach the gospel he called men from the various vocations of life, among others from the occupation of fishing; he called twelve men, whom he ordained apostles. He inspired these men with the gift of revelation and with a knowledge of God. He placed them in communication with God, so that they had revelation from him and were enabled to teach the laws of life. He breathed upon them and said—"Receive ye the Holy Ghost"; and they received it, and that Holy Ghost took of the things of God and showed them unto them, it drew aside the curtains of futurity, whereby they were enabled to penetrate into the invisible world and comprehend the things of God. This was the position they occupied and the kind of gospel they had.

THE TESTING OF JESUS' TEACHINGS.—Well, how did they operate with it? Jesus told them to go out and preach it; and he called seventy men and inspired them, too; and told them to go out and heal the sick, cast out devils, and preach the gospel. They were furthermore to go without purse and scrip, he saying unto them—"freely ye have received, freely give." (Matthew 10:8.) They went out in this kind of way, without purse and scrip, to preach the gospel. By and by a number of them returned, and he asked them how they had fared. They told him they had been preaching, and healing the sick, and even devils were subject to them in his name. Said he—"Rejoice, not that devils are subject to you; but rather rejoice that your names are written in heaven,"[1] that you are the Lord's, that God is your friend. Rejoice that you have been brought into communication with God, and that you have received the everlasting gospel, which brings life and immortality to light. This was their position, and they listened to the teachings of Jesus, and we all—that is all of these various parties of which I have spoken,—believe that Jesus was the Son of God. . . .

I sometimes reflect and wonder whether the same effects would follow if we had that religion today, or whether truth has turned into fiction, or has falsehood turned into truth. How is it, if that was the gospel then, and God is the same yesterday, today, and forever, and, as they say in the Church of England— "As it was in the beginning, is now and ever shall be, worlds without end, amen?"—if that is true, then we ought to expect the same things today as they had then, that is, if we profess the same gospel. This is the way I reason, I cannot get at it any other way; I cannot arrive at any other conclusion. It is reasonable, rational, and philosophical. It agrees with every principle of science, with every principle of intelligence that God has communicated to man.—*JD*, 16:303-309, November 16, 1873.

## THE MYTH OF MODERNITY

THE WORLD ORGANIZED ON ETERNAL PRINCIPLES.— Some men will stultify themselves with the idea that in ages gone and past the human race was in a semi-civilized or barbarous condition, and that any kind of religion would do for the people in those days; but with the progress of intelligence, the march of intellect, the development of the arts and sciences and the expansion of the human mind, it is necessary that we should have something more elevated, refined, and intellectual than that which existed then. To me such notions are perfect foolishness. If I read my Bible aright and believe in it, known unto God were all things from before the foundation of the world. . . . Yet men will boast that they know things independent of God whereas unless they had been aided by the Spirit of the Lord, and unless the principles had existed, they never could have been found out, for no man could have originated them himself. All that man has ever done, with all his boasted intelligence, has been simply to

---

[1]Compare Luke 10:20.

develop or find out a few of the common principles of nature
that always have existed, and always will exist, for these things
and every principle of nature are eternal. The gospel is also
eternal.—*JD*, 13:223-225, May 6, 1870.

## INTELLIGENCE AND THE PHILOSOPHY
## OF THE WORLD

Speaking of philosophy, . . . I was almost buried up in it
while I was in Paris. I was walking about one day in the *Jardin
des Plantes*—a splendid garden. There they had a sort of exceedingly light cake. It was so thin and light that you could blow
it away, and you could eat all day of it, and never be satisfied.
Somebody asked me what the name of that was. I said, I don't
know the proper name, but in the absence of one, I can give it
a name—I will call it philosophy, or fried froth, whichever you
like. It is so light you can blow it away, eat it all day, and at
night be as far from being satisfied as when you began. . . .

I will risk our elders among the world, if they will only
brush up their ideas a little. I will take any of you rough-look-
ing fellows, put you in a tailor's shop a little, and start you out
like gentlemen, as large as life. I tell you there is great difference
between our people and others. Many others have a nice little
finish on them; they may be compared to scrimped-up dandies.
But everything is on the outside, and nothing in the inside.

Our folks who are operating round here in the canyons,
and on the land, are listening to the servants of God and studying
principles of eternal truth. They are like young rough colts, with
plenty of bone, sinew, and nerve in them. All they want is
rubbing down a little, and they will come out first-rate. I believe
in the polish, and a little of everything else. . . .

INTELLIGENCE GAINED BY FAITH AND STUDY.—I have
found that all intelligence is good, and there is a good deal in
the world, mixed up with all their follies. It is good for the
elders to become acquainted with the languages, for they may
have to go abroad, and should be able to talk to the people, and
not look like fools. I care not how much intelligence you have,
if you cannot exhibit it, you look like an ignoramus. Suppose
a Frenchman should come upon this stand to deliver a lecture
upon botany, astronomy, or any other science, and could not
speak a word of English, how much wiser would you be? You may
say, I thought the Lord would give us the gift of tongues. He won't
if we are too indolent to study them. I never ask the Lord to
do a thing I could do for myself. We should be acquainted with

all things, should obtain intelligence both by faith and by study. We are instructed to gather it out of the best books, and become acquainted with governments, nations, and laws. The elders of this church have need to study these things, that when they go to the nations, they may not wish to return home before they have accomplished a good work.—*JD*, 1:27, August 22, 1852.

## SOME MORMON PHILOSOPHY

IF ALL NATURE IS UNDER LAW, WHY NOT MAN.—According to the eternal laws of God and the eternal fitness of things as they exist with him in the eternal worlds and as they exist here upon the earth, all of us are . . . as much obligated to listen to his law and be governed by his counsels and advice . . . [as] we would be in making a grain of wheat to grow. . . . Being the God and Father of the spirits of all flesh, and having made a world for all flesh to inhabit, and having made provision for the sustenance of that flesh, for their food, clothing, comfort, convenience and happiness, and having given them intelligence and told them to go forth and manipulate the abundance of nature to their use, has he not a right to lead and direct us, to ask obedience to his law? Would not that be a legitimate right, when we reflect upon it? The world says, No, he has no right; I am my own master, etc. Some of the Latter-day Saints almost say the same thing; not quite, but they would like to get near it. "I am a free man; I will be damned if I don't do as I please," etc. Well, I will tell you another part of that story. You will be damned if you do act as you please unless you please to do and to keep the laws of God. We cannot violate his laws with impunity nor trample under foot these eternal principles which exist in all Nature. If all Nature is compelled to be governed by law or suffer loss, why not man?

Now, then, he has revealed unto us the gospel. He has gathered us together from among the nations of the earth for the accomplishment of his purposes. For this he has used higher measures and more exalted principles than are associated with some of the lower orders of nature. . . . It is for us to learn this lesson and to find out that there is a God who rules in heaven, and that he manages, directs and controls the affairs of the human family. We are not our own rulers. We are all the children of God. He is our Father and has a right to direct us, not only us, but has a perfect right to direct and control the affairs of all the human family that exist upon the face of the earth for they are all his offspring. Now, he feels kindly towards them and knows what kind of people they are, and also what we are, and he would do everything he could for them even if in his almighty wisdom he has to kill them off in order to save them. He destroyed the antediluvian world on that account, because they were not filling the measure of their creation. They had corrupted themselves to such an extent that it would have been an injustice to the spirits in the eternal worlds if they had to come through such a corrupt lineage to be subject to all the trouble incident thereunto. And therefore God destroyed them. He cut off the cities of Sodom and Gomorrah in consequence of their corruptions, and by and by he will shake all the inhabitants of the earth, he will shake thrones and will overturn empires and desolate the land and lay millions of the human family in the dust. Plagues and pestilence will stalk through the earth because of the iniquities of men, because of some of these corruptions . . . namely, the perversion of the laws of nature between the sexes, and the damnable murders that exist among men.—JD, 21:113-116, November 28, 1879.

# BOOK TWO

## THE GOSPEL MESSAGE

*"The gospel is calculated to lead us on from truth to truth, and from intelligence to intelligence, until that scripture will be fulfilled which declares that we shall see as we are seen and know as we are known, until one will not have to say to another, know ye the Lord, but all shall know him from the least unto the greatest, until the light and intelligence of God shall beam forth upon all, and all shall bask in the sunlight of eternal truth."*
—JOHN TAYLOR,
*JD,* 11:217,
*April 7, 1866.*

# CHAPTER IX

# THE MEANING OF THE GOSPEL

## THE GOSPEL OF JESUS CHRIST

A COMPREHENSIVE SUBJECT.—The gospel of Jesus Christ is perhaps one of the most comprehensive subjects that mankind can reflect upon. It not only embraces things as they now exist, associated with the human family, but it takes us back to days that are past and gone, to the organization of this world and of other worlds, and by the principle of revelation it develops, unfolds, and makes manifest unto the human family the great purposes of God as they shall transpire throughout every succeeding age. There are thousands of details or minutiae mixed up with these great projects, purposes, and designs; some of them we comprehend correctly, or think we do; others are not so clear and comprehensible to our minds.—*JD*, 10:123, March 1, 1863.

Without the gospel it would be impossible for men to have any knowledge of God, or of Jesus Christ whom he hath sent.—*JD*, 11:161-162, October 7, 1865.

NEED OF THE GOSPEL.—There is no adhesive principle sufficiently powerful to unite the people of any portion of the earth, similar to the one that has sprung forth in our day and right among this people; if there is anything of that sort abroad in the world, I am not acquainted with it. Then it follows, as a natural consequence, that if there is nothing to unite the people together they are deficient in some principle, doctrine, faith or practice. Philosophy has not united the people together; politics has never done it; no social principles have ever accomplished it. —*JD*, 10:124-125, March 1, 1863.

SIGNIFICANCE OF THE GOSPEL.—We, under the inspiration of the Almighty, will introduce the laws of God that exist in the heavens and upon the earth, and form a nucleus of truth, of virtue and intelligence, of law and order, of principles pertaining to morals, to philosophy, to politics, to religion, and to everything that is pure, exalting, and ennobling, and the kingdom will be the Lord's. And we will operate together, we will try to frustrate the works of darkness and the powers of the adversary, to save the living and redeem the dead, having our hearts turned towards our fathers who have lived before us who have been ignorant of the principles of life and salvation which God has been pleased to confer upon us, while the brethren behind the veil are feeling after us who are their children. The Lord will turn the hearts of the fathers to the children, and the hearts of the children to the fathers through Elias who was to come, which if not accomplished, it is written, "the earth would be smitten with a curse."[1]—*JD*, 21:97, April 13, 1879.

THE LEAVEN OF THE GOSPEL.—The gospel is like a little leaven put into a certain portion of meal, and it is working and operating, and the ultimate result will be that the whole lump will be leavened. Not that everybody that is in the world will obey the gospel; but the Lord will have his own way in manipulating his affairs, and great tribulation will overtake the inhabitants of the earth. As you have heard, many of the wicked will slay the wicked. But after these things have taken place the good, the honorable, the virtuous, the pure, those that are desirous to serve God, will all have their position, and that thing will be fulfilled which was spoken of by Jesus—"Blessed are the meek for they shall inherit the earth."—*JD*, 24:124, April 8, 1883.

DIVINITY OF THE GOSPEL.—We have embraced the gospel of the Son of God, and God has taught us how to organize his church. Had he not taught us we should not have known anything about its organization. Joseph Smith knew nothing about it; Brigham Young knew nothing about it; I could not have known anything about it, nor any of the twelve, nor any man living on the earth, until God introduced it and taught us in all these things.—*JD*, 25:265, August 17, 1884.

THE GOSPEL IS TANGIBLE.—In relation to the gospel of Jesus Christ, it is something that is full of importance and information, and is associated with our present and eternal welfare, it enters into all the ramifications of life where we can understand it. It is not a sing-song sort of a thing, such as we hear taught among the sectarians; but there is something tangible about it. It consists of eternal principles, unfolding light and intelligence, and is adapted to the nature of man as a mortal and immortal being—principles that affect us in time and in eternity, in life, in health, in sickness, in death, and which lead to life everlasting.—*JD*, 5:259, September 20, 1857.

THE EVERLASTING GOSPEL: REVEALED FROM THE HEAVENS.—The everlasting gospel, or the everlasting priesthood, was not known till the Lord revealed it from the heavens by the voice of his angel, and when we receive these principles and they abide in us, we shall then have the principles of eternal life.

---

[1]See Malachi 4:6.

It was small when it first began, but you see the spirit of God has caused it to grow and become a mighty tree, and its branches cover the whole earth. Without the principle of eternal life, the principle of eternal knowledge never could be imparted as a blessing to the human family; and when once the key was turned, when the door was unlocked, and the seed once sown, truth began to grow, and the communication opened between the heavens and the earth, which placed men in a situation to converse with beings that surround the throne of God. The Melchizedek priesthood holds the keys that unfold the purposes of Jehovah, and drag into daylight the secret of God, the mystery of godliness, as well as the secret abominations of the wicked. Yes, "life and immortality are brought to light through the gospel."—*MS*, 8:89, July 6, 1845.

THE GOSPEL AND REALITY.—When men obey the gospel with pure hearts—when they are baptized in the name of Jesus Christ for the remission of sins, and have hands laid upon them for the gift of the Holy Ghost, and have received that Spirit and live in obedience to the dictates of that Spirit, it will bring things past and present to their remembrance, lead them into all truth, and show them things to come. This is part and parcel of our belief.

What is the reason we do not always comprehend things right? Because, in many instances, we give way to temptation. We let our old prepossessions, feelings, and influences, by which we have been governed heretofore, predominate over the Spirit of God, and we fall into error and darkness; and "If therefore the light that is in thee be darkness, how great is that darkness!" (Matthew 6:23.) It is not enough, then, that we are baptized and have hands laid upon us for the gift of the Holy Ghost. It is not enough even that we go further than this, and receive our washing and our anointings, but that we daily and hourly and all the time live up to our religion, cultivate the Spirit of God, and have it continually within us "as a well of water springing up unto everlasting life," unfolding, developing, making manifest the purposes and designs of God unto us, that we may be enabled to walk worthy of the high avocation whereunto we are called, as sons and daughters of God to whom he has committed the principles of eternal truth and the oracles of God in these last days.—*JD*, 6:106-107, December 6, 1857.

EFFECT OF THE GOSPEL.—The principles of the gospel, to the unbeliever, have neither worth nor efficacy. But with us, who believe them, they comprehend everything pertaining to the well-being of man in time and eternity. With us the gospel is the alpha and omega, the beginning and the end. It is interwoven with all our interests, happiness, and enjoyment, whether in this life or that which is to come. We consider that, when we enter into this church and embrace the new and everlasting covenant, it is a lifelong service and affects us in all the relationships of time and eternity. And as we progress, these ideas which, at first, were a little dim and obscure, become more vivid, real, life-like, tangible and clear to our comprehensions, and we realize that we stand upon the earth as the sons and daughters of God, the representatives of heaven. We feel that God has revealed to us an everlasting gospel, and that associated with that are everlasting covenants and relationships. The gospel, in the incipient stages of its operations, begins, as the prophet said it should, to "turn the hearts of the fathers to the children and the hearts of the children to the fathers." We no longer have to ask, as in former times, "Who am I?" "Where did I come from?" "What am I doing here?" or "What is the object of my existence?" for we have a certainty in relation to these things. It is made plain to us by the fruits of the gospel—by the truths which God has revealed through the medium of revelation by the inspiration of the Almighty, that we are "saviors on Mount Zion and that the kingdom is the Lord's." . . . It is the knowledge of these things and of many more of a similar nature that leads us to pursue the course that we do. It is this which prevents us from bowing to the notions, caprices, ideas and follies of men. Having been enlightened by the spirit of eternal truth, having partaken of the Holy Ghost, and our hope having entered within the veil, whither Christ, our forerunner, has gone, and knowing that we are the children of God and that we are acting in all things with reference to eternity, we pursue the even tenor of our way independent of the smiles and careless of the frowns of men.—*JD,* 14:186-187, March 20, 1870.

## THE NATURE OF THE GOSPEL

Is THE LORD CHANGEABLE?—To those who have not reflected seriously upon the dealings of God and his laws, the Lord appears to be changeable in his way of saving the human family. In the different dispensations from Adam until Christ, they suppose that he has adopted as many different ways of salvation.

We are told by Christian divines of the dispensation that existed before the flood; we are informed of the Patriarchal dispensation, the Mosaic dispensation, and finally of the Christian dispensation; and it is a prevailing idea among the uninformed that each of these dispensations presented a different system of salvation adopted by the Almighty in teaching the human family, in enlightening their minds, and in giving unto them correct information in regard to God and eternity. Hence I have often heard eminent divines refer to the dispensation before the flood as a day of almost utter darkness; then to the Patriarchal dispensation as one in which a faint glimmer of light began to be made manifest; of the Mosaic dispensation as a time in which the sun began to rise a little above the horizon; and of the Christian dispensation, as it now exists in the world, as being the fulness of light and intelligence, or the full blaze of gospel day. These views of the different dispensations generally obtain among professors of Christianity.

I entertain a very different opinion of the Almighty. God, like his Son, Jesus Christ, is "the same yesterday, today, and for ever,"—the same in intelligence, the same in purity, the same in his projects, plans, and designs. He is, in short, unchangeable. And I apprehend, if the saints who had communication with him in ancient days were to appear on this earth at the present time, they would find the same medium of communication, the same way of imparting intelligence, and the same unchangeable Being that existed one thousand eight hundred, four thousand, or six thousand years ago.

It is true mankind have not at all times been susceptible of receiving and appreciating the same degree of light, truth, and intelligence that they have at other times. God has in certain instances withdrawn the light of his countenance—his Holy Spirit—the light and intelligence that proceeds from him, in a certain degree, from the human family; but his laws are immutable, and he is the same eternal, unchangeable Being. . . .

THE GOSPEL IS ETERNAL.—As the gospel is a principle that emanates from God, like its author, it is "the same yesterday, today, and for ever,"—eternal and unchangeable. God ordained it before the morning stars sang together for joy, or ere this world rolled into existence, for the salvation of the human race. It has been in the mind of God, and as often as developed it has been manifested as an eternal, unchangeable, undeviating plan by which to save, bless, exalt, and dignify man, and to accomplish this end by one certain, unalterable method of salvation, according to its degree or manifestation.

I speak of the gospel of Jesus Christ in its fulness and of the blessings associated therewith. It is perfect folly to entertain the idea that the gospel has only existed about one thousand eight hundred years, and yet this foolish idea is strongly entertained and almost universally believed throughout Christendom. This mistake is for want of calm reflection and correct information upon that subject. . . .

MORE THAN THE NEW TESTAMENT.—We are told the gospel is the New Testament. I do not find any such declaration even in the New Testament itself. There are certain records in the New Testament giving an account of the birth, life, suffering, and death of our Lord and Savior Jesus Christ. It contains also an account of the doctrines he taught, the discourses he delivered, and the moral sentiments he inculcated. It gives us an account of the organization of his church, and of the teachings of his apostles, and the manner of their administration, etc. But this is not the gospel.

*The gospel is a certain living, abiding, eternal principle.* That which is written in the New Testament is like a chart of a country, if you please; but the gospel is the country itself. A man having the map of the United States in his possession would be considered foolish if he supposed he possessed the United States; and because a man may have the Old and New Testament in his possession, it does not follow that he has the gospel. But is it not written in some of our good Bibles, "The Gospel according to St. John," "The Gospel according to St. Matthew," etc.? Certainly. But what has that to do with it? The gospels according to Matthew, Mark, Luke, and John describe certain teachings and instructions which Jesus gave, and among the rest the officers constituting his church are named. "And God hath set some in the church, first apostles, secondarily prophets, thirdly teachers, after that miracles, then gifts of healings, helps, governments, diversities of tongues." (1 Corinthians 12:28.) These are the living substance of which they write an account.

Well, but the gospel is contained in the Old and New Testament. It is not, nor in the Book of Mormon, nor in the revelations we have received. These are simply records, histories, commandments, etc. The gospel is a living, abiding, eternal, and unchangeable principle that has existed co-equal with God, and always will exist, while time and eternity endure, wherever it is developed and made manifest.—*JD*, 7:360-362, January 15, 1860.

THE NATURE OF THE GOSPEL.—And what is the nature of the gospel? It is the same as that taught on the day of Pentecost by the apostles, when they cried out to the multitude, "Repent, and be baptized every one of you in the name of Jesus Christ for the remission of sins, and ye shall receive the gift of the Holy Ghost." (Acts 2:38.) That was the testimony which they bore to the people. That is the testimony which the elders of this church bear. There is something about this that is reasonable, that is intelligent, and that is susceptible of proof. It was a very fair proposition for the apostle to make, promising the people who would obey the requirements which the gospel imposes upon its adherents, that they should receive the Holy Ghost. And what should this do for them? It was to cause their old men to dream dreams and their young men to see visions, daughters prophesy; it was to bring things past to their remembrance, to lead them into all truth, and to show them things to come. . . .

THE GOSPEL AND EXPERIMENTAL EVIDENCE.—Now here is a principle of the gospel that will admit of as strong evidence as anything in nature. What is it? "Repent, and be baptized every one of you in the name of Jesus Christ for the remission of sins, and ye shall receive the gift of the Holy Ghost." Or in other words, sow wheat and you reap wheat; plant corn and you gather corn. It was a bold position to take. I remember that on these points I questioned the elder who brought the gospel to me. I asked, What do you mean by this Holy Ghost? . . . Will it give you the permeating influence of the Spirit of the living God, and give you a certain knowledge of the principles that you believe in?

"Yes," he answered, "and if it will not, then I am an impostor." Said I, "That is a very fair proposition." Finding the doctrine to be correct, I obeyed, and I received that Spirit through obedience to the gospel which gave me a knowledge of those principles which I simply believed before, because they were scriptural, reasonable and intelligent, according to that scripture which saith, "If any man will do his will, he shall know of the doctrine, whether it be of God, or whether I speak of myself." —JD, 23:50-51, 52, April 9, 1882.

FAITH AND ACTION NEEDED.—The Zion of God must consist of men that are pure in heart and pure in life and spotless before God. At least that is what we have got to arrive at. We are not there yet, but we must get there before we shall be prepared to inherit glory and exaltation. Therefore a form of godliness will amount to but little with any of us, for he that knoweth the master's will and doeth it not shall be beaten with many stripes. It is "Not every one that saith unto me, Lord, Lord, shall enter into the kingdom of heaven; but he that doeth the will of my Father, which is in heaven." (Matthew 7:21.) These are doctrines of the gospel as I understand them. And it is not enough for us to embrace the gospel and to be gathered here to the land of Zion, and be associated with the people of God, attend our meetings and partake of the sacrament of the Lord's supper, and endeavor to move along without much blame of any kind attached to us. For notwithstanding all this, if our hearts are not right, if we are not pure in heart before God, if we have not pure hearts and pure consciences, fearing God and keeping his commandments, we shall not unless we repent, participate in these blessings about which I have spoken and of which the prophets bear testimony.—*JD*, 26:92, February 12, 1882.

ETERNAL NATURE OF THE GOSPEL.—There is not a principle associated with the gospel of the Son of God but what is eternal in its nature and consequences, and we cannot with impunity trample upon any principle that is correct without having to suffer the penalty thereof before God and the holy angels, and in many instances before men. The principles of the gospel being eternal, they were framed and originated with the Almighty in eternity before the world was according to certain eternal laws, and hence the gospel is called the everlasting gospel.—*JD*, 21:112, November 28, 1879.

JOSEPH SMITH'S MISSION.—Joseph Smith's mission was to restore this same gospel in its fulness. He brought back the same gospel that Jesus taught, the same faith and repentance, the same baptism for the remission of sins, and the same laying on of hands for the gift of the Holy Ghost, and the same Holy Ghost with all its powers and blessings. This is the doctrine and these the principles we profess to believe in. We do not profess to have received our authority from the Church of England or any other sect: it came directly from God by the ministration of holy angels. The gospel that we preach is the everlasting gospel; it reaches back into the eternities that are past; it exists in time and it stretches forward into the eternities to come, and everything connected with it is eternal. . . .—*JD*, 13:17-19, March 14, 1869.

CONSEQUENCES OF THE PROPHET'S MISSION.—Why is it that the world rage? Why is it that the priests of the day are angry—that politicians are mad? It is because the Lord has set forth his hand to accomplish his purposes and bring to pass the things spoken of in the holy prophets.

As one of old has said:

Why do the heathen rage, and the people imagine a vain thing?
The kings of the earth set themselves, and the rulers take counsel together, against the Lord, and against his anointed, saying,
Let us break their bands asunder, and cast away their cords from us.
He that sitteth in the heavens shall laugh: the Lord shall have them in derision.
Then shall he speak unto them in his wrath, and vex them in his sore displeasure." (Psalm 2:1-5.)

The Lord will bring to pass his strange purpose, and accomplish the thing he has designed. It is for us to live our religion, to fully appreciate the gospel we possess, and fully obey its requirements, submit to its laws, and yield to its dictations, following the direction of the holy priesthood, which holds the keys of the mysteries of the revelations of God, magnifying our callings, and honoring our God, that we may be prepared to fulfil our destiny upon the earth, and be enabled to be a blessing to those around us, and to pour blessings upon our posterity, and spread forth the great principles of eternity, which are calculated to bless, enlighten, ennoble, and exalt all who will yield obedience to their dictates.—*JD, 7:370, January 15, 1860.*

## PRIESTHOOD AND THE GOSPEL

CO-ETERNITY OF THE GOSPEL, PRIESTHOOD, REVELATION. —Wherever the gospel existed, there existed also the power of God and the revelations of God, and therein men had a knowledge of God, and "therein was revealed the righteousness of God from faith to faith." But let me make another remark here concerning the priesthood. We are told it holds the mysteries of the revelations of God. These are sayings we have a right to look into and investigate, to find out upon what principle they are based.

ADAM'S KNOWLEDGE.—How did Adam get his information of the things of God? He got it through the gospel of Jesus Christ, and through this same priesthood of which we have been speaking. God came to him in the garden and talked with him. We are told that no man can see the face of God and live. How was it that he obtained his knowledge of God? Through the gospel; and he was the first man upon this earth that had the gospel and the holy priesthood; and if he had it not, he could not have known anything about God or his revelations. But God revealed himself to him and told him what he might do and what he might not do, what course he was to pursue and what course not to pursue; and when he transgressed the laws which the Lord gave to him, he was driven from the face of God, and left in a measure to grope in the dark.

ENOCH.—Let us pass on to Enoch's day. The Bible only gives a very short account of Enoch. We are told that he "walked with God: and was not; for God took him." (Genesis 5:24.) Then he had the gospel, for it is through the gospel that "the righteousness of God is revealed from faith to faith." It is that which holds the keys of the mysteries of the revelations of God. It is that which imparts a knowledge of the priesthood, and it is by the gospel that mankind can commune with God: it is that which is the power of God unto salvation to every one that believeth. Enoch had this through the gospel. Being in possession of this, he was enabled to communicate with God— had revelations from him. And further revelations which have been given in these last days go to show us that Enoch built a city, and that he taught the citizens of that city the great principles of eternal truth as they emanated from God; that God communed with them—taught them correct principles; and that, by-and-by, when the people waxed full of iniquity and the earth became ripe for destruction, Enoch and his city were caught up into heaven. . . .

THE GOSPEL KEY.—The great principle I wish to keep before your minds is, that men in those different ages of the world did have a knowledge of God, and they obtained it through revelation and a knowledge of the gospel.—*JD, 7:363-364,* January 15, 1860.

## THE HOLY GHOST: DIFFERENCE BETWEEN SECTS AND THE GOSPEL

What difference is there between the gospel and the beliefs of other sects and creeds? The gospel always did and always will "bring life and immortality to light." That is the difference. While others are groping in the dark, though their intentions in many instances are to do good and work righteousness, so far as they know, yet they cannot come to a knowledge of God, nor become acquainted with eternal things without the gospel; without the gift of the Holy Ghost, the spirit of revelation which proceeds from God. And who are to have this? All who obey. "But I thought," say some, "that that was confined to some one or two, or to half a dozen or a dozen, as the case may be, and that the whole people had nothing to do with it." This is a very great mistake, and I will now show you the difference between . . . the position that we occupy and the position that the world occupy.

The world, as I have told you, unaided by the gift of the Holy Ghost, unaided by the gospel and the light of revelation, are left to grope a good deal in the dark. But not so with the saints of God; no matter in what age of the world they may have lived, they have been placed under other circumstances; they have had the light of truth to guide them, and revelation direct from the Lord. And here is the difference between one and the other. When Nicodemus came to Jesus, he went to him by night. He was much like some men are in this our day, with respect to their private feelings for the Mormons. They respect the Mormons, they cannot help doing so. But they do not want it known for the Latter-day Saints, like the former-day saints, are not popular. In fact, we are considered by many as they were, to be of disreputable character, a people with whom it would not be considered proper to associate. This was the character that the Savior bore among the self-righteous but hypocritical religionists of his day. Yet we call him the Son of God. And we find Nicodemus, a prominent man, a man of discernment and ability, creeping around the back door, not wishing it to be known that he had called upon the Mormons—oh, no!—Jesus of Nazareth; yet he wished to find out something respecting him, for he believed that no man could do the things that he did except God were with him. Jesus in explaining the gospel to him, told him that he, in order to understand his teachings and his works, would have to be born again. Nicodemus could not appreciate this saying. He knew not what the Savior meant, thinking the saying referred to a man's natural birth. The Savior then told him, that unless a man was born of the water and of the Spirit, he could not enter the kingdom of God; that he could not comprehend it; that he could not even see it; that he could not understand the relationship that existed between God and man without the gift of the Holy Ghost.—*JD*, 23:372-373, February 11, 1883.

## THE SCOPE OF THE GOSPEL

COMPREHENSIVE CHARACTER.—In regard to our religion, I will say that it embraces every principle of truth and intelligence pertaining to us as moral, intellectual, mortal and immortal beings, pertaining to this world and the world that is to come. We are open to truth of every kind, no matter whence it comes, where it originates, or who believes in it. Truth, when preceded by the little word "all," comprises everything that has ever existed or that ever will exist and be known by and among men in time and through the endless ages of eternity. And it is the duty of all intelligent beings who are responsible and amenable to God for their acts, to search after truth, and to permit it to influence them and their acts and general course in life, independent of all bias or preconceived notions, however specious and plausible they may be.

We, as Latter-day Saints, believe, first, in the gospel, and that is a great deal to say, for the gospel embraces principles that dive deeper, spread wider, and extend further than anything else that we can conceive. The gospel teaches us in regard to the being and attributes of God. It also teaches us our relationship to that God and the various responsibilities we are under to him as his offspring. It teaches us the various duties and responsibilities that we are under to our families and friends, to the community, to the living and the dead. It unfolds to us principles pertaining to futurity. In fact, according to the saying of one of the old disciples, it "brings life and immortality to light," brings us into relationship with God, and prepares us for an exaltation in the eternal world. There is something grand, profound, and intellectual associated with the principles of the gospel as it stands connected with the salvation and exaltation of man.

A man in search of truth has no peculiar system to sustain, no peculiar dogma to defend or theory to uphold. He embraces all truth, and that truth, like the sun in the firmament, shines forth and spreads its effulgent rays over all creation. If men will divest themselves of bias and prejudice, and prayerfully and conscientiously search after truth, they will find it wherever they turn their attention. But in regard to the leading principles of the gospel, there are some distinctive features connected therewith, which, like all the laws of nature and of nature's God, require implicit obedience and compliance therewith in order to insure a realization of the results which flow therefrom. The earth on which we live, the matter of which it is composed, the elements with which we are surrounded, as well as the planetary system, have certain inscrutable, eternal, unchangeable laws connected with them that can not be departed from.—*JD*, 16:369, February 1, 1874.

# CHAPTER X

# THE DISPENSATIONS OF THE GOSPEL

## THE PURPOSE AND THE PLAN

There were certain great principles involved in the organization of this earth, and one was that there might be a place provided whereon the children of our Heavenly Father could live and propagate their species, and have bodies formed for the spirits to inhabit who were the children of God; for we are told that he is the God and Father of the spirits of all flesh. It was requisite, therefore, that an earth should be organized. It was requisite that man should be placed upon it. It was requisite that bodies should be prepared for those spirits to inhabit, in order that the purposes of God pertaining to his progeny might be accomplished, and that those spirits might be enabled, through the medium of the everlasting gospel, to return unto the presence of their Heavenly Father, as Gods among the Gods.

GOOD AND EVIL IN THE WORLD'S HISTORY.—There have been different agencies at work throughout this world's history. Lucifer has been and is one of these agencies. There was a garden planted, and Adam and Eve were placed in it, and there they had communion with God. There was another being whose name was Lucifer, who is called in some places, "the son of the morning." Job speaks of a time at the creation of this earth when "the morning stars sang together, and all the sons of God shouted for joy." (Job 38:7.) As it was necessary that there should be a God, a man, an earth and a heaven, it was also necessary that there should be a devil, that man might be tried, and by trial be instructed. Indeed, in the economy of God, it was not only necessary that man, but the Savior also should be perfected by suffering. It is written: "For it became him, for whom are all things, and by whom are all things, in bringing many sons unto glory, to make the captain of their salvation perfect through sufferings." (Hebrews 2:10.) It was further necessary that there should be a Redeemer according to the plan which was devised from before the foundation of the world, and also that man might be a free agent to act and operate for himself, to receive the good and reject the evil, or reject the good and be governed by the evil. And there were certain rewards promised to those who would obey the laws of God, and keep his commandments, and certain punishments inflicted upon those who would not. Satan has made very great ravages among the human family in trying to accomplish his purposes; for he has been the enemy of God, and the enemy of man, and in ages past he wrought upon mankind, until after a certain period he had contrived to get the great majority of them on his side. Nevertheless, they had the priesthood among them in those early days as we have among us today. . . .

And in these latter days God has introduced these same principles with the same object in view. He has revealed the same principles of heaven, and as heretofore, in the interest of humanity.—JD, 25:303-305, October 6 and 7, 1884.

THE LAW OF TESTING.—In the economy of God and the plan proposed by the Almighty, it was provided that man was to be placed under a law apparently simple in itself, yet the test of that law was fraught with the gravest consequences. The observance of that law would secure eternal life, and the penalty for the violation of that law was death. . . .

Men could not have been tested without a law. The penalty for the violation of that law was death. If the law had not been broken, man would have lived; but would man thus living have been capable of perpetuating his species, and of thus fulfilling the designs of God in preparing tabernacles for the spirits which had been created in the spirit world? And further, could they have had the need of a mediator, who was to act as a propitiation for the violation of this law, which it would appear from the circumstances was destined to be broken or could the eternal increase and perpetuity of man have been continued, and his high exaltation to the Godhead been accomplished, without the propitiatory atonement and sacrifice of the Son of God?—MA, 128-129.

ADAM AND EVE AND THE LAW.—Adam and Eve both considered that they had gained, instead of suffered loss, through their disobedience to that law; for they made the statement, that if it had not been for their transgression they never would "have known good and evil." And again, they would have been incapable of increase; and without that increase the designs of God in relation to the formation of the earth and man could not have been accomplished; for one great object of the creation of the world was the propagation of the human species, that bodies might be prepared for those spirits who already existed, and who, when they saw the earth formed, shouted for joy.

Secondly. By pursuing the course they did, through the atonement, they would see God as they had done before; and furthermore, they would be capable of exaltation, which was made possible only through their fall, and the atonement of Jesus Christ; and also, they might have the comforting influence of the Spirit of God, and his guidance and direction here, as well as eternal lives and exaltations in the world to come.—*MA,* 130.

THE LAW AND THE ATONEMENT.—Was it known that man would fall? Yes. We are clearly told that it was understood that man should fall, and it was understood that the penalty of departing from the law would be death, death temporal. And there was a provision made for that. Man was not able to make that provision himself, and hence we are told that it needed the atonement of a God to accomplish this purpose; and the Son of God presented himself to carry out that object. And when he presented himself for this position he was accepted by his Father, just the same as any man who owes a debt, if he is not able to pay that obligation, and somebody steps forward and says, I will go security for him. If the persons to whom he is indebted are willing to take him as security, they will receive the security's note or obligation to meet the debt. So Jesus offered himself. Now, man could not have done that. Man could do all that he is capable of doing. But there was an eternal law of God violated and it needed an eternal, infinite sacrifice to atone therefor; and Jesus offered himself as that sacrifice to atone for the sins of the world; and hence it is written, he was the Lamb slain from before the foundation of the world.

THE PRINCIPLE OF SACRIFICE.—Now, to carry out this view of indebtedness a little further. We will suppose that a man has given his note to pay a certain amount in a certain given time, and in order to keep that note good, he agrees to pay interest on it. Now, when Jesus gave himself up as security for the sins of mankind, and God accepted of his security, what was done then? Why, sacrifices were introduced as types of the sacrifice of the Son of God, to show that the ancient servants of God recognized this principle which had existed in the heavens, and many of them understood the principle with great clearness. We find that Adam offered sacrifices, and when he did this, he said in answer to a question put to him by an holy angel, I do not know why I do it, only the Father has commanded it. And then the angel commenced to explain to him that this rite was a type of the sacrifice of the Only Begotten of the Father who should come in the meridian of time to offer himself as a sacrifice for the sins of the world; and said he, "Wherefore, thou shalt do all that thou doest in the name of the Son, and thou shalt repent and call upon God in the name of the Son forevermore." (Pearl of Great Price, Moses 5:8.) When Adam and Eve ate of the forbidden fruit, the mercy of God was extended to them, and they perceived as Eve expressed it, that if there had been no fall, they would have had no posterity, and that they would have been deprived of many joys and blessings relating both to this life and the life to come. And so Adam and Eve rejoiced in their hearts that God had provided the plan, and although they were fallen, yet in this life, through the atonement, they would have joy, and by and by they would return to their Father, and there rejoice exceedingly in the abundant mercy of God, and in the redemption wrought out for them by the Son of God.

THE POWERS STRIVING WITH MEN.—We find that from that time Satan began to operate and to use his influence against God, seeking to introduce rebellion on the earth as he had done in heaven. He succeeded but too well in his operations. And when Cain and Abel offered up their sacrifice, Cain would not have done it if the devil had not urged him; but we are told that Cain loved Satan better than he loved God, and that he departed from the laws of God. Satan requested Cain to offer up a sacrifice, which he did, and the Lord rejected it, but he accepted his brother Abel's. Why did the Lord refuse one and accept the other? Because the Lord knew that Cain had departed from him, and that he was not sincere in his offering, as we sometimes are not sincere in our offerings and in our worship, and therefore he rejected it. Then Satan came again and whispered to Cain, "I could have told you all about it before; God is an unrighteous God; he gathers where he has not strewn; he reaps where he has not sown. He was unjust to me in heaven, and therefore I rebelled against him; and I advise you to do so also." And Cain listened to the advice of Satan, and as the devil was a murderer and a liar from the beginning, so he induced Cain to become the same, and he instigated him to kill his brother Abel. Here were the two powers represented in the two men, that of God in Abel, and that of Satan in Cain; and thus the warfare commenced, and the opposition was inaugurated, for we are told it was necessary there should be an opposition in all things. And furthermore, we are told that it became him of whom are all things, and by whom are all things, in bringing many sons unto glory, to make the Captain of their salvation perfect through suffering.

Now, these things spread and grew. It was necessary and proper that there should be good and evil, light and darkness, sin and righteousness, one principle of right opposed to another of wrong, that man might have his free agency to receive the good and reject the evil, and by receiving the good (through the atonement of Jesus Christ and the principles of the gospel, which he introduced, and which were advocated long before he himself appeared on the earth), they might be saved and exalted to the eternal Godhead, and go back to their Father and God, while the disobedient would have to meet the consequences of their own acts.

THE DESTRUCTION OF THE WICKED: THE OPERATION OF JUSTICE.—This warfare continued; and as men began to increase upon the earth, so wickedness increased, until it was decided that they should be destroyed, that they might be deprived of the privilege of perpetuating their species. Why? Let us go back to the time when Satan rebelled against the Almighty and drew away one-third of the hosts of heaven. We find that there were pure spirits that stood that test and who had given to them the promise of bodies on this earth. Let us suppose that you and I were there as spirits, awaiting the privilege of taking bodies, and that we could see the wickedness and corruption that was going on upon the earth, and that we could see prophets going about teaching the principles of righteousness and warning the people of judgments that should come, of the flood that should overwhelm them, and of the prisons prepared in which the ungodly should be cast. And we say, "Father, you see the people on the earth that they are wicked and depraved, fallen and corrupt! Yes. Is it right and just that we who have done no wrong should have to enter into such corrupt bodies and partake of the influences with which they are surrounded?" "No," says the Father, "it is not just, and I will cut them off; I will cause the floods to come upon them to destroy them, and I will send those wicked and disobedient spirits into prison," which he did.

Here was an act of justice. Some men who profess to be very wise, think God was unjust in thus destroying so many of his creatures. They know nothing about it because they do not comprehend the law of God and the purposes of God. It was an act of justice and righteousness according to the eternal justice that dwells in the bosom of the Father.—*JD*, 22:300-302, August 28, 1881.

## THE ROLE AND REALITY OF SATAN

THE SATANIC EFFORT.—Satan has tried from the beginning of the world to overturn the works of God and in some instances he has apparently succeeded admirably. He was the cause at one time of all the people of the earth being destroyed except a little seed which was saved to propagate the human species. Probably the devil would laugh pretty heartily over that, thinking that he had accomplished his purposes. However, that was not the end. It is true that the judgments of God overtook them. It is true they were destroyed by a flood in the flesh, and were shut up in prison in the spirit. But it is also true that the same Savior who is our Savior, when he was put to death in the flesh, was quickened by the spirit, and that he visited those spirits in prison opening up the door of salvation to them that they might be redeemed and come forth and accomplish certain purposes which God had designed. And hence we find the Savior operating among all that body of people that the devil thought were destroyed, but through this visitation were placed within the reach of deliverance. But has Satan prevailed to a great extent? He has. Has darkness spread itself over the earth? Yes. Have people wandered away from God and forsaken him and his laws? They have. But then the Lord will be merciful towards them, they not having received the light that we have, hence he feels towards them as a father feels towards his children, being desirous to promote their happiness as far as it lies in his power; and if he could not save them while in the flesh, he understands certain eternal laws and principles whereby they may hereafter be redeemed. The judge of all the earth will do right. And while the priesthood behind the veil are operating and preaching to the spirits that are in prison that have been there from the different ages, he calls upon us to build temples that we may administer for the bodies of these people that have died without the gospel, that they may be judged according to men in the flesh and live after God in the spirit.—*JD,* 21:96, April 13, 1879.

REBELLION AGAINST GOD.—Satan, we are told, rebelled against God; and he wanted to introduce something that was contrary to the law of God and to the counsel of God; as much as to say, "O, you do not know much about it; I will go and save all; wherefore give me thy glory." Some of our folks nowadays feel and say sometimes they have a portion of the priesthood, and they think they are almighty personages. They think they know better than anybody else, better than the bishop, better than the twelve, better than the presidency of the church. They are puffed up and filled with their vain imaginations. Say they, "Let me have my say; and then, I want you to give me your honor to help me to carry it out." Or, in other words, "I want to fight against the work of God and against the priesthood of God, and I want you to give me power and influence to accomplish it." They do not tell you that in so many words; but those are the facts.

Now, we are told that Satan rebelled against God. He could not rebel against a law if that law had not been given. He could not have violated a commandment if that commandment did not exist. And we are told that he sought to take away the agency of man, to make man a poor miserable serf; and then to take his own course in regard to the destiny of the human family. But God would not have it so. . . . He cast Lucifer out of heaven and with him one-third of the hosts of heaven, because of their departure from God and his laws, and because they sought to pervert the counsel of God and violate those principles which he had introduced for the salvation of the world which was to be, and upon which we now dwell.—*JD*, 22:299-300, August 28, 1881.

It was not for drunkenness, theft nor any other act of immorality that Satan was hurled from heaven, but for resisting authority, and trying to subvert the order of God.—*TS*, 5:662, 1844.

LUCIFER'S INFLUENCE.—When man was placed upon the earth, Lucifer, or Satan, still manifested the same animus and spirit; and through his influence he operated upon Cain, for Cain listened to his wiles, and being controlled by him, he also rebelled against his father and his God. Thus the rebellion in the heavens was transmitted to a rebellion on the earth, and all who became subject to this influence placed themselves in a state of enmity and antagonism to God, and one of the first results exhibited was covetousness and murder, even the murder by Cain of his brother Abel.—*MA*, 68.

THE DEVIL.—God has had a certain design to accomplish, associated with the human family; and I suppose that everything which has taken place has been just. I am not going to find fault with God or the devil. I suppose the devil is as necessary as any other being, or he would not have been.—*JD*, 6:23, November 1, 1857.

WILL THE DEVIL BE SAVED?—Some people will ask if we think the devil will be saved. You must ask him, for I have nothing to say about it. I have gone far enough in my remarks. I believe God will accomplish all his purposes, and Satan will not have power to frustrate his designs in any way whatever; for if he did, he would be more powerful than God.—*JD*, 1:159, June 12, 1853.

## THE DISPENSATIONS OF THE GOSPEL

OUTLINE OF THE DISPENSATIONS.—We have had in the different ages various dispensations; for instance what may be called the Adamic dispensation, the dispensation of Noah, the dispensation of Abraham, the dispensation of Moses and of the prophets who were associated with that dispensation; the dispensation of Jesus Christ, when he came to take away the sins of the world by the sacrifice of himself, and in and through those various dispensations, certain principles, powers, privileges and priesthoods have been developed. But in the dispensation of the fulness of times a combination or a fulness, a completeness of all those dispensations was to be introduced among the human family. If there was anything pertaining to the Adamic, (or what we may term more particularly the Patriarchal) dispensation, it would be made manifest in the last days. If there was anything associated with Enoch and his city, and the gathering together of his people, or of the translation of his city, it would be manifested in the last days. If there was anything associated with the Melchizedek priesthood in all its forms, powers, privileges and blessings at any time or in any part of the earth, it would be restored in the last days. If there was anything connected with the Aaronic priesthood, that also would be developed in the last times. If there was anything associated with the apostleship and presidency that existed on this continent, it would be developed in the last times, for this is the dispensation of the fulness of times, embracing all other times, all principles, all powers, all manifestations, all priesthoods and the powers thereof that have existed in any age, in any part of the world. For, "those things which never have been revealed from the foundation of the world, but have been kept hid from the wise and prudent, shall be revealed unto babes and sucklings in this, the dispensation of the fulness of times." (D. & C. 128:18.)

ROLE OF THE FATHER AND THE SON.—And who was to originate this? It originated with God the Father, and it was sustained by Jesus, the Mediator of the new covenant, and it was sanctioned by all the prophets, patriarchs, apostles and men of God who held the priesthood in former ages. And finally, when all the preparations were made and everything was ready, or the time had fully come, the Father and the Son appeared to the youth Joseph Smith to introduce the great work of the latter days. —JD, 22:298-299, August 28, 1881.

INSIGHTS INTO THE ADAMIC PERIOD.— . . . The offering of sacrifices . . . was a usual ceremony, and as it belonged to the priesthood and to the promised seed to offer sacrifices, it would be reasonable to suppose that Adam did . . . officiate in that rite. Indeed, it was stated by the Prophet Joseph Smith, in our hearing, while standing on an elevated piece of ground or plateau near Adam-ondi-Ahman (Daviess County, Missouri), where there were a number of rocks piled together, that the valley before us was the valley of Adam-ondi-Ahman; or in other words, the valley where God talked with Adam, and where he gathered his righteous posterity, as recorded in the above revelation, and that this pile of stones was an altar built by him when he offered up sacrifices, as we understand, on that occasion. If Adam then offered up sacrifices in the presence of these prominent men, he being the president of these high prists, he would officiate for them as well as for himself; while it is quite reasonable to believe that they assisted in the offerings made upon that altar. —MA, 69-70.

THE CITY OF ENOCH.—It would appear that the translated residents of Enoch's city are under the direction of Jesus, who is the Creator of worlds; and that he, holding the keys of the government of other worlds, could, in his administrations to them, select the translated people of Enoch's Zion, if he thought proper, to perform a mission to these various planets, and as death had not passed upon them, they could be prepared by him and made use of through the medium of the holy priesthood to act as ambassadors, teachers, or messengers to those worlds over which Jesus holds the authority.—*MA, 76.*

Each kingdom, or planet, and the inhabitants thereof, were blessed with the visits and presence of their Creator, in their several times and seasons.

It is recorded that to Jesus has been given all power in heaven and in earth, and . . . he evidently had power which he used to commission the citizens of the Zion of Enoch to go to other worlds on missions.—*MA, 77.*

NOAH AND THE ANTEDILUVIANS.—The flood came and destroyed the unrighteous, and their spirits were confined in prisons, as they are termed. And I think I hear the devil laughing, as some of them did when we were driven away from our homes, thinking that Mormonism had gone to perdition. But we live yet; and they were mistaken; and so was the devil. For although they were destroyed in the body, yet when Jesus came and was put to death in the flesh, yet quickened by the spirit, he went and preached to the spirits in prison that were disobedient in the days of Noah. And then the devil put on a long face and said, I imagined I had got rid of these fellows; but they are going to have a chance yet that I did not think of. And after the flood we are told that the curse that had been pronounced upon Cain was continued through Ham's wife, as he had married a wife of that seed. And why did it pass through the flood? Because it was necessary that the devil should have a representation upon the earth as well as God; and that man should be a free agent to act for himself; and that all men might have the opportunity of receiving or rejecting the truth and be governed by it or not, according to their wishes, and abide the result; and that those who would be able to maintain correct principles under all circumstances might be able to associate with the Gods in the eternal worlds. It is the same eternal program. God knew it, and Adam knew it.

Now, with regard to Noah and his day. God made arrangements beforehand and told Methuselah that when the people should be destroyed, that a remnant of his seed should occupy the earth and stand foremost upon it. And Methuselah was so anxious to have it done that he ordained Noah to the priesthood when he was ten years of age. Noah then stood in his day as the representative of God; and after him Abraham was selected to take the lead in relation to these matters pertaining to man's salvation.—*JD, 22:303-304, August 28, 1881.*

NOAH RECOGNIZED THE ATONEMENT.—The first act after the destruction of the world by a flood was a recognition of the great expiatory principle of the atonement, which was to be made by the Only Begotten Son of God, as revealed by the angel to Adam. And as God recognized Adam's and Abel's offerings, so he also recognized that of Noah; and as a result, the patriarch obtained great promises, in which the people of all ages, then to come, would be interested.—*MA, 82.*

ABRAHAM.—We were informed that Abraham was a man that followed after righteousness, and that he sought to obtain more righteousness; that he searched the records of his fathers as they had come down to him, and traced them back until the days of Adam, and even before the world was. Before the world was? Yes. God, we are told, talked with him, and told him of certain noble spirits who stood in his presence in the beginning, whom he had determined to make his rulers; "and thou, Abraham," said he, "art one of them." He was not only a prince on the earth but a prince in the heavens, and by right came to the earth in his time to accomplish the things given him to do. And he found by tracing his genealogy that he had a right to the priesthood, and when he ascertained that, he prayed to the Lord, and demanded an ordination. And he was ordained (as we are told by Joseph Smith) under the hands of Melchizedek to the holy priesthood. (Doctrine & Covenants 84:14.) And afterwards, we are informed, he came in possession of the Urim and Thummin by which he could obtain a knowledge of God and of his laws, and all things pertaining to the earth and the heavens. And God revealed himself unto him; and he told him that in blessing, he would bless him; and in multiplying, he would multiply him, and that in him and in his seed all the families of the earth should be blessed. And has this been so? Yes; from that time forth, by that lineage the blessings of heaven have flowed to the children of men.

ABRAHAM'S POSTERITY.—Let us examine a few things. Who were Isaac and Jacob? Heirs of the same promises as himself. Who was Joseph, who was sold into Egypt? A descendant of Abraham. Who was Moses, who delivered the people from Egyptian bondage? A descendant of Abraham. Who was Aaron, who was associated with the Aaronic priesthood, and who presided over it? A descendant of Abraham. Who were the prophets that we read of in this Bible? They were descendants of Abraham. Who was Jesus, who as the Son of God, taketh away the sins of the world? A descendant of Abraham according to the flesh. Who were the twelve apostles, commissioned to preach the gospel to all nations? Descendants of Abraham. And who were the twelve apostles that lived upon this continent? Descendants of Abraham. Who was Joseph Smith, to whom the gospel was revealed in these last days? A descendant of Abraham. And it had been predicted of him that his name should be Joseph, and that his father's name should also be Joseph, and that he should be a descendant of that Joseph who was sold into Egypt. And who are the present twelve? Just the same kind of people. And who are we gathering to Zion? A remnant of that seed, with a considerable mixture of grizzly, gray, and all kinds. But Jesus said, My sheep hear my voice, and they know me, and a stranger they will not follow, because they know not the voice of a stranger. And why do not the millions of the inhabitants of the earth embrace the gospel? Because they are not sheep; that is all. And if the goats kick up and cut a few antics, you need not be astonished. It is the nature of goats, is it not?—*JD*, 22:304-305, August 28, 1881.

ABRAHAM AND THE PRIESTHOOD.—In examining the records, tracing them back through the flood, clear away back unto Adam's day, Abraham . . . found he had a right to the priesthood. I need not stop to tell you what that is, you Latter-day Saints. You understand it is the rule and government of God, whether in the heavens or on the earth, and when we talk of the kingdom of God, we talk of something that pertains to rule, government, authority, and dominion; and that priesthood is the ruling principle that exists in the heavens or on the earth, associated with the affairs of God. . . .

It was this priesthood, that would be the means of introducing him into the presence of God, that Abraham found that he was a rightful inheritor of. . . . And what then? The next that we read of is that he had the Urim and Thummim, and thus he sought unto God for himself, and while searching unto him, God revealed himself unto Abraham and said: "And I will bless them that bless thee, and curse them that curseth thee: and in thee shall all families of the earth be blessed." (Genesis 12:3.) There is something very remarkable about this when we reflect upon it, and when we examine the position that he occupied, and that his seed occupied, we can see the fulfilment of these things. Afterwards, the Lord revealed himself to him from time to time, communicated his will to him, and he was made acquainted with the designs of the Almighty. The Lord showed unto him the order of the creation of this earth on which we stand, and revealed unto him some of the greatest and most sublime truths that ever were made known to man. He got these through revelation from God and through the medium of the gospel of the Son of God.—*JD*, 21:159-160, December 7, 1879.

THE LAW OF MOSES AND RELIGIOUS PRACTICES OF THE NEPHITES.—First, the law of Moses, with all its rites, ordinances and sacrifices, was strictly observed by the faithful Nephites from the time of their arrival on the promised land, until it was fulfilled in Christ, and by his command ceased to be observed.

Second, that when the Nephites brought any of the Lamanites to the knowledge and worship of the true God, they taught them to observe this law.

Third, that those who apostatized from the Nephites, as a general thing, ceased to observe this law.

Fourth, that the true import of the law of Moses, and of its ceremonies and sacrifices, as typical of the atonement yet to be made by our Lord and Savior, was thoroughly taught by the priesthood among that people, and very generally understood by them.

Fifth, that associated with the observance of this law, there were continued admonitions given that salvation was in Christ and not in the law, which was but the shadow and type of that of which he was the prototype and reality.

Sixth, that temples were erected of the same pattern as that of Solomon at Jerusalem, evidently for the reason that they were to be used for the same purposes.

Seventh, that the gospel was preached in connection with the law, and churches were established and organized according to the gospel requirements, and that the higher priesthood, although not fully organized in all its parts, ministered to the Nephites as well as the lesser.

Eighth, it appears indubitable from the two records, the Bible and the Book of Mormon, that the intent and true meaning of the law of Moses, of its sacrifices, etc., were far better understood and comprehended by the Nephites than by the Jews. But in this connection it must not be forgotten that a great many most plain and precious things, as the Book of Mormon states, have been taken from the Bible, through the ignorance of uninspired translators or the design and cunning of wicked men.—*MA*, 109-110.

THE CHRISTIAN DISPENSATION.[1]—Jesus came here according to the foreordained plan and purpose of God, pertaining to the human family, as the Only Begotten of the Father, full of grace and truth. He came to offer himself a sacrifice, the just

---

[1]See also the following chapter, for detail.

for the unjust; to meet the requirements of a broken law which the human family were incapable of meeting. . . .—*JD,* 22:140, July 3, 1881.

THE DISPENSATION OF THE FULNESS OF TIMES.—We are living in peculiar times. We are operating in an eventful era. We are associated with a peculiar dispensation, and we have a labor to perform which in many respects differs from that of all other ages or times. The dispensation that we are connected with is called in scripture the dispensation of the fulness of times in which, it is recorded, God will gather together all things in one, whether they be things on the earth or things in the heavens. There are ideas associated with this dispensation that are in many respects distinct and dissimilar from those that have been enunciated and proclaimed in former ages and dispensations; and inasmuch as the present dispensation is to embrace everything that has been connected with all past dispensations, all the prominent features as well as the minor ones that characterized the church and kingdom of God in former days, that were essentially necessary to its growth and development, must reappear in connection with the work of God in this our day. If the manifestations and developments of other dispensations have been made known to us, we have had revealed to us doctrines, theories, organizations, and systems that have existed among the whole of them, because it is emphatically the dispensation of the fulness of times. If they had anything that was peculiarly characteristic in the days of the ancient patriarchs, we have the same revealed to us. If they had anything prominent and important in the dispensation of Noah, we have it; and if Noah was called upon to preach the gospel to the world in his day, before its destruction, so are we.

If in the Abrahamic or Mosaic dispensations, God revealed important principles, we have a clear knowledge of those things made known to us, and the reasons, the whys and wherefores, pertaining to them. If they had anything among the ancient prophets and men of God, we have the same principles developed. If in the days of Jesus they had manifestations, revelations, doctrines, or organizations, those things are made known to us. Or if the people upon this continent, to whom God revealed his will—either the people that came from the Tower of Babel, or those who came from Jerusalem during the reign of Zedekiah —if anything was revealed to them, we have had it revealed unto us.—*JD,* 23:28-29, March 5, 1882.

THE FINAL SALVATION OF MAN.—It would appear that, when everything shall have been accomplished pertaining or relating to the sacrifice and atonement of the Son of God, in the time of the restitution of all things the sons of Levi will offer up an acceptable offering unto the Lord. What this offering' will be does not distinctly appear. There are many things associated with the final salvation of man, and the working out and accomplishment of the purposes of God in relation to the human family, which lie yet in the future: the peculiar position which the children will occupy, also the position of the heathen who have died without law, and of those who have been translated, and who it would appear have a specified labor to perform associated with their mission to the terrestrial worlds; the letting loose of Satan after the thousand years, and many other things which it is not permitted for us at the present time to comprehend in full. These will all be revealed in the due time of the Lord.—*MA*, 119-120.

# CHAPTER XI

# THE MEDIATION AND ATONEMENT OF CHRIST

## FOUNDATIONS OF THE CHRISTIAN FAITH

THE MEMORIAL OF THE SACRAMENT OF THE LORD'S SUPPER.—It would seem that the coming of the Savior to the world, his suffering, death, resurrection, and ascension to the position he occupies in the eternal world before his Heavenly Father has a great deal to do with our interests and happiness; and hence this continued memorial that we partake of every Sabbath. This sacrament is the fulfilment of the request of Jesus Christ to his disciples. "For as often as ye eat this bread, and drink this cup, ye do shew the Lord's death till he come." (1 Corinthians 11:26.) Faith in this ordinance would necessarily imply that we have faith in Jesus Christ, that he is the Only Begotten of the Father, that he came from the heavens to the earth to accomplish a certain purpose which God had designed—even to secure the salvation and exaltation of the human family. All this has a great deal to do with our welfare and happiness here and hereafter. The death of Jesus Christ would not have taken place had it not been necessary. That this ceremony should be instituted to keep that circumstance before the minds of his people, bespeaks its importance as embracing certain unexplained purposes and mysterious designs of God. They are explained in part, but they are not fully comprehended why it was necessary that Jesus Christ should leave the heavens, his Father's abode and presence, and come upon the earth to offer himself up a sacrifice; that he should, according to the scripture saying, Take away sin by the sacrifice of himself. Why this should be, why it was necessary that his blood should be shed, is an apparent mystery. It is true that we are told that without the shedding of blood there is no remission of sins. But why this? Why should such a law exist? It is left with us as a matter of faith, that it was necessary he should come and, being necessary, he shrank not from the task, but came to take away sin by offering up himself.—*JD*, 10:114, February 22, 1863.

Jesus Christ is spoken of in the scriptures as "The Lamb of God, which taketh away the sin of the world." (John 1:29.) What sins of the world did he take away? We are told that it is the sin which Adam committed. We do not know much about Adam nor what he did. But we know that this sacrifice took place and that we are in the position we now occupy, and we are ready to believe from the testimonies we have received in relation to this sacrifice that it was the will of God he should thus offer himself up and that he came here for that purpose. He was "the only begotten of the Father, full of grace and truth." (John 1:14.) He suffered his body to be broken and his blood to be spilled, doing not his own will but the will of him that sent him, not to accomplish his own purpose particularly but the purpose of him that sent him, and hence we are told to observe this rite (the sacrament) until he comes again.

THE SECOND ADVENT.—There is something also to be looked to in the future. The Son of God has again to figure in the grand drama of the world. He has been here once and in his humiliation his judgment was taken away. It would seem that his ancient disciples upon this continent or upon the continent of Asia actually looked forward to the time when Jesus would come again and hence he is frequently spoken of in the scriptures having a reference to his second advent, that to those who look for him he would appear the second time without sin unto salvation. Again, Isaiah, in speaking of him, says:

All we like sheep have gone astray; we have turned every one to his own way; and the Lord hath laid on him the iniquity of us all.
He was oppressed, and he was afflicted, yet he opened not his mouth: he is brought as a lamb to the slaughter, and as a sheep before her shearers is dumb, so he openeth not his mouth.
He was taken from prison and from judgment: and who shall declare his generation? for he was cut off out of the land of the living: for the transgressions of my people was he stricken. . . . (Isaiah 53:6-8.)

Again, the same prophet spoke of him as coming in power, glory and dominion, and as having his wrath and indignation kindled against the nations of the earth.

Who is this that cometh from Edom, with dyed garments from Bozrah? this that is glorious in his apparel, travelling in the greatness of his strength? I that speak in righteousness, mighty to save.
Wherefore art thou red in thine apparel, and thy garments like him that treadeth in the winefat?
I have trodden the winepress alone; and of the people there was none with me: for I will tread them in mine anger, and trample them in my fury; and their blood shall be sprinkled upon my garments, and I will stain all my raiment.
For the day of vengeance is in mine heart, and the year of my redeemed is come. (Isaiah 63:1-4.)

Jesus accomplished what he was sent to do, and feeling satisfied of this, when he was about to leave the earth he said he had finished the work his Father gave him to do. But there was another work, another event that was to transpire in the latter days, when he should not be led as a lamb to the slaughter or be like a sheep before the shearers; when he would not act in that state of humiliation and quiescence, but when he will go forth as a man of war and tread down the people in his anger and trample them in his fury, when blood should be on his garments and the day of vengeance in his heart, when he would rule the nations with an iron rod and break them to pieces like a potter's vessel.

REASONS FOR CHRISTIAN MEMORIAL CAME BY REVELATION.—There must be some reason why he was allowed to suffer and to endure; why it was necessary that he should give up his life a sacrifice for the sins of the world, and there must be a reason why he should come forth in judgment to execute vengeance, indignation, and wrath upon the ungodly. In these reasons we and all the world are intimately concerned; there is something of great importance in all this to us. The whys and wherefores of these great events are pregnant with importance to us all. When he comes again, he comes to take vengeance on the ungodly and to bring deliverance unto his Saints. "For the day of vengeance," it is written, "is in mine heart, and the year of my redeemed is come." (Isaiah 63:4.) It behooves us to be made well aware which class we belong to, that if we are not already among the redeemed, we may immediately join that society, that when the Son of God shall come the second time with all the holy angels with him, arrayed in power and great glory to take vengeance on them that know not God and obey not the gospel, or when he shall come in flaming fire, we shall be among that number who shall be ready to meet him with gladness in our hearts and hail him as our great deliverer and friend. In relation to all events that have transpired and to the designs of God connected with the earth and all grades of men upon it, and to the events that transpired before we came into this existence, if there is anything we cannot clearly comprehend, we can leave it for the future to reveal. True, it is the privilege of a certain class of people to have the Holy Ghost that Jesus said should bring things past, present, and to come to their remembrance and lead them into all truth. We can have a portion of that Spirit by which we can draw back the veil of eternity and comprehend the designs of God that have been hidden up for generations past and gone. We can go back to our former existence and contemplate the designs of God in the formation of this earth and all things that pertain to it; unravel its destiny and the designs of God in relation to our past, present, and future existence. . . .

KNOWLEDGE OF CHRIST TO COME BY REVELATION.—No matter what ability and talent a man may possess, all must come under this rule if they wish to know the Father and the Son. If knowledge of them is not obtained through revelation it cannot be obtained at all. . . . This principle alone can give the knowledge of God which is life eternal and the only power by which a man can stand unscathed in the trying hour. Those who possess this principle are one with Jesus Christ and one with the Father, as says Jesus, "That they all may be one; as thou, Father, art in me, and I in thee, that they may be one in us: . . . that they may be one, even as we are one." (John 17:21-22.) They are baptized with the same baptism, they are baptized with the same Spirit; they are in possession of the same knowledge; and they knew God, whom to know is life everlasting. When built upon this rock the storms may blow, the rains may descend and beat upon the house, but it cannot fall because it is founded upon a rock. These are some of my reflections in relation to this ordinance of the sacrament of the Lord's supper.—*JD*, 10:115-117, February 22, 1863.

THE WORK OF GOD.—The work of God and the glory of God is to bring to pass the immortality and eternal life of man, as it is written: "For behold, this is my work and my glory—to bring to pass the immortality and eternal life of man." (Pearl of Great Price, Moses 1:39.) The creation of man and the multiplication of man was one thing; the immortality and eternal life of man and his exaltation is another thing; and in the organization of the world, and in the calculations of the Almighty pertaining to this immortality and eternal life, it would seem that it was decreed that the Only Begotten Son was provided for the purpose of accomplishing this object; and hence Christ was the Lamb slain, according to the eternal purposes of God, before the foundation of the world.—*MA*, 88-89.

## THE DIFFUSION OF THE CHRISTIAN IDEA

The ideas of a general atonement and redemption, entertained by ancient heathen nations, were derived originally from the teachings of earlier servants of God.—*MA*, 190.

THE TESTIMONY OF MYTH AND TRADITION.—We gather that men who have written in relation to the various gods or virgins who have, each in her turn, conceived and borne a god or a messiah, would argue that the accounts of the birth, ministry, death, resurrection, etc., of the Savior, were simply a backing up and resuscitating of some of the old legends of heathen mythology which had been in existence in ages long antecedent to his advent, and that, therefore, the account of the life and works of the Redeemer was simply an act of priestcraft, to introduce another messiah and another establishment of religion in the interests of the projectors, and that Christianity was simply a copy of the old paganisms that had exhibited themselves in the forms above referred to. Whereas the reverse is clearly demonstrated. . . . The fact is clearly proved, instead of Christianity deriving its existence and facts from the ideas and practices of heathen mythologists, and from the various false systems that had been introduced by apostacy, unrecognized pretensions and fraud, that those very systems themselves were obtained from the true priesthood and founded on its teachings from the earliest ages to the advent of our Lord and Savior Jesus Christ; that those holy principles were taught to Adam, and by him to his posterity; that Enoch, Noah, Abraham, and the various prophets had all borne testimony of this grand and important event, wherein the interest and happiness of the whole world were concerned, pertaining to time and to eternity. The gospel is a system, great, grand, and comprehensive, commencing in eternity, extending through all time, and then reaching into the eternities to come. And the ideas with regard to these disjointed materials, that are gathered together from the turbid waters of heathen mythology, are so much claptrap and nonsense, calculated only to deceive the unwary, superstitious, and ignorant, and are as far below those great and eternal principles of heavenly truth which permeate through all time, penetrate into the heavens, and are interwoven with all the interests, happiness, and exaltation of man, as the earth is below the heavens above. The object of placing this statement before our brethren, is to prove and demonstrate . . . that these truths should grow together unto the confounding of false doctrines, and laying down of contentions.—*MA*, 204-205.

MODERN REVELATION AND KNOWLEDGE OF THE ATONEMENT.—Modern revelation has restored another most important key to unlock the mystery of the almost universal knowledge of the Redeemer and of the plan of the atonement. It is found in the statement that Jesus, after his resurrection, visited at least the inhabitants of two distinct portions of the earth who could not have been reached through the ministry of his Jewish apostles. These two peoples were the Nephites on this land, and the ten tribes in their distant northern home. The knowledge that the Mexicans and other aboriginal races of America had, at the time of their discovery by the Spaniards, of the life of the Savior was so exact that the Catholics suggested two theories (both incorrect, however) to solve the mystery. One was that the devil had invented an imitation gospel to delude the Indians; the other, that the Apostle Thomas had visited America and taught its people the plan of salvation.—*MA*, 200-201.

## THE POSITION OF CHRIST

HOLDS ALL POWER BY VIRTUE OF THE ATONEMENT.— From the facts in the case and the testimony presented in the scriptures it becomes evident that through the great atonement, the expiratory sacrifice of the Son of God, it is made possible that man can be redeemed, restored, resurrected, and exalted to the elevated position designed for him in the creation as a Son of God. . . .

The Savior thus becomes master of the situation—the debt is paid, the redemption made, the covenant fulfilled, justice satisfied, the will of God done, and all power is now given into the hands of the Son of God—the power of the resurrection, the power of the redemption, the power of salvation, the power to enact laws for the carrying out and accomplishment of this design. Hence life and immortality are brought to light, the gospel is introduced, and he becomes the author of eternal life and exaltation. He is the Redeemer, the Resurrector, the Savior of man and the world; and he has appointed the law of the gospel as the medium which must be complied with in this world or the next, as he complied with his Father's law; hence "He that believeth and is baptized shall be saved; but he that believeth not shall be damned." (Mark 16:16.)

The plan, the arrangement, the agreement, the covenant was made, entered into, and accepted before the foundation of the world; it was prefigured by sacrifices, and was carried out and consummated on the cross.

Hence being the mediator between God and man, he becomes by right the dictator and director on earth and in heaven for the living and for the dead, for the past, the present, and the future, pertaining to man as associated with this earth or the heavens, in time or eternity, the captain of our salvation, the apostle and high priest of our profession, the Lord and giver of life.—*MA*, 170, 171.

DISTINCTIONS BETWEEN THE POSITION OF CHRIST AND HIS FOLLOWERS.—It may here be asked, what difference is there between the Son of God, as the Son of God, the Redeemer, and those who believe in him and partake of the blessings of the gospel?

One thing, as we read, is that the Father gave him power to have life in himself: "For as the Father hath life in himself; so hath he given to the Son to have life in himself." (John 5:26.) And further, he had power, when all mankind had lost their life, to restore life to them again; and hence he is the resurrection and .the life, which power no other man possesses.

Another distinction is, that having this life in himself, he had power, as he said, to lay down his life and to take it up again, which power was also given him by the Father. This is also a power which no other being associated with this earth possesses.

Again, he is the brightness of his Father's glory and the express image of his person. Also, he doeth what he seeth the Father do, while we only do that which we are permitted and empowered to do by him.

He is the elect, the chosen, and one of the presidency in the heavens, and in him dwells all the fulness of the Godhead bodily, which could not be said of us in any of these particulars.

Another thing is, that all power is given to him in heaven and upon earth, which no earthly being could say.

It is also stated that Lucifer was before Adam; so was Jesus. And Adam, as well as all other believers, was commanded to do all that he did in the name of the Son, and to call upon God in his name for ever more; which honor was not applicable to any earthly being.

He, in the nearness of his relationship to the Father, seems to occupy a position that no other person occupies. He is spoken of as his well beloved Son, as the only begotten of the Father—does not this mean the only begotten after the flesh? If he was the firstborn and obedient to the laws of his Father, did he not inherit the position by right to be the representative of God, the Savior and Redeemer of the world? And was it not his peculiar right and privilege as the firstborn, the legitimate heir of God, the Eternal Father, to step forth, accomplish, and carry out the designs of his Heavenly Father pertaining to the redemption, salvation, and exaltation of man? And being himself without sin (which no other mortal was), he took the position of Savior and Redeemer, which by right belonged to him as the firstborn. And does it not seem that in having a body specially prepared, and being the offspring of God, both in body and spirit, he stood preeminently in the position of the Son of God, or in the place of God, and was God, and was thus the fit and only personage capable of making an infinite atonement?—*MA,* 135-137.

## THE ACT OF THE ATONEMENT

Of Central Importance.—In reality, this act of the atonement was the fulfilment of the sacrifices, of the prophesying, of the Passover, and of all the leading, prominent acts of the patriarchs and prophets relating thereto; and having performed

this, the past and the future both centered in him. Did these
worthies offer sacrifices? They prefigured his appearing and
atonement. Did they prophecy? It was of him, for the testimony
of Jesus is the spirit of prophecy. Did they keep the Passover?
He himself was the great expiatory offering. Were the people
called upon afterwards to commemorate this event? They
did it in remembrance of him, as a great memorial among
all of his disciples in all nations, throughout all time; of the
sacrifice of his broken body and spilt blood; the antitype of the
sacrificial lamb slain at the time of the Passover; of him; as
being the Mediator, the Messiah, the Christ, the Alpha and Omega,
the Beginning and the End: the Son of the living God.—*MA*, 126.

THE SHEDDING OF BLOOD.—Again, there is another phase
of this subject that must not be forgotten. From the commencement of the offering of sacrifices the inferior creature had to
suffer for the superior. Although it had taken no part in the
act of disobedience, yet was its blood shed and its life sacrificed,
thus prefiguring the atonement of the Son of God, which should
eventually take place. The creature indeed was made subject to
vanity not willingly, but by reason of him who hath subjected
the same in hope. Millions of such offerings were made, and
*hecatombs* of these expiatory sacrifices were offered in view of
the great event that would be consummated when Jesus should
offer up himself. With man this was simply the obedience to a
command and a given law, and with him might be considered
simply a pecuniary sacrifice. With the animals it was a sacrifice
of life.

But what is the reason for all this suffering and bloodshed,
and sacrifice? We are told that without shedding of blood is no
remission of sins. This is beyond our comprehension. Jesus had
to take away sin by the sacrifice of himself, the just for the unjust,
but, previous to this grand sacrifice, these animals had to have
their blood shed as types, until the great antitype should offer
up himself once for all. And as he in his own person bore the
sins of all, and atoned for them by the sacrifice of himself, so
there came upon him the weight and agony of ages and generations, the indescribable agony consequent upon this great sacrificial atonement wherein he bore the sins of the world, and suffered
in his own person the consequences of an eternal law of God
broken by man. Hence his profound grief, his indescribable
anguish, his overpowering torture, all experienced in the submission to the eternal fiat of Jehovah and the requirements of an
inexorable law.—*MA*, 149-150.

THE SUFFERING OF CHRIST.—The suffering of the Son of
God was not simply the suffering of personal death; for in assuming the position that he did in making an atonement for the sins

THE MEDIATION AND ATONEMENT OF CHRIST

of the world he bore the weight, the responsibility, and the burden of the sins of all men, which, to us, is incomprehensible. —*MA*, 150.

And again, not only did his agony affect the mind and body of Jesus, causing him to sweat great drops of blood, but by reason of some principle, to us unfathomable, his suffering affected universal nature.

> World upon world, eternal things,
> Hang on thy anguish, King of kings.

When he gave up the ghost, the solid rocks were riven; the foundations of the earth trembled; earthquakes shook the continents and rent the isles of the sea; a deep darkness overspread the sky; the mighty waters overflowed their accustomed bounds; huge mountains sank and valleys rose; the handiwork of feeble men was overthrown; their cities were engulfed or consumed by the vivid shafts of lightning; and all material things were convulsed with the throes of seeming dissolution. . . .

Thus, such was the torturing pressure of this intense, this indescribable agony, that it burst forth abroad beyond the confines of his body, convulsed all nature, and spread throughout all space.—*MA*, 151-152.

> Then opened he their understanding, that they might understand the scriptures,
> And said unto them, Thus it is written, and thus it behooved Christ to suffer, and to rise from the dead the third day:
> And that repentance and remission of sins should be preached in his name among all nations, beginning at Jerusalem.
> And ye are witnesses of these things. (Luke 24:45-48.)

WHY THIS SUFFERING?—One great and very striking statement is here made by the Lord himself, to the effect that it behooved Christ to suffer, and the question at once presents itself before us, why did it behoove him? Or why was it necessary that he should suffer? For it would seem from his language, through his sufferings, death, atonement, and resurrection, "that repentance and remission of sins" could be preached among all nations, and that consequently if he had not atoned for the sins of the world, repentance and remission of sins could not have been preached to the nations. A very important principle is here enunciated, one in which the interests of the whole human family throughout all the world are involved. That principle is the offering up of the Son of God as a sacrifice, an atonement, and a propitiation for our sins.—*MA*, 8-9.

> Giving thanks unto the Father, which hath made us meet to be partakers of the inheritance of the saints in light:
> Who hath delivered us from the power of darkness, and hath translated us into the kingdom of his dear Son:

In whom we have redemption through his blood, even the forgiveness of sins:
Who is the image of the invisible God, the firstborn of every creature: . . .
And he is the head of the body, the church: who is the beginning, the firstborn
from the dead; that in all things he might have the preeminence.
For it pleased the Father that in him should all fulness dwell;
And, having made peace through the blood of his cross, by him to reconcile
all things unto himself; by him, I say, whether they be things in earth, or things
in heaven. (Colossians 1:12-15, 18-20.)

From the above passage (Colossians 1:12-15, 18-20) we learn that our redemption is obtained through the blood of Jesus; that he is in the image of God; again, that he is "the firstborn of every creature;" also that he is "the firstborn from the dead"; and furthermore, that he stands preeminent as the representative of God in the interests of humanity pertaining to this world, or the world which is to come, and that he is the head of the church, the grand medium through which all blessings flow to the human family.—*MA*, 31.

THE POWER AND EFFECTS OF THE ATONEMENT.—If it were not for the atonement of Jesus Christ, the sacrifice he made, all the human family would have to lie in the grave throughout eternity without any hope. But God having provided, through the atonement of the Lord Jesus Christ, the medium whereby we can be restored to the bosom and presence of the Father, to participate with him among the Gods in the eternal worlds—he having provided for that, has also provided for the resurrection. He proclaimed himself the resurrection and the life. Said he, "I am the resurrection, and the life: he that believeth in me, though he were dead, yet shall he live." (John 11:25.) By and by the tombs will be opened and the dead will hear the voice of the Son of God, and they shall come forth, they who have done good to the resurrection of the just, and they who have done evil to the resurrection of the unjust.—*JD*, 22:356, January 29, 1882.

THE RESURRECTION.—The great prerequisites having been fulfilled, it now becomes our duty to enquire what next had to be done to consummate the great object obtainable through the fulfilment of this law, or what was accomplished by the atonement.

First, the resurrection. The penalty of the broken law in Adam's day was death; and death is passed upon all. The word of the Lord was, ". . . in the day that thou eatest thereof thou shalt surely die." (Genesis 2:17.) The atonement made by Jesus Christ brought about the resurrection from the dead, and restored life. And hence Jesus said: "I am the resurrection, and the life; he that believeth in me, though he were dead, yet shall he live;" (John 11:25.) and Jesus himself became the first fruits of those who slept.

The next question that arises is, how far does this principle extend and to whom is it applicable? It extends to all the human family; to all men of every nation.—*MA*, 177-178.

PROGRESS TOWARD GODHOOD MADE POSSIBLE.—The next question for us to examine is, how, and in what manner are men benefited by the atonement and by the resurrection? In this, that the atonement, having restored man to his former position before the Lord, has placed him in a position and made it possible for him to obtain that exaltation and glory which it would have been impossible for him to have received without it; even to become a son of God by adoption; and being a son, then an heir of God, and a joint heir with Jesus Christ; and that, as Christ overcame, he has made it possible, and has placed it within the power of believers in him also to overcome; and as he is authorized to inherit his Father's glory which he had with him before the world was, with his resurrected body, so through the adoption may we overcome and sit down with him upon his throne, as he has overcome and has sat down upon his Father's throne.—*MA*, 179.

FOR THE BENEFIT OF ALL THE WORLD.—That the world might be benefited through the redemption brought about by Jesus Christ, he called and ordained twelve apostles, and commanded them to go forth into all the world, and preach the gospel to every creature.—*MA*, 180.

Thus it would seem that the redeemed of the Lord from all nations and peoples are indebted to the Lord Jesus Christ, through his atonement, for the position that they will occupy in the state of exaltation here referred to. And if they are exalted to be kings and priests unto God, it is through the ordinances which he has appointed for the accomplishment of this object, as the wise will understand.—*MA*, 35.

THE ATONEMENT AND LITTLE CHILDREN.—Without Adam's transgression those children could not have existed. Through the atonement they are placed in a state of salvation without any act of their own. These would embrace, according to the opinion of statisticians, more than one-half of the human family who can attribute their salvation only to the mediation and atonement of the Savior. Thus, as stated elsewhere, in some mysterious, incomprehensible way, Jesus assumed the responsibility which naturally would have devolved upon Adam; but which could only be accomplished through the mediation of himself, and by taking upon himself their sorrows, assuming their responsibilities, and bearing their transgressions or sins.—*MA*, 148.

## THE ATONEMENT AND THE CHRISTIAN'S LIFE

ALL THINGS TO BE DONE IN THE NAME OF THE SON.—
To Adam it was said, "Wherefore, thou shalt do all that thou
doest, in the name of the Son, and thou shalt repent and call upon
God in the name of the Son forevermore." (Pearl of Great Price,
Moses 5:8.) The same principle continued both on the Asiatic
and on this continent, and was recognized by all men of God
holding the Melchizedek priesthood, and will be recognized
throughout all time until the final consummation of all things,
when every knee shall bow, and every tongue confess that Jesus
is the Christ, to the glory of God, the Father.—*MA*, 33.

These scriptures evidently show that the testimony of Jesus
was the very principle, essence, and power of the spirit of prophecy
whereby the ancient prophets were inspired.—*MA*, 12.

MEDIATION AND THE SCHOOL OF HUMAN EXPERIENCE.—
It is necessary, then, that we pass through the school of suffering, trial, affliction, and privation, to know ourselves, to know
others, and to know our God. Therefore it was necessary, when
the Savior was upon the earth, that he should be tempted in all
points, like unto us, and "be touched with the feeling of our
infirmities," to comprehend the weaknesses and strength, the per-
fections and imperfections of poor fallen human nature. And
having accomplished the thing he came into the world to do;
having had to grapple with the hypocrisy, corruption, weakness,
and imbecility of man; having met with temptation and trial
in all its various forms, and overcome; he has become a "faithful
high priest" to intercede for us in the everlasting kingdom of
his Father. He knows how to estimate and put a proper value
upon human nature, for he, having been placed in the same position as we are, knows how to bear with our weaknesses and infirmities, and can fully comprehend the depth, power, and strength
of the afflictions and trials that men have to cope with in this
world. And thus understandingly and by experience, he can
bear with them as a father and an elder brother.—*JD*, 1:148,
June 12, 1853.

CHAPTER XII

# THE GOSPEL RESTORED

## THE RESTORATION OF THE GOSPEL AND KEYS OF THE PRIESTHOOD

JOSEPH SMITH.—We all look upon Joseph Smith as being a prophet of God. God called him to occupy the position that he did. How long ago? Thousands of years ago before this world was formed. The prophets prophesied about his coming, that a man should arise whose name should be Joseph, and that his father's name should be Joseph, and also that he should be a descendant of that Joseph who was sold into Egypt. This prophecy you will find recorded in the Book of Mormon. He had very great and precious promises made to him by the Lord. I have heard him say on certain occasions, "You do not know who I am." The world did not like him. The world did not like either the Savior or the prophets; they have never liked revealed truth; and it is as much as a bargain for the Saints even to bear the truth.

REFERRED TO THE SON.—In the commencement of the work, the Father and the Son appeared to Joseph Smith. And when they appeared to him, the Father, pointing to the Son, said, "This is My Beloved Son. Hear Him!" (Pearl of Great Price, Joseph Smith 2:17.) As much as to say, "I have not come to teach and instruct you; but I refer you to my Only Begotten, who is the Mediator of the New Covenant, the Lamb slain from before the foundation of the world; I refer you to him as your Redeemer, your High Priest and Teacher. Hear him."

PRINCIPLES AND PRIESTHOOD.—What next? Then came men who had held the priesthood before. Who were they? Moroni, an ancient prophet who had lived upon this continent and who had charge of the records from which the Book of Mormon was translated—a fitting person to introduce the same principles again. Afterwards it was necessary that the priesthood should be conferred; and John the Baptist came and laid his hands upon Joseph Smith and Oliver Cowdery, saying, "Upon you, my fellow servants, I lay my hands, and confer upon you the Aaronic Priesthood, which shall never be taken from the earth again until the sons of Levi offer an acceptable offering before me."[1] That

---

[1] Paraphrased from D. & C. 13.

was the lesser priesthood — the Aaronic — appertaining to the bishopric. And why was John the Baptist chosen to confer this priesthood? Because he was the last that held this holy priesthood upon the earth. And why did he come? Because the priesthood administers in time and eternity; both the Aaronic and Melchizedek. And he, holding the keys of that priesthood, came and conferred it upon Joseph Smith. When he had conferred this priesthood upon Joseph Smith, other things had to be conferred; that is, what is called the Melchizedek priesthood. But you understand but very little about that; as the Indian would say, about so much (meaning the point of the finger.) If you did, you would think and act differently from what you do. Who held the keys of that priesthood? Peter, James, and John, who were three presiding apostles. Did they confer this priesthood upon Joseph Smith? Yes. . . .

KEYS OF THE GATHERING.—What next? They built a temple by and by, as we are doing now, in Kirtland, Ohio. And in that temple the Lord Jesus Christ appeared to them again, the account of which you may read for yourselves in the Doctrine and Covenants. Jesus appeared there, and Moses appeared there, and Moses conferred upon Joseph the keys of the gathering of Israel from the four quarters of the earth, and also the ten tribes. And you are here because that priesthood was conferred upon the elders who came to you with the gospel; and when they laid their hands upon your heads, among other things you received the Holy Ghost and the spirit of the gathering. But you did not know what it was that was working in you, like yeast sometimes under certain conditions, producing an influence causing you to come to Zion. Yet you could not help it. If you had wanted to help it, you could not while you were living your religion and were governed thereby. For that spirit brought that influence and power along with it, and it carries it with it wherever it goes. And as men received the Holy Ghost so they received the spirit of the gathering, which was conferred by Moses upon Joseph Smith, and by him upon others, and which created that anxiety you all felt to gather to Zion.—JD, 26:106-7, October 20, 1881.

The people that are independent, who think they can get along without religion or without God, will find that in time or eternity they will have to come to the priesthood of God.—JD, 26:109, October 20, 1881.

# THE PURPOSE OF THE RESTORATION

TO GATHER AN UPRIGHT PEOPLE.—God has introduced the system of things that we have been speaking of for the purpose of gathering together a people who would listen to his voice, and they are the only people on the earth today who will listen thereto, and then it is as much as the bargain for many of us to do it. God expects to have a people who will be men of clean hands and pure hearts, who withhold their hands from the receiving of bribes, who will swear to their own hurt and change not, who will be men of truth and integrity, of honor and virtue, and who will pursue a course that will be approved by the Gods in the eternal worlds, and by all honorable and upright men that ever did live or that now live, and having taken upon us the profession of sainthood, he expects us to be Saints, not in name, not in theory, but in reality.—*JD*, 23:26, December 11, 1881.

To Bring "Life and Immortality to Light."—God has restored the gospel for the purpose of bringing life and immortality to light; and without the knowledge of the gospel there is no knowledge of life and immortality; for men cannot comprehend these principles only as they are made known unto them, and they cannot be revealed only through the medium of the gospel, and through obedience to the laws of salvation associated therewith. . . . Hence when the heavens were opened and the Father and Son appeared and revealed unto Joseph the principles of the gospel, and when the holy priesthood was restored and the Church and kingdom of God established upon the earth, there were the greatest blessings bestowed upon this generation which it was possible for man to receive. If they could comprehend it, it was the greatest blessing which God could confer upon humanity. Then he sent his servants forth to proclaim this gospel to the nations of the earth, and he is now sending them forth to preach the gospel of the Son of God, to deliver the testimony that he has given unto us. And, speaking for the priesthood, have we done it? We have, and we have done it in the name of Israel's God; and he has been with us and I know it.—*JD*, 22:218, June 27, 1881.

To Make Men Free.—God has committed to us the gospel and the high priesthood, which is not intended, as some suppose, to bring men into bondage or to tyrannize over the consciences of men, but to make all men free as God is free; that they may drink of the streams "whereof shall make glad the city of God"; that they may be elevated and not debased; that they may be purified and not corrupted; that they may learn the laws of life and walk in them, and not walk in the ways of corruption and go down to death.—*JD*, 22:292, October 9, 1881.

To Introduce the Rule and Government of God on Earth.—Now, it is the rule of God which is desired to be introduced upon the earth, and this is the reason why the Father and

the Son appeared to Joseph Smith, why John the Baptist conferred the Aaronic priesthood, why Peter, James, and John conferred the Melchizedek priesthood, why Moses came to bestow
the dispensation of the gathering, and why other manifestations
have been given unto us as a people, his elect, whom he has chosen
from among the nations. This is an honorable position for us
to occupy. We are called to fill various duties that God requires
at our hands. And our position is not a nominal thing; it is a
reality. . . .

We are here to do the will of God, to build up the kingdom
of God, and to establish the Zion of God.—*JD*, 23:323, 324,
November 23, 1882.

## JOSEPH SMITH AS A RESTORER[1]

JOSEPH'S OWN STORY.—Joseph Smith came forward
telling us that an angel had administered to him and had revealed
unto him the principles of the gospel as they existed in former
days, and that God was going to set his hand to work in these
last days to accomplish his purposes and build up his kingdom,
to introduce correct principles, to overturn error, evil, and corruption, and to establish his Church and kingdom upon the earth.
I have heard him talk about these things myself. I have heard
him tell over and over again, to myself and others, the circumstances pertaining to these visions and the various ministrations
of angels, and the development of the purposes of God towards
the human family. And what does he do? Bring us something
different? Yes, in many respects, but not different in regard to
our connection with God. Different as regards the age in which
we live and the circumstances with which he was surrounded, but
not different as it regards bringing men to a knowledge of God.
He taught precisely the same principles and doctrine and ordinances
that were taught by Jesus and his disciples in their day.—*JD*,
14:365, March 17, 1872.

JOSEPH'S TESTIMONY TO JOHN TAYLOR.—Now, we will
come to other events, of later date; events with which we are
associated—I refer now to the time that Joseph Smith came among
men. What was his position and how was he situated? I can
tell you what he told me about it. He said that he was very
ignorant of the ways, designs, and purposes of God, and knew
nothing about them; he was a youth unacquainted with religious
matters or the systems and theories of the day. He went to the
Lord, having read James' statement, "If any of you lack wisdom,
let him ask of God, that giveth to all men liberally, and up-

---

[1] See also Chapter 35, "About Joseph Smith."

braideth not; and it shall be given him." (James 1:5.) He believed that statement and went to the Lord and asked him, and the Lord revealed himself to him together with his Son Jesus, and pointing to the latter, said: "This is My beloved Son, Hear Him!" He then asked in regard to the various religions with which he was surrounded. He inquired which of them was right, for he wanted to know the right way and to walk in it. He was told that none of them was right, that they had all departed from the right way, that they had forsaken God the fountain of living waters, and hewed them out cisterns, broken cisterns, that could hold no water.

Afterwards the Angel Moroni came to him and revealed to him the Book of Mormon, with the history of which you are generally familiar, and also with the statements that I am now making pertaining to these things.—*JD,* 21:161, December 7, 1879.

NEED FOR THE RESTORATION.—Now, what condition was the world in before the gospel we now preach was introduced? Many of you older men here . . . lived when the gospel was not upon the earth. I did, and many others did. Where could we find anything resembling that which was taught by Jesus? Nowhere on the face of the wide earth. Apostles, prophets, pastors, teachers, etc., were nowhere to be found. Do I know this? I do know it, for I lived in the world at that time! I knew what was going on. I was mixed up with their teachers and was well acquainted with the different societies and organizations. Did they have the gospel as laid down in the scriptures? No. I remember reading with very great interest the remarks of one of the Wesleys—I do not remember now whether it was Charles or John—in some poetry of his:

> From chosen Abraham's seed the new apostles choose
> O'er isles and continents to spread the soul reviving news.

He knew very well that they did not have apostles, nor those officers that used to exist in the Church, and he felt it keenly, as did many others. I, myself, mixed up with a society of gentlemen before I heard the fulness of the gospel, who were searching the scriptures to find out the true way, for we did not find any men who professed to be inspired. We were told that all inspiration had ceased, and yet there were men professing to be called of God to preach the gospel. Now, that is a very singular thing. How can a man be called of God, if God has ceased to speak? If a man is called of God, he must be called either by the voice or Spirit of God, or by somebody who is authorized of God, and knows something about his ways. If he does not receive his calling in this way, how is he going to get it? There is one other

way—that is, if God has had a regular priesthood upon the
earth, unbroken, uncorrupted, and uncontaminated, then it might
come down from one to another through the different ages. The
Church of Rome professes to trace its authority down from the
days of the apostles until the present. But unfortunately there
is a scripture that rather interferes with them and with others,
namely: "Whosoever transgresseth, and abideth not in the doctrine of Christ, hath not God. He that abideth in the doctrine
of Christ, he hath both the Father and the Son." (2 John 9.)
I will tell you what Joseph Smith told me personally. Said he:
"You are going out to preach the gospel, and if you can find
a people anywhere as you wander through the world . . . having
the doctrines of Christ, you need not baptize them." . . . But I never
found anywhere, wherever I went, any persons holding the
doctrines of Christ as taught by him, with apostles and prophets
and inspired men under the influence of the Holy Ghost, and
with an organization similar to that which was introduced by
our Lord and Savior Jesus Christ. Therefore I had to call upon
all men everywhere to repent, for I could not find the kind of
people Joseph said I need not baptize.—JD, 25:261-263, August
17, 1884.

# BOOK THREE

## PRIESTHOOD: THE GOVERNMENT OF GOD

*"To define all the laws of the
priesthood would be impossible,
for it is living power, not a
dead letter, and although these
instructions may be of general
use, the living priesthood must
regulate its own affairs."*
—JOHN TAYLOR,
*MS,* 9:326,
*November 1, 1847.*

# CHAPTER XIII

# THE NATURE OF PRIESTHOOD

## WHAT IS PRIESTHOOD?

PRIESTHOOD—THE GOVERNMENT OF GOD.—What is priesthood? Without circumlocution, I shall briefly answer that it is the government of God, whether on the earth or in the heavens, for it is by that power, agency, or principle that all things are governed on the earth and in the heavens, and by that power that all things are upheld and sustained. It governs all things—it directs all things—it sustains all things—and has to do with all things that God and truth are associated with. It is the power of God delegated to intelligences in the heavens and to men on the earth; and when we arrive in the celestial kingdom of God, we shall find the most perfect order and harmony existing, because there is the perfect pattern, the most perfect order of government carried out, and when or wherever those principles have been developed in the earth, in proportion as they have spread and been acted upon, just in that proportion have they produced blessings and salvation to the human family. And when the government of God shall be more extensively adopted, and when Jesus' prayer, that he taught his disciples is answered, and God's kingdom comes on the earth, and his will is done here as in heaven, then, and not till then, will universal love, peace, harmony, and union prevail.—*MS, 9:321, November 1, 1847.*

THE PRIESTHOOD TO DEVELOP THE ORDER OF THE KINGDOM OF GOD.—The priesthood is placed in the church for this purpose, to dig, to plant, to nourish, to teach correct principles, and to develop the order of the kingdom of God, to fight the devils, and maintain and support the authorities of the church of Christ upon the earth. It is our duty all to act together to form one great unit—one great united phalanx, having sworn allegiance to the kingdom of God; then everything will move on quietly, peaceably, and easily, and then there will be very little trouble.—*JD, 9:14, April 6, 1861.*

THE PRIESTHOOD IN THE HEAVENS.—There is a priesthood in the heavens, and we have the same priesthood on the earth, but there should be a closer communion between the priesthood on the earth and the priesthood in the heavens; it is desirable that we should be brought into closer proximity; we want to be advancing as Enoch advanced.—*JD*, 25:307, October 6 and 7, 1884.

POWER IN THE PRIESTHOOD.—It is the intercourse and communication of the priesthood in heaven, that gives power, life, and efficacy to the living priesthood on the earth, and without which they would be as dead and withered branches: and if any man has life, or power, it is the power and life of the priesthood, the gift and power of God communicated through the regular channels of the priesthood, both in heaven and on earth; and to seek it without, would be like a stream seeking to be supplied with water when its fountain was dried up, or like a branch seeking to obtain virtue when the trunk of the tree was cut off by the root: and to talk of a church without this is to talk of a thing of naught—a dried fountain, a dead and withered tree.—*MS*, 9:323, November 1, 1847.

The power manifested by the priesthood is simply the power of God, for he is the head of the priesthood, with Jesus as our President and great High Priest; and it is upon this principle that all the works of God have been accomplished, whether on the earth or in the heavens; and any manifestation of power through the priesthood on the earth is simply a delegated power from the priesthood in the heavens, and the more the priesthood on the earth becomes assimilated with and subject to the priesthood in the heavens the more of this power shall we possess.—*MA*, 87-88.

## WHY THE PRIESTHOOD?

AN ORGANIZED POWER TO BUILD ZION.—Now, God has ordained his holy priesthood upon the earth with presidents, apostles, bishops, high councils, seventies, high priests, and the order and organization of the church and kingdom of God in its fulness and completeness, more complete, perhaps, than it ever was since the world was framed. Why? Because it is the dispensation of the fulness of times, embracing all other times that have ever existed since the world was, and he has gathered us together for that purpose.—*JD*, 21:117-118, November 28, 1879.

I would further ask: What is this priesthood given us for? That we may be enabled to build up the Zion of our God. What for? To put down wrong and corruption, lasciviousness, lying, thieving, dishonesty, and covetousness, with every kind of evil, and also to encourage faith, meekness, charity, purity, brotherly kindness, truthfulness, integrity, honesty, and everything that is calculated to exalt and ennoble mankind, that we may be the true and proper representatives of God our Father here upon the earth, that we may learn to know his will and do it; that his will may be done on earth as in heaven. And hence, Zion is spoken of as being the pure in heart. . . .

TO ESTABLISH THE KINGDOM OF GOD THROUGH CHURCH ORGANIZATION.—Now, then, God has gathered us together for a purpose, and that purpose is to build up Zion and to establish his kingdom on the earth, and he could not do it in any other way that I know of than the way in which he is doing it. He may, however, have some other way, but if he has I am not acquainted with it. It is sufficient for us to know that he has chosen this way. Very well. We are taking hold and are doing a great many good things.

THE PROBLEM: TO GOVERN OURSELVES AND TRUST OTHERS TO GOD.—We are here, then, to build up Zion. . . . Now, while we have no disrespect for the world, no disrespect for the nations in which we live, or for the authorities thereof, if they act wisely, well. If they do not act wisely, it is not so well. No matter about that; we can trust them in the hands of God.

LIBERTY AND RIGHTS OF ALL TO BE MAINTAINED.—We are the friends of all men, and are the friends of this nation. We are the friends and supporters of the Constitution of this nation. We are the friends of right, of freedom, and of good administration and good men everywhere, and that on the principle . . . of freedom, liberty, believe, and let believe, worship, and let others worship, worship as you please according to the dictates of conscience, and let others do the same. It is for us to be governed by correct principles, and as far as it lies in our power, to extend to all men this right, and then maintain, on correct principles, our own rights, the rights of others and the rights of God. These are my feelings in relation to this matter.

PRIESTHOOD TO TEACH THE GOSPEL SO THAT LIBERTY CAN PREVAIL.—But the world do not comprehend our principles; they cannot. But we can afford to teach them the gospel even if we are abused for doing it. We can deal justly with them, and then suffer their abuse. No matter. We can do all this and a good deal more, and also advocate the rights of men, look after our own interests and welfare, and the interest of the community we are associated with, and sustain all just laws and correct principles.—*JD*, 22:9-11, January 9, 1881.

THE ATTITUDE REQUIRED.—If we understand ourselves and our position, it ought to be with us, the kingdom of God first and ourselves afterwards. If we can learn to accomplish a little thing, the Lord will probably tell us to do a greater, because we are prepared to do it. . . . If we are the people of God, and he is trusting to us to accomplish these great purposes, we have got to do a little more than we have done, and we have got to be willing and obedient to the dictation of the Spirit of the Lord and his servants whom he had placed over us. If we do this, every labor we engage in will be joyous and pleasant to us, peace will reign in our bosoms and the peace of God will abide in our habitations; the Spirit of the Lord will brood over us, and we shall be full of joy and rejoicing all the day long, and so it will be to the end of the chapter. I know of no other way to accomplish all this work, only to be taught of the Lord, and for that purpose he has organized his holy priesthood.—*JD*, 10:150-151, April 6, 1863.

PRIESTHOOD TO BRING ABOUT THE RESTITUTION OF ALL THINGS.—To bring about this desirable end—to restore creation to its pristine excellency and to fulfil the object of creation—to redeem, save, exalt, and glorify man—to save and redeem the dead and the living, and all that shall live according to its laws, is the design and object of the establishment of the priesthood on the earth in the last days. It is for the purpose of fulfilling what has not heretofore been done—that God's works may be perfected—that the times of the restitution of all things may be brought about, and that, in conjunction with the eternal priesthood in the heavens (who without us, nor we without them, could not be made perfect), we may bring to pass all things which have been in the mind of God, or spoken of by the Spirit of God, through the mouth of all the holy prophets since the world was. . . .

The priesthood in the heavens are uniting with us to bring. about these purposes, and as they are governed by the same principle, that our works may agree—that there may be a reciprocity of action, and that God's will (so far as we are concerned) may be done on the earth as it is in heaven. It is this which we have to learn, and this which we must do to fulfil our calling, and render our works acceptable in the sight of God and of the holy angels, and also in the sight of our brethren, who are associated with us in the priesthood in the kingdom of God on the earth.—*MS*, 9:321-322, November 1, 1847.

## CALLINGS IN THE PRIESTHOOD

THE PRINCIPLE.—There are different callings, and offices, and stations, and authorities in the holy priesthood, but it is all the same priesthood; and there are different keys, and powers, and responsibilities, but it is the same government; and all the priesthood are agents in that government, and all are requisite for the organization of the body, the upbuilding of Zion, and the government of his kingdom; and they are dependent one upon another, and the eye cannot say to the ear I have no need of thee, nor the head to the foot I have no need of thee. It is for every one to abide in the calling whereunto he is called, and magnify his office and priesthood, and then will he have honor of his brethren and be honored of God and of the holy angels.

HONOR PROCEEDS FROM WORKS, NOT FROM OFFICE.—I have noticed some in my travels, those, who, like the disciples of Jesus of old, evince a great desire for power, and manifest a very anxious disposition to know who among them shall be greatest. This is folly, for honor proceeds not from office, but by a person magnifying his office and calling. If we have any honor proceeding from or through the priesthood, it comes from God, and we certainly should be vain to boast of a gift when we have no hand in the gift, only in receiving it. If it comes from God, he ought to have the glory and not us, and our magnifying our calling is the only way or medium through which we can obtain honor or influence.—*MS*, 9:322, November 1, 1847.

## LABOR IN THE PRIESTHOOD

"THE WORK IS HARDLY BEGUN."—Some men who have been ordained to the priesthood have remarked that they have nothing to do. I have heard some foolish remarks of that kind. They will find plenty to do before they get through. They need not be troubled on that score. There will be plenty for them to do if they are only prepared to do it. There is a great work to perform in preaching the gospel to the nations of the earth. Then as we build our temples we shall want a great many people to administer in them, and I have seen some people quite pleased at the idea. Some elders, seventies, and high priests have said—"What can I do? I am getting old and gray-headed. Still I would like to do something." We shall require quite a number to administer in the temples as we get them built. . . .

You need not be concerned about having nothing to do. We will find plenty for the seventies to do. You need not think there are any too many of them. The nations of the earth have yet to be preached to. The work is not all through. It is hardly begun. We are just getting ready for the labor, and so you may prepare yourselves, you seventies, you high priests, and you elders, for missions to the nations of the earth.—*JD*, 25:185-186, May 18, 1884.

"LET THE RULE AND GOVERNMENT OF GOD BE ESTABLISHED."—We have a labor before us. You, seventies; you, high priests, you are not here to find out what you shall eat or drink, or wherewithal you shall be clothed. You are not here to quarrel over little things and to have your own way. Jesus said, "Father, Thy will be done." He said, he came not to do his own will, but the will of his Father who sent him. And when his disciples came to him and said, Lord, "Teach us how to pray, as John taught his disciples," he said, pray, "Our Father which art in heaven, Hallowed be thy name: Thy kingdom come. . . ." (Matthew 6:9-10.) Let the rule and government of God be established.

"Thy kingdom come. Thy will be done in earth, as it is in heaven." (Matthew 6:10.) This was his feeling, and this is the feeling of all good saints and faithful elders in Israel.

And what did Joseph Smith come to do? The will of his Father, to learn that will and do it. What was the duty of Brigham Young? The same. What is mine? The same. What is the duty of the twelve? To follow the counsel of the presidency. What is the duty of the presidents of stakes? To follow the counsel of the presidency. What is the duty of the bishops? To follow the counsel of the presidents of stakes and of their presiding bishop. I have had men frequently come to me and want to pass by the presidents of stakes. I pass them back again! I tell them to go to their presidents. Again I have men come to me who wish to pass by their bishops; I send them back to their bishops, as I wish to honor all men in their place. I have enough to do without interfering with the little details of others: and so on from them to the elders, priests, teachers and deacons, every man in his place.—*JD*, 22:310, August 28, 1881.

"REGULATE, TEACH, INSTRUCT, AND ENTER INTO ALL THE RAMIFICATIONS OF LIFE."—We need teaching continually, line upon line, precept upon precept, here a little and there a little. Hence we have our various organizations of the priesthood, calculated to oversee, to manipulate, to regulate, to teach, to instruct, and to enter into all the ramifications of life whether they pertain to this world or the world to come.—*JD*, 21:62, January 4, 1880.

## PRIESTHOOD AND THE WELFARE OF SOCIETY

PRIESTHOOD TO PURGE CORRUPTION.—We call upon you to honor your calling and priesthood and purge from your midst corruption of every kind. And we call upon the presidents of stakes and their counselors, upon the bishops and their counselors, and upon the priests, teachers and deacons, to magnify their offices, and not to be partakers of other men's sins. For as sure as I live and as God lives, if you do, God will require it at your hands. And therefore, I call upon presidents and men in authority, where men do not magnify their calling, to remove them from their positions of responsibility and replace them by men who will; and let us have correct principles and the order of God carried out in Zion.

TO DISCERN AND SUSTAIN TRUTH.—Apostles, prophets, pastors, teachers, and evangelists were placed in the church of old for what? "For the perfecting of the saints, for the work of the ministry, for the edifying of the body of Christ:

"Till we all come in the unity of the faith, and of the knowledge of the Son of God, unto a perfect man, unto the measure of the stature of the fulness of Christ." (Ephesians 4:12, 13.) It is so today. My brethren who have spoken have told you plainly of many evils that exist in our midst; but we can scarcely perceive them, many of us. Sometimes it is very difficult to discern between a saint and a sinner, between one who professes to fear God and one who does not. It is for us to straighten out these matters. And you men in authority will be held responsible, and the twelve will be held responsible, and I hold you responsible, and God will hold you responsible for your acts.—*JD*, 22:1-2, October 7, 1879.

ORDER IN PRIESTHOOD PURPOSES.—You and I may violate our covenants. You and I may trample upon the principles of the gospel, and violate the order of the priesthood and the commands of God. But among the hosts of Israel there will be thousands and tens of thousands who will be true to the principles of truth and God in the heavens; the holy angels and the ancient priesthood that now live where God lives are all united together, for the accomplishment of this purpose. The Lord will roll forth his purposes in his own way and in his own time. And having thus organized, as I before stated, it is not for us to act as we may think individually, but as God shall dictate. We have a regular order in the Church. You brethren, who hold the holy priesthood, understand these things.—*JD*, 25:307-308, October 6 and 7, 1884.

## SPIRITUAL MANIFESTATIONS: RESTORATION OF THE PRIESTHOOD

SPIRITUAL MANIFESTATIONS REQUISITE TO CIRCUMSTANCES.—I have heard some remarks in the temple pertaining to these matters, and also here, and it has been thought, as has been expressed by some, that we ought to look for some peculiar manifestations. The question is, What do we want to see? Some peculiar power, some remarkable manifestations? All these things are very proper in their place; all these things we have a right to look for; but we must only look for such manifestations as are requisite for our circumstances, and as God shall see fit to impart them.

PURPOSE OF THE FIRST VISION.—Certain manifestations have already occurred. When our Heavenly Father appeared unto Joseph Smith, the Prophet, he pointed to the Savior who was with him, (and who, it is said, is the brightness of the Father's glory and the express image of his person) and said: "This is my beloved Son, hear Him." There was an evidence manifested through his servant to the world, that God lived, that the Redeemer, who was crucified and put to death to atone for the sins of the world, also lived, that there was a message which had to be communicated to the human family, and that the Son was the personage through which it should be communicated. The key thus being turned, authority given by the highest source in the heavens in relation to the purposes of God on the earth, the holy priesthood began to be developed. Why? Because there was no priesthood on the earth; there was nobody who was authorized to operate and officiate in the name of the Lord.

RESTORATION OF THE AARONIC PRIESTHOOD.—Therefore John the Baptist came as the representative of the Aaronic Priesthood, having held the keys thereof in his day, and he placed his hands upon the heads of Joseph Smith and Oliver Cowdery, and . . . imparted the Aaronic Priesthood . . . It being already conferred, it is not now necessary that John the Baptist should return for the accomplishment of that purpose. He had delivered his testimony; he had turned the key; he had introduced the power and authority to administer in that priesthood; so that those upon whom it was conferred were able to perform the several duties associated therewith.

RESTORATION OF THE MELCHIZEDEK PRIESTHOOD.—Then Peter, James and John appeared and conferred upon Joseph Smith and Oliver Cowdery the Melchizedek priesthood. . . . It is not necessary that Peter, James and John should come again to do the thing that is already done.

PRIESTHOOD—THE KEY TO ALL BLESSINGS.—The priesthood has been restored, with which are connected all the blessings that ever were associated with any people upon the face of the earth; and if we know today so little in regard to the things of God, and the principles associated with eternity, with the heavens and with the angels, it is because we have not improved our privileges as we might, nor lived up to those principles which God has revealed unto us, and because we are not yet prepared for further advancement.—*JD*, 25:177-178, May 18, 1884.

## RESPONSIBILITY OF THE PRIESTHOOD

SAINTS MAY FAIL BUT THE KINGDOM WILL NOT.—It has been asked by Brother Brigham whether this kingdom will fail. I tell you in the name of Israel's God it will not fail. I tell you in the name of Israel's God it will roll forth, and that the things spoken of by the holy prophets in relation to it will receive their fulfilment. But in connection with this I will tell you another thing: A great many of the Latter-day Saints will fail, a great many of them are not now and never have been living up to their privileges, and magnifying their callings and their priesthood, and God will have a reckoning with such people, unless they speedily repent.

There is a carelessness, a deadness, an apathy, a listlessness that exists to a great, extent among the Latter-day Saints, and there never was a stronger proof of this than that which was exhibited here yesterday. I asked myself, as I looked over the empty benches, where are all the bishops? Have they not time to attend the quarterly conference? Oh, shame on such men! are they worthy to hold a place in the bishopric, and associate with the holy priesthood of God? They are desecrating the holy principles by which they ought to be governed. Where are their counselors, I asked myself, and where are the priests and teachers and deacons? Is there no interest manifested in the church and kingdom of God, or in the Zion he is about to establish? Not much with many of them. Where were these thousands of seventies and high priests and elders? The great majority of them were not here; but today they are, and I thought I would talk to them while here, and not when absent.

UNFAITHFUL PRIESTHOOD TO BE REMOVED.—Are the things of God of so small importance—are the issues of life, the destinies of the world, and the salvation of the living and the dead of so small importance, that we cannot afford time to spend a day once a quarter in attending to the duties of our office, in representing our different districts, and in fulfilling the duties of our priesthood and the obligations God has placed upon us? I tell you, ye elders of Israel, who neglect these things and who shirk your duties, that God will remove your candlestick out of its place, and that speedily, unless you repent. And I say so to the bishops, and I say so to all Israel who hold the priesthood. We are not here to do our own will, but the will of our Heavenly Father who sent us. God has placed an important mission upon us; he expects us to fulfil it. If we treat it lightly and neglect our duties, he will remove us and others will take our crown.— *JD*, 20:20-21, July 7, 1878.

PRIESTHOOD HOLDS THE DESTINY OF THE HUMAN FAMILY. —This exhibits a principle of adjudication or judgment in the hands, first, of the great High Priest and King, Jesus of Nazareth, the Son of God; secondly, in the hands of the twelve apostles on the continent of Asia, bestowed by Jesus himself; thirdly, in the twelve disciples on this continent, to their peoples, who it appears are under the presidency of the twelve apostles who ministered at Jerusalem; which presidency is also exhibited by Peter, James, and John, the acknowledged presidency of the twelve apostles; they, holding this priesthood first on the earth, and then in the heavens, being the legitimate custodians of the keys of the priesthood, came and bestowed it upon Joseph Smith and Oliver Cowdery.

It is also further stated that the saints shall judge the world. Thus Christ is at the head, his apostles and disciples seem to take the next prominent part; then comes the action of the saints, or other branches of the priesthood, who it is stated shall judge the world. This combined priesthood, it would appear, will hold the destiny of the human family in their hands and adjudicate in all matters pertaining to their affairs; and it would seem to be quite reasonable, if the twelve apostles in Jerusalem are to be the judges of the twelve tribes, and the twelve disciples on this continent are to be the judges of the descendants of Nephi, that the brother of Jared and Jared should be the judges of the Jaredites, their descendants; and, further, that the first presidency and twelve who have officiated in our age, should operate in regard to mankind in this dispensation, and also in regard to all matters connected with them, whether they relate to the past, present, or future, as the aforementioned have done in regard to their several peoples; and that the patriarchs, the presidents, the twelve, the high priests, the seventies, the elders, the bishops, priests, teachers and deacons should hold their several places behind the veil, and officiate according to their calling and standing in that priesthood. In fact, the priesthood is called an everlasting priesthood; it ministers in time and in eternity. . . .

Thus shall we also become legitimately and by right, through the atonement and adoption, kings and priests—priests to administer in the holy ordinances pertaining to the endowments and exaltations; and kings, under Christ, who is King of kings and Lord of lords, to rule and govern, according to the eternal laws of justice and equity, those who are thus redeemed and exalted.— *MA*, 156-157, 158-159.

# CHAPTER XIV

# THE MELCHIZEDEK PRIESTHOOD

## MELCHIZEDEK AND THE MELCHIZEDEK ORDER OF PRIESTHOOD

THE KEY TO REVELATION.—The Melchizedek priesthood holds the mysteries of the revelations of God. Wherever that priesthood exists, there also exists a knowledge of the laws of God; and wherever the gospel has existed, there has always been revelation; and where there has been no revelation, there never has been the true gospel.—*JD*, 13:231, May 6, 1870.

THE PATRIARCHAL ORDER.—We find that after the days of Noah an order was introduced called the patriarchal order, in which every man managed his own family affairs. And prominent men among them were kings and priests unto God, and officiated in what is known among us as the priesthood of the Son of God, or the priesthood after the order of Melchizedek. Man began again to multiply on the face of the earth, and the heads of families became their kings and priests, that is, the fathers of their own people. And they were more or less under the influence and guidance of the Almighty. We read, for instance, in our revelations pertaining to these matters, of a man called Melchizedek, who was a great high priest. We are told that there were a great many high priests in his day, and before him and after him; and these men had communication with God, and were taught of him in relation to their general proceedings, and acknowledged the hand of God in all things with which they were associated.— *JD*, 17:207, October 7, 1874.

MELCHIZEDEK.—There was Melchizedek, for instance, who was called the king of Salem and the prince of peace, of whom Paul makes some curious remarks, among which was that Christ was a priest forever, after the order of Melchizedek. If he was, then of course, Melchizedek was a priest after the order of Christ. And as Christ introduced the gospel, so Melchizedek had the gospel, and had and held and administered in the same priesthood that Jesus did. And we read, too, according to some men's ideas, a very singular thing concerning him, that he was "without father, without mother, without descent, having neither beginning of days, nor end of life, but made like unto the Son of God; abideth a priest continually." (Hebrews 7:3.) He must be,

indeed a very singular man, to be without father and without
mother and without descent, and yet that he should be a priest
forever. Well, how is it? You generally understand it; but
I will inform those who do not that the Apostle Paul referred
to the priesthood that Melchizedek held. . . . The Melchizedek
priesthood . . . had nothing to do particularly with either father or
mother, it being without descent. Therefore, people holding it
were not altogether dependent upon their father or mother or
descent for this authority; but on that priesthood, administering
in time and in eternity. And this is what Paul referred to by
way of contradistinction to the Aaronic priesthood which then
existed.—*JD*, 21:244, March 21, 1880.

JOHN, PETER, NEPHI, MORONI, HELD THIS PRIESTHOOD.
—This priesthood was held by John the revelator, by Peter, by
Moroni, one of the prophets of God on this continent. Nephi,
another of the servants of God on this continent, had the gospel
with its keys and powers revealed unto him.—*JD*, 18:139,
October 10, 1875.

PRIESTHOOD FUNCTION: ANCIENT AND MODERN.—Those
who have held the Melchizedek priesthood, many of whom had
the gifts of the Holy Ghost, and much of the spirit of prophecy,
even where there was no organization of priesthood or of the
kingdom of God upon the earth, stood as isolated characters in
the world, and maintained their integrity before God. But we
have a kingdom, the pattern of which has been revealed from the
great God, given for our own happiness and salvation. And with
the laying of the foundation of his kingdom on the earth there
is a promise given unto us that the powers of darkness and all
the power of hell combined shall not prevail against this kingdom.
In this respect we differ from all others.—*JD*, 8:98, June 17,
1860.

## MELCHIZEDEK PRIESTHOOD CALLINGS:
## THE PRESIDENCY OF THE HIGH PRIESTHOOD

JURISDICTION.—The presidency of the high priesthood, after
the order of Melchizedek, have a right to officiate in all the offices
in the church.

Now, will you show me an office, or calling, or duty, or
responsibility, temporal or spiritual, that does not come under
this statement? From this I think this presidency have something
to do with the bishops and temporal things as well as with the
Melchizedek priesthood and spiritual things, and with all things
pertaining to the interests and welfare of Zion. That is the way
I understand these matters.—*JD*, 21:364, August 8, 1880.

THE TWELVE AND FIRST PRESIDENCY.—It is gratifying to me to be able to state that now all the various organizations of the church are provided for. For some time the twelve have been operating in the capacity of a First Presidency, and it was very proper that they should have acted in that capacity. . . . This was the course adopted at the time when the Prophet Joseph Smith left us. The twelve then stepped forward into the position of the First Presidency, and operated for about three years in that capacity. And when President Young left us, it was thought proper that the same course should be pursued. The twelve, I believe, have in this respect magnified their calling and taken a course that is approved by the Lord, and I think also by the brethren, judging from the vote given here today.

Had it not been our duty to have the church organized fully and completely in all its departments, I should have much preferred to have continued with the brethren of the twelve, speaking of it merely as a matter of personal feeling. But there are questions arising in regard to these matters that are not for us to say how they shall be, or what course shall be pursued. When God has given us an order and has appointed an organization in his church, with the various quorums of priesthood as presented to us by revelation through the Prophet Joseph Smith, I do not think that either the First Presidency, the twelve, the high priests, the seventies, the bishops, or anybody else, have a right to change or alter that plan which the Lord has introduced and established. And as you heard Brother Pratt state this morning, one duty devolving upon the twelve is to see that the churches are organized correctly. And I think they are now thus organized throughout the land of Zion. The churches generally are organized with presidents of stakes and their counselors, with high councils, with bishops and their counselors, and with the lesser priesthood, according to the order that is given us.

Then we have the high priests, seventies, and elders occupying their places according to their priesthood, position, and standing in the church. And the First Presidency seemed to be the only quorum that was deficient. And it is impossible for men acquainted with the order of the holy priesthood to ignore this quorum, as it is one of the principal councils of the church. While the twelve stand as a bulwark ready to protect, defend, and maintain, to step forward and carry out the order of God's kingdom in times of necessity, such as above referred to, yet when everything is adjusted and matters assume their normal condition, then it is proper that the quorum of the First Presidency, as well as all other quorums, should occupy the place assigned it by the Almighty.

These were the suggestions of the Spirit of the Lord to me. I expressed my feelings to the twelve, who coincided with me, and indeed, several of them had had the same feelings as those with which I was actuated. It is not with us, or ought not to be, a matter of place, position, or honor, although it is a great honor to be a servant of God. It is a great honor to hold the priesthood of God. But while it is an honor to be God's servants, holding his priesthood, it is not honorable for any man or any set of men to seek for position in the holy priesthood. Jesus said, Ye have not called me, but I have called you. And as I said before, had I consulted my own personal feelings, I would have said, things are going on very pleasantly, smoothly, and agreeably; and I have a number of good associates whom I respect and esteem, as my brethren, and I rejoice in their counsels. Let things remain as they are. But it is not for me to say, it is not for you to say what we would individually prefer, but it is for us holding the holy priesthood to see that all the organizations of that priesthood are preserved intact and that everything in the church and kingdom of God is organized according to the plan which he has revealed. Therefore we have taken the course which you have been called upon to sanction by your votes today.—*JD,* 22:38-40, October 10, 1880.

PRINCIPLES AND PRACTICES IN ORGANIZING THE FIRST PRESIDENCY.—And now let me refer with pride to my brethren of the twelve here, which I do by saying that while they as a quorum held the right by the vote of the people to act in the capacity of the First Presidency, yet when they found, as Brother Pratt expressed it this morning, that they had performed their work, they were willing to withdraw from that presidency, and put it in the position that God had directed, and fall back into the place that they have always held, as the twelve apostles of the Church of Jesus Christ of Latter-day Saints. I say it is with pride that I refer to this action and the feeling that prompted it. I very much question whether you could find the same personal exhibition of disinterested motives and self-abnegation, and the like readiness to renounce place and position in deference to principle, among the same number of men in any other place. They saw the necessity of this action; a motion was made in that council; and the vote was unanimously adopted that the First Presidency be reorganized, and afterwards the brethren to fill this quorum were selected.

The next step was to present the matter to the church, and it was laid before the priesthood at a meeting, when there were present a representation of all the important authorities of the church in the different stakes in Zion. After having done that, lest some difficulty might exist somewhere, it was thought proper to pursue the course taken today—that each organization of the priesthood, embracing all the quorums, should be seated in a quorum capacity by themselves, and separately have the opportunity of voting freely and fully without control of any kind, and of expressing their feelings, and, finally, that the whole congregation should have the same opportunity. This is emphatically the voice of God, and the voice of the people; and this is the order that the Lord has instituted in Zion, as it was in former times among Israel. God gave his commandments; they were delivered by his Prophet to the people and submitted to them, and all Israel said, Amen. You have all done this by your votes, which vote, so far as we can learn, has been without a dissenting voice, either among the separate quorums or in the vote of the combined quorums and people.

Now, continue to be united in everything as you are in this thing, and God will stand by you from this time henceforth and forever. And any man who opposes principles of this kind is an enemy of God, an enemy of the church and kingdom of God upon the earth, an enemy to the people of God, and an enemy to the freedom and rights of man. The Lord has selected a priesthood that he might among all Israel make known his mind and will through them, and that they might be his representatives upon the earth. And while he does this he does not wish men to be coerced or forced to do things contrary to their will. But where the Spirit of God is, there are union, harmony, and liberty, and where it is not there are strife, confusion, and bondage. Let us then seek to be one, honor our God, honor our religion, and keep the commandments of God, and seek to know his will, and then to do it.—*JD*, 22:40-41, October 10, 1880.

DISORGANIZATION OF THE FIRST PRESIDENCY.—Supposing that I, as president of the church, were to resign, or anything occur to me. What would be the result? My counselors would drop into their former place in the quorum of the twelve, and whoever succeeded me would have the selection of his own counselors with the approval of the general conference. He might and he might not retain as his counselors those whom I have chosen. It is proper that we should understand these things in order that the right kind of feeling may exist, and no improper reflection be cast upon any person.—*JD*, 24:33, January 21, 1883.

# THE APOSTLESHIP

THE TWELVE AS PROPHETS, SEERS, AND REVELATORS.— You voted yesterday that the twelve should be prophets, seers, and revelators. This may seem strange to some who do not comprehend these principles, but not to those who do. The same vote was proposed by Joseph Smith and voted for in the temple in Kirtland, so long ago as that; consequently there is nothing new in this. And, as you heard this morning, this is embraced in the apostleship, which has been given by the Almighty, and which embraces all the keys, powers, and authorities ever conferred upon man. I do not wish to enter into the details of this matter; you will find them in the Doctrine and Covenants, very clearly portrayed, and I refer you there for the evidences on these points. —*JD*, 19:124, October 7, 1877.

THE APOSTOLIC CALLING.—The twelve are set apart as special witnesses to the nations of the earth, and are empowered and authorized to open up the gospel, to introduce it, and to turn the keys thereof to all people, and the word to the apostles—and to others associated with them—to the elders of Israel generally is, "Go ye into all the world, and preach the gospel to every creature. He that believeth and is baptized shall be saved; and he that believeth not shall be damned." (Mark 16:15-16.) This is just as it was in former ages.—*JD*, 24:288-289, October 7, 1883.

Now then, what are we called to do? What, for instance, is the duty of an apostle? We used to understand it to be our duty to go to the ends of the earth and preach the gospel; and I may say we have traveled hundreds of thousands of miles to accomplish that object. But some of us are getting white-headed. . . . And it is so with many of the twelve; they have got past that some time ago. But the twelve went out, and were always ready to go out, and are today if required. And I will say of my brethren who are around me, I do not know of a better set of men in existence, nor could I tell where they can be found. I will bear this testimony concerning my brethren of the twelve. They are ready to do what God requires of them at any time.— *JD*, 20:45, August 4, 1878.

SEVENTIES TO ASSIST THE TWELVE.—To assist the twelve in the labors in which they are engaged, are the seventies, who are called as special witnesses to the nations of the earth. What for? Who organized these seventies, and these twelve, and who dictated their duties and responsibilities? The Lord. Why did he do it? Because, as in former ages, he felt interested in the welfare of the human family, and it is not and never was the will of God, that mankind should perish, but that they all might be brought to a knowledge of the truth, and to an obedience thereof, if they saw proper, and if not, when the twelve, the seventies, the elders, and the various officers who have been ordained and set apart to preach the gospel, have fulfilled their missions to the nations of the earth; they have done just what the Lord has required at their hands, and no more. I further wish to state to the twelve and to the seventies, and to the elders, that they are not responsible for the reception or the rejection by the world of that word which God has given to them to communicate. It is proper for them to use all necessary diligence and fidelity, and plainly and intelligently, and with prayer and faith, to go forth as messengers to the nations, as the legates of the skies, clothed upon with authority from the God of heaven, even the authority of the holy priesthood, which is after the order of the Son of God, which is after the order of Melchizedek, which is after the power of an endless life. He has endowed them, as you have heard, with authority to call upon men to repent of their sins, and to be baptized in the name of Jesus for the remission of sins, and then he has told them to lay hands on the people thus believing, and thus being baptized, and to confer upon them the gift of the Holy Ghost, and when they have performed their labors, and fulfilled their duties, their garments are free from the blood of this generation, and the people are then left in the hands of God, their Heavenly Father, for the people, as before stated, will be held responsible to God for their rejection of the gospel, and not to us.—*JD*, 24:289, October 7, 1883.

THE TWELVE AND THE SEVENTIES.—It devolves upon the twelve apostles and the seventies to see that the gospel is carried, and to carry it themselves, to all the nations of the earth—first unto the gentiles and then to the Jews. This is their especial calling, and they should keep it constantly before them.—*JH*, March 31, 1886, p. 11; Salt Lake *Herald*, March 31, 1886.

DUTIES OF SEVENTIES.—Now let us go on to the seventies. There are large numbers of them, and there has been a great desire to push men into quorums, without regard sometimes to their worth and fitness. Now what is their duty? Why, to go abroad and preach the gospel to all nations. How many do this? Very few. Well, say some, we go when called upon. That is all true. The seventies have, as a rule, been on hand to go forth and preach. But I am speaking more particularly of the nature of the priesthood they hold and the duties which devolve upon them. They should be always ready, kind of minute men under the immediate direction of the twelve, to go forth as the messengers of life and salvation to all nations on the earth. . . .

THE SEVENTY AND THE HIGH PRIEST.—We talk about and wonder who the biggest man is—the seventy or the high priest? Let us seek to know who of us is living nearer to God and acting in such a manner as to call down upon us the power of God, and angels will administer to us. We cannot tell which member of the body is most useful to us, which we can best afford to spare—the leg or the arm, the eye or the nose. All are necessary to render the body perfect.—*JD*, 19:141, October 14, 1877.

## PATRIARCHS[1]

THE OFFICE OF PATRIARCH TO THE CHURCH.—In regard to the office of patriarch, William Smith has been ordained patriarch to the church; but he is not the only patriarch, but would act as a senior patriarch, holding the keys of that priesthood; and his labors would be more especially connected with the church in Zion; and he would take the lead, priority, or presidency of the patriarchal office in this place; and in this capacity, if there should be a council of patriarchs, he as a matter of course would preside by right of office. But every legally ordained patriarch has the same right to bless that he has, and their administrations are just as legal as his are. Every ordinance that is administered by a legal administrator, is legal. A priest has just as much right to baptize a person for the remission of sins as an elder, a high priest, or an apostle; but he cannot lay on hands for the gift of the Holy Ghost, because he does not possess the authority to do it; but an elder does, and an elder's administration would be just as legal as the administration of any of the beforementioned persons, or as that of the president of the church.

RIGHTS OF FATHERS TO ACT AS PATRIARCHS.—Every father, after he has received his patriarchal blessing, is a patriarch to his own family, and has the right to confer patriarchal blessings upon his family; which blessings will be just as legal as those conferred by any patriarch of the church: in fact it is his right; and a patriarch in blessing his children, can only bless as his mouthpiece.

A patriarch to the church is appointed to bless those who are orphans, or have no father in the Church to bless them. Not as stated inadvertently, in the editorial above alluded to "to bless all, and such as have not a father to do it," for this he could not do, where the church is so extensive: the burden would be too onerous; hence other patriarchs have been ordained, both in this country, and in England, to assist the patriarch to the church, and hence the provision made in the Doctrine and Covenants: "It is the duty of the Twelve, in *all* large branches of the church, to ordain *evangelical ministers*, [patriarchs] as they shall

---

[1]This article was especially prepared by Elder Taylor for the *Times and Seasons* to correct a previous editorial by W. W. Phelps. It is a most significant statement.

be designated unto them by revelation." (D. & C. 107:39.) And should any of those patriarchs remove here, they have just as much right to administer in their patriarchal office under the direction of the patriarch to the church, as an elder or priest would, who should remove from one of the branches to this place, under the direction of the presidency. Brother William Smith, however, "holds the keys of the patriarchal blessings upon the heads of all my people," and would of necessity have the seniority, and of course the priority and presidency; yet it would be left for those who wished to be administered to, to make their choice; just as much as it would for a candidate for baptism to choose who should administer to him.

The above is the true doctrine of the church in regard to this matter, and we speak of it for the information of the brethren at large, lest those who may have received their patriarchal blessings from other sources, or from their fathers, might be tempted to think they were of no avail, and also, to set at rest this agitated question.

THE PATRIARCH DOES NOT PRESIDE OVER THE PRIESTHOOD OR THE CHURCH.—We now proceed to answer some of the remarks which we have heard:

We have been asked, "Does not patriarch *over* the *whole* church" place Brother William Smith at the head of the *whole* church as president?

Answer. No. Brother William is not patriarch *over* the *whole* church, but patriarch to the church, and as such he was ordained. The expression "over the whole church," is a mistake made by W. W. Phelps. He is patriarch to the church of Jesus Christ of Latter-day Saints. The twelve are commanded to ordain evangelical ministers in all large branches of the church abroad, and who has charge over them? The patriarch? No. Those who ordained them. And to whom is committed the power and authority to regulate all the affairs of the churches abroad? And who has the charge of the whole priesthood here? Answer. The presidency of the church, and not the patriarch.

But does not the Doctrine and Covenants say:

"*First*, I give unto you Hyrum Smith to be a patriarch unto you to hold the sealing blessings of my church, even the Holy Spirit of promise, whereby ye are sealed up unto the day of redemption, that ye may not fall notwithstanding the hour of temptation that may come upon you."[1] (D. & C. 124:124.)

Yes, but that is in regard to seniority not in regard to authority in priesthood, for it immediately follows, "I give unto you my servant Joseph to be a *presiding elder* over *all* my church,

---

[1]All italics are added by John Taylor.

to be a translator, a revelator, a seer, and a prophet."[1] (D. & C. 124:125.) In the Doctrine and Covenants we read "the duty of President of the office of the high priesthood is to preside over the whole church, and to be like unto Moses." (D. & C. 107:91.) And from this it is evident that the president of the church, not the patriarch, is appointed by God to preside.

But does not the patriarch stand in the same relationship to the church as Adam did to his family, and as Abraham and Jacob did to theirs? No. This is another mistake which is made by our junior, and one that may be very easily made inadvertently. Adam was the *natural* father of his posterity, who were his family and over whom he presided as patriarch, prophet, priest, and king. Both Abraham and Jacob stood in the same relationship to their families. But not so with Father Joseph Smith, Hyrum Smith, or William Smith. They were not the natural fathers of the church, and could not stand in the same capacity as Adam, Abraham, or Jacob; but inasmuch as there had been none to bless for generations past, according to the ancient order, they were ordained and set apart for the purpose of conferring patriarchal blessings, to hold the keys of this priesthood, and unlock the door, that had long been closed upon the human family: that blessings might again be conferred according to the ancient order, and those who were orphans, or had no father to bless them, might receive it through a patriarch who should act as proxy for their father, and that fathers might again be enabled to act as patriarchs to their families, and bless their children. For like all other ordinances in the church, this had been neglected and must needs be restored. But Father Joseph Smith was not president of the church, nor the president's counsel. Nor was Hyrum Smith either president or president's counsel. He was once counsel, but when he was ordained patriarch he gave it up and another was ordained in his stead, [William Law] and in all probability if Brother William magnifies his calling, he will not be able henceforth to attend to the duties of an apostle; but officiate in the same capacity in regard to blessing as his brother Hyrum did—not as president of the church, but as patriarch to it.

The president of the church presides over all patriarchs, presidents, and councils of the church; and this presidency does not depend so much upon genealogy as upon calling, order, and seniority. James and Joses were the brothers of Jesus, and John was his beloved disciple, yet Peter held the keys and presided over all the church. Brother William was in the quorum of the twelve yet he was not president of the twelve during his brother's lifetime, nor since; and if being ordained a patriarch would make

---
[1] All italics are added by John Taylor.

him president of the church, it would have made Father Joseph Smith and Hyrum Smith presidents over the church instead of Joseph.

Brother William understands the matter, and were it not for the folly of some men there would be no necessity for these remarks.

A patriarch is what is termed in scripture an evangelist, and Brother William acts in that capacity, and God placed in the church "first apostles,' not first evangelists, but the president stands in the same relationship to the church as Moses did to the children of Israel, according to the revelations.

Again, who ordained Father Smith to the office of patriarch? His son Joseph, and Father Smith ordained Hyrum, and the twelve (of whom Brother William is one) ordained him. Who are appointed to ordain evangelical ministers? It is the duty of the Twelve, in all large branches of the church, to ordain evangelical ministers, as they shall be designated unto them by revelation. (D. & C. 107:39.) Can a stream rise higher than its fountain? No. . . .

We think that everyone will see that Brother William Smith's patriarchal office will not exalt him higher in regard to priesthood than he was before, as one of the twelve; but will rather change the nature of his office.

But will it take any thing from his priesthood? it may be asked. No. You cannot take any man's priesthood away without transgression. Brother William will still retain the same power, priesthood, and authority that he did before, and yet will hold in connection with that the patriarchal office and the keys of that priesthood, and as one of the twelve must maintain his dignity as one of the presidents of the church,[1] of whom President Brigham Young is the president and head, and presides over all patriarchs, presidents, and councils of the church.—*TS,* 6:921-922, June 1, 1845.

## HIGH PRIESTS

QUORUM OF HIGH PRIESTS IN EACH STAKE.—We have a quorum of high priests in each stake, and it is for them to exercise themselves and their influence individually and as a quorum in the interests of righteousness and virtue and the maintenence of the principles connected with the kingdom of God. They have no particular position or calling; they are ordained to the high priesthood, and it is for their president to meet with them and

---

[1]This occurred during the apostolic interregnum of 1844-1847 when the twelve, Brigham Young at their head, were sustained as "presidents of the church."

have them humble themselves before God, and seek for the
guidance of his holy Spirit and the light of revelation. "Which
ordinance" we are told in the Doctrine and Covenants, "is instituted for the purpose of qualifying those who shall be appointed
standing presidents or servants over different stakes scattered
abroad;

"And they may travel also if they choose, but rather be
ordained for standing presidents; this is the office of their calling,
saith the Lord your God." (D. & C. 124:134, 135) That they
may comprehend the principles of law, of government, of justice,
and equity, and watch over, not only themselves, but their families
and friends, associations and neighborhoods, and act as fathers
in Israel, looking after the welfare of the people and exerting a
salutary influence over the saints of the Most High God.—*JD,*
23:219, August 6, 1882.

HIGH PRIESTS TO INSTRUCT EACH OTHER IN CHURCH
GOVERNMENT.—The high priests occupy a position in their
priesthood whereby they are enabled to perform the various duties
that they may be called upon to fill. You will find in reading
the Doctrine and Covenants the following statement regarding
the quorum of high priests: "Which ordinance is instituted for
the purpose of qualifying those who shall be appointed standing
presidents or servants over different stakes scattered abroad." (D.
& C. 124:134.) That is, it is the duty of high priests to preside;
the principle of presidency is connected with them. . . . What is the
duty of that quorum? To meet together to instruct one another
in regard to the principles of the government of the church and
kingdom of God; that its members may understand the various
organizations of the church, the laws, and the principles of
government thereof, and the various duties they may be called
upon to fill. It may be to occupy the position of a president of
a stake. It may be a counselor to the president. It may be a high
counselor. It may be a bishop or his counselor. There are divers
positions that high priests are called to occupy, as deaths and other
changes often transpire, and new stakes and wards are being
organized. But the changes do not affect the status of the individual at all. . . . Here is Brother Shurtliff called from acting as bishop
to be the president of a stake. Have we a right to do that? Yes.
Who is the bishop? A high priest. His place being vacated, that
position needs supplying, and who shall supply it? These things
are left for the counsel and the deliberation of the proper authorities to operate in for the welfare of the church as far as they know
how, and according to the best judgment they possess; and then
they should be presented to the people for them to vote upon.
But in dropping a president it drops his counselors. They were

selected to be his counselors, not somebody else's; and when some one else takes his place, then he should have his own counselors. These are the views entertained on this subject, and they are correct and very proper. The order of the church is for us to fulfil and magnify the calling to which we are called, and do it with an eye single to the glory of God, each man fulfilling the various duties and responsibilities of his office.—*JD,* 24:33-34, January 21, 1883.

The high priests are a sort of normal school to prepare the people to preside. They have hardly fulfilled this. Perhaps if they had been more active, and become acquainted with principles for which they are organized, we should not have to ordain so many high priests from the elders' quorum to make presidents of stakes, bishops, high councils, etc. But as it was, we had to pick up the material where we could, and I hope we will have better material next time.—*JD,* 19:147, October 21, 1877.

## SEVENTIES AND HIGH PRIESTS

A HIGH PRIEST MAY TRAVEL AND A SEVENTY PRESIDE!— There has been, sometimes, a little feeling manifested between the seventies and high priests, as to who has the greatest authority, and some of the seventies have manifested a desire to be united with the high priests' quorum, thinking thereby to obtain a greater degree of priesthood. This is folly, for, as I stated before, it is not the office but the magnifying of an office that makes a man honorable. But in relation to their offices, they are called to move in other spheres, and fulfil other callings, rather than possessing different power and authority. Brother Carter thought that some of the seventies were out of their place, because they were appointed to preside over conferences, whereas they have as much right to preside, when legally appointed, as an high priest or an apostle. The seventies have the high priesthood, and many of them have received ordinances in the temple, qualifying them to build up the kingdom of God, if every other officer were dead or killed, and so have the high priests. So far, then, as authority is concerned, they both have authority, but it is the especial business of the seventies to preach to all the world, introduce and spread the gospel; while it is the duty of the high priests more especially to preside. Yet a high priest is not precluded from traveling and preaching, and introducing the gospel (nor a seventy from presiding.)

AN ANALOGY.—You have your officers in the army and navy; they may be equal in authority, but act in different callings. The military officer, if at sea, while the navy is engaged in a fight with an enemy, would assist with his men to vanquish the enemy; while on the other hand the naval officer would assist the military in storming a garrison and taking possession of territory. They are both engaged in the same cause, and are fighting for the interests of the same kingdom or government; and so it is with the high priests and seventies—they are both empowered to do good, and although their callings differ in some respects, they can both act legally in whatsoever situation they are placed by authority. And though it is the especial duty of the seventies to preach, yet some of the high priests are much more competent to do it than they; and although it is the especial duty of an high priest to preside, yet a wise man who fulfils and magnifies his calling among the seventies is much more competent to preside than a foolish or ignorant high priest, who does not magnify his calling.—*MS*, 9:324-325, November 1, 1847.

We have a great number of seventies, and the question has often arisen, Which is the bigger, they or the high priests? I say I don't think it makes much difference as to which is the greater or smaller. I think the body of Christ was not one member but composed of many parts. Now which member of your body would you like to be without? An arm or a leg? No, you want both. So does the church. But which is the most useful? If you can tell me which of those members is most useful to you, I will let you know which is the more useful to the church, the high priests or seventies. We ought to magnify the priesthood we hold, and be satisfied with the positions we hold.—*JD*, 19: 147, October 21, 1877.

THE QUORUMS OF SEVENTIES.—Again, we have our organization of seventies, and they ought to see that there is no iniquity among their quorums—no drunkenness, no whoredom, no fraud, nothing that is wrong or improper, unholy or impure; but that they are men of God chosen and set apart as messengers to the nations of the earth, and wherever they reside it is their duty, and it is the duty of all men in Israel, to see that there is no iniquity, to use their influence on the side of right, and to put down wrong. —*JD*, 23:219, August 6, 1882.

## THE ELDERS

STANDING MINISTERS.—Then again, the same thing will apply to elders. The elder is ordained in many instances to act as a standing minister among the people, to preach to them, to instruct them as we are doing and as your missionaries are doing and as others are doing, preaching among the people at home, and frequently going abroad as circumstances may require.—*JD*, 23:219, August 6, 1882.

A HERALD OF SALVATION.—Talking of the elder, why he is a herald of salvation. He is a legate of the skies. He is commissioned of the great Jehovah to bear a message to the nations of the earth, and God has promised to sustain him. He has always sustained his faithful elders, and he always will. And what of the elder? He is commanded to call upon men to believe in Jesus Christ, to repent of their sins, and to be baptized for the remission of sins, promising them the gift of the Holy Ghost; and all who obey the requirements receive this divine gift. . . .

Is there any greater position that man can occupy upon the earth than to be engaged as a herald of salvation, commissioned of the great Jehovah to proclaim the words of life to a fallen world, and to call upon them to repent and be baptized in the name of Jesus for the remission of sins, promising them if they do it that they shall receive the Holy Ghost? This is the position occupied by our elders, as well as that occupied by seventies and high priests. They go forth in the name of the Lord; and people believe their testimony and gather here.—*JD*, 24:35-36, January 21, 1883.

CHALLENGE.—We want some manhood, and some priesthood and power of God to be manifested in Israel, and the Spirit of God to be poured out upon Israel and upon the elders thereof. And I pray God, the Eternal Father, to waken up these elders, that the spirit of their mission may rest upon them, and that they may comprehend their true position before God.—*JD*, 20:23, July 7, 1878.

# CHAPTER XV

# THE AARONIC PRIESTHOOD

## RESPONSIBILITY OF THE LESSER PRIESTHOOD

IMPORTANCE OF PRIESTS, TEACHERS, AND DEACONS.—
There is as much devolving upon the priests, the teachers, and the
deacons, and those of the lesser priesthood as there is upon any
other members of the church. When they do not fulfil their
duties, what is the result? People go to the twelve, or to the First
Presidency; they pass the more immediate authorities; and confusion and disorder exist; and valuable time is occupied almost
needlessly; and those who will work may work until they are
broken down ready to cease their earthly labors; and all this for
the want of men's knowing their duties and doing them.

TO INTRODUCE RIGHTEOUSNESS.—But while we are contending over little things what becomes of us? We are losing
sight of our callings; we forget that this kingdom was established
upon the earth for the purpose of introducing righteousness and
the laws of heaven upon the earth, and of blessing mankind and
of saving the living and the dead. We forget what we are here
for, and what the kingdom of God is established for. It is not
for you or for me or anybody else alone; it is for the interests
of the world and the salvation of mankind. We are expected,
every one of us, to perform the various duties and responsibilities
devolving upon us. If we neglect them, are we not guilty before
God? Whence come the difficulties that we have in our midst?
Because as I have said in many instances the priesthood do not
perform their duties, are not vigilant and faithful.—*JD*, 19:54,
June 17, 1877.

## ITEMS ON THE AARONIC PRIESTHOOD[1]

AN HISTORICAL SKETCH.—It seems . . . that Moses had
the greater or Melchizedek priesthood; that when he was taken, the
keys went with him; that the Aaronic priesthood ruled until
Christ, and the people were under the law; that when Christ came
he introduced a better covenant and restored the gospel; and that
the bishopric was, and the Aaronic priesthood is, under the Melchizedek, and an appendage thereto, as are also all elders appendages

---

[1]From *Items on Priesthood.*

to the Melchizedek priesthood. And it is also evident that the presidency of that priesthood presides over all, as did Melchizedek, Moses, Joseph Smith, etc., with Jesus at the head, as the great Presiding High Priest. . . .

Yet the Aaronic priesthood, as the Melchizedek, is an everlasting priesthood, as before exhibited, and continueth forever as an appendage to the Melchizedek priesthood. Hence in the old apostolic days, when under an organization of the Melchizedek, the latter is the most prominent, and very little is said about the Levitical or Aaronic, probably on account of the peculiar traditions and superstitions of the Jews, which made it almost impossible for them to comprehend the greater or Melchizedek. Yet the Aaronic cannot be ignored, and in the dispensation of the fulness of times it again comes forth, as one of the grand aids or appendages to the Melchizedek priesthood. Hence, in the ushering in of this dispensation, John the Baptist appears on the stage and confers the Aaronic priesthood upon Joseph Smith and Oliver Cowdery. —*IP, 7, 16-17.*

SOME SUMMARY ITEMS.—First.—We find that there are two distinctive general priesthoods, namely, the Melchizedek and Aaronic, including the Levitical priesthood.

Second.—That they are both conferred by the Lord; that both are everlasting, and administer in time and eternity.

Third.—That the Melchizedek priesthood holds the right of presidency, and has power and authority *over all the offices in the church,* in all ages of the world, *to administer in spiritual things.*

Fourth.—That the second priesthood is called the priesthood of Aaron, because it was conferred upon Aaron and his seed throughout all their generations.

Fifth.—That the lesser priesthood is a part of, or an appendage to the greater, or the Melchizedek priesthood, and has power in administering outward ordinances. The lesser or Aaronic priesthood can make appointments for the greater in preaching; can baptize, administer the sacrament, attend to the tithing, buy lands, settle people on possessions, divide inheritances, look after the poor, take care of the properties of the church, attend generally to temporal affairs; act as common judges in Israel, and assist in ordinances of the temple, under the direction of the greater or Melchizedek priesthood. They hold the keys of the ministering of angels and administer in outward ordinances, *the letter of the gospel,* and the baptism of repentance for the remission of sins.

Sixth.—That there is a presidency over each of these priesthoods, both over the Melchizedek and the Aaronic.

Seventh.—That while the power of the higher, or Melchizedek, is to hold the keys *of all* the spiritual *blessings of the church;* to have the privilege of receiving the mysteries of the kingdom of heaven, to have the heavens opened to them, to commune with the general assembly and church of the firstborn and to enjoy the communion and presence of God the Father, and Jesus the Mediator of the new covenant, and to preside over all the spiritual officers of the church, yet the *presidency* of the high priesthood, after the order of Melchizedek, have a right to officiate in *all the offices in the church,* both spiritual and temporal.

> Then comes the High Priesthood, which is the greatest of all.
> Wherefore, it must needs be that one be appointed of the High Priesthood to preside over the Priesthood, and he shall be called president of the High Priesthood of the church;
> Or, in other words, the Presiding High Priest over the High Priesthood of the Church.—(D. & C. 107, 64-66.)

It is thus evident that this priesthood presides over all presidents, all bishops, including the presiding bishop; over all councils, organizations, and authorities in the whole Church, in all the world.

That the bishopric is the presidency of the Aaronic priesthood, which is "an *appendage* to the greater or Melchizedek priesthood," and that no man has a legal right to hold the keys of the Aaronic priesthood, which presides over all bishops and all the lesser priesthood, except he be a literal descendant of Aaron. But, that "as a high priest of the Melchizedek priesthood has authority to officiate in all the lesser offices, he may officiate in the office of bishop . . . if *called, set apart, and ordained unto this power* by the hands of the presidency of the Melchizedek priesthood."

We may here notice that John the Baptist conferred this priesthood upon Joseph Smith, and that therefore, as he held it, he had the power to confer it upon others.

Eighth.—That there are bishops holding different positions: Bishop Partridge was a general bishop over the land of Zion; while Bishop Whitney was a general bishop over the church in Kirtland, Ohio, and also over all the eastern churches until afterwards appointed as presiding bishop [to the church]. That there are also ward bishops, whose duties are confined to their several wards. That there are also bishops' agents, such as Sidney Gilbert and others.

That the position which a bishop holds, depends upon his calling and appointment, and that, although a man holding the bishopric is eligible to any office in the bishopric, yet he cannot officiate legally in any, except by selection, calling, and appointment.

Ninth.—That the power and right of selecting and calling

of the presiding bishop and general bishops is vested in the First Presidency, who also must try those appointed by them in case of transgression, except in the case of a literal descendant of Aaron; who, if the firstborn, possesses a legal right to the keys of this priesthood; but even he must be sanctioned and appointed by the First Presidency. This arises from the fact that the Aaronic is an appendage to the Melchizedek priesthood.

That the presiding bishop, who presides over all bishops, and all of the lesser priesthood, should consult the First Presidency in all important matters pertaining to the bishopric.

Tenth.—That in regard to the appointment and trial of ward bishops, it appears that they stand in the same relationship to the presidents of stakes as the early bishops did to the First Presidency, who presided over the stake at Kirtland; but that those presidents should consult with the First Presidency on these and other important matters, and officiate under their direction in their several stakes.

That in regard to the office and calling of bishops, it is very much like the office and calling of high priests. All high priests are eligible to any office in the church, when called, ordained, and appointed to fill such office. The First Presidency are high priests. The twelve are high priests; high councilors are high priests; presidents of stakes are high priests, and all their counselors; bishops and their counselors are high priests: but it does not follow that all high priests are first presidents, members of the twelve apostles, presidents of stakes, high councilors, bishops or bishops' counselors; they only obtain these offices by selection and appointment from the proper source, and when not appointed to any specific calling, they are organized in a stake quorum, under a president and council.

So although the bishopric is eligible to fulfil any office to which they may be appointed, all are not presiding bishops, all are not general bishops, or special bishops, or ward bishops, or even bishops' agents; they occupy their several offices, as do the high priests, by selection, appointment, as well as ordination, and that the presidency of the Melchizedek priesthood presides over, calls, directs, appoints, and counsels all. It is further evident that as the Melchizedek priesthood holds the keys of all the spiritual blessings of the church, and that the presidency thereof has a right to officiate in all the offices of the church, therefore that presidency has a perfect right to direct or call, set apart, and ordain bishops, to fill any place or position in the church that may be required for that ministry to perform in all the stakes of Zion, or throughout the world. Thus, after going through the whole matter, we come back to a term frequently used among us: Obey counsel!—*IP*, 36-40.

# THE LEVITICAL PRIESTHOOD

WHAT IS THE LEVITICAL PRIESTHOOD?—There were in the days of Moses a tribe of the children of Israel set apart to officiate in some of the lesser duties of the Aaronic priesthood, and their office was called the Levitical priesthood.—*JD*, 21:364, August 8, 1880.

THE LEVITICAL PRIESTHOOD AN APPENDAGE TO THE AARONIC.—Aaron and his sons held the Aaronic priesthood, and the Levites were given unto them to minister unto them to keep his charge, the charge of the congregation, to do the service of the tabernacle, keep the instruments of the tabernacle, and the charge of the children of Israel. . . . They seemed to have been an appendage to the Aaronic priesthood to assist in the service of the tabernacle and other duties. Aaron and his male descendants were selected for the priesthood, the other Levites as assistants, or an appendage.—*IP*, 40-41.

SUMMARY.—From the above it would seem—

First.—That the Levites were selected in the place of the firstborn whom the Lord called his own.

Second.—That they were given to Aaron to assist him in the minor or lesser duties of the priesthood; but that Aaron and his sons officiated in the leading offices of the priesthood, and not the Levites.

Third.—That there was a tithing paid to them by the whole house of Israel for their sustenance.

Fourth.—That they paid a tithe of this to Aaron.

Fifth.—That on assuming the higher duties of the priesthood of Aaron, the judgments of God overtook them.

Sixth.—That their priesthood was only an appendage to the Aaronic priesthood, and not that priesthood itself as held by Aaron and his sons.—*IP*, 43.

# WORK OF THE LESSER PRIESTHOOD

WARD TEACHING.—Much depends in these days of trial upon those who bear the lesser priesthood. They have opportunities which are of unequaled advantage. They visit or should visit the people at their homes. They talk to them by their firesides. They can see their inner lives, and learn where they need strengthening and guiding in order to be more efficient Latter-day Saints. When priests and teachers understand their duties and seek to enjoy the spirit of their offices, they can do an immense amount of good; for they are brought directly into contact with the people. They learn their wants, are made familiar with their weaknesses, and are in a position to check the growth of evil tendencies in parents and in children.

There is, in many instances, doubtless, too much formality in the character of these visits—a disposition to drop into routine and to ask stereotyped questions, without conversing in a way to bring out the real feelings and spirit of the households which they visit. Visits of this character are comparatively barren of results. To make them as productive of good as they should be, live, active men should be used as priests and teachers. The best ability in the various wards can find ample field for usefulness in performing these duties. Young men who have not had experience should be associated with those who have had experience, and they should be impressed with the importance of seeking for the Spirit of God to rest upon them in power, to dictate to them the very things that should be said to the family which they visit. The teachings which might be appropriate to one family would not perhaps be so suitable for another family. Therefore, the necessity of having the guidance of the Spirit of God is apparent.—*Epistle of The First Presidency,* April 8, 1887; *JH,* April 8, 1887, p. 2; *DN,* April 8, 1887.

THE DUTY OF THE TEACHER AND PRIEST.—The organization of the church is after the plan that exists in heaven and according to the principles that God has revealed in the interest of his church upon the earth and for the advancement and rolling forth of his kingdom. We start in with the teacher and with the priest, whose duty it is to know the position of all the members in their several districts. If they do their duty they will know really and truly the position of all those who come under their charge. Their duty is very simple. What is it? They are to see that there is no hard feeling existing in the breasts of the saints one towards another; that there are no dishonest or fraudulent acts, no lasciviousness or corruption, no lying, false accusations, profanity, or drunkenness; and that the people call upon God in prayer in their various households—the father and mother and children, and that all perform their various duties and do right.

I look upon it that the teachers and the priests occupy a very important position in the church and kingdom of God. . . . For it is their right and privilege to look after these things, and not only their right and privilege but their duty. And if they do not fulfil this, they are not magnifying their calling and priesthood. But if they are and people are disposed to listen to them, then everything will be right in regard to this matter. And if there are those who are not disposed to listen to them and to do right, then it becomes the duty of the teachers, after pleading with them and doing the best they can, to report them to their bishop. Then it devolves upon him to do his part, not in anger or animosity or in the spirit of vindictiveness, but as a savior, and the teacher and the priest ought to act in the same way. And while God has organized his church upon the earth after the plan that exists in the heavens, it is for the various officers in the church to fulfil the duties devolving upon them, acting in all kindness, long-suffering, and mercy before the Lord, yet with justice and judgment that the law of God may be honored, that the principles of righteousness may be exalted, that the workers of iniquity may be ashamed, that the meek may increase their joy in the Lord, and the poor among men may rejoice in the Holy One of Israel; that righteousness and truth may prevail among the people of God; and we may act not in name only, but in reality as the saints of God, without rebuke, in the midst of a crooked and perverse generation.

APPEALS.—If any persons then should feel that they are aggrieved by the acts of the teacher or the bishop, if they should think that they have been unnecessarily harshly dealt with, they have the right of appeal to the high council—high priests selected from among the people and set apart because of their fidelity, their integrity, their honor, and their justice—at least these are the kinds of qualifications necessary to fill this calling. And if upon an appeal to the high council on any of these matters (of course, including drunkenness), they find there has been unnecessary harshness, it would be for them to remedy the evil, to see that justice is done, and that no man is oppressed; on the contrary that all have their rights, freedom, liberty, and equal justice in righteousness without fear or favor.—JD, 23:216-218, August 6, 1882.

PRIESTS.—What is the duty of the priests? Only to hold office? No; it is to visit the members of the various wards, and to see that there are no hard feelings, troubles, or difficulty among the people, to anticipate the occurrence of anything of that sort, put things right, and see that the ordinances of the church are carried out.—JD, 19:142, October 14, 1877.

TEACHERS.—Then the teachers, who are helps to the priests, whose duty it is to go among the people and talk to them on their duties—not like so many parrots, but full of the Spirit of God. And where there may be difficulties to settle, and it is not within the power of the teachers to satisfactorily adjust them, report them to the bishop, who sits as a common judge in Israel, and to adjudicate all such matters. If thy brother offend thee, go and say to him, "Brother, you have done so and so," and if he will not listen to you nor ask forgiveness for the offense he has given you, take another man with you—one who you think has influence with him, and one whom you think he will listen to—and let him talk. And if the offending person will not listen to him, report him, to be dealt with according to the order of the church. And if he continues obdurate and stubborn, then he does not belong to us. Let us always feel like operating together for the good of each other and for the kingdom we are identified with.—*JD*, 19:142, October 7, 1877.

Some of us think that our teachers are of very little importance. I will tell you how I regard them. If the teachers do not come to visit me as often as I think they should, I do not like it very well. When they do come, I acquaint my family with it, call them together, and then tell our visitors that we are all under their jurisdiction, ready and anxious to hear from them the words of eternal life. That is how I feel towards the teachers, and in the same manner I respect all the priesthood in the various positions they occupy. Shall I assume to dictate to those who are above me? No, never. Will you? That is for you to say, not for me.— *JD*, 18:285, November 5, 1876.

# CHAPTER XVI

# PRIESTHOOD AND THE GOVERNMENT OF THE CHURCH

## THE PURPOSE AND ORGANIZATION

TO BUILD THE CHURCH AND THE KINGDOM OF GOD.— The Lord has given us a certain work to accomplish; and the feelings or ideas of men in the world in relation to this work have but little to do with us. We are gathered here for the express purpose of building up the church and kingdom of God upon the earth.—*JD*, 21:373, October 7, 1879.

THE NECESSITY OF ORGANIZATION.—It would be found very difficult for any individual left to himself to do right, to think right, to speak right, and to fulfil the will and law of God upon the earth; and hence the necessity of the organization of the church and kingdom of God upon the earth, of the properly-organized priesthood, of the legitimate channel, check, bounds, laws, and governments that the Almighty has introduced into his church and kingdom for the guidance, instruction, protection, welfare, up-building, and further progress of his church and kingdom upon the earth. As in a school it requires a man more competent to be a teacher than those who are taught, so in the church of God; and hence the various grades and positions of the priest-hood. When a president, bishop, or those having authority live up to their religion and cleave unto God, it is expected by us at all times that they will comprehend things under their immediate jurisdiction—things that they control; know the wants of the people and the best course for them to pursue, better than the individuals they teach; and this extends throughout all the various ramifications of the church of God, from the First Presidency down. And indeed, between the First Presidency and the Lord of Hosts there is a regularly organized channel through which the blessings of his kingdom flow unto his Saints when they are found in obedience to his laws.—*JD*, 6:107, December 6, 1857.

THE TWO PRIESTHOODS AND CHURCH GOVERNMENT.— God has ordained two priesthoods upon the earth—the Melchi-zedek and the Aaronic. The Melchizedek presides more especially over the spiritual affairs of the church, and has done in all ages when it has existed upon the earth. You will find this provided for in the Doctrine and Covenants. . . . The Aaronic priesthood is presided over by the presiding bishop. If we had a literal descendant of Aaron, he would have a right to preside over the bishopric, and to operate and manage and direct these things without the aid of counselors. In the absence of such men, the Lord has directed us to take men from the high priesthood and set them apart to be bishops to administer in temporal things. This Aaronic priesthood is an appendage to the Melchizedek priesthood, and its province is to administer in temporal affairs. One reason why we want men of this class to administer in temporal things is because there is a special provision made for it. Nevertheless a high priest that is after the order of Melchizedek may be set apart to administer in temporal things, *having a knowledge of them by the spirit of truth.* And before a man attempts to administer in Zion in temporal things, he ought to obtain a knowledge of that spirit of truth to administer according to the intelligence which that spirit of truth imparts. Thus we have the Aaronic priesthood in its place; the Melchizedek priesthood in its place. And in all the various functions it is necessary to enter into all the various organizations. It is on one or two particular points that I wish to speak now.

THE PRINCIPLE OF PRESIDENCY.—In the first place, the Lord requires certain things to be done to meet his approbation; and everything has to be done under the direction of the presidency of the twelve,[1] both temporal things and spiritual things. The bishops and the presidents of stakes and all the officers in the church of God are subject to this authority and they cannot get around it. And when any officer of this church who by virtue of his calling does things without counseling with the proper authorities of the church, he takes upon himself things that he has no right to do, and such a course cannot be acceptable before God and the priesthood.

ADMINISTRATION OF TEMPORAL AFFAIRS.—Now then, we come to the bishopric. Ought the bishops to be consulted in regard to temporal things? Yes, they ought. And as an example, let me tell you that for the last year Bishop Hunter has associated with the council of the twelve[1] whenever they have met to consider temporal matters. And I may say we have been pleased to have his company, because it was his place to understand the position of temporal things, that we may know his feelings, and counsel with him and he with us, that everything may be done according to the order and laws of God, that there may be perfect unanimity. With this view he was placed as one of the counselors to the trustee-

---

[1]At this time (1879) the council of the twelve was the presiding council of the church. What is said applies equally to the First Presidency when it exists.

in-trust—because the trustee-in-trust thought it belonged to him
to hold that position, and thinks so today. But then, does he
preside over the Melchizedek priesthood? No, he does not. Who
and what is he? A high priest ordained and set apart to the
bishopric. By whom? The presidency. Does he control the
presidency? No, he is set apart by them; as bishop he is an
appendage to the higher priesthood, and does not control it. No
man controls it. I remember a remark made on one occasion by
Joseph Smith, in speaking with Bishop Partridge. He was a
splendid good man, as Bishop Hunter is. But he got some crooked
ideas into his head; he thought he ought to manage some things
irrespective of Joseph, which caused Joseph to speak rather sharply
to him. Joseph said, I wish you to understand that I am president
of this church, and I am your president, and I preside over you
and all your affairs. Is that correct doctrine? Yes. It was true
then and it is true today.

RESPONSIBILITY OF INSTITUTIONS CLAIMING CHURCH
CONNECTION.—Well, it is necessary that we should have an
understanding of these things, that we may make no mistakes in
our administration. I want, then, in all our operations to confer
with our bishops. And if this institution of ours is "Zion's Cooperative," then it should be under the direction of Zion, under
the direction of the priesthood; and if it is not "Zion's" Cooperative, then it is a living lie. But do we wish to interfere
with them? No, we do not. Do we wish to interrupt them in
any of their operations? No, we want to help them; we want
to unite them and all the people into one, with God at our head,
governed by the holy priesthood. Have they rights? Yes. Do
we respect them? Yes. Have the people rights? Yes. Shall the
people be respected in their rights? Yes, they shall, all the people
in all the stakes; and while we sustain them they must sustain us;
and if they expect to have our support, they must give us theirs.—
*JD*, 21:35-36, April 9, 1879.

## AUTHORITY IN THE CHURCH

PRINCIPLES OF PRESIDENCY, APOSTLESHIP, QUORUMS, AND
COUNSELORSHIPS.—When Joseph Smith was living, he was the
president of all councils, and all authorities in the church; he
stood as prophet, seer, and revelator, and apostle; the chief apostle
of the Church of Jesus Christ of Latter-day Saints. He stood
before God as the representative of his church on the earth.
In his absence, the twelve being next in authority, stepped in; not
to deprive him of his place, which he still occupies in the heavens,
but to fulfil their office and calling, and the relationship which

they sustain to the church; but why did not his counselors occupy his place? Because they were not ordained to that authority, and they, therefore, could not act in it, no more than the king's cabinet could reign over the nation after the king's death. On the demise of a king it is necessary that another should be crowned in his stead, and this must be the rightful heir. It is not enough that he is his companion or counselor.

And here let me remark that there is a material difference between a counselor and a president. There are some quorums in the church wherein so much difference does not exist, as the high council and the twelve, and, with some few exceptions the seventies, high priests, elders, teachers, and deacons; but the bishops have their counselors, so had Joseph, and so have some of those others. The high council, however, and twelve, have not, further than the whole quorums are counselors to each other and to their president. And in relation to the twelve, their president became such, not on account of election or choice, but because of seniority, or age, hence when Thomas B. Marsh was in good standing he was the oldest, and consequently the presiding officer; but when he apostatized the next oldest took it, which was President Brigham Young. He had the same priesthood before and the same authority, but was not the president or mouth-piece of the others, who are all presidents in all the world, *without other ordinations,*[1] and in this respect differ from the council of Joseph. The twelve standing next to Joseph, on his death the charge of the church necessarily fell upon them, and President Young being their president, of course presided, and became the mouth-piece and president, not only of the twelve but of the church.—*MS,* 9:324, 1847.

"FOR THE PERFECTING OF THE SAINTS."—The Lord has placed in his church apostles and prophets, high priests, seventies, elders, etc. What for? For the perfecting of the Saints. Are we all perfect to begin with? No. These various officers are for perfecting of the Saints. What else? For the work of the ministry, that men might be qualified and informed and be full of intelli-gence, wisdom, and light, and learn to proclaim the principles of eternal truth and to bring out from the treasury of God things new and old, things calculated to promote the welfare of the people. Now, then, these offices having been placed in the church, every man ought to be respected in his office. I know some of you think we can respect some, and some we cannot respect; we can respect some of the prominent authorities—I do not know

---

[1]Italics added by the compiler. It should also be observed that in the church, the law of common consent is equally binding with that of ordination, in ascending to new responsibility or authority.

who they are, do you? You remember when Jesus was upon the earth, some of his followers were contending as to who was the greatest: and he took a little child and placed it in their midst, and said, he that can be most like this little child, is the greatest in the kingdom of heaven. And I will tell you more than that, that the teacher or deacon who fulfils his duties is a great deal more honorable than a president or any of the twelve who does not. And there are duties and responsibilities devolving on all of us pertaining to these matters; and we ought to be very careful in all our acts that we do not transgress the laws of God.—*JD*, 21:209, March 1, 1880.

A PRINCIPLE OF CHURCH GOVERNMENT.—Brother Joseph F. Smith spoke rightly this morning when he said, that no man could guide this kingdom. He cannot unless God be with him and on the side of the elders of Israel. But with him on their side, all things will move on aright, and the intelligence and the revelations of God will be poured out. His law will be made known and the principles of truth be developed; or it is not the kingdom of God. And we all of us ought to humble ourselves before God, and seek for the guidance of the Almighty.

THE FORCES THAT UNDERMINE ALL GOVERNMENT.— There are forces at work in the world that will in time overturn the world, which are today sapping the foundation of all governments and eating as a canker the foundation of all rule and dominion; and by and by their thrones will be cast down and nations and empires will be overturned, for God will arise to purge the world from its iniquities, its evils, and corruptions. And we have more or less of the principles of insubordination among us. But there is a principle associated with the kingdom of God that recognizes God in all things, and that recognizes the priesthood in all things, and those who do not do it had better repent or they will come to a stand very quickly; I tell you that in the name of the Lord. Do not think you are wise and that you can manage and manipulate the priesthood, for you cannot do it. God must manage, regulate, dictate, and stand at the head, and every man in his place. The ark of God does not need steadying, especially by incompetent men without revelation and without knowledge of the kingdom of God and its laws. It is a great work that we are engaged in, and it is for us to prepare ourselves for the labor before us, and to acknowledge God, his authority, his law and his priesthood in all things.

THE ORDER OF THE KINGDOM.—I have men come to me sometimes with some great complaints to make about their bishop. I hear them, but I either send them back to their bishop or to their president (of their stake) as circumstances dictate. Then I have bishops come to me finding fault with their presidents. I send them back to their presidents, and write to those whose business it is to attend to it. I acknowledge every man in his place and office, whether president, bishop, priest, teacher or deacon; and then they should acknowledge everybody over them . . . in the name of the Lord. I know what I am saying. I tell you it is the word and the will of the Lord. Do not be wise above what is written. Do not be too anxious to be too smart, to manage, and manipulate, and to put things right; but pray for those that God has placed in the different offices of this church that they may be enabled to perform their several duties. The Lord will sustain his servants and give them his Holy Spirit and the light of revelation, if they seek him in the way that he has appointed, and he will lead them and lead you in the right path. This is the order of the kingdom of God, as I understand it, and not the other. And it is for us to learn that order and be obedient to it.— *JD*, 23:220-221, August 6, 1882.

This is an order, as I understand it, that is introduced by the Almighty, and by him alone. It is not of man, nor did it proceed from man, neither can it progress nor be perfected by man without the direction of the Almighty. In fact, with all these helps, with all these organizations, with all these principles, owing to the weakness and infirmities of man, we find it difficult to preserve in purity those sacred institutions that God has given unto us, and we continually need the greatest care, humility, self-denial, perseverance, watchfulness, and reliance upon God.— *JD*, 22:7, January 9, 1881.

## SOME PROBLEMS OF GENERAL CHURCH ADMINISTRATION

FUNCTIONS OF A GENERAL CONFERENCE.—We are met here in a conference capacity, and have assembled ostensibly, and in reality, to confer together about the general interests of the church and kingdom of God upon the earth. The authorities from the distant settlements are here to represent themselves and their people, and a great many are here from the surrounding settlements to listen to the teachings that may be given, to the business that may be transacted, to the doctrines that may be promulgated, and in general to make themselves acquainted with the spirit of the times, with the obligations that devolve upon them; and the various responsibilities that rest upon all parties.

We meet, then, as I have said, to consult on the general

interests of the Church and kingdom of God upon the earth, and not upon our own peculiar ideas and notions, to carry out any particular favorite theme or to establish any special dogma of our own devising. Nor do we meet here to combine against men, but to seek, by all reasonable and proper means, through the interposition and guidance of the Almighty, and under the influence of his Holy Spirit, to adopt such means and to carry out such measures as will most conduce to our individual happiness, the happiness of the community with which we are associated, to the establishment of correct principles, to the building up of our faith, and strengthening us in the principles of eternal truth, to our advancement and progress in the ways of life and salvation, and to devise such measures and carry out such plans as will best accord with the position and relationship we occupy to God, to the world we live in, and to each other.—*JD*, 14:245, October 8, 1871.

THE SCOPE OF A GENERAL CONFERENCE.—The object of our meeting is not altogether for religious purposes, but to consult upon all matters for the interest of the church and kingdom of God upon the earth. On these occasions it is quite common for missionaries to be appointed to the different nations of the earth, and it is also usual to discuss the principles and doctrines that we believe in, and to attend to any business that may have to be presented from the different parts of this territory, and from all parts of the earth; and we try to build up the people in their most holy faith. We meet also to consult upon the best course for us to pursue with regard to temporal things as well as spiritual things; for as we possess bodies as well as spirits, and have to live by eating, drinking, and wearing, it becomes necessary that temporal matters should be considered and discussed in our conferences, and that we should deliberate upon all things that are calculated to benefit, bless, and exalt the Saints of God, whether they refer to our spiritual affairs or to our avocations and duties in life as husbands and wives, as parents and children, as masters and servants; whether they refer to the policy we should pursue in our commercial relations, to protecting ourselves against the incursions of savages, or to any other matter affecting us as human beings composing part of the body politic of this nation or as citizens of the world. The idea of strictly religious feelings with us, and nothing else, is out of the question; yet we do everything in the fear of God. Our religion is more comprehensive than that of the world; it does not prompt its votaries with the desire to "sit and sing themselves away to everlasting bliss," but it embraces all the interests of humanity in every conceivable phase, and every truth in the world comes within its scope.—*JD*, 11:353-354, April 6, 1867.

ADVICE ON CHURCH VOTING.—We have got through presenting the various quorums comprising the authorities of the Church of Jesus Christ of Latter-day Saints. . . . and I believe there has been a unanimous feeling to sustain all those officers presented in their respective positions. . . . If there are those among us that feel a little crossways, thinking that some other way might be better; yet there is so much of the feeling to the contrary that the opposition is readily brought to acquiesce in the popular vote, whether the opposers really feel so or not. But they generally feel like it. Still there is a lesson that we have been learning that none of us is perfect in. Our judgment is not perfect and as we are not perfect in our sphere, we need not expect to find others perfect in theirs. And as we are not perfect ourselves, we may have need to come to the throne of mercy and ask for wisdom and support, and we can come to the Lord with faith and full assurance. If we have need to come to the Lord, so have you. Be careful, then, how you judge. We can say to all, with what judgment ye judge, ye shall be judged; and with what measure ye mete, it shall be measured to you again.—*JD*, 9:8-9, April 6, 1861.

THE METHOD OF VOTING FOR PRESIDENT OF THE CHURCH.—It is gratifying to me, and it is no doubt satisfactory to you, to see the unanimity and oneness of feeling and the united sentiment which have been manifested in our votes. Those votes being taken first in their quorum capacity, each quorum having voted affirmatively, then by the vote of the presidents of the several quorums united, and afterwards by the vote of the quorums and people combined, men and women, among the many thousands assembled who have participated in this vote, having a full and free opportunity, uncontrolled by any influence other than the Spirit of God, to express their wishes and desires, there has not been, from all that we could discover, one dissenting vote. . . .

We have had an example here today of the unanimity which characterizes those possessed of the spirit of the gospel, and it ought to be a pattern for us in all of our affairs.—*JD*, 22:40, October 10, 1880.

PRINCIPLES UNDERLYING CONFIDENCE IN CHURCH LEADERSHIP.—Why have this people confidence in President Young and others? Because they have seen them leave their homes and go forth and endure every privation to promote their welfare in time and in eternity. . . .

Furthermore, this people have confidence in their leaders, because in times of trouble and trial they have stemmed the torrents and been foremost in the battle. It is not a kind of soft, smooth eloquence to tickle the ears of men, but it is stern matters of fact that the people know.—*JD*, 5:247, September 13, 1857.

## LOCAL CHURCH GOVERNMENT

JURISDICTIONAL SPHERES.—When we have a stake organization, . . . the presidency of the stake presides over all bishops,
high councils, and all authorities of the stake. The several bishops
preside over their respective wards and manage their affairs, under
the direction of the stake presidency, who in their office and
calling are responsible to the First Presidency of the church. The
bishops are also under the direction of presiding Bishop Hunter
in all affairs connected with the temporal interests of the church.
And Bishop Hunter is under the direction of the First Presidency,
the Aaronic priesthood being an appendage to the Melchizedek
priesthood. It is however, the special duty of the Aaronic priesthood to attend to temporal matters; but then the First Presidency
presides over all bishops, all presidents, all authorities, and lastly
God presides over all.

Now we are sometimes fond, that is, some of us are, of
talking about our authority. It is a thing I care very little about.
I tell you what I want to do if I can: I want to know the will
of God so that I may do it; and I do not want to dictate or
domineer or exercise arbitrary control. Then again, all men ought
to be under proper control to the presidency and priesthood presiding over them. If I were a bishop, I should want to know what
the president of my stake desired, and I should confer with him.
—*JD*, 21:365, August 8, 1880.

THE RESPONSIBILITY OF ADMINISTRATIVE OFFICERS.—
To you, brethren, who, as presidents of stakes, high councilors and
bishops, hold in your keeping the purity of the lives of the members of the Church, we again repeat the warnings and admonitions
of our former epistles and say, upon you lies the responsibility
of the keeping of God's house in order, each according to his
calling, ordination, and appointment, and to the extent and scope
of the duties imposed upon him. In these duties you cannot be
negligent without incurring the displeasure of the Lord and losing
his spirit. The Lord holds each man responsible for that portion
of his flock which is placed in his care.—*JH*, March 31, 1886,
p. 11; Salt Lake Herald, April 7, 1886.

PRESIDENTS OF STAKES.—The presidents of stakes have
important positions. They preside over all the interests of the
church where they are placed, and they should feel like acting for
God, and they and their counsel should have continually with
them the light of revelation, be full of the Holy Ghost, and quick
to discern. There is no officer in the church who acts with a
single eye to the glory of God but what will have wisdom given
him according to his capacity. The president of the stake presides

over the high council, a set of men appointed and ordained to adjudicate all matters in dispute that may come before them, and they should act in all meekness, humility, and wisdom, seeking intelligence from the Foundation of Light, so that they can act in righteousness and give righteous judgment.—*JD*, 19:141-142, October 14, 1877.

RESPONSIBILITY OF STAKE PRESIDENTS AND OTHERS.— It is expected that these presidents of stakes be full of the Holy Ghost and the power of God, that they feel and realize that they are the servants of Jehovah, engaged in his work, and that he will require at their hands an account of their stewardships. It is necessary also that the high councils and the bishops act in the same way, together with the high priests, seventies, elders, and all those of the Aaronic priesthood, and that all operate together in the fear of God, for his eye is over you, and he expects you to work righteousness, and purge the church from iniquity, and teach the people correct principles and lead them in the paths of life. This is what God requires at your hands.—*JD*, 19:125, October 7, 1877.

SELECTION OF BRANCH PRESIDENTS.—It is not always wisdom to appoint the highest [priesthood] officer in a branch to preside. It frequently happens that a priest or teacher is more competent to preside over a branch than an elder; and it is the privilege of the president of the conference to appoint such to preside, with the consent of the church, according to the regulations of the Doctrine and Covenants; and, if he is a man full of the Holy Ghost, he will be able to select such as are most competent.—*MS*, 9:325, November 1, 1847.

POPULAR GOVERNMENT: PURPOSE OF STAKE CONFERENCES.—We convene in conference in the various stakes that everything pertaining to the interests of the stakes may be considered in those conferences, and that all matters may be properly represented, and all the saints have the privilege of voting for or against those officers who are presented to the conference for their acceptance. It is also usual to vote for the officers of wards in the wards over which they preside, such as bishops and their counselors, with all the lesser priesthood, so that there may be perfect unanimity in all our acts. Because the church of God is based upon the principle of perfect freedom of action. . . . It is proper that all of these authorities should be presented from time to time before the people, that all the people everywhere, not only in a stake, but in all the stakes, as well as at the general conference, may have the opportunity if they know of anything wrong, anything immoral or unrighteous associated with the acts of any of the leading authorities of the church, of speaking of it, that everything and everybody may be properly presented and that the conduct of all men may be intelligently scrutinized; for, if we cannot bear the scrutiny of our brethren upon earth, how shall we be able to meet the scrutiny and investigations of our Heavenly Father when we shall stand before him. And if there is anything immoral or unrighteous, of any kind, it is proper and expedient that it be righted; and this applies quite as much to the presidency, the twelve, and the leading authorities as to any other individual in the church, in order that everything may be presented in its proper form, and everybody have a full opportunity of offering his ideas and views in regard to these matters.—*JD*, 24:32-33, January 21, 1883.

## THE RESPONSIBILITY OF CHURCH LEADERS

A LESSON FROM TEMPLE WORK.—This temple . . . is a place where, among other things, eternal covenants and obligations are entered into, and the question is, how and in what manner shall they be performed, and who are worthy and who are unworthy? There are some things that we find it exceedingly difficult to decide upon. Why? Because the parties that are dead are not here to speak for themselves, and we cannot have them misrepresented or robbed of their rights in any shape. But if they have violated the laws of God, what then? Now, here comes a question to which I desire to draw attention. There are many men who ought to have been cut off the church. But they have not been; the bishops have been negligent, the teachers have been negligent, and perhaps the president of the stake has been negligent. I am speaking in general terms. I speak of it to draw the attention of presidents of stakes, bishops, elders, priests, teachers and deacons, and those who officiate in the church of God, and all men who are set to watch over the fold of Christ. If some of these men, that I have referred to, had been brought up on certain occasions, they might have repented of their sins and placed themselves right. But because these officers did not do their duty themselves, and did not see that other men did theirs, things have passed along out of order, and the parties in question have gone behind the veil. What account can we give of ourselves if we are found thus negligent? If people do wrong, let them be brought up, and let the teachers, priests, and bishops clear their garments of them, and feel that they have done their duty, and purified the church so far as they could.

The presidents of stakes should see that these things are carried out according to the laws of God. This is a standard we must attain to, so that when people say, can we go into the temple of the Lord? we may know exactly their status, what position they occupy, and what to do with them, without having to take up the records of the dead. These are responsibilities devolving upon us.

RESPONSIBILITY FOR THE LIVING.—Our elders go abroad to preach the gospel and to gather in the people. When they are thus gathered, the presidents of stakes, the bishops, priests, teachers, and deacons are expected to watch over them, and see that they are fulfilling their obligations, or that they are not fulfilling them. If they fail to do their duty, let them be brought to account; let them be dealt with according to the laws of God. If they repent, forgive them; but it is expected that all who have taken upon them the name of Christ will obey the laws of God, and walk in obedience to his commands. These are some things that we all of us have to be responsible for, and therefore I, occupying the position that I do, feel it my duty to lay these things before you and to require them at your hands—that is at the hands of the president of the stake and his counselors, at the hands of the bishops and their counselors, at the hands of the high council, and at the hands of the priests, teachers, and deacons; for I don't want to carry myself the sins of the people. God expects us to purge ourselves from iniquity, that we may become the chosen of the Lord, and our offspring with us, not in name or in theory, but in deed and in truth, and according to the laws of life, and the spirit that dwells in Jesus Christ, our Savior, which every one of us ought to have dwelling in us and dwelling and abiding in our habitations, that we may feel that we are devoted to our God, blameless before the Lord, and keeping his commandments.— *JD*, 25:164-165, June 15, 1884.

RINGS AND CLIQUES IN CHURCH GOVERNMENT.—But there are those in our midst, who, although they have a name and a standing in the church, disregard the authority of the priesthood, both local and general. I hear sometimes of parties, and of cliques, and of rings in our midst. What! a party in the church and kingdom of God? What! rings associated with the principles of eternal truth—associated with the celestial law that emanates from our Heavenly Father? The devil got up a ring and was cast out of heaven for getting it up, as also a third part of the spirits who associated themselves with him. They were cast out because they devised principles that were in opposition to the word and will and law of God, and every man who follows in their footsteps, unless he speedily repent, will be placed in the same position —will also be cast out. The law of God must be put in force against the transgressor. No man who professes to be a Latter-day

Saint can transgress with impunity. The priesthood of God cannot be disregarded with impunity. . . .

ALL TO BE GOVERNED BY THE LAW OF GOD.—If I violate any law of the Church, bring me up for it. If any one else does, bring him up for it. But don't go sneaking around back-biting and misrepresenting. Let us act as men, at least, if we won't be saints. But we should be true to our calling and profession and honor our God.

THE WORK DURING THE MILLENNIUM.—There is nothing new in all this. The spirit of rebellion has gone on ever since the devil and his angels were cast out of heaven. He and they have been making war against the saints, and will continue to do so; but Satan will finally be overcome. Before that, however, Satan will be bound for a thousand years, and during that time we will have a chance to build temples and to be baptized for the dead, and to do a work pertaining to the world that has been, as well as to the world that now is, and to operate under the direction of the Almighty in bringing to pass those designs which he contemplated from the foundation of the world.—*JD*, 24:233-235.

No "WHITEWASHING"—JUST PLAIN TALK.—Brethren and sisters, God bless you and lead you in the paths of life. Do I talk plainly? God expects me to talk plainly. I have not come here to daub you with untempered mortar, but I tell you the truth. And while he has called us to high privileges, to thrones and principalities and dominions, and to be saviors on Mount Zion, and to be kings and priests unto God, and our wives, queens and priestesses unto their husbands, while God has ordained us for this, in the name of Israel's God we will try and carry it out.—*JD*, 22:311, August 28, 1881.

RESPONSIBILITY IN SUSTAINING AUTHORITY.—We have been voting for our officers and for those holding places in the church and kingdom of God in this stake of Zion. And it is well for us sometimes to understand what we do in relation to these matters. We hold up our right hand when voting in token before God that we will sustain those for whom we vote. And if we cannot feel to sustain them, we ought not to hold up our hands, because to do this would be to act the part of hypocrites. And the question naturally arises, how far shall we sustain them? Or in other words, how far are we at liberty to depart from this covenant which we make before each other and before our God? For when we lift up our hands in this way, it is in token to God that we are sincere in what we do, and that we will sustain the parties we vote for. This is the way I look at these things. How far then should we sustain them, and how far should we not? This is a matter of serious importance to us. If we agree to do a thing and do not do it, we become covenant-breakers and violators of our obligations, which are, perhaps, as solemn and binding as anything we can enter into.

WHAT IT MEANS TO SUSTAIN.—We frequently pass by many of those important things which we have engaged to abide by, and sometimes begin to whisper by way of complaining or finding fault one with another after we have entered into solemn obligations that we will not do it. What is meant by sustaining a person? Do we understand it? It is a very simple thing to me, I do not know how it is with you. For instance, if a man be a teacher, and I vote that I will sustain him in his position, when he visits me in an official capacity I will welcome him and treat him with consideration, kindness, and respect. If I need counsel, I will ask it at his hand, and I will do everything I can to sustain him. That would be proper and a principle of righteousness. I would not say anything derogatory to his character. If that is not correct, I have it yet to learn. And then if anybody in my presence were to whisper something about him, disparaging to his reputation, I would say, look here! are you a Saint? Yes. Did you not hold up your hand to sustain him? Yes. Then why do you not do it? Now, I would call an action of that kind sustaining him. If any man makes an attack upon his reputation —for all men's reputations are of importance to them—I would defend him in some such way.

TO VOTE IS TO COVENANT.—When we vote for men in the solemn way in which we do, shall we abide by our covenants? or shall we violate them? If we violate them, we become covenant-breakers. We break our faith before God and our brethren, in regard to the acts of men whom we have covenanted to sustain.

WHEN THE AUTHORITY VIOLATES THE TRUST.—But supposing he should do something wrong, supposing he should be found lying or cheating, or defrauding somebody, or stealing or anything else, or even become impure in his habits? Would you still sustain him? It would be my duty then to talk with him as I would with anybody else, and tell him that I had understood that things were thus and so, and that under these circumstances I could not sustain him. If I found that I had been misinformed, I would withdraw the charge; but if not, it would then be my duty to see that justice was administered to him, that he was brought before the proper tribunal to answer for the things he had done; and in the absence of that I would have no business to talk about him.—*JD*, 21:207-208, March 1, 1880.

## THE CHURCH JUDICIAL SYSTEM

CHURCH LAW AND ORDER.—No man shall hold a standing in the church and kingdom of God, or preside in that church who will violate the laws of God, and seek to the ungodly, inasmuch as God has laws by which he expects us to be governed. . . . God has given us laws to regulate these matters and all our matters before our high councils, under the direction of inspired men who have been ordained to the holy priesthood to judge in matters brought before them. And when we turn to the ungodly, we sell ourselves to the devil, which we will not permit men to do, and maintain the fellowship of the saints and a standing in the church and kingdom of God.—*JD*, 22:311, August 28, 1881.

. . . Again we hear of fraudulent acts sometimes, and we permit them to be passed over. What are laws for? What are bishops' courts and high councils for? That when men transgress the laws of God, they shall be tried according to the laws of the church, and if found guilty, and are worthy of such action, they shall be cast out; that the pure and the righteous may be sustained, and the wicked and corrupt, the ungodly and impure, be dealt with according to the laws of God. This is necessary in order to maintain purity throughout the Church, and to cast off iniquity therefrom.—*JD*, 24:169-171, May 19, 1883.

THE BISHOPS' COURTS, THE COMMON COURTS.—Every bishop should be first ordained a high priest, and then set apart to the bishopric by the proper authority; and the bishop's counselors, if not already ordained to the high priesthood, should be, and then set apart to act in their capacity, as first and second counselors to the bishop. These three then form a quorum, and a court, and are qualified to sit in judgment upon all matters that may come before the bishop, as a common judge in Israel, which pertain to his ward. They are then properly authorized to act in this capacity, and they ought to be upheld and sustained in the position they occupy, and in all of their doings, inasmuch as they are characterized by righteousness and sound judgment, and, as the scriptures say, with humility and faith, and long-suffering and wisdom, and according to the principles laid down in the book of Doctrine and Covenants, which the Spirit of God would dictate to men occupying such a position.

THE HIGH COUNCILS.—And then if there is an appeal from this court, it goes to the high council which is also composed of high priests, set apart to this office by the First Presidency or the twelve, to be presided over by the presidency of the stake. For the lack of this more perfect organization all kind of confusion has prevailed among the brethren in many instances; all kinds of little differences are taken to the high council, which ought to be taken to the bishop's court. People sometimes quarrel about little things, very trivial affairs that do not represent more than ten or twenty dollars in monetary matters, and they are not satisfied unless the high council try such cases. And what is the result? Instead of having these little matters settled by the teachers or bishops in their own wards, they occupy the time of the fifteen men composing the council, besides their own and that of the witnesses, who generally number from five to fifteen. But these men work for nothing and board themselves, and therefore it costs the disputants nothing for the adjudication of their differences, whereas in such cases the high council would prefer to put their hands in their pockets and pay the amount in dispute rather than listen to their nonsense. And it would seem that some men are so inconsiderate, that they would impose upon them, because they are willing to give their time.

ARBITRATION AND PERSONAL RECONCILIATION.—Such cases should not come before the high council; they more properly belong to the lesser priesthood, to the priests and teachers and to the bishop's court. Such men do not realize their position before God and their brethren. If men have differences, they should try to settle them amicably among themselves. But if they cannot do this, let them take the first steps as directed in the church covenants, let them then come together as brethren having a claim upon the Spirit and power of God which would attend them if they lived their religion, and then, provided the priests and teachers did their duty and were filled with wisdom and the spirit of their office and calling, ninety-nine cases out of every hundred might be satisfactorily settled without either troubling the bishop's court or the high council.—*JD*, 19:53-54, June 17, 1877.

## THE WOMEN OF THE CHURCH

WORK OF THE WOMEN.—A great deal of credit is due to our sisters. God has provided them as helpmates to their husbands, and it is the duty of the latter to cherish and protect those whom God has given unto them, and show them how to make themselves happy. Teach them—our wives and daughters—the pure principles of the gospel that the daughters of Zion may be lovely and shine as the light and glory of the age in which we live. Sisters, put away from you the vanities and frivolities of the world, administer to the poor and the afflicted. The sisters know how to sympathize with and administer to those who are poor, afflicted, and downcast; and let the brethren help them in their kindly ministrations.—*JD*, 19:142, October 14, 1877.

I am glad there is a little spirit among our sisters, and that they dare say their souls are their own.—JD, 14:270, December 17, 1871.

THE RELIEF SOCIETY.—We have here our Relief Societies, and they have done a good work. And people are desirous to know something of these organizations. I was in Nauvoo at the time the Relief Society was organized by the Prophet Joseph Smith, and I was present on the occasion. At a late meeting of the society held in Salt Lake City I was present, and I read from a record called the Book of the Law of the Lord, the minutes of that meeting.

WOMEN CALLED TO LABOR, TO EXPOUND SCRIPTURES.— At that meeting the Prophet called Sister Emma to be an elect lady. That means that she was called to a certain work; and that was in fulfilment of a certain revelation concerning her. She was elected to preside over the Relief Society, and she was ordained to expound the scriptures. In compliance with Brother Joseph's request, Sister Whitney, wife of Bishop Newel K. Whitney, and Sister Cleveland, wife of Judge Cleveland, were selected to be her counselors.

WOMEN HOLD PRIESTHOOD IN CONNECTION WITH THEIR HUSBANDS.—Some of the sisters have thought that these sisters mentioned, were, in this ordination, ordained to the priesthood. And for the information of all interested in this subject, I will say, it is not the calling of these sisters to hold the priesthood, only in connection with their husbands, they being one with their husbands. Sister Emma was elected to expound the scriptures, and to preside over the Relief Society; then Sisters Whitney and Cleveland were ordained to the same office, and I think Sister Eliza R. Snow to be secretary. A short time ago I attended a meeting in Salt Lake City, where Sister Snow and Sister Whitney were set apart. I happened to be the only member of the twelve in town at the time, the other members of the quorum being unavoidably absent. I went to this meeting and set apart Sister Whitney and Sister Snow who were two of those I set apart some forty years ago, in Nauvoo. And after I had done so, they reminded me of the coincidence. At this meeting, however, Sister Snow was set apart to preside over the Relief Societies in the land of Zion, and Sister Whitney, her counselor, with Sister Zina D. Young, her other counselor. I speak of this for the information of the sisters, although I presume they may have read of it in their paper, The Exponent.

WORK OF THE RELIEF SOCIETIES.—With regard to those Societies, I will say, they have done a good work and are a great assistance to our bishops, as well as being peculiarly adapted to console, bless, and encourage those of their sisters who need their care, and also to visit the sick, as well as to counsel and instruct the younger women in the things pertaining to their calling as children and saints of the Most High. I am happy to say that we have a great many honorable and noble women engaged in these labors of love, and the Lord blesses them in their labors, and I bless them in the name of the Lord. And I say to our sisters, continue to be diligent and faithful in seeking the well-being and happiness of your sex, instruct and train your own daughters in the fear of God, and teach your sisters to do likewise, that we may be the blessed of the Lord and our offspring with us.—*JD,* 21:367-368, August 8, 1880.

## THE PROBLEM OF PROGRESS

THE SAINTS FORGET; THE WORK LAGS.—We do not all of us sufficiently comprehend the great blessings that God has conferred upon us. We forget, sometimes, that we are the Saints of God; we forget that we have dedicated ourselves to the Lord, with all that we have; and we forget our high calling and our future destiny. We forget, sometimes, that we are engaged, with many others, in establishing righteousness and planting the kingdom of God upon the earth; and we condescend to little meannesses, and become forgetful of the great and glorious calling to which we are called. Many of us give way to temptation; we falter and get into darkness, and lose the Spirit of the Lord. We forget that God and angels are looking upon us; we forget that the spirits of just men made perfect and our ancient fathers, who are looking forward for the establishment of the kingdom of God upon the earth, are gazing upon us, and that our acts are open to the inspection of all the authorized agencies of the invisible world.

And, forgetting these things sometimes, we act the part of fools, and the Spirit of God is grieved; it withdraws from us, and we are then left to grope our way in the dark. But if we could live our religion, fear God, be strictly honest, observe his laws and his statutes, and keep his commandments to do them, we should feel very different. We should feel comfortable and happy. Our spirits would be peaceful and buoyant. And from day to day, from week to week, and from year to year, our joys would increase.

OTHER CAUSES.—Other causes also operate to retard the Saints in their progress. Most of us have come out of and been mixed up with the world. We have been associated with, and have received our education and ideas in the midst of corruptions of

every kind, and we have sucked it in as with our mother's milk.
Even our religion has been corrupt, and our ideas of morality
have been wrong; our politics, law, and philosophy have all been
wrenched, twisted, and perverted; our customs, habits, and associations have been wrong; and all that we have come out from is
vanity, evil, corrupting, and damnable in its nature.

Is it surprising, then, that we should find it difficult to live
according to the light and intelligence that dwells in the bosom
of God and that is manifested partially unto us, his people? Is
it surprising that, surrounded as we have been, and wallowing
in corruption all the day long, that we should have partaken more
or less of these things, and that they should still cling to us?

PROPHECY AND POPULAR PREJUDICE.—When Joseph
Smith had anything from God to communicate to the children of
men or to the Church, what was it he had to fight against all
the day long? It was the prejudices of the people; and, in many
instances, he could not and dared not reveal the word of God to
the people, for fear they would rise up and reject it. How many
times has he faltered? It was not that he was particularly afraid;
but he had to look after the welfare and salvation of the people.

If the Prophet Joseph had revealed everything which the
Lord manifested to him, it would have proved the overthrow of
the people in many instances; hence, he had to treat them like
children, and feed them upon milk, and unfold principles gradually, just as they could receive them.

Was all this because it was so hard to comprehend correct
principles? No; it was because we were babes and children, and
could not understand.

How is it now, under the administration of President Young?
Much the same, in this respect. He has often found it very
difficult to make the people understand things as the Lord has
revealed them unto him.

We ourselves have not got rid of our evils. We have so
much professed righteousness and foolish tradition within us,
that we feel indignant many times at righteous principles, when
God reveals them. Have you not felt so, brethren and sisters?
I know you have, and you know you have.

What is the reason of this? It is because you do not understand celestial laws, nor the principles that govern intelligences
in the eternal worlds; it is because you do not understand what
is best calculated to elevate, ennoble, and exalt you both in this
world and in the world to come; and hence many falter and
stumble and fall by the way.—*JD*, 6:164-166, January 17, 1858.

We could progress a great deal faster, and could prosper a

thousand times more than we do if we would be one in carrying out the counsels given us by the Lord through his servants.—*JD,* 11:357, April 6, 1867.

Remember the race is not to the swift, nor the battle to the strong; but to those who trust in the Lord.—*TS,* 6:797, 1845.

# CHAPTER XVII

# SUCCESSION IN THE PRIESTHOOD[1]

## INFORMATION FOR THE "ELDERS OF ISRAEL"

THE PRINCIPLE OF SUCCESSION.—There are two or three things that I wish to speak about for the information of the elders of Israel. Since the death of President Young, of the first seven presidents of the seventies, the question has been asked who shall occupy his place. There are a number of men pretty well up in years who are associated with the first seven presidents over the seventies. Some have been of the opinion, as these men are aged, that it would be perhaps better to have some younger person appointed to fill the vacancy as presiding president over the seven presidents of seventies, occasioned by Brother Joseph Young's death. However, there seems to be an order in the priesthood pertaining to these matters that we cannot well ignore. It has been usual heretofore, in cases of this kind, both in regard to the quorum of the twelve and also in regard to high councils— not always, perhaps, carried out in regard to high councils, but acted upon in numerous instances—that is, that the members preside according to priority of ordination and seniority of age, and the two, I think, would probably go together. The twelve, when they were first organized, were directed to have the oldest man selected for their president, who was Thomas B. Marsh. There were similar arrangements made in many instances in regard to high councilors, and in such cases they were regulated, if my memory serves me aright, in the same way. This is my understanding of the order in the early history of the church. This has been the case in regard to the twelve, and there may be other circumstances that I may refer to connected with this order; but I wish to speak of this subject before I come to the other, in order that we may have a just and clear conception of the position we occupy in relation to these matters.

THE RELATIONSHIP BETWEEN THE TWELVE AND THE SEVENTY.—Joseph Young, Sen., who was known as President

---

[1] A discourse by President John Taylor, delivered at the priesthood meeting, held in the Salt Lake Assembly Hall, Friday evening, October 7, 1881. Reported by George F. Gibbs. The First Presidency had been reorganized after an apostolic interregnum of three years, and several problems had to be faced and solved. The entire discourse is reproduced, at the expense of some duplications, for its historic significance in resolving these problems. It is of importance to all members of the church and especially those holding the priesthood.

Joseph Young, occupied the position of president over the first seven presidents of the seventies . . . until his death. . . . A peculiar connection exists between the seventies and the twelve. The twelve are a traveling high council, whose business it is to preach the gospel, or to see it preached, in all the world; that is their special calling and appointment by revelation. The seventies also possess a mission of a similar nature. This mission is to preach the gospel to all the world. They are placed under the direction of the twelve, who are authorized to call upon them to go forth to the nations of the earth; thus their mission in this respect is similar to the mission of the twelve. The same responsibilities rest upon them in regard to these duties as those which rest upon the twelve, so far as their priesthood and calling go. The high priesthood, as you are aware, differs from the priesthood of the seventies in this respect—the high priests are expected to preside. It is a part of their office and calling to do that. Their organization in a quorum capacity is, as stated, an ordinance "instituted for the purpose of qualifying those who shall be appointed standing presidents or servants over different stakes scattered abroad." (D. and C., 124:134.) It is not the special business of the seventies to preside, but to preach the gospel, and we understand that it is their duty, whenever called upon, to go forth and fulfil missions under the directions of the twelve. And it is so far imperative upon them that the twelve are told first to call upon the seventies,[1] and, in the event of their not being prepared to perform this labor, then they may call upon others. But the seventies seem to be the especial helps, assistants, and fellow-laborers of the twelve. This being the case, if a rule of the kind that has been referred to in regard to age and priority of ordination exists among the twelve, the question would naturally arise: Would it not be quite as proper that the same principle should exist among the seventies, who possess a mission and calling so similar in its duties and responsibilities to that of the twelve? This seems to be reasonable, proper, and correct. There is a fitness about

---

[1]D. and C., see sec. 107, v. 38; sec. 124, v. 139, 140. (Footnote by President John Taylor) These passages are as follows: "It is the duty of the traveling high council to call upon the Seventy, when they need assistance, to fill the several calls for preaching and administering the gospel, instead of any others." D. & C. 107:38. "And again, I give unto you Joseph Young [etc.] . . . to preside over the quorum of Seventies;

"Which quorum is instituted for traveling elders to bear record of my name in all the world, wherever the traveling high council, mine apostles, shall send them to prepare a way before my face.

"The difference between this quorum and the quorum of elders is that the one is to travel continually, and the other is to preside over the churches from time to time; the one has the responsibility of presiding from time to time, and the other has no responsibility of presiding saith the Lord your God." D. & C. 124:138-140.

many of these things that it is well for us to comprehend. Joseph Young died awhile ago, that is, what we call death. But he lives; and where is he? He has gone behind the veil. Are there any other seventies gone behind the veil before him? I think there are a great many. Do they expect to hold their priesthood and position behind the veil? Yes, if they understand themselves they do, just as much as here. For if the priesthood is everlasting and administers in time and in eternity, then what has been sealed upon the earth by the proper authorities upon the heads of men is also sealed in the heavens. I so read it. And if it is sealed in the heavens, then Joseph Young would take his place in the heavens and operate in his calling and priesthood there, as he did here, and preside over the seventies who have been ordained in this dispensation in their administrations in the other world.

If we look at some statements made in the Doctrine and Covenants, we find these things very plainly set forth—that is, the same ideas; and they are principles that are understood by all intelligent elders of Israel. However, there is no harm to speak about them that we may all see eye to eye and comprehend alike.

THE PRINCIPLE OF SUCCESSION BASED ON ETERNITY OF THE PRIESTHOOD.—The Doctrine and Covenants, in referring to the twelve, mentions their names and that of their president. It then mentions the names of the presiding officers in the seventies. It mentions the names of the members of the high council that was then organized. And in speaking about David Patten, one of the twelve, it is written: "behold, his priesthood no man taketh from him; but, verily I say unto you, another may be appointed unto the same calling." (D. and C., 124:130.) But his being dead made no difference in regard to his priesthood. He held it just the same in the heavens as on the earth. There is another man mentioned. Referring to the high council, it is stated: "Seymour Brunson I have taken unto myself; no man taketh his priesthood, but another may be appointed unto the same priesthood in his stead." (D. and C., 124:132.) Then there is something said concerning Joseph Smith, Sen., the father of the Prophet Joseph Smith, of whom it is said that he sitteth with Abraham, at his right hand. (See D. and C., 124:19.) Who was Abraham? A patriarch. Who was Father Joseph Smith? A patriarch. It is quite fitting, therefore, that he should associate with Abraham, who was and is also a patriarch; and, perhaps, if we had the full details given, we should have an account of other patriarchs as well. But here is a place alluded to, where he went when he left this world.

I have now referred to men holding three different callings in the priesthood on the earth who are indicated as being provided for in their proper positions in the heavens. If the priesthood administers in time and in eternity, and if quorums of this kind are organized upon the earth, and this priesthood is not taken away, but continued with them in the heavens, we do not wish, I think, to break up the order of the priesthood upon the earth; and it would seem to be necessary that these principles of perpetuity or continuity should be held sacred among us. . . .

SUCCESSION AMONG THE SEVENTY.—Now, because some of these brethren of the first seven presidents of seventies are feeble, aged, or infirm, it is not for us to deprive them of their rights and privileges, and put some others in their places while they remain true and faithful and good members in the church. And, therefore, the proper way, as I understand it, would be to take the senior member of that quorum, that is, the senior president of the seven presidents of seventies, and allow him to preside. The senior president is Levi W. Hancock. Let these brethren then get together and consult over these things, the senior president taking his place among them, and whatever business they may have to transact associated with the seventies, they can all operate together, each performing in his own duties as directed by counsel, as when President Joseph Young was here, each retaining his proper standing, office, calling, and priesthood. I presume my counselors agree with me in that. [Presidents George Q. Cannon and Joseph F. Smith both answered, "Yes, sir."] The first presidency are agreed; and I presume the twelve would be. This seems to be the proper way, that all may be respected and honored in their office.

SUCCESSION IN THE TWELVE—SOME HISTORY.—Another subject that I wished to speak about is in regard to the twelve, and the changes that have taken place from time to time in the church since the organization of that quorum. I desire to show the reason for these changes, that we may understand things properly and intelligently.

As I stated, the twelve, when they were called, were placed on the same footing that I have referred to, and Thomas B. Marsh was the senior in that quorum. Hence he was appointed and he is spoken of in the revelations as their president.

At the time of his apostasy, there was another change made. David W. Patten would have been the next, had he lived, but he was killed in Missouri before Thomas B. Marsh apostatized. Had he lived, he would have been president of the twelve, instead of Brigham Young. But he died, and consequently Brigham Young, being the senior member of the twelve, was appointed in his place.

Now, in regard to the apostasy of Thomas B. Marsh, I will get Brother Reynolds to read in what his apostasy consisted. It was a horrible affair, as I look at it.

(The affidavit of Thomas B. Marsh was then read, as follows:)

### AFFIDAVIT OF THOMAS B. MARSH

They have among them a company, considered true Mormons, called the Danites, who have taken an oath to support the heads of the Church in all things that they say or do, whether right or wrong. Many, however, of this band are much dissatisfied with this oath, as being against moral and religious principles. On Saturday last, I am informed by the Mormons, that they had a meeting at Far West, at which they appointed a company of twelve, by the name of the Destruction Company, for the purpose of burning and destroying, and that if the people of Buncombe came to do mischief upon the people of Caldwell, and committed depredations upon the Mormons, they were to burn Buncombe; and if the people of Clay and Ray made any movement against them, this destroying company were to burn Liberty and Richmond.

The plan of said Smith, the Prophet, is to take this state; and he professes to his people to intend taking the United States, and ultimately the whole world. This is the belief of the Church, and my own opinion of the Prophet's plans and intentions. The Prophet inculcates the notion, and it is believed by every true Mormon that Smith's prophecies are superior to the laws of the land. I have heard the Prophet say that he would yet tread down his enemies, and walk over their dead bodies; that if he was not let alone, he would be a second Mohammed to this generation, and that he would make it one gore of blood from the Rocky Mountains to the Atlantic Ocean; that like Mohammed, whose motto in treating for peace was "the Alcoran or the Sword," so should it be eventually with us, "Joseph Smith or the Sword." These last statements were made during the last summer. The number of armed men at Adam-Ondi-Ahman was between three and four hundred.

Thomas B. Marsh

Sworn to and subscribed before me, the day herein written.

Henry Jacobs,
J. P., Ray County, Missouri.

Richmond, Missouri, October 24, 1838.

### AFFIDAVIT OF ORSON HYDE

The most of the statements in the foregoing disclosure I know to be true; the remainder I believe to be true.

Orson Hyde

Richmond, October 24, 1838.
Sworn to and subscribed before me, on the day above written.

Henry Jacobs, J. P.

Testimonies from these sources are not always reliable, and it is to be hoped, for the sake of the two brethren, that some things were added by our enemies that they did not assert, but enough was said to make this default and apostasy very terrible.

I will here state that I was in Far West at the time these affidavits were made, and was mixed up with all prominent church affairs. I was there when Thomas B. Marsh and Orson Hyde left there; and there are others present who were there at the same time. And I know that these things, referred to in the affidavits, are not true. I have heard a good deal about Danites, but I never heard of them among the Latter-day Saints. If there was such an organization, I never was made acquainted with it. The fact of a president of the twelve, who ought to be true to his trust, apostleship, and calling, and the guardian and protector of the people, making such statements, is truly infamous and is to be deplored by all correct feeling people. It is not unusual for lawyers to say, when speaking of any crime, that such a man, instigated by the devil, did so and so. Thomas B. Marsh was unquestionably "instigated by the devil" when he made this statement which has been read in your hearing. The consequence was, he was cut off the church. When he was cut off, he seemed to have lost all the spirit and power and manhood that he once enjoyed. I was acquainted with him before this. I was acquainted with him soon after I came into the church. With the Prophet Joseph Smith and Sidney Rigdon, he visited Upper Canada at the time I was presiding there, in the year 1837. I was with them for some time. I procured from a sister, a carriage, which was a very good one, and Brother Joseph Horne, who may be present, supplied the team, and, I think, acted as teamster. In it we visited the churches. I rode with them in the same carriage. They were with us for some time, visiting the various churches and holding meetings and conferences. Thomas B. Marsh many of you knew as he was here in the valleys, and some of you perhaps knew him at that time. At that earlier period, he was a pretty fair average man in regard to intelligence, speech, good, sound reason, etc. I have heard some people say he was a fool, but I did not so understand it. [Brother Woodruff said: "I did not, either."] Until the time of his apostasy, he was a fair average man in regard to intelligence. But when he took the steps he did, it was a shocking course for a man to pursue, occupying the position that he did. I remember a circumstance that occurred. A number of us had been out to a place called Di-Ahman. Its proper name was Adam-Ondi-Ahman. In coming into Far West, I heard about him and Orson Hyde having left. It would be here proper to state, however, that Orson Hyde had been sick with a violent fever for some time, and had not yet fully recovered therefrom, which, with the circumstances with which we were surrounded and the influence of Thomas B. Marsh, may be offered as a slight palliation for his default. Brother Heber C. Kimball and I were together, and I said to him: "I have a notion to take a team and follow after these brethren, and see if I cannot persuade them to come back," speaking particularly of Brother Marsh. "Well," said he, "if you knew him as well as I do, you would know that if he had made up his mind to go, you could not turn him." With that I gave up the idea, knowing that Brother

Kimball was better acquainted with him than I was, and I did not go. The result was that he did this deed. I am here reminded of the words of Joseph in exhorting the twelve. He said:

O ye Twelve, and all Saints, profit by this important key, that in all your trials, troubles, and temptations, afflictions, bonds, imprisonment and death, see to it that you do not betray heaven, that you do not betray Jesus Christ, that you do not betray your brethren, and that you do not betray the revelations of God, whether in the Bible, Book of Mormon, or Doctrine and Covenants, or any of the word of God. Yes, in all your kicking and floundering, see to it that you do not this thing, lest innocent blood be found on your skirts, and you go down to hell. We may ever know by this sign that there is danger of our being led to a fall and apostasy, when we give way to the devil so as to neglect the first known duty. But, whatever you do, do not betray your friends. (*History of Joseph Smith*, June 2, 1839.)

Thomas B. Marsh, of course, was cut off from the church for this, as he ought to be, and so was Orson Hyde. I will give you a little further history of Thomas B. Marsh. On my way, I think, from a mission in Europe—I do not now remember the time—I met him in Florence, Nebraska. He hunted me up, and he looked a broken-down man. He spoke to me and asked me about affairs in the mountains, and told me what a wretched position he was in, in consequence of the course he had taken, and said he: "I want to go out there, and I would like to have your opinion as to how the people will receive me." I replied: "In regard to that, I do not think the people will entertain any hard or harsh feelings about you; they realize your position as you realize it; they would feel disposed to treat you properly and kindly; but as regards your ever occupying the position you once held, that to me would be impossible." He answered: "I do not look for anything of that kind," and I do not know but what he said that he did not deserve anything of the kind. I don't remember, however. But he did say: "I want to have a place among the brethren there. I want to stand in the position of a private member, or anywhere that shall be allotted to me. I want to die there."

His circumstances were poor, and I relieved, in part, his present necessities. After his arrival here, I remember hearing him talk in the Fourteenth Ward meetinghouse. It seemed to me about the most foolish and ridiculous talk, devoid of common sense, common intelligence, and common manhood, that I had heard for a long time. Said I to myself: "There is a specimen of apostasy." I remember I was once driving north out of the city. I think it was rather cold. I saw a man tottering along, I thought he was hardly fit to be out in such weather, and when I drew near to him, I found it was Brother Marsh. I asked him to get into my carriage. He had started for Bountiful, but I do not think he could have reached there alone. He appeared to be so weak and feeble.

Perhaps you remember, in the Old Tabernacle, he got up when something was said in regard to apostasy, and said: "If any of you want to see the effects of apostasy, look upon me." You will perhaps remember that. [A number of voices in the congregation, "Yes, sir."] He lived in that way, and died in that way. He might have been at the head of the church, but he died in that miserable condition. I refer to this, because all of these things, when you reflect upon them, have a bearing upon our history, and on the propriety of the course that has been taken in these matters. Did the twelve feel bad towards him? No. I remember that on learning that he was in poor circumstances, they proposed to give him a new suit of clothes, and assist in relieving his wants. But President Young, hearing of it, desired to do it himself, and he supplied his necessities. These are some little reminiscences associated with him. It was real apostasy, and I wanted his affidavit read to show that it was apostasy, that there was nothing wrong or unjust in regard to the treatment that he received. After his apostasy, President Young, by reason of his seniority, necessarily took the position of president of the twelve.

When the twelve arrived in England, a meeting of the quorum was held in Preston. Brother Woodruff has an account of the whole concern. [Brother Woodruff—"Yes, sir."] And there was a vote taken by the twelve at that meeting, and the vote was unanimous, that Brigham Young should be accepted as the president of the twelve apostles. Afterwards, you will find, in a revelation given concerning the twelve, that President Young's name is mentioned as being president of the twelve. It is in that revelation given concerning the Nauvoo House, January 19th, 1841. His name is mentioned as being president of the twelve, and then follow the names of the other members then belonging to that quorum.

I will now go a little back and trace up some other things associated with this subject.

There was a time when there was a large amount of apostasy in Kirtland; it was in 1837, I think. There was a very bitter feeling gotten up by a number of men who had apostatized. Parley P. Pratt was one who was affected. He, however, did not go to the length that some did; and Orson Pratt had partaken more or less of that spirit. I speak of these things as facts. Parley mentions it himself in his own autobiography, which he published, or at least prepared for publication. And then he speaks about his bitter repentance and his reconciliation with Joseph Smith, when the thing was made right. He says:

> About this time, after I had returned from Canada, there were jarrings and discords in the Church at Kirtland, and many fell away and became enemies and apostates. There were also envyings, lyings, strifes, and divisions, which caused much

trouble and sorrow. By such spirits I was also accused, misrepresented, and abused. And at one time, I also was overcome by the same spirit in a great measure, and it seemed as if the very powers of darkness which war against the Saints were let loose upon me. But the Lord knew my faith, my zeal, my integrity of purpose, and he gave me the victory.

I went to Brother Joseph Smith in tears, and with a broken heart and contrite spirit, confessed wherein I had erred in spirit, murmured, or done or said amiss. He frankly forgave me, prayed for me, and blessed me. Thus by experience I learned more fully to discern and to contrast the two spirits, and to resist the one and cleave to the other. And being tempted in all points, even as others, I learned how to bear with and excuse and succor those who are tempted. (*Autobiography of Parley P. Pratt*, page 183.)

PRESIDENT TAYLOR'S CALL TO THE TWELVE.—But there were four of the twelve who did apostatize.—William E. McLellin, Luke Johnson, John F. Boynton, and Lyman Johnson. When they apostatized, the following revelation was given:

*Revelation given through Joseph Smith, the Prophet, at Far West, Missouri, July 8th, 1838, in response to the supplication: Show us thy will, O Lord, concerning the Twelve, etc.*

Verily, thus saith the Lord: Let a conference be held immediately; let the Twelve be organized; and let men be appointed to supply the place of those who are fallen.

Let my servant Thomas remain for a season in the land of Zion, to publish my word.

Let the residue continue to preach from that hour, and if they will do this in all lowliness of heart, in meekness and humility, and long-suffering, I, the Lord, give unto them a promise that I will provide for their families; and an effectual door shall be opened for them, from henceforth.

And next spring let them depart to go over the great waters, and there promulgate my gospel, the fulness thereof, and bear record of my name.

Let them take leave of my saints in the city Far West, on the twenty-sixth day of April next, on the building-spot of my house, saith the Lord.

Let my servant John Taylor, and also my servant John E. Page, and also my servant Wilford Woodruff, and also my servant Willard Richards, be appointed to fill the places of those who have fallen, and be officially notified of their appointment. (D & C. 118.)

I will state that I was living in Canada at the time, some three hundred miles distant from Kirtland. I was presiding over a number of churches in that region, in fact, over all of the churches in Upper Canada. I knew about this calling and appointment before it came, it having been revealed to me. But not knowing but that the devil had a finger in the matter, I did not say anything about it to anybody. [Brother Woodruff here spoke up and said that he was on the Fox Islands, which were farther away still; and also knew, by the Spirit, that he would be called to the apostleship.] A messenger came to me with a letter from the First Presidency, informing me of my appointment, and requesting me to repair forthwith to Kirtland, and from there to go to Far West. I went according to the command.

When I reached Far West, John E. Page, another one mentioned in the revelation just read to you, was there also. John E. Page and I were ordained into the quorum of the twelve at the same meeting. Brother Woodruff was ordained, after the scenes of the war at Far West; but I think it was right in the midst of the war when Brother Page and I were ordained. Brother Woodruff was ordained on the cornerstone of the foundation of the temple in Far West, on the 26th of April, 1839, when we went to fulfil this same revelation that you have heard read, and I helped to ordain him. Brother George A. Smith was ordained at the same time, and I am informed that he took the place of Thomas B. Marsh, who apostatized. I had not retained this fact in my memory, but I think it is correct. There were two other men ordained at the same time [to the office of seventy], one by the name of Darwin Chase, the other Norman Shearer. The former joined Conner's company and was in the fight on Bear River, where he was shot and shortly afterwards died at Camp Douglas. These are some reminiscences associated with this affair.

REORGANIZATIONS WITHIN THE TWELVE.—Now we come to some other events. When the twelve were reorganized, there were some changes made. For instance, in the case of John E. Page, it was not long before he apostatized. Willard Richards was ordained into the twelve at Preston in Lancashire, England, at the same time and place as President Young was voted for and accepted as president of the twelve. Through some inadvertence, or perhaps mixed up with the idea of seniority of age taking the precedence, Wilford Woodruff's name was placed on the records of the time, and for many years after, before that of John Taylor. This matter was investigated some time afterwards by President Young and his council, sanctioned also by the twelve, whether John Taylor held the precedence and stood in gradation prior to Brother Wilford Woodruff, and it was voted on and decided that his name be placed before Wilford Woodruff's, although Wilford Woodruff was the older man. The reason assigned for this change was that although both were called at the same time, John Taylor was ordained into the twelve prior to Wilford Woodruff; and another prominent reason would be that as John Taylor assisted in the ordination of Elder Wilford Woodruff, he therefore must precede him in the council.

Another question arose afterwards on this same subject: Orson Hyde and Orson Pratt had both of them been disfellowshipped and dropped from their quorum, and when they returned, without any particular investigation or arrangement, they took the position in the quorum which they had formerly occupied, and as there was no objection raised, or investigation had on this subject, things continued in this position for a number of years. Some ten or twelve years ago, Brother George A. Smith drew my attention to this matter. I think it was soon after he was appointed as counselor to the first presidency; and he asked me if I had noticed the impropriety of the arrangement. He stated at the same time that these brethren having been dropped from the quorum could not assume the position that they before had in the quorum; but that all those who remained in the quorum when they had left it must necessarily take the precedence of them in the quorum. He stated, at the same time, that these questions might become very serious ones, in case of change of circumstances arising from death or otherwise; remarking also, that I stood before them in the quorum. I told him that I was aware of that, and of the correctness of the position assumed by him, and had been for years, but that I did not choose to agitate or bring up a question of that kind. Furthermore, I stated that, personally, I cared nothing about the matter, and, moreover, I entertained a very high esteem for both the parties named; while, at the same time, I could not help but see, with him, that complications might hereafter arise, unless the matters were adjusted. Some time after, in Sanpete, in June, 1875, President Young brought up the subject of seniority, and stated that John Taylor was the man that stood next to him; and that where he was not, John Taylor presided. He also made the statement that Brother Hyde and Brother Pratt were not in their right positions in the quorum. Upon this statement, I assumed the position indicated.

Thus our positions at that time seemed to be fully defined; and what had been spoken of by Elder George A. Smith, without any action of mine, was carried out by President Young. I occupied the senior position in the quorum, and occupying that position, which was thoroughly understood by the quorum of the twelve, on the death of President Young, as the twelve assumed the presidency, and I was their president, it placed me in a position of president of the church, or, as expressed in our conference meeting: "As president of the quorum of the twelve apostles, as one of the twelve apostles, and of the presidency of the church of Jesus Christ of Latter-day Saints." In this manner, also, was President Brigham Young sustained, at the general conference held in Nauvoo, in the October following the martyrdom of the Prophet Joseph Smith. We find the following recorded in the minutes of that conference:

Elder W. W. Phelps moved that we uphold Brigham Young, the President of the Quorum of the Twelve, as one of the Twelve, and First Presidency of the Church.

Thus I stood in the same position that President Young did when called to occupy the same place at the death of the Prophet Joseph Smith.

It may be proper here to again say a few words with regard to Brother Orson Hyde, whose endorsement of the terrible charges made by Thomas B. Marsh, in his affidavit, has already been read. Suffice it to say, in addition to what has previously been

stated, he was cut off the church, and of course lost his apostleship; and when he subsequently returned, and made all the satisfaction that was within his power, he was forgiven by the
authorities and the people, and was again re-instated in the
quorum. But having been cut off from the quorum, and having
remained in that condition for some time, he of course lost his
former position as to seniority, and that necessarily placed me
in advance of him.

Orson Pratt also had some difficulties while we were in
Nauvoo, arising out of the introduction of the celestial order
of marriage. It seems, from remarks made in a conversation that
I had with him afterwards, that he did not fully realize or
comprehend the situation. But, at the time of the occurrence,
when I saw that he was very severely tried, as I had always held
pleasant relations with him, I took every pains that I possibly
could to explain the situation of things, to remove his doubts,
and to satisfy his feelings, but without avail. At one time I talked
with him for nearly two hours, to prevent, if possible, his apostasy
or departure from the church. But he was very sorely tried, and
was very self-willed and stubborn in his feelings, and would not
yield. His feelings were bitter towards the Prophet Joseph Smith
and others, and the result was that he was dropped from his
position in the quorum. But I am not aware of his ever having
written or published anything against the church. On the contrary, when Dr. John C. Bennett, who had apostatized, sent a
letter to Sidney Rigdon, wherein he denounced President Smith,
and stated that he was a villain and a scoundrel, and that a requisi-
tion would be made for him by the State of Missouri, and requested him to show this letter to Orson Pratt; although Sidney
Rigdon, who was the first counselor to Joseph, did not show
this statement unfolding this conspiracy to him [the Prophet],
yet, as soon as Sidney Rigdon handed the letter to Orson Pratt,
he immediately took it to the Prophet Joseph. And thus, while
Sidney Rigdon withheld this information from one to whom
he was in honor and duty bound, as his first counselor, to make
it known, yet Orson Pratt, although at the time disfellowshipped,
immediately made Joseph acquainted with the conspiracy that was
being plotted against him, and thus exhibited a manhood and
integrity that were so woefully deficient in Sidney Rigdon. In
reference to Brother Pratt's severance from the council of the twelve,
the following items from the life of President Young are in-
teresting:

August 8, 1842.—Assisted by Elders H. C. Kimball and George A. Smith, I spent
several days laboring with Elder Orson Pratt, whose mind became so darkened by the
influence and statements of his wife, that he came out in rebellion against Joseph,
refusing to believe his testimony or obey his counsel. He said he would believe his

wife in preference to the Prophet. Joseph told him if he did believe his wife and follow her suggestions, he would go to hell.

We reported to the Prophet that we had labored with Brother Orson diligently, in a spirit of meekness, forbearance, and long-suffering. He requested us to ordain Brother Amasa Lyman in Brother Orson's stead. After receiving these instructions, we met Brother Orson near my house, and continued to labor with him. He said to us: "There is Brother Amasa Lyman in your house, Brother Young; he has been long in the ministry: go in and ordain him in my stead."

August 20.—Brother Orson Pratt was cut off from the Church, and, according to the Prophet's direction, Brothers H. C. Kimball, George A. Smith, and I ordained Brother Amasa Lyman in his stead. (*History of Brigham Young.*)

Of Brother Pratt's integrity, indefatigable labors, purity of life, zeal for the cause of God, and untiring devotion in proclaiming the word of the Lord, I cannot speak in terms of too high praise or affectionate regard; and these other matters, painful though they be, are only mentioned now because they are necessary to make plain to your minds an important principle, and without these details you would not so readily nor fully understand my position, and the position of the twelve, at the present time.

Having said so much on these matters, I will talk a little on some other things.

We are told in the Doctrine and Covenants, that when the people are united, or the priesthood are united, and are moved upon by the Holy Ghost, their teachings "shall be scripture, shall be the will of the Lord, shall be the mind of the Lord, shall be the word of the Lord, shall be the voice of the Lord, and the power of God unto salvation." (D. and C. 68:4.) That is the case, and I have not seen greater unanimity than we have had, both in the selection of the twelve and in that of the First Presidency afterwards. And if the united voice of a few elders is the will of God, and the word of God, and the law of God, the question is, is not the voice of the whole Church the law of God and the will of God? I speak of this for your information, that you may comprehend the ground upon which you stand, speaking not of persons, but of the principle. Speaking of myself, who am I? Just like you. Who are you? Just like me—poor, feeble, weak, erring humanity. Can I do anything without the aid of the Almighty? No; I could not leave this stand without his assistance, nor could any of you leave this house if God was to say, no, and was to withdraw the breath which you breathe, which you received from him. But God has called all of us to a high calling; and there is a regular organization in the church and kingdom of God which ought to be respected. . . .—(*L. D. S. Pamphlets*, Vol. 31, Widtsoe Collection.)

CHAPTER XVIII

# PRIESTHOOD QUESTIONS AND PROBLEMS

## SOME GENERAL PROBLEMS

RELATIONS BETWEEN THE FIRST PRESIDENCY AND THE PRESIDING BISHOPRIC.—I will here read on this subject a passage which people take up sometimes, without understanding it, and consequently, when they do so, they are apt to make quite a number of mistakes. The passage to which I will refer you, is the twenty-second verse of the sixty-eighth section, in the Doctrine and Covenants. After reading it, you would think you had got the whole answer, but then you might not have it, although you might think you had.

And again, no bishop or high priest who shall be set apart for this ministry shall be tried or condemned for any crime, save it be before the First Presidency of the church.

Now, does not that look very plain? It does, when apart from the context, and if we do not examine the other parts associated therewith. I will further read some more pertaining to this matter, which will be found in the Doctrine and Covenants, section sixty-eight, verses fourteen to seventeen:

There remain hereafter, in the due time of the Lord, other bishops to be set apart unto the church, to minister even according to the first;

Wherefore they shall be high priests who are worthy, and they shall be appointed by the First Presidency of the Melchizedek Priesthood, except they be literal descendants of Aaron.

And if they be literal descendants of Aaron they have a legal right to the bishopric, if they are the firstborn among the sons of Aaron.

For the firstborn holds the right of the presidency over this priesthood, and the keys or authority of the same.

Now, I desire to draw your attention to one thing very distinctly, that you may comprehend. "For the firstborn holds the right of presidency over this priesthood." Over what priesthood? The bishopric. There is a presidency in that priesthood; and this firstborn of the literal descendants of Aaron would have a legal right to that presidency. No man has a legal right to this office, to hold the keys of this priesthood, except he be a literal descendant of Aaron, and the firstborn among his sons. Then, he would have a legal right to it. . . . But [I wish to speak of one or two leading principles pertaining to this subject; and] as a high priest of the Melchizedek priesthood has authority to officiate in all the lesser offices, he may officiate in the office of bishop when no literal descendant of Aaron can be found, and it is stated, and they shall be set apart "under the hands of the First Presidency of the Melchizedek Priesthood." (D. & C. 68:19.) To what authority? To what power? To what calling? To what bishopric? To the presiding bishopric. This is what is here referred to:

And a literal descendant of Aaron, also, must be designated by this Presidency, and found worthy, and anointed, and ordained under the hands of this Presidency, otherwise they are not legally authorized to officiate in their priesthood.

But, by virtue of the decree concerning their right of the priesthood descending from father to son, they may claim their anointing, if at any time they can prove their lineage, or do ascertain it by revelation from the Lord under the hands of the above named Presidency. (D. & C. 68:20, 21.)

Without that the presiding bishop could not be set apart, because there is where the authority is placed.

And again, no bishop or high priest who shall be set apart for this ministry shall be tried or condemned for any crime, save it be before the First Presidency of the church;

In regard to what ministry? Why, the Presidency of the Aaronic Priesthood. That is what is here spoken of.

And inasmuch as he is found guilty before this Presidency, by testimony that cannot be impeached, he shall be condemned;

And if he repent he shall be forgiven, according to the covenants and commandments of the church. (D. & C. 68:22-24.)

Now, then, I will read you something more on the same subject, which will be found in the Doctrine and Covenants.

There are, in the church, two priesthoods, namely, the Melchizedek and Aaronic, including the Levitical Priesthood.

Why the first is called the Melchizedek Priesthood is because Melchizedek was such a great high priest.

Before his day it was called *the Holy Priesthood, after the order of the Son of God.*

But out of respect or reverence to the name of the Supreme Being, to avoid the too frequent repetition of his name, they, the church, in ancient days, called that priesthood after Melchizedek, or the Melchizedek Priesthood.

All other authorities or offices in the church are appendages to this priesthood.

But there are two divisions or grand heads—one is the Melchizedek Priesthood, and the other is the Aaronic, or Levitical Priesthood.

The office of an elder comes under the priesthood of Melchizedek.

The Melchizedek Priesthood holds the right of presidency, and has power and authority over all the offices in the church in all ages of the world, to administer in spiritual things. (D. & C. 107:1-8.)

Now here is a principle developed that I wish to call your attention to, and that is, that it is the especial prerogative of the Melchizedek priesthood, and has been "in all ages of the world, to administer in spiritual things," and to have the right of presidency in those things.

But then, here is another distinction that I wish to call your attention to, at the same time, which is found in the next verse:

The Presidency of the High Priesthood, after the order of Melchizedek, have a right to officiate in all the offices in the church.

But there is a difference between the general authority of the Melchizedek priesthood and the one that is designated, which presides over them all: and that which presides over the whole has the right to administer in all things. The Aaronic priesthood is an appendage unto the Melchizedek priesthood, and is under its direction. I mention these things that you bishops, and you seventies, and you high priests, and you elders, and you high councilors, and you presidents of stakes and councilors, may comprehend the position of things, as here indicated; and, as was said formerly, I think it was by Paul, that you may be able to rightly divide the word of truth, and give to every man his portion in due season. These principles are written here, and are very plain, if they are understood, but if not understood, then they are mysterious, and it is required of us to make ourselves acquainted with the principles inculcated and herein developed. The things which I have mentioned are plain to the minds of all intelligent Latter-day Saints, who have studied the Doctrine and Covenants on these points.

High priests after the order of the Melchizedek Priesthood have a right to officiate in their own standing, under the direction of the presidency, in administering spiritual things, and also in the office of an elder, priest (of the Levitical order), teacher, deacon, and member. (D. & C. 107:10.)

That is the reason why, as soon as they possess this priesthood and right, if they are appointed to any particular office in the Church, they have a right to administer in that office.

I will now speak a little upon the high priesthood. This high priesthood, we are told, has held the right of presidency in all ages of the world. But there is a difference between the general powers of the priesthood, and the particular office and calling to which men are set apart; and you, when I tell you, will understand it very easily; for instance, the presidency of the priesthood, or the presidency of the church, are high priests. The twelve are high priests. The presidents of stakes and their counselors, the high council of a stake, and of all the stakes, are high priests. The bishops are ordained and set apart through the high priesthood, and stand in the same capacity; and thus bishops and their counselors are high priests. Now, these things you all know. There is nothing mysterious about them.

ALL PRIESTHOOD FUNCTIONS UNDER DIRECTION IN CHURCH CAPACITY.—There is another question associated with this matter. Because a man is a high priest, is he an apostle? No. Because a man is a high priest, is he the president of a stake, or the counselor to the president of a stake? No. Because he is a high priest, is he a bishop? No, not by any means. And so on, in all the various offices. The high priesthood holds the authority to administer in those ordinances, offices, and places, when they are appointed by the proper authorities, and at no other time; and while they are sustained also by the people. Now these are the distinctions which I wish to draw, simply to classify them. And when there is anything said about a high priest, you say, "I am a high priest, and if such a man has authority, I have it!" You have if you have been appointed to it, or you have not if you have not. You have it if you are appointed to fill the office, and are properly called and set apart to that office; but unless you are, you have not got that office, but still you are a high priest; and high priests after the order of the Melchizedek priesthood have a right to officiate in their own standing under the direction of the presidency, in administering spiritual things, but they must be under that direction or presidency. Now here is where the question comes in. Is it not plain when you look at it? To me it is very distinct and pointed, and it is to you who are intelligent and have studied these things. It is not because a man holds a certain class of priesthood that he is to administer in all the offices of that priesthood. He administers in them only as he is called and set apart for that purpose. . . .—*JD*, 22:193-196, July 18, 1880.

## FULFILLING CALLINGS IN THE HIGH PRIESTHOOD

HIGH PRIESTS.—Why are you organized as a high priesthood? Read the Doctrine and Covenants. What does it say? It says "Which ordinance is instituted for the purpose of qualifying those who shall be appointed standing presidents or servants over different stakes scattered abroad." (D. & C. 124:134.) It is a kind of normal school, where they may be taught lessons in the presidency, and be prepared to judge and act in the various places which they may be called to. Do the priesthood fulfil their calling? No, they do not. When the stakes were being organized, we had to call upon seventies and elders, and all classes of men to hold positions which high priests should have held. But there are some who talk about being great big high priests, who, when they should have been called upon to be bishops, or bishops' counselors, were found to be incompetent because they had not prepared themselves to occupy these offices associated with their calling, and been dabbling with the world and had been led by its influence, instead of being wide awake and full of the life and power and revelations of God. If they had magnified their priesthood, then God would have been with them, and they would have been selected, until all those places would have been filled.

SEVENTIES.—Then, how is it in regard to the seventies? Just the same. . . . How many of them, if they were called today, are prepared to go to the nations of the earth to preach the gospel? You are not prepared to do it any more than the high priests were prepared to magnify their calling. The twelve are commanded first to call upon the seventies, but when they do so, they frequently find they with one consent begin to make excuses. I know it is so, if you do not. Very well, what then? As there are other appendages to the Melchizedek priesthood, the twelve are obliged to call upon the elders, and high priests, and others, to go and perform duties which should be performed by the seventies, but which they neglect to do. . . . Now, notwithstanding this being the case, the work of God cannot stand still. The nations must be warned. The word of God must go forth, or the twelve would be held responsible, if these things were not done; and we have to keep doing it, doing it!

CALLING SEVENTIES FOR MISSIONS.—Now, as a sample of the excuses that men make who are called to go on missions, I will tell you what people tell me. One man says, "I have been building a house, and have not got the roof on it." Another comes, and says, "I have just been entering some land, and I am afraid I shall be placed in difficulty if I go; I pray you have me excused." And one man said he was so engaged in merchandising, and he was so much interested in the people's welfare, that he was afraid they would suffer very materially in their temporal interests if he ceased to keep store—that it would not be well to take him away. Another has bought five yoke of oxen, and is proving them, and prays to be excused. And another has married a wife and he cannot go. . . . Well, it is rather a lamentable story to tell. Yet, while we hold this important priesthood, it is a sorry way of treating it. . . .

THE LABOR NOT FOR ONE OR A DOZEN.—Now, the idea is not that one or a dozen men have to bear off this kingdom. For what is the priesthood conferred upon you? Is it to follow the "devices and desires of your own hearts," as I used to hear them say in the Church of England when I was a boy? Is it to do that? I think not. Or were we enlisted to God, for time and eternity? I think we were; and we want to wake up to the responsibilities which devolve upon us, and honor our calling and magnify our priesthood. . . .—*JD*, 22:201-203, July 18, 1880.

BROTHERLY CONCERN.—Let us seek to promote one another's welfare, and feel that we are brethren, that we are the representatives of God upon the earth. Our Heavenly Father is desirous to promote the happiness and welfare of the whole of the human family; and if we, any of us, hold any priesthood, it is

simply for that same purpose, and not for our personal aggrandizement, or for our own honor, or pomp, or position; but we hold it
in the interest of God and for the salvation of the people, that
through it we may promote their happiness, blessing, and prosperity, temporal and spiritual, both here and in the world to
come. That is why the priesthood is conferred upon us, and if
we do not use it in this way, then there is a malfeasance in office;
then we violate our obligations before God, and render ourselves
unworthy of the high calling that the Lord has conferred upon
us. The priesthood always was given for the blessing of the
human family. People talk about it as though it was for the
special benefit of individuals. . . .—*JD*, 22:230, June 26, 1881.

PRIESTHOOD AND TEMPLE WORK.—Elijah, it was prophe-
sied, should come and turn the hearts of the fathers to the children
and the hearts of the children to the fathers. That prophecy has
been fulfilled, and while millions and myriads of the human
family had died without a knowledge of the gospel, we are instructed what our duty is towards them. And while we are engaged in building temples and administering therein both for
the living and the dead, the everlasting priesthood in the heavens
are engaged in operating in the same way in the interests of all
humanity, not only of those who now live but those who have
lived. We need, it is true, the assistance and guidance of the
Almighty, and the holy priesthood behind the veil also requires
our assistance and our help. Paul, who understood these things,
said that they without us should not be made perfect, and we
without them cannot be made perfect. They in their day had
obtained a knowledge of God and his law, and we are permitted
to obtain the same. God has been pleased to restore the same
principles and to place us in communion with him and them.
Hence, while they are operating in the heavens we are operating
here upon the earth. We build temples and administer in them.
They are attending to those who have died without a knowledge
of the gospel, and who will communicate from time to time with
us to show us our duty.

It is written that saviors shall come upon Mount Zion. How
can a man be a savior if he saves nobody? And how can they
save unless God shows them how? How can they build temples
unless they have a knowledge of the work in which they are
engaged? And how can they administer in these temples unless
God instructs them? They cannot do it; we cannot do it; nobody can do it; and therefore it is necessary that we should all
the time be under the guidance and direction of the Almighty, for
without him we can do nothing.—*JD*, 22:292-293, October 9,
1881.

ETERNITY OF THE PRIESTHOOD.—And are the priesthood operating behind the veil? Yes, and we are operating here. And we have a priesthood here, and they have one there. Have we a presidency? They have one there. Have we a twelve? So they have there. Have we seventies here? They have there. Have we high priests here? They have there. Have we various quorums? Yes, and we operate in them; and when we get through we join our quorums above. . . .—*JD*, 22:308, August 28, 1881.

## INTER-STAKE DIFFICULTIES

I shall now refer to what is known as Utah Lake and Jordan River Dam water question. . . . President Angus M. Cannon showed me a letter in which it was stated that a law-suit was commenced in regard to the affair, some of the parties thereto being outside of the church and sóme inside. . . . Brother Cannon (who is president of the Salt Lake Stake) came to me and wanted to know what to do. He said he could not regulate these matters as his jurisdiction did not extend beyond Salt Lake Stake, nor could President Smoot because his jurisdiction did not go beyond Utah Stake. Here was a dilemma. What shall be done? Could I show him a way out of the difficulty?

I told him I could; that a council had been provided through the Prophet Joseph Smith for just such cases. Some people don't know anything about that, but yet that is a fact. They did not know that it had ever been used before. It is a council of twelve high priests over which the First Presidency of the church should preside to adjudicate upon difficult cases that might arise in the church, and this should be the highest council in the church, and from which there should be no appeal. We called together this council and met here in this house, and the parties were heard—some outside of the church and some inside. Finally we got the matter adjusted, and I am informed that the decision is satisfactory to all parties. . . . I and Brother George Q. Cannon presided in all the meetings of the council.[1] In selecting the council we selected men from the two counties who were conversant with

---

[1]The council was composed of the following brethren, *viz.*: Abraham O. Smoot, president of Utah Stake; Angus M. Cannon, president of Salt Lake Stake; Warren N. Dusenberry, Probate Judge of Utah County; Elias A. Smith, Probate Judge of Salt Lake County; Jonathan S. Page and A. D. Holdaway, Selectmen of Utah County; Ezekiel Holman and Jesse W. Fox, Jr., Selectmen of Salt Lake County; Presiding Bishop Wm. B. Preston; John T. Caine, Delegate to Congress from Utah; Bishops Thos. R. Cutler, and John E. Booth.

After the first session of the council, in consequence of Hon. John T. Caine's being required at Salt Lake City on official business, Elder L. John Nuttall was appointed a member of the council in place of Elder Caine.

county affairs, and both counties were equally represented. But some people will say—how is it the high council could not settle the question? Because the high council in Utah Stake has no jurisdiction over affairs in Salt Lake Stake, nor has the high council of Salt Lake Stake any jurisdiction over affairs in Utah Stake, and the other council was formed just to meet such an emergency. I speak of this for your information; and, as I have said, when the matter is thoroughly completed, it will prove to be satisfactory to all parties.—*JD*, 26:73-74, November 30, 1884.

ADVICE TO A HIGH COUNCIL.—Now, I will tell you of a principle taught by Joseph Smith. It may be of use to you as a high council, and it will not hurt anybody else. In speaking of the discernment of spirits, said he, a man may have the gift of the discernment of spirits; he may see what is in the heart; but because that has been revealed to him, he has no business to bring that as a charge against any person. The man's acts must be proved by evidence and by witnesses.—*JD*, 26:359, February 20, 1884.

# BOOK FOUR

## THE KINGDOM OF GOD

*"We are here to do the will of God, to build up the kingdom of God, and to establish the Zion of God."*
—JOHN TAYLOR,
*JD,* 23:324.

# CHAPTER XIX

# THE MEANING OF THE KINGDOM OF GOD

## THE IDEA OF THE KINGDOM OF GOD

A THEORY OF GOVERNMENT.—We talk a good deal about the church and kingdom of God. I sometimes think we understand very little about either. The kingdom of God means the government of God. That means, power, authority, rule, dominion, and a people to rule over. But that principle will not be fulfilled, cannot be entirely fulfilled, until, as we are told in the scriptures, the kingdoms of this world are become the kingdoms of our Lord and his Christ, and he will rule over them, and when unto him every knee shall bow and every tongue confess that he is Christ, to the glory of God, the Father. That time has not yet come, but there are certain principles associated therewith that have come; namely, the introduction of that kingdom, and the introduction of that kingdom could only be made by that Being who is the King and Ruler, and the Head of that government, first communicating his ideas, his principles, his laws, his government to the people. Otherwise we should not know what his laws were.

The world has been governed in every kind of form; we have had every species of government. Sometimes we have had patriarchal government; at other times we have had unlimited monarchies or what may be called despotic governments, where the power to rule is in the hands of one individual. At other times we have had limited monarchies such as exist in many places now upon the face of the earth. In other places and at different ages we have had what is termed republican governments where the voice of the people has ruled and governed and managed the people's affairs. There have been various forms independent of these . . . but nowhere have we had the government of God. It is true that for a limited period among a very small people in early days, among the Jews, they professed to be under the guidance of God for a certain length of time. But they were continually departing therefrom.—*JD*, 21:63-64, January 4, 1880.

A CHRISTIAN CONCEPT.—"Thy kingdom come." . . . This was taught by Jesus to his disciples when they came to him, saying, teach us to pray. . . . Thy kingdom come. What kingdom? What is the meaning of "thy kingdom come"? It means the rule of God. It means the law of God. It means the government of God. It means the people who have listened to and who are willing to listen to and observe the commands of Jehovah. And it means that there is a God who is willing to guide and direct and sustain his people. Thy kingdom come, that thy government may be established, and the principles of eternal truth as they exist in the heavens may be imparted to men; and that, when they are imparted to men, those men may be in subjection to those laws and to that government, and live in the fear of God, keeping his commandments and being under his direction. Thy kingdom come, that the confusion, the evil, and wickedness, the murder and bloodshed that now exist among mankind may be done away, and the principles of truth and right, the principles of kindness, charity, and love as they dwell in the bosom of the Gods, may dwell with us.—*JD*, 23:177-178, July 24, 1882.

MORMON POLITICAL THOUGHT.—We differ from the world with regard to our political views, for they are based on our religious faith; we believe in God, and therefore we fear him; we believe he has established his kingdom upon the earth, and therefore we cling to it; we believe that he is designing to turn, and overturn, and revolutionize the nations of the earth, and to establish a government that shall be under his rule, his dominion, and authority, and shall emphatically be called the government of God, or, in other words, the kingdom of God. There is nothing strange, however, in this; for a great many parties, both in the United States and in the governments of the old world, have believed in the kingdom of God being established in the last days; it has been a favorite doctrine, both among socialists and Christians, and much has been said and written about it, theoretically. The difference between them and us is, they talk about something to come; we say that it has commenced, and that this is that kingdom.—*JD*, 11:89-90, March 5, 1865.

PRIESTHOOD: THE GOVERNMENT OF THE KINGDOM OF GOD.—What is the kingdom of God? It is God's government upon the earth and in heaven. What is his priesthood? It is the rule, authority, administration, if you please, of the government of God on the earth or in the heavens; for the same priesthood that exists upon the earth exists in the heavens, and that priesthood holds the keys of the mysteries of the revelations of God; and the legitimate head of that priesthood, who has communion with God, is the prophet, seer, and revelator to his church and people on the earth.

When the will of God is done on earth as it is in heaven, that priesthood will be the only legitimate ruling power under the whole heavens; for every other power and influence will be subject to it. When the millennium . . . is introduced, all potentates, powers, and authorities—every man, woman, and child will be in subjection to the kingdom of God; they will be under the power and dominion of the priesthood of God: then the will of God will be done on the earth as it is done in heaven.—*JD*, 6:25, November 1, 1857.

A LITERAL OR SPIRITUAL KINGDOM.—Will God's kingdom be a literal or a spiritual kingdom? It would be almost unnecessary to answer such a question as the above, were it not for the opinions that are entertained in the world concerning a purely spiritual kingdom. . . . But I have introduced this merely to meet some questions that exist in the minds of many, relative to a spiritual kingdom, arising from certain remarks of our Savior's, where he says, "My kingdom is not of this world"; (John 18:36) and again, the "kingdom of God is not meat and drink; but righteousness, and peace, and joy in the Holy Ghost"; (Romans 14:17) and again, "the kingdom of God is within [or among] you." (Luke 17:21.)

The kingdom of God, as I have already stated, is the government of God, whether in the heavens or on the earth. Hence Jesus taught his disciples to pray, "Thy kingdom come, thy will be done in earth, as it is in heaven." And when the kingdom of God is established on the earth, and prevails universally, then will the will of God be done on earth, and not till then; then will the reign of God exist on the earth, as it now does in heaven. It is this reign we are speaking of, a reign of righteousness. But whenever God's laws are established, or his kingdom is organized, and officers selected, and men yield obedience to the laws of the kingdom of God, to such an extent does God's kingdom prevail.— GG, 83, 1852.

I have demonstrated . . . that the kingdom of God would be literally established on the earth. It will not be an aerial phantom, according to some visionaries, but a substantial reality. It will be established, as before said, on a literal earth, and will be composed of literal men, women, and children; of living saints who keep the commandments of God, and of resurrected bodies who shall actually come out of their graves, and live on the earth. The Lord will be king over all the earth, and all mankind literally under his sovereignty, and every nation under the heavens will have to acknowledge his authority, and bow to his sceptre. Those who serve him in righteousness will have communications with God, and with Jesus; will have the ministering of angels, and will know the past, the present, and the future; and other people, who may not yield full obedience to his laws, nor be fully instructed in his covenants, will, nevertheless, have to yield full obedience to his government.[1] For it will be reign of God upon the earth, and he will enforce his laws, and command that obedience from the nations of the world which is legitimately his right. Satan will not then be permitted to control its inhabitants, for the Lord God will be king over all the earth, and the kingdom and greatness of the kingdom under the whole heaven will be given to the saints.—*GG*, 87-88, 1852.

God has introduced *his* kingdom after *his* order, and it is for him to guide that kingdom and direct it, and manage it, and manipulate it in the interest of the honest in heart, and of all nations. He has commenced it among us that he might have a little nucleus where he could communicate and reveal his will, composed of such as would carry that will out, and do his bidding and obey his behests.—*JD*, 21:60, September 21, 1878.

JOHN TAYLOR'S BELIEF.—Well, we are here struggling and trying to introduce correct principles, and to advance not only the interests of the church of God, but the kingdom of God, for God will have a kingdom, . . . and he will have rule and dominion, for this earth belongs to him and he will possess it, and his saints will inherit it at last. We did not use to be afraid of talking about these things. In former times they told us that the saints of the Most High should finally take the kingdom and the greatness of the kingdom, which should be given to the saints of the Most High God. Do you believe it? I happen to be one who believes it. And I prophesy that it will be fulfilled.—*JD*, 21:216, March 1, 1880.

## RELATION TO THE CHURCH AND PRIESTHOOD

A KINGDOM OF PRIESTS.—We are today a kingdom of priests holding to a very great extent the holy priesthood; and it is essential that we submit ourselves to the laws of that priesthood and be governed by them in all of our actions.—*JD*, 21:358, August 8, 1880.

THE PRIESTHOOD TO FACILITATE THE KINGDOM OF GOD.—Here then, God was desirous of introducing his kingdom upon the earth, and he had, in the first place, to organize his church, to organize the people that he had scattered among the nations and to bring them together, that there might be one fold and one shepherd, and one Lord, one faith, and one baptism, and one God, who should be in all and through all, and by which all should be governed. To facilitate this object, he organized his

---

[1]Their free agency, however, will be respected; likewise their freedom to organize in terms of their own belief (see Book V, *passim,* below). However there will be full and frank recognition of the role of Christ_and his government, as the following pages will clarify.

holy priesthood as it existed in the heavens, and he gave a pattern of these things, just as much as he did in the days of Moses, only more so.—*JD*, 18:138, October 10, 1875.

MEANING OF THE RELATIONSHIP.—This is a work that is not popular among men. They want their ideas, their theories, and their notions; we want the ideas and theories, the word and will, and the guidance and direction of the Almighty; and if we are connected with his kingdom, if there is such a thing as the kingdom of God upon the earth, it means the rule and government of God.

Peradventure some will say, "We won't let you do it." Now, don't stop the Lord, will you? No matter about the theories, ideas, and notions of men. God has committed to us certain principles, and by the help of God we mean to carry them out. In doing this it devolves upon us to send the gospel to every creature under heaven. . . . And let the twelve, let the seventies, let the high priests, and let the elders work up to the dignity and importance of their calling, and feel that they are under command, as the servants of God, to do his will in spreading the gospel of life and salvation to the nations of the earth. The world will hate you. No matter—they hated your Master before you. They persecuted him before they persecuted you. He endured it; we will try to.—*JD*, 22:293-294, October 9, 1881.

THE LEGITIMATE OFFICERS OF THE CHURCH AND KINGDOM.—You should understand that when you have been voting here to sustain the presidency of the Church of Jesus Christ of Latter-day Saints, the twelve apostles, the high council, the bishops, and other quorums, you have been voting to sustain the legitimate and authorized officers of the church and kingdom of God, whose right it is to rule and govern whenever and wherever the Almighty has a people upon the earth.—*JD*, 9:12-13, April 6, 1861.

RESPONSIBILITY OF ORGANIZATION.—It is not correct to suppose that the whole duty of carrying this kingdom devolves upon the twelve or the First Presidency, as the case may be, or upon the presidents of the stakes, or upon the high priests, or upon the seventies, or upon the bishops, or upon any other officer in the church and kingdom of God; that to the contrary, all of us have our several duties to perform. And I may go farther in regard to the duties of men, and also in regard to those of women; all have their duties to perform before God. The organization of this church and kingdom is for the express purpose of putting every man in his place, and it is then expected that every man in that place will magnify his office and calling.—*JD*, 21:359-360, August 8, 1880.

THE CHURCH OF GOD A FORERUNNER TO THE KINGDOM
OF GOD.—We talk sometimes about the church of God, and why?
We talk about the kingdom of God, and why? Because, before
there could be a kingdom of God, there must be a church of God,
and hence the first principles of the gospel were needed to be
preached to all nations, as they were formerly when the Lord
Jesus Christ and others made their appearance on the earth. And
why so? Because of the impossibility of introducing the law of
God among a people who would not be subject to and be guided
by the spirit of revelation. Hence the world have generally made
great mistakes upon these points. They have started various
projects to try to unite and cement the people together without
God; but they could not do it. Fourierism, communism—another
branch of the same thing—and many other principles of the same
kind have been introduced to try and cement the human family
together. And then we have had peace societies, based upon the
same principles. But all these things have failed, and they will
fail, because, however philanthropic, humanitarian, benevolent,
or cosmopolitan our ideas, it is impossible to produce a true and
correct union without the Spirit of the living God and that Spirit
can only be imparted through the ordinances of the gospel. Hence
Jesus told his disciples to go and preach the gospel to every creature,
baptizing them in the name of the Father, Son, and Holy Ghost,
and said he—"lo, I am with you alway, even unto the end of
the world." (Matthew 28:20.) It was by this cementing, uniting spirit, that true sympathetic, fraternal relations could be introduced and enjoyed.—JD, 18:137, October 10, 1875.

And let me say a little farther on a subject that I before
referred to, that is, that God could not build up a kingdom on
the earth unless he had a church and a people who had submitted
to his law and were willing to submit to it; and with an organization of such a people, gathered from among the nations of the
earth under the direction of a man inspired of God, the mouth-
piece of Jehovah to his people; I say that, with such an organization, there is a chance for the Lord God to be revealed, there is
an opportunity for the laws of life to be made manifest, there is
a chance for God to introduce the principles of heaven upon the
earth and for the will of God to be done upon earth as it is done
in heaven.—JD, 18:140, October 10, 1875.

THE CHURCH, A SCHOOL FOR THE KINGDOM OF·GOD.—
You cannot teach the arts and sciences without necessary preparation for their introduction, nor can you teach people in the government of God unless they are placed in communication with
him, and hence comes the church of God, and what is meant by
that? A school, if you please, wherein men are taught certain
principles, wherein we can receive a certain spirit through obedience to certain ordinances.—JD, 21:65, January 4, 1880.

## THE ROLE OF THE PEOPLE

THE LATTER-DAY SAINTS.—The kingdom of God will be built up. The will of God must be done on the earth as it is in heaven. Will such a thing as that ever take place on the earth? Yes, as surely as you and I are here today it will. Then, if the kingdom of God is to come, if the will of God is ever to be done on the earth as it is done in heaven, where can it commence except it is among the Latter-day Saints; for there is no other people under the heavens who acknowledge the authority of God? They do not really acknowledge the rule of God, or the government of God, anywhere among all the nations of the earth; and if his will is ever done on earth as it is done in heaven, where shall it start but in the land of Zion, and among the people of Zion?— *JD*, 24:355-356, December 9, 1883.

"SOME ACTION IS REQUIRED."—We have been talking for years about the rule and government of the kingdom of God and its final establishment upon the earth, in peace and righteousness; and also about the time when every creature which is in the heavens and on the earth, and under the earth, and such as are in the sea, and all that are in them will be heard saying, "Blessing, and honor, and glory, and power, be unto him that sitteth upon the throne, and unto the Lamb for ever and ever." (Revelation 5:13.) We have been talking about these things, but there is much to be done in the intermediate space between the present and that impenetrable period in the great future. It is not all a matter of faith, but there is some action required; it is a thing that we have got to engage in ourselves, individually and collectively as a people, and it is a matter of no small concern.—*JD*, 9:341, April 13, 1862.

THE POWER OF THE PEOPLE OF THE EARTH.—It is in vain for the elders of Israel to teach the principles of truth unless the people are prepared to receive them; and it is vain for the Lord to communicate his will unto the people unless the people possess a portion of his Spirit, to comprehend something of that will and the designs of God towards them, and towards the earth upon which they dwell. Nor can the Lord work with them unless they are prepared to cooperate with him in the establishment of his kingdom upon the earth.—*JD*, 11:158-159, October 7, 1865.

THE INDIVIDUAL'S PLACE.—How is the world going to be redeemed, think you? If the kingdom of God is ever built up, the Almighty will have to dictate things himself. Through what medium will he do this? Is he going to send his angels to gather the people? He has thousands of them, but he has his own way of doing things and that is through the priesthood. If we are teachers, we think faithful people ought to listen to us. If we are bishops, we of course think that the people ought to respect our counsel, and if presidents, we are anxious to see the people obedient. If so, is it not right for us to listen to those that are over us? All people in this government should listen to the head, for that is the order of God.

It is all very nice; it is a beautiful theory; everybody under our rule must submit; our wives and our children must yield obedience; we all admire the beauty and order and harmony of the church of God until it comes to touch us, and we are the only people exempt. We are very apt to show that we like a little of our own way, and that although God's government is very good for others, that we do not like to be interfered with so much. If this be our feeling, why do we act hypocritically? Why exact of others that which we will not do or yield ourselves? Why not, if we are the rich men we profess to be, be on hand, show our willingness at all times to do what is required of us, seek the Spirit of the Lord, for when we get that, we will be willing to yield to its dictates.

It is very easy to submit to law, and doubtless we should all be ready enough to submit if the Almighty should come and speak to us face to face. But he chooses to speak by his messengers; to them we must yield obedience. Jesus said, in his day, what is true in this: he that receiveth you receiveth me, and receiveth him that sent me, and he that rejecteth you rejecteth me and rejecteth him that sent me.—*JD*, 9:345, April 13, 1862.

What is a man's duty here? It is obedience to the oracles of God that are in our midst; and so long as we keep the commandments of God, we need not fear any evil; for the Lord will be with us in time and in eternity.

"But," says one, "I have got a son, who has gone out upon the Plains, and perhaps the soldiers will kill him." . . . Did you ever know your sons were in possession of eternal life, and that this is only a probation or a space between time and eternity? We existed before, in eternity that was, and we shall exist in eternity that is to come; and the question only is, whether it is better to die with the harness on, or to be found a poor, miserable coward. All that I said to my son Joseph, after blessing him, before he went out, was, "Joseph, do not be found with a hole in your back." I do not want any cowardice—any tremblings or feelings of that kind.

What of our friends who have gone behind the veil—are they dead? No; they live, and they move, in a more exalted sphere. Did they fight for the kingdom of God when here? Yes, they did. Are they battling for it now? Yes; and the time is approaching when the wicked nations have to be destroyed; and the time is near when every creature is to be heard saying, "Blessing, and honour, and glory, and power, be unto him that sitteth upon the throne, and unto the Lamb for ever and ever." (Revelation 5:13.) We have got to bring this about, whether we do it in this world or that which is to come.—*JD*, 5:191, August 30, 1857.

OBEDIENCE IN THE KINGDOM OF GOD.—If the Lord can have a people to listen to his law, there may be a chance to establish his kingdom upon the earth. If not, the only way he can establish his kingdom is to remove them from the earth, or give up his kingdom until another time; for it is impossible to establish his kingdom without having a people obedient to him. What does that obedience imply? Obedience in all things, —that the twelve should be obedient to the presidency, the seventies to the twelve, and so on through all the ramifications of the priesthood—obedience of wives to husbands, children to parents—and that a general order of this kind should be established in every neighborhood, in every house, and in every heart.

Well, this is the feeling that ought to exist; and where this feeling does not exist the Spirit of God does not exist; and where there is not a feeling of obedience, the Spirit of God will be withdrawn. People cannot retain it and be in rebellion against the authorities and counsels of the church and kingdom of God.

When the kingdom of God is established and his word is listened to, the spirit of obedience extends through the ramifications of the body of Christ, even as the sap extends through the trunk of a tree till it reaches to the extreme branches and twigs, and to every part of it.—*JD*, 5:265, September 20, 1857.

PREACHING VERSUS PRACTICE IN DEVELOPING THE KINGDOM.—Some people think that preaching is the greatest part of the business in building up the kingdom of God. This is a mistake. You may pick out our most inferior elders, in point of talent and ability, and send them to England to preach and preside, and they think they are great men there. Their religion teaches them so much more than the gentiles know, that they are received as the great men of the earth. Anybody can preach. He is a poor simpleton that cannot. It is the easiest thing in the world. But, as President Young says, it takes a man to practice. . . .

We are becoming notorious in the eyes of the nations. And the time is not far distant when the kings of the earth will be glad to come to our elders to ask counsel to help them out of their difficulties; for their troubles are coming upon them like a flood, and they do not know how to extricate themselves.—*JD*, 1:18-19, August 22, 1852.

SOME PRACTICAL CONSIDERATIONS.—If the kings and princes of the earth have got to come and gaze upon the glory of Zion, we must have some of that principle in ourselves that will attract the attention and admiration of surrounding nations. If we do not put ourselves in a way to get in possession of these principles, how can we ever arrive at them? It is impossible.— *JD*, 10:279-280, October 25, 1863.

THE GREAT MISSION.—We have a great mission to perform —we have to try to govern ourselves according to the laws of the kingdom of God, and we find it one of the most difficult tasks we ever undertook, to learn to govern ourselves, our appetites, our dispositions, our habits, our feelings, our lives, our spirits, our judgment, and to bring all our desires into subjection to the law of the kingdom of God and to the spirit of truth. It is a very critical thing to be engaged in the upbuilding of the kingdom of God—a nucleus of which we have here.—*JD*, 9:12, April 6, 1861.

THE ESTABLISHMENT OF THE KINGDOM OF GOD.—There is one thing very certain, very certain indeed, and that is, whatever men may think, and however they may plot and contrive, that this kingdom will never be given into the hands of another people. It will grow and spread and increase, and no man living can stop its progress.—*JD*, 25:348, October 19, 1884.

THE RISE OF THE KINGDOM.—How are the nations going to be redeemed? How is the kingdom of God going to be planted upon the earth? Will it be by preaching, or by power? Will it be by the natural course of events, or by moral suasion? Will it be by the outpouring of the judgments of God on the nations? Will it be by kingdoms being overthrown and empires crumbling to ruins? How is it going to be done? I answer, these things will be accomplished by the guidance of the Lord through his prophets who are in our midst. Don't you see this, brethren?—*JD*, 6:167, January 17, 1858.

What is the first thing necessary to the establishment of his kingdom? It is to raise up a prophet and have him declare the will of God; the next is to have people yield obedience to the word of the Lord through that prophet. If you cannot have these, you never can establish the kingdom of God upon the earth.—*JD*, 6:25, November 1, 1857.

THE MEANS OF ESTABLISHING THE KINGDOM.—In making a brief summary of what we have said before in relation to the means to be employed for the establishment of the kingdom of God, we find the following:—

First.—That it will be not only a spiritual kingdom, but a temporal and literal one also.

Second.—That if it is the kingdom of heaven, it must be revealed from the heavens.

Third.—That a standard is to be lifted up, by the Lord, to the nations.

Fourth.—That an angel is to come with the everlasting gospel, which is to be proclaimed to every nation, kindred, people, and tongue; that it is to be the same as the ancient one, and that the same powers and blessings will attend it.

Fifth.—That not only will the ancient gospel be preached, but there will accompany it a declaration of judgment to the nations.

Sixth.—That there will be a literal Zion, or gathering of the Saints to Zion, as well as a gathering of the Jews to Jerusalem.

Seventh.—That when this has taken place, the Spirit of God will be withdrawn from the nations, and they will war with and destroy each other.

Eighth.—That judgments will also overtake them, from the Lord, plague, pestilence, famine, etc.

Ninth.—That the nations, having lost the Spirit of God, will assemble to fight against the Lord's people, being full of the spirit of unrighteousness, and opposed to the rule and government of God.

Tenth.—That when they do, the Lord will come and fight against them himself; overthrow their armies; assert his own right; rule the nations with a rod of iron; root the wicked out of the earth; and take possession of his own kingdom. I might here further state, that when the Lord does come to exercise judgment upon the ungodly, to make an end of sin, and bring in everlasting righteousness, he will establish his own laws, demand universal obedience, and cause wickedness and misrule to cease. He will issue his commands, and they must be obeyed; and if the nations of the earth observe not his laws, "they will have no rain." And they will be taught by more forcible means than moral suasion, that they are dependent upon God; for the Lord will demand obedience, and the scriptures say, time and again, that the wicked shall be rooted out of the land, and the righteous and the meek shall inherit the earth.

The Lord, after trying man's rule for thousands of years, now takes the reins of government into his own hands, and makes use of the only possible means of asserting his rights. For if the wicked never were cut off, the righteous never could rule; and if the devil was still suffered to bear rule, God could not, at the same time; consequently after long delay, he whose right it is takes possession of the kingdom; and the kingdom, and the greatness of the kingdom under the whole heavens, shall be given to the saints of the Most High God; and the world will assume that position for which it was made. A king shall rule in righteousness, and princes shall decree judgment. The knowledge of the Lord will spread, and extend under the auspices of this government. Guided by his counsels, and under his direction, all those purposes designed of him, from the commencement, in relation to both living and dead, will be in a fair way for their accomplishment.—GG, 103-105, 1852.

## SOME EFFECTS OF ESTABLISHING THE KINGDOM

What will be the effects of the establishment of Christ's kingdom, or the reign of God on the earth? . . .

THE RESTITUTION.—It is the doing away with war, bloodshed, misery, disease, and sin, and the ushering in of a kingdom of peace, righteousness, justice, happiness, and prosperity. It is the restoration of the earth and man to their primeval glory and pristine excellence; in fact, the "restitution of all things spoken of by all the prophets since the world began."—GG, 105-106, 1852.

THE BUILDING OF ZION.—We believe that we shall rear splendid edifices, magnificent temples, and beautiful cities that shall become the pride, praise, and glory of the whole earth. We believe that this people will excel in literature, in science and the arts, and in manufactures. In fact, there will be a concentration of wisdom, not only of the combined wisdom of the world as it now exists, but men will be inspired in regard to all these matters in a manner and to an extent that they never have been before. . . .—JD, 10:147, April 6, 1863.

THE GLORY OF ZION.—When Zion is established in her beauty and honor and glory, the kings and princes of the earth will come, in order that they may get information and teach the same to their people. They will come as they came to learn the wisdom of Solomon.—JD, 6:169, January 17, 1858.

ESTABLISHING THE KINGDOM: THE GREAT COUNCIL AT ADAM-ONDI-AHMAN.—A great council will then be held to adjust the affairs of the world, from the commencement, over which Father Adam will preside as head and representative of the human family. . . .
Then they will assemble to regulate all these affairs, and all that held keys of authority to administer will then represent their

earthly course. And, as this authority has been handed down from one to another in different ages, and in different dispensations, a full reckoning will have to be made by all. All who have held the keys of priesthood will then have to give an account to those from whom they received them. Those that were in the heavens have been assisting those that were upon the earth; but then, they will unite together in a general council to give an account of their stewardships, and as in the various ages men have received their power to administer from those who had previously held the keys thereof, there will be a general account.

Those under the authorities of the Church of Jesus Christ of Latter-day Saints have to give an account of their transactions to those who direct them in the priesthood; hence the elders give an account to presidents of conferences; and presidents of conferences to presidents of nations. Those presidents and the seventies give an account to the twelve apostles; the twelve to the First Presidency; and they to Joseph, from whom they, and the twelve, received their priesthood. This will include the arrangements of the last dispensation. Joseph delivers his authority to Peter, who held the keys before him, and delivered them to him; and Peter to Moses and Elias, who endowed him with this authority on the Mount; and they to those from whom they received them. And thus the world's affairs will be regulated and put right, the restitution of all things be accomplished, and the kingdom of God be ushered in. The earth will be delivered from under the curse, resume its paradisiacal glory, and all things pertaining to its restoration be fulfilled.

Not only will the earth be restored, but also man; and those promises which, long ago, were the hope of the Saints, will be realized. The faithful servants of God who have lived in every age will then come forth and experience the full fruition of that joy for which they lived, and hoped, and suffered, and died. The tombs will deliver up their captives, and reunited with the spirits which once animated, vivified, cheered, and sustained them while in this vale of tears, these bodies will be like unto Christ's glorious body. They will then rejoice in that resurrection for which they lived, while they sojourned below.

Adam, Seth, Enoch, and the faithful who lived before the flood, will possess their proper inheritance. Noah and Melchizedek will stand in their proper places. Abraham, with Isaac and Jacob, heirs with him of the same promise, will come forward at the head of innumerable multitudes, and possess that land which God gave unto them for an everlasting inheritance. The faithful on the continent of America will also stand in their proper place; but, as this will be the time of the restitution of all things, and all things will not be fully restored at once, there will be a distinction between the resurrected bodies, and those that have not been resurrected; and, as the scriptures say that flesh and blood cannot inherit the kingdom of God, neither doth corruption inherit incorruption; and although the world will enjoy just laws—an equitable administration, and universal peace and happiness prevail as the result of this righteousness; yet, there will be a peculiar habitation for the resurrected bodies. This habitation may be compared to paradise, whence man, in the beginning, was driven.

When Adam was driven from the garden, an angel was placed with a flaming sword to guard the way of the tree of life, lest man should eat of it and become immortal in his degenerate state, and thus be incapable of obtaining that exaltation which he would be capable of enjoying through the redemption of Jesus Christ, and the power of the resurrection, with his renewed and glorified body. Having tasted of the nature of the fall, and having grappled with sin and misery, knowing, like the Gods, both good and evil, having, like Jesus, overcome the evil, and through the power of the atonement having conquered death, hell, and the grave, he regains that paradise from which he was banished, not in the capacity of ignorant man, unacquainted with evil, but like unto a God. He can now stretch forth, and partake of the tree of life, and eat of its fruits, and live and flourish eternally in possession of that immortality which Jesus long ago promised to the faithful: "To him that overcomes, will I grant to sit with me in my throne; and eat of the tree of life which is in the midst of the paradise of God."—GG, 115, 116-118, 1852.

## THE KINGDOM OF GOD AND THE NATION— STATE SYSTEM[1]

THE KINGDOM A CHURCH AND STATE.—Was the kingdom that the prophets talked about, that should be set up in the latter times, going to be a church? Yes. And a state? Yes, it was going to be both church and state, to rule both temporally and spiritually. It may be asked, How can we live under the dominion and laws of the United States and be subjects of another kingdom? Because the kingdom of God is higher, and its laws are so much more exalted than those of any other nation,[2] that it is the easiest thing in life for a servant of God to keep any of their laws; and, as I have said before, this we have uniformly done.—JD, 6:23-24, November 1, 1857.

---

[1]For a detailed examination of this stirring problem, see Book Five.
[2]But compare this with doctrinal developments concerning the United States and its constitution, below and in Book Five.

THE AMERICAN CONSTITUTION AND THE KINGDOM OF GOD.—We are not taking any steps contrary to the laws and the Constitution of the United States. But in everything we are upholding and sustaining them.—*JD*, 5:157-158, August 23, 1857.

REALITY OF THE KINGDOM: TO UPHOLD THE CONSTITUTION OF THE UNITED STATES.—When the people shall have torn to shreds the Constitution of the United States, the elders of Israel will be found holding it up to the nations of the earth and proclaiming liberty and equal rights to all men, and extending the hand of fellowship to the oppressed of all nations. This is part of the program, and as long as we do what is right and fear God, he will help us and stand by us under all circumstances.—*JD*, 21:8, August 31, 1879.

PROBLEMS OF CHURCH AND STATE.—We are under the United States. But the United States is not the kingdom of God. It does not profess to be under his rule, nor his government, nor his authority. Yet we are expected as citizens of the United States to keep the laws of the United States, and hence we are, as I said before, an integral part of the government. Very well, what is expected of us? That we observe its laws, that we conform to its usages, that we are governed by good and wholesome principles, that we maintain the laws in their integrity and that we sustain the government. And we ought to do it.

But there is a principle here that I wish to speak about. God dictates in a great measure the affairs of the nations of the earth, their kingdoms and governments and rulers and those that hold dominion. He sets up one and pulls down another, according to his will. That is an old doctrine, but it is true today. Have we governors? Have we a president of the United States? Have we men in authority? Yes. Is it right to traduce their characters? No, it is not. Is it right for us to oppose them? No, it is not. Is it right for them to traduce us? No, it is not. Is it right for them to oppress us in any way? No, it is not. We ought to pray for these people, for those that are in authority, that they may be led in the right way, that they may be preserved from evil, that they may administer the government in righteousness, and that they may pursue a course that will receive the approbation of heaven. Well, what else? Then we ought to pray for ourselves that when any plans or contrivances or opposition to the law of God, to the church and kingdom of God, or to his people, are introduced, and whenever we are sought to be made the victims of tyranny and oppression, that the hand of God may be over us and over them to paralyze their acts and protect us. . . .—*JD*, 21:68, January 4, 1880.

THE FUTURE.—Now as to the great future, what shall we
say? Why, a little stone has been cut out of the mountains without hands, and this little stone is becoming a great nation, and
it will eventually fill the whole earth.    How will it fill it?
Religiously?   Yes, and politically too, for it will have the rule,
the power, the authority, the dominion in its own hands. . . .
JD, 9:343, April 13, 1862.

# CHAPTER XX

# ON THE ROLE AND PURPOSE OF THE CHURCH

## THE PURPOSE OF THE WORK

TO BUILD THE ZION OF THE LATTER DAYS.—We are here to build up the church of God, the Zion of God, and the kingdom of God, and to be on hand to do whatever God requires— first to purge ourselves from all iniquity, from covetousness and evil of every kind, to forsake sin of every sort, cultivate the Spirit of God, and help to build up his kingdom; to beautify Zion and have pleasant habitations, and pleasant gardens and orchards, until Zion shall be the most beautiful place there is on the earth. Already Zion is attracting the attention of the people of the world. I have all kinds of people calling on me—lords, admirals, senators, members of the House of Representatives, members of the Parliament of England, of the Reichstag of Germany, and the Chamber of Deputies of France—all classes come and they say, "You have a most beautiful place here!" Why, yes. And by and by the kings of the earth will come to gaze upon the glory of Zion, and we are here to build it up under the instruction of God our Heavenly Father. Zion shall yet become the praise and the glory of the whole earth.—*JD*, 24:201, June 18, 1883.

THE LORD'S WORK TEMPORAL.—A great amount of the work the Lord is going to accomplish is what is generally called temporal, because it belongs to the earth. That is, the government, laws, and general direction of affairs among the nations that are not now fallen under the control of the Almighty, will have to be so changed and altered as to come under his entire control, government, and dictation in every respect. He has shown to his prophets and people long ago, to a certain extent, what kind of rule and government he would have in the last days. He showed them that a time would come when every knee should bow, and every tongue should confess unto the Lord, no matter whether they were priests or people, rulers or ruled, lawyers or doctors, no matter what position they held in the world, to him every knee shall bow, and every tongue shall confess that he is the Lord of all to the glory of God the Father.—*JD*, 10:278-279, October 25, 1863.

TO ESTABLISH THE KINGDOM OF GOD.—You have been ordained kings and queens, and priests and priestesses to your

Lord; you have been put in possession of principles that all the kings, potentates, and power upon the earth are entirely ignorant of; they do not understand it; but you have received this from the hands of God. . . .

What are we going to do, then? We are going to establish the kingdom of God upon the earth.—*JD,* 5:189-190, August 30, 1857.

We are all interested in the great latter-day work of God, and we all ought to be co-workers therein.—*JD,* 18:196, April 6, 1876.

ANOTHER MISSION OF THE CHURCH: TO PERPETUATE THE LIBERTY AND RIGHTS OF MAN.—Besides the preaching of the gospel, we have another mission, namely, the perpetuation of the free agency of man and the maintenance of liberty, freedom, and the rights of man. There are certain principles that belong to humanity outside of the Constitution, outside of the laws, outside of all the enactments and plans of man, among which is the right to live. God gave us the right and no man: No government gave it to us, and no government has a right to take it away from us.

We have a right to liberty—that was a right that God gave to all men; and if there has been oppression, fraud, or tyranny in the earth, it has been the result of the wickedness and corruptions of men and has always been opposed to God and the principles of truth, righteousness, virtue, and all principles that are calculated to elevate mankind.

The Declaration of Independence states that men are in possession of certain inalienable rights, among which are life, liberty, and the pursuit of happiness. They belong to us; they belong to all humanity. I wish, and the worst wish I have for the United States, is, that they could have liberality enough to give to all men equal rights, and, while they profess to have delivered the black slaves, that they strike off the fetters of the white men of the South who have been ground under the heel of sectional injustice, and let them feel that we are all brothers in one great nation, and deliver all people from tyranny and oppression of every kind, and proclaim, as they did at the first, liberty throughout the land and to all people. That is the worst wish I have for them. And when I see them take another course I feel sorry for it. . . .

I preach the gospel to the world. What is it? Force, tyranny, and oppression? No; it is all free grace, and it is all free will. Is anybody coerced? Did anybody coerce you, Latter-day Saints? Are any of you forced to continue Latter-day Saints if you do not want to? If you think you are, you are all absolved today. We know of no such principle as coercion; it is a matter of choice. The principle that I spoke of before—that is, men receive the Holy Ghost within themselves—is the cementing, binding, uniting power that exists among the Latter-day Saints.—*JD*, 23:63-64, April 9, 1882.

THE WORK OF GOD.—We have the gospel to preach to the nations, a message that the Lord has given unto us to promulgate to all peoples. . . . Our mission has principally been to preach the first principles of the gospel, calling upon men everywhere to believe in the Lord God of heaven, he that created the heavens and the earth, the seas, and the fountains of waters; to believe in his Son, Jesus Christ, repenting of their sins, to be baptized for the remission of the same; and then we have promised them the Holy Ghost. In doing this the Lord has stood by us, sustaining those principles that we have advanced; and when we have ministered unto men the ordinances of the gospel; they have received for themselves the witness of the Spirit, even the Holy Ghost, making known to them for a surety that the principles that they had received were from God. And in regard to this I can say as Paul said on a certain occasion—"Ye are my witnesses," for this whole congregation, with few exceptions, know this to be true.—*JD*, 23:235-236, August 20, 1882.

## THE ORDER OF THE CHURCH

RESPECT FOR OFFICERS.—I do not know that I have ever disobeyed the requests of a bishop. Why? Because he presided over me in a ward capacity, and if he had a right to respect me as an apostle, I had a right to respect him as a bishop, and I always felt a desire to comply with all the requirements that were made of me by any of the proper authorities. I feel and always have felt the same towards teachers. If a teacher came to my house —or teachers, they generally come two at a time—if I happened to be there, I have told them that I felt happy to meet with them, and I called together the members of my family that were within my reach, and told them that the teachers had come to instruct us. Permit me here to ask, have not I a right—say as the president of the Church, or as an apostle, which I was for many years —have not I a right, or my family a right to possess the same privileges that others possess, and to have the teachers come to inquire after my welfare and that of my family, and to see that there is no wrong existing—have not I that right? I think I have. If they are the servants of God, have not I a right to listen to them? Yes, I have, and I feel it my duty to receive them kindly, treat them properly, and listen to their teaching.

On the other hand, when the teachers got through, I might give them a little instruction, say as an apostle, or as a brother—put it any way you like; that while I and my family were receiving benefits from them, it was my duty, on the other hand, to teach and instruct them in some things that I thought might benefit them.

Now, these are correct principles in the church and kingdom of God. The teacher occupies his place; the priest and deacon occupy their places; the elder occupies his place; the bishop his place; the high council their places; the presidents of stakes their places, and every one in his position ought to be honored—the twelve in their place, the First Presidency in their place—each one yielding proper respect and courtesy and kindness to the other. And when we talk about great big personages, there is no such thing. We are none of us anything only as God confers blessings upon us, and if he has conferred anything upon us, we will give him the glory.—*JD*, 26:130-132, October 6, 1883.

CALLING OF THE MINISTRY.—Jesus, in selecting his disciples, took one man here and another there—a tax gatherer, a fisherman, and others who it was thought were the most unlikely of any men to carry out the purposes of God. He left the great men out of the question, that is the high priests and the popular and pious of all classes, and he selected his own laborers to perform his own work; and he subsequently told them, You have not chosen me, but I have chosen you and set you apart unto this mission.

When a message had to be proclaimed to the world in these last days, the agents were chosen on the same principle. There was any amount of teachers of divinity, any amount of professors of theology, any amount of reverend, and right reverend fathers and all classes of religious men and religious teachers; but God did not recognize them. He chose a young, uneducated man and inspired him with the spirit of revelation, and placed upon him a mission and required him to perform it; and he was obedient to that requirement.—*JD*, 23:259, October 8, 1882.

# CHAPTER XXI

# THE MEANING OF CHURCH MEMBERSHIP

## THE PHILOSOPHY UNDERLYING CHURCH MEMBERSHIP

We believe that God has set his hand in these last days to accomplish his purposes, to gather together his elect from the four winds, even to fulfil the words which he has spoken by all the holy prophets, to redeem the earth from the power of the curse, to save the human family from the ruin of the fall, and to place mankind in that position which God designed them to occupy before this world came into existence, or the morning stars sang together for joy. We believe in and realize these things. We feel them, we appreciate them, and therefore are we thus assembled together.—*JD*, 1:147, 148, June 12, 1853.

OBJECTS OF MORMONISM.—We are seeking, in the first place, to regenerate ourselves, and then, under the guidance and direction of the Almighty, to regulate the world in which we live. We know that this is not very popular; but that makes no difference to us. So far as we, ourselves, are concerned we know precisely where we stand. So far as the world is concerned, as to the reception of our ideas by them, that is their business, and God's business. They have to do with him, and we have to do with him. We are in his hands, and all the world of mankind are in his hands, and he will manage and control them and dictate and regulate them according to the dictates of his will, and not according to my theories or yours or any other person's, and the judge of all the earth will do right.—*JD*, 14:339-340, March 3, 1872.

REQUIREMENTS OF GOD'S FOLLOWERS.—There is an inexorable law of God that requires from his professed followers the principles of virtue, honor, truth, integrity, righteousness, justice, judgment, and mercy.—*MA*, 162.

NO CENSORSHIP OF TRUTH.—No people upon the face of the earth are blessed to the same extent as this people. It is our privilege to have knowledge of all doctrines and principles that are taught, and if we do not have this knowledge, we are living below our privileges. It is said in one of the revelations that the voice of the people is the voice of God; this is because they are taught alike; they are taught correct principles and when they are united, then their voice in regard to any principle becomes the voice of God, for it brings us into connection with him and his Spirit.—*JD*, 9:344, April 13, 1862.

THE MISSION OF THE MEMBERS.—We have a great and important mission committed unto us, and it is for us to seek to comprehend that mission and fulfil the various duties and responsibilities devolving upon us. The Lord has given unto us a form of government, an organization, priesthood, and authority to enable us to perform these several duties, and he has certain plans, purposes, and designs to accomplish pertaining to us, pertaining to this nation, to other nations, and to the world in which we live—pertaining to those who have lived and are now in another state of existence, and also pertaining to those who shall yet live.—*JD*, 23:258, October 8, 1882.

I am not going to preach. I wish to tell my feelings, and look at you, and think about what we have done, and what we are going to do, for it is not all done yet. We have only commenced the great work of the Lord, and are laying the foundation of that kingdom which is destined to stand forever. What we shall do is yet in the future. We have commenced at the little end of the horn, and by and by we will come out at the big end.—*JD*, 1:16, August 22, 1852.

We are here to serve God and keep his commandments; and if we will purge ourselves from our iniquities, live our religion, and keep the commandments of God, there is no power on this side of hell, nor on the other, that can harm us, for God will be on our side to protect us in the position we occupy.—*JD*, 22:3, October 7, 1879.

## THE MEANING OF WORSHIP

OBJECTS OF MEETING TOGETHER.—We meet together, as intelligent beings, desirous of understanding something of our common origin, our present existence, and our future destiny. We meet to find out something in relation to our Heavenly Father, in relation to his providential dealings with the human family, in relation to his policy and designs pertaining to us, and in relation to the object of our creation; and to know something, if possible, pertaining to that world that lies beyond our present scene of action. These are some things among the many that we are desirous to know, to comprehend, to find out, if possible.

We further wish to pursue a course that shall be acceptable to our God and Father. Having partaken of a portion of his Holy Spirit, we are desirous to be taught more perfectly the things pertaining to the kingdom of God. We are desirous of cultivating his Holy Spirit, and to draw from the fountain of light and intelligence; from the spirit of revelation that flows from God, and the spirit that dwells in us, comfort, consolation, and intelligence, that we may feel that we are the sons and daughters of God, that we are walking in the light of his countenance, that we are doing the things that are pleasing and acceptable in his sight, that our own consciences are producing satisfactory evidence to our minds, that our conduct and acts are acceptable before the Lord, and that the Holy Ghost also bears testimony to us that we are his children, doing his will, walking in the light of his countenance, helping to establish his kingdom on the earth, and to fulfil the varied duties we are placed here upon the earth to attend to.—*JD*, 11:20, December 11, 1864.

SACRAMENT MEETINGS.—In meeting together on Sabbath days we assemble generally for the purpose of renewing our spirit-. ual strength by partaking of the emblems of the broken body and shed blood of our Lord and Savior Jesus Christ, communing with our own hearts and reflecting upon things pertaining to the kingdom of God, and of speaking and listening to those things that have a tendency to enlighten our minds and establish us in the faith, to increase and confirm our hopes, and to enable us to press onward with avidity, confidence, and renewed determination in the path which the Lord' has marked out for us to travel in.—*JD*, 18:278, November 5, 1876.

We have met to partake of the sacrament of the Lord's supper, and we should endeavor to draw away our feelings and affections from things of time and sense. For in partaking of the sacrament we not only commemorate the death and sufferings of our Lord and Savior Jesus Christ, but we also shadow forth the time when he will come again and when we shall meet and eat bread with him in the kingdom of God. When we are thus assembled together, we may expect to receive guidance and blessings from God.—*JD*, 14:185, March 20, 1870.

This ceremony has been attended to throughout generations that are past, and still it is attended to. Jesus said also, "do this until I come again." Notwithstanding the great falling off—the great apostasy since the days of Christ and his apostles, this ordinance has generally been adopted by the Christian churches, so called, however they may err in many other principles of faith and doctrine. This ordinance has been renewed to us, and is part and parcel of the new covenant God has made with his people in the latter days. It was practiced among the ancient saints who resided upon this continent, long before it was discovered by Columbus, as well as upon the continent of Asia among the saints that lived there. When we attend to this ordinance, we do it upon the same principle that they did anciently, whether among the Saints of God on the Asiatic continent or among the Saints on the American continent.—*JD*, 10:113, February 22, 1863.

WORSHIP "IN SPIRIT AND IN TRUTH."—The best of us are not too good; we all of us might be better, and do better, and enjoy life better, having more of the Spirit of the Lord in our own homes and in our own hearts, and do more to promote the welfare of all who come within our reach and influence. To serve the Lord is one of the great objects of our existence; and I appreciate as a great privilege the opportunity we enjoy of worshiping God on the Sabbath day. And when we do meet to worship God, I like to see us worship him with all our hearts. I think it altogether out of place on such occasions to hear people talk about secular things; these are times, above all others perhaps, when our feelings and affections should be drawn out towards God. If we sing praises to God, let us do it in the proper spirit; if we pray, let every soul be engaged in prayer, doing it with all our hearts, that through our union our spirits may be blended in one, that our prayers and our worship may be available with God, whose Spirit permeates all things, and is always present in the assemblies of good and faithful Saints.—*JD*, 22:226, June 26, 1881.

What then shall we do? We will do everything which God requires at our hands. Have we families? We will try to train them up in the fear of God. Have we wives? We will treat them as we would angels of God, and be their protectors and guardians and make them comfortable and happy. And then, as was remarked, we will dedicate our houses and lands to God, and ourselves to God, and our wives and children and everything we have, and feel that we are the children of God and our offspring with us. Again, if I were a woman, I would try to treat my husband right and to make a heaven of my home, and would try to make everything pleasant around me. You husbands now and then quarrel with your wives, and you wives quarrel with your husbands. . . . I will say, cease such folly, and have another kind of feeling; and treat everybody not as he always treats us, for that would not always be right; but let us do unto all men as we would have them do unto us.—*JD*, 22:220, 221, June 27, 1881.

## PROFESSIONS AND PROBLEMS OF THE LATTER-DAY SAINTS

PROFESSIONS IN GENERAL.—We profess that this is the work of God in which we are engaged, and our profession is strictly correct. When we say this is the church and kingdom of

God, we believe it, and so it is. And it is the only Church and the only kingdom that he has on this earth in this generation that we know anything about. We profess to know that God has revealed his law, that he has restored the holy priesthood, and that he is communicating his will to the human family. We profess to believe that the kingdom of God will overrule and prevail over every other power and every other form of government, and that it will go on from strength to strength, from power to power, from intelligence to intelligence, from knowledge to knowledge; and that in the due course of events it will rule over the whole earth, until every creature upon the earth and under the earth and on the sea will be subject to the law of God, to the kingdom of God, to the dominion of God, and to the rule of the holy priesthood. This is our profession. We believe it: at any rate we profess to believe it; and if we do not, we are hypocrites.—*JD,* 1:371, 372, April 19, 1854.

A DAILY REMINDER.—How many of us have fallen on the right hand and on the left; those we have judged to be men of intelligence, some of them have stepped aside in one shape and some in another. Some have given way to their corrupt appetites and passions, and have fallen in an evil hour, have lost the Spirit of God, have destroyed themselves, and have destroyed others. Corrupted, weak, fallen, degenerate, and abominable, they have sunk to their own place. How much of this has there been both among men and women, to the violation of the most sacred covenants they have made before God, angels, and men. They have broken their covenants, corrupted themselves, departed from the right way, lost the Spirit of God, and they are anxious to go here and there, and everything is wrong with them, and every place fails to yield them comfort, because a consciousness of their guilt is continually with them; everything is out of place to them; and their understandings are darkened. At one time they were quick to comprehend truth by the light of the Spirit, but now they walk in darkness. . . .

Have you forgotten who you are, and what your object is? Have you forgotten that you profess to be Saints of the Most High God, clothed upon with the holy priesthood? Have you forgotten that you are aiming to become kings and priests to the Lord, and queens and priestesses to him? Have you forgotten that you are associated with the Saints of God in Zion, where the oracles of truth are revealed, and the truths of God are made manifest, and clearly developed; where you and your posterity after you can learn the ways of life and salvation; where you are placed in a position that you can obtain blessings from the great Elohim, that will rest upon you and your posterity worlds without end? Have you forgotten these things, and begun to turn again to the beggarly elements of the world, and become blind, like others we have spoken of, turning like the sow that was washed to her wallowing in the mire? We ought to reflect sometimes upon these things, and understand our true position.—*JD*, 1:372, April 19, 1854.

AN ITEM OF FAITH.—There has been something said about men turning away from the Church of Christ. If a man has not the witness in himself, he is not governed by the principles of eternal truth, and the sooner such people leave this Church the better.—*JD*, 10:260-261, October 10, 1863.

We cannot run our own way and have the blessing of God. Every one who attempts it will find he is mistaken. God will withdraw his Spirit from such, and they will be left to themselves to wander in the dark, and go down to perdition. It is expected of us that we shall move on a higher plane, that we shall feel that we are the children of God, that God is our Father, and he will not be dishonored by disobedient children, or by those who fight against his laws and his priesthood. He expects us to live our religion, to obey his laws and keep his commandments.— *JD*, 25:164, June 15, 1884.

DOING "As THEY DARNED PLEASE."—Some men who think they are doing pretty well, and doing, according to their own expression, "as they darned please," will wake up to find they have not been doing the will of God. They may have thought that they had wives and children, but they will wake up to find that they have not got them, and that they are deprived of many of those great blessings they anticipated enjoying. With all of our mercy, kindness, and tender feelings towards our brethren and sisters, and towards all people, we cannot violate the law of God, nor transgress those principles which he has laid down with impunity. He expects us to do those things that are acceptable before him, and if we don't, we must pay the penalty of our departure from correct principle.—*JD*, 25:163, June 15, 1884.

HUMAN WEAKNESSES.—What do you think about a lying elder, a swearing high priest, a Sabbath-breaking seventy, and a covetous Saint? The souls of such men ought to be inspired with the light of revelation, and they ought to be living witnesses, epistles known and read of all men! Do you think you can live your religion, have the Spirit of God and obtain eternal life, and follow after these things? I tell you, Nay.

It was said of olden time—"Love not the world, neither the things that are in the world. If any man love the world, the love of the Father is not in him." (1 John 2:15.) That is as true today as it was eighteen hundred years ago. It is proper that we, as elders of Israel, and as heads of families, should reflect upon these things, for in many instances we are setting examples before our children that will tend to plunge them to perdition. Is this what we are gathered here for? I tell you, Nay; we are gathered here to serve God and keep his commandments, and to build up his Zion upon the earth.—*JD*, 18:141-142, October 10, 1875.

HONESTY IN WORSHIP.—There is one great principle by which, I think, we all of us ought to be actuated in our worship, above everything else that we are associated with in life, and that is honesty of purpose. . . .

It is proper that men should be honest with themselves, that they should be honest with each other in all their words, dealings, intercourse, intercommunication, business arrangements, and everything else. They ought to be governed by truthfulness, honesty, and integrity, and that man is very foolish indeed who would not be true to himself, true to his convictions and feelings in regard to religious matters. We may deceive one another, as in some circumstances, counterfeit coin passes for that which is considered true and valuable among men. But God searches the hearts and tries the reins of the children of men. He knows our thoughts and comprehends our desires and feelings. He knows our acts and the motives which prompt us to perform them. He is acquainted with all the doings and operations of the human family, and all the secret thoughts and acts of the children of men are open and naked before him, and for them he will bring them to judgment.

These ideas are believed in by men generally, who, with very few exceptions, whatever their general conduct or ideas on religious matters may be, believe in an all-seeing eye which penetrates and is enabled to weigh the actions and motives of the children of men. This is an idea that will not be disputed by any race of men now existing upon the earth, nor perhaps by any who have existed heretofore, for whatever may have been the theories or notions of men in former times, they have generally had a reverence for, and a belief in, an all-wise, supreme, omnipotent Being, who, they supposed, was greater than all of them, and who governed and controlled by their actions. A feeling of this kind is frequently made manifest in the scriptures, and it is nothing new in our age to believe in a God of this character.—*JD*, 16:301-302, November 16, 1873.

## THE MORMON POSITION

TO BE "IN THE WORLD, BUT NOT OF THE WORLD."—
We have separated ourselves from the world in which we live.
We have been baptized, by immersion in water, for the remission
of sins. We have had hands laid upon us for the gift of the
Holy Ghost; and the question with us now is, shall we condescend
to go again into the beggarly elements of the world, or shall we
continue in obedience to the law of God? If we do not obey the
law which the Lord has given for our guidance, we shall go
down to destruction, and our second state will be far worse
than the first. We are now laying a foundation for ourselves
and our posterity; and what is it that will flash upon our minds
if we turn away from the truth? We shall think of the time
when we thought we were the Saints of God. We shall think
of our associations with this people, and these reflections will
greatly increase our misery.—*JD*, 8:99-100, June 17, 1860.

TOLERATION.—It is a mistaken notion, let me say here,
that some people entertain that because men persecute us, we must
persecute them: that because men would proscribe us in our religious faith, we must persecute them in theirs. There is no such principle associated with God, or with those who dwell in the love
of God, or who are actuated by the Spirit of God. Everything
of that kind proceeds from beneath and not from above. God is
interested in the welfare of all people, all nations, all kindreds, and
all tongues.—*JD*, 22:290-291, October 9, 1881.

As intelligent beings it is for us to comprehend all truth
so far as we are capable of understanding it.—*JD*, 26:87, February 12, 1882.

PROMISES TO THE SAINTS.—If there have been any blessings
enjoyed by men in former dispensations of the world, they will
also be given to you, ye Latter-day Saints, if you will live your
religion and be obedient to the laws of God. There is nothing
hidden but what shall be revealed, says the Lord. He is prepared
to unfold all things, all things pertaining to the heavens and the
earth, all things pertaining to the peoples who have existed, who
now exist or will exist, that we may be instructed and taught
in every principle of intelligence associated with the world in
which we live, or with the Gods in the eternal worlds.—*JD*,
25:184, May 18, 1884.

Now, then, if we are blessed we have not to thank any
man, or any set of men for it. If we are provided for, we
have not obtained it from anybody else, but from the Lord God
of Israel, who has watched over and protected his people just as
he said he would do. He said it was his business to take care of

his saints, but, then, it is our business to be saints.—*JD,* 26:69, November 30, 1884.

I will tell you the only thing I am afraid of about the saints is that they will forget their God and that they will not live their religion. Then again I have not that fear, because I know the generality of them will. I know this kingdom will not be given into the hands of another people. I know that it will continue to progress and continue to increase in spite of all the powers of the adversary, in spite of every influence that exists now, or that ever will exist on the face of this wide earth. God is our God, and he will bring off Israel triumphant.—*JD,* 14:367, March 17, 1872.

THE ONLY FEAR.—The only fear I have for the Latter-day Saints is that they will not live their religion. And I call upon you here today to lay aside your covetousness, your greed, and your avarice, and act honorably and justly one with another as your brethren; humble yourselves before God and seek unto him for his guidance; and he will help you; he will bless you sustain you; and he will deliver you.—*JD,* 21:6, August 31, 1879.

"IT IS GOOD TO BE A SAINT."—It is good to be a Saint. When we get the Spirit of the Lord upon us, we feel to rejoice exceedingly, and sometimes when we don't have much of  that, it feels rather what we used to call hard-sledding. But there is nothing that makes things go so well among the saints of God as living their religion and keeping the commandments of God, and when they don't do that, then things go awkward and cross and every other way but the right way. But when they live their religion and keep the commandments, "their peace flows as a river, and their righteousness as the waves of the sea."—*JD,* 26:71, November 30, 1884.

# CHAPTER XXII

# MISSIONARY WORK (PROSELYTING THE KINGDOM)

## PROCLAIMING THE GOSPEL

THE MISSIONARY SPIRIT.—I rejoice in proclaiming this glorious gospel, because it takes root in the hearts of the children of men, and they rejoice with me to be connected with, and participate in, the blessings of the kingdom of God. I rejoice in afflictions, for they are necessary to humble and prove us, that we may comprehend ourselves, become acquainted with our weakness and infirmities; and I rejoice when I triumph over them, because God answers my prayers; therefore I feel to rejoice all the day long.—*JD*, 1:17, August 22, 1852.

I, myself, have traveled hundreds of thousands of miles preaching the gospel; and without purse or scrip, trusting in the Lord. Did he ever forsake me? Never, no never. I always was provided for, for which I feel to praise God my Heavenly Father. I was engaged in his work, and he told me that he would sustain me in it. He has been true to his trust; and if I have not been true to mine, I hope he will forgive me and help me to do better. But the Lord has been true and faithful, and I have never needed anything to eat or drink or wear, and was never prevented for want of means of traveling where I pleased.—*JD*, 21:95, April 13, 1879.

THE GREAT RESPONSIBILITY.—Our duty is to preach the gospel to all men. Who, the First Presidency? Yes, if there is nobody else. The twelve? Yes, it is their especial calling to preach it themselves or see that it is preached to all the world. And, then, the seventies, it is their duty to go forth at the drop of the hat, as minute men, to preach the gospel to all nations, under the guidance of the twelve. And, then, it is for those who are in Zion, the high priests, and others to go and preach the gospel.

"TURN NOW TO ISRAEL."—And we are doing this in spite of the opposition of men, and in the name of God we will do it until he who directs us shall say, "It is enough: turn now to Israel." When he says that, then we will quit. And if they love the devil better than God, they can do so and sup trouble and sorrow and calamity and war and bloodshed. For nation will rise against nation, country against country; and thrones will be cast down; and empires will be scattered to the four winds, and the powers of the earth everywhere will be shaken; and the Lord will come forth by and by to judge the nations; and it behooves us to know what we are doing, and while we profess to be the saints of God not to be hypocrites, but be full of truth and full of integrity and magnify our calling and honor our God.

This is what God expects of us. And then to build temples, and what then? Administer in them. Send the gospel to the nations of the earth. And then gather the people in. What then? Build more temples. What then? Have men administer in them. And when we get through with our relatives and friends, and trace back our ancestry as far as we can, then we will call upon God to give us information as to who need to be administered for in the heavens; and we will work at it for a thousand years, until all the purposes of God shall be accomplished, and everything spoken of in the prophets shall be fulfilled.—*JD*, 26:110, October 20, 1881.

FOR THE BENEFIT OF THE WORLD.—The gospel was then revealed, what for—for you and me, or for this man and that man? No; it was for the benefit of the world; it was in the interests of humanity; and it was to be proclaimed to every nation, kindred, people, and tongue, by men commissioned of God to do so. . . .

And we are still struggling on, in the face of a general opposition, trusting in our God to sustain us, while we shall continue to sow the precious seed of the everlasting gospel, and maintain in our own midst the principles of life eternal, and freedom, liberty, and equality to the human race. And our sons who have grown up are now doing what we have done; and they too are full of the Spirit, full of life, light, and intelligence, having, as we had and still have, the interests of humanity at heart, as they move among the people as messengers of life and salvation.

Our course is onward; and are we going to stop? No. Zion must be built up, God has decreed it, and no power can stay its progress. Do you hear that? I prophecy that in the name of the Lord Jesus Christ. For Zion must and will be built up despite all opposition, the kingdom of God established upon the earth in accordance with the designs and purposes of God. That is true, and you will find it to be true if you live long enough, and if you die, you will find it to be true; it will make no difference.—*JD*, 23:33-34, March 5, 1882.

THE COMMAND OF GOD.—We are sending the gospel to the nations of the earth. Why? Because God has commanded it.

What are the seventies for? For this purpose. What are the twelve for? For this purpose. What are the elders for? When there is a deficiency among the seventies they are chosen for this purpose; and the high priests have to assist in the same way. What to do? To teach, to instruct, to enlighten, to bless, and to lead the people of the world in the ways of life.—*JD*, 25:95, February 10, 1884.

TESTS OF MORMONISM.—I have generally taken the liberty of applying the word of God to principles of religion whether taught by the Methodists, Church of England, Roman Catholics, or any others; and when Mormonism was presented to me, my first inquiry was, "Is it scriptural? Is it reasonable and philosophical?" This is the principle I would act upon today. No matter how popular the theories or dogmas preached might be, I would not accept them unless they were strictly in accordance with the scriptures, reason, and common sense.

I used to be told when investigating religious principles that it was dangerous to do so, and I had better let them alone; but I did not think so. I believe it is good to investigate and prove all principles that come before me. Prove all things, hold fast that which is good, and reject that which is evil, no matter what guise it may come in. I think if we, as Mormons, hold principles that cannot be sustained by the scriptures and by good sound reason and philosophy, the quicker we part with them the better, no matter who believes in them or who does not. In every principle presented to us, our first inquiry should be, "Is it true? Does it emanate from God?" If he is its author, it can be sustained just as much as any other truth in natural philosophy; if false, it should be opposed and exposed just as much as any other error. Hence upon all such matters we wish to go back to first principles.—*JD*, 13:14-15, March 14, 1869.

## TRENDS IN MISSIONARY WORK

"PURSE AND SCRIP."—We used to be in the habit of going without purse or scrip. That is the way I have traveled hundreds and thousands of miles; but then we felt as the disciples of old did. When we returned, if asked if we had lacked anything, we could say verily no. But there was a time afterwards when Jesus said—Let him that has a purse take it with him, and let him that has no sword sell his coat and buy one. We do not always remain in *status quo*. At that time we were the poorest people in the world. But now we are better off than the generality of mankind and we are able to help one another, and there is no necessity for our missionaries to go under the circumstances they have done heretofore. And since it is the counsel that they shall not, why let us do what we can to help them.—*JD*, 12:48, May 19, 1867.

REASONING UNDERLYING THE PERPETUAL EMIGRATION FUND.—We have expended millions upon millions in gathering the poor to this land, by what is known as the Perpetual Emigration Fund. We may ask, why did this people in these valleys expend such large sums? Was it because they were sending for relatives and friends? No, but because they were of the family of Christ, the sons and daughters of God, and desired to come to Zion. We have sent as much as five hundred teams at a time to help out the poor. You have done it, and many of you have either sent your sons or gone yourselves, and you have carried provisions for them as well as bringing them here. I do not think there is very much harm in that.

And what then? When these same men who had received the message of truth in far-off lands, and who had been gathered here, had been further instructed, we have sent them back again to the nations from whence they came, to proclaim to their kindred and friends, to their tongue and nation, what God had done for them. After fulfilling their missions they return again. What to do? To slumber and sleep away their time? No, but to continue their work in reclaiming the waste places, and to build temples in the interest of humanity, as the friends of God and of the world.—*JD*, 19:127, October 7, 1877.

DEVELOPMENTS IN MISSIONARY WORK: A PROPHETIC INSIGHT.—There is a terrible time approaching the nations of the earth, and also this nation, worse than has ever entered into the heart of man to conceive of—war, bloodshed, and desolation, mourning and misery, pestilence, famine, and earthquakes, and all those calamities spoken of by the prophets will most assuredly be fulfilled, and they are nearer by forty years than they were forty years ago. And it is for us, Latter-day Saints, to understand the position we occupy. . . .

Among the honorable men I have referred to, there are some things that make it extremely difficult for men sometimes to perform the kind of missions that they did formerly, owing to age, infirmities, and circumstances. Yet I have frequently felt ashamed when I have seen the acts of many of these quorums to which I refer, when they have been called upon to go on missions. One has one excuse, and another, another. It was easier some twenty years ago to raise two or three hundred men than it is now among all those thousands in Israel. How do you account for this? Partly in consequence of an apathy that exists in the different organisms of the priesthood; and partly from circumstances with which we have been surrounded.

We have been grappling with these difficulties in common with others; and the Lord has placed us in this position to try us to see what material we are made of. Or, to use a common saying, to see who would be found at the rack, hay or no hay. But the general feeling seems to be—and I suppose it is so with us in Salt Lake and other places—that we would rather go to the rack when there was plenty of hay. But there is such a thing as having faith in God.

I will tell you how I have viewed these things. A great many have been thrown into circumstances that without distressing their families it would be extremely difficult to pick themselves up and go on missions. We did not use to think about this; but there should be in this, as in other things, a cooperation, a united order, if you please. We have found, in looking over some of our affairs, that these pinching times have reached to England. And lately when our elders have returned home after having been absent two or three years, they themselves not having the means to pay their way home, they have had to give their notes for the money; and the consequence was they would return with a load of debt upon their shoulders. The council have considered this matter, and decided to cancel such indebtedness. It amounted to some fifty thousand dollars. And then we contrived with Brother Staines and the presidency in Liverpool to try to make such arrangements that when our brethren return home from missions, they shall come free. How do you feel? All who are in favor say aye. [The congregation said aye.]—JD, 20:46-47, August 4, 1878.

## TO ALL THE NATIONS

I never see the elders go forth on missions to preach the gospel, but I consider that they are going forth to take part in one of the greatest works ever committed to the human family.

Whatever their feelings may be, they go forth as the angels of mercy bearing the precious seeds of the gospel, and they shall be the means of bringing many from darkness to light, from error and superstition to life, light, truth, and intelligence, and finally, to exaltation in the celestial kingdom of our God.

"TO COMBAT THE ERRORS OF AGES."—When these brethren go forth, it may be a new work to them. They will have to combat the errors of ages, to contend with the prejudices which they themselves state to you held such a powerful influence over them; they will also have to preach to and reason with men who have no regard for truth, much less for the religion which we have embraced, yet these elders go forth as the sent messengers of the Lord Jesus Christ. They go to proclaim that God has established his work upon the earth, that he has spoken from the heavens, and that the visions of the Almighty have been opened to our view; the light of ages is being revealed to the servants of the Most High, the darkness which has enshrouded the world for ages is being dispersed; and these chosen elders of Israel are sent forth to proclaim these glad tidings of salvation to the dark and benighted nations of the earth. I consider it a great privilege for any man to be set apart to so honorable, so praiseworthy, and so important a mission. . . . They go forth and they shall come back rejoicing, bearing precious sheaves with them, and they will bless the name of the God of Israel, that they have had the privilege of taking a part in warning this generation.

THE FAMILIES AT HOME.—As regards the circumstances of their families, it is proper and correct that men should have some feelings for those they have left at home. It is true there ought to be sympathy and some care for those with whom they have been immediately associated. Yet their families as well as our families, and all of us and our affairs, are in the hands of God, and, inasmuch as they go forth putting their trust in the living God, all will be peace, and they will find peace and contentment from this time forth until they return, inasmuch as they will magnify their callings and lean upon their God. In this is their safety, in order that they may be enabled to bear a faithful testimony to the world among whom they may travel to deliver their message of warning and of glad tidings of great joy to the honest in heart.—*JD*, 10:36-37, April 27, 1862.

THE MISSIONARIES.—We want men to preach the gospel who are honorable and upright men, and full of the Holy Ghost. And when such men go, they go with our faith, carrying with them our esteem and love and affection; and if they need anything, we will give it to them. If their families need anything, we will have them looked after; we will feed them and clothe them and take care of them, and consider that they are our brethren and not that they are poor, miserable paupers, or that their wives and families are a trouble to us. We want to do away with all such feelings. Let us cultivate the spirit of magnanimity and kindness, and as the Lord blesses us, let us bless others; and that is all the things of the earth are worth. Do good to all men, especially to the household of faith. And by and by, as was the case formerly, those who go forth weeping, bearing precious seed, will return rejoicing, bringing their sheaves with them.—*JD*, 20:178, April 8, 1879.

## INSTRUCTIONS TO MISSIONARIES

"FULFIL YOUR MISSION."—I would say to these brethren —let it be your study to fulfil your mission. Never mind the world, never mind the dollars and cents, the pounds, shillings, and pence. You cleave to God, live your religion, magnify your callings, humble yourselves before God, call upon him in secret, and he will open your path before you, and you shall have food and clothing, and your every want will be supplied, and you will be able to accomplish a good work and return to Zion in peace and safety. These are my feelings.—*JD*, 12:397, April 14, 1867.

PRAYER AND STUDY.—In relation, again, to these elders, I will tell you the first thing I used to do when I went preaching, particularly when I went to a fresh place—and that was to go aside to some place, anywhere I could get, into a field, a barn, into the woods, or my closet, and ask God to bless me and give me wisdom to meet all the circumstances with which I might have to contend; and the Lord gave me the wisdom I needed and sustained me. If you pursue a course of this kind, he will bless you also. Do not trust in yourselves, but study the best books —the Bible and Book of Mormon—and get all the information you can, and then cleave to God and keep yourselves free from corruption and pollution of every kind, and the blessings of the Most High will be with you.—*JD*, 12:398, April 14, 1867.

THE HUMBLE SPIRIT.—There is a very great difference between our mode of promulgating the gospel and that pursued by the world. . . . The grand difference between us and them is that we go forth in the name of Israel's God, sustained by his power, wisdom, and intelligence, to proclaim the principles of eternal truth communicated to us by him, while they go forth . . . having learned what they call the Science of Divinity; they consider themselves qualified to teach it anywhere and under all circumstances. They have nothing more to learn and nothing more to teach. When our elders go forth, they have no preparation beyond the common rudiments of education that all are supposed to learn; but it is not words they go to teach, it is principles. And although before an audience learned in the laws of God, they may feel a good deal of tremor and bashfulness in trying to express themselves, yet, when they go forth and stand before congregations in the world, the Spirit of the Lord God will go with them, the Lord will sustain them, and will give unto them wisdom, "that all their adversaries will not be able to gainsay nor resist." That is the promise made to the servants of the Lord who go forth trusting in him.

I have a great deal more confidence in men who rise feeling their weakness and inability than I have in those who feel that they are well informed and capable of teaching anything and everything. Why? Because when men trust to themselves they trust in a broken reed, and when they trust in the Lord, they will never fail. I have been out when I was . . . young . . . , before my head was gray, and I had to learn to trust in God. When we go forth into the world, we do not go among friends, for sometimes they do not treat us very friendly. I would say to these brethren, they will meet with enemies on every hand who will oppose and persecute them, malign their characters, and say all manner of evil about them, and who will try to overturn the principles they advocate, unless there is a very great change in the world since the time that I used to preach among them.

At the same time they will find many very good people who will bless them, feed and clothe them, and take care of them. And.the Lord is over all, he watches over his people, and if these brethren will continue to trust in God . . . his Spirit will rest upon them, enlighten their minds, enlarge their capacities, and give to them wisdom and intelligence in time of need. They need not be under any apprehension with regard to the wisdom of the world, for there is no wisdom in the world equal to that which the Lord gives to his Saints; and as long as these brethren keep from evil, live their religion, and cleave to the Lord by keeping his commandments, there is no fear as to the results; and this will apply to all the Saints as well as to these brethren.

SEARCH THE SCRIPTURES.—I would say, however, to those going on missions, that they should study the Bible, Book of Mormon, Doctrine and Covenants, and all our works, that they may become acquainted with the principles of our faith. I would also say to other young men who are not now going on missions, but who will probably have to go at some time in the future, that these things are of more importance to them than they realize at the present time. We ought to be built up and fortified by the truth. We ought to become acquainted with the principles, doctrines, and ordinances pertaining to the church and kingdom of God. We are told, in the Doctrine and Covenants, to search after wisdom as we would for hidden treasures, both by study and by faith, to become acquainted with the history and laws of the nation we live in, and of the nations of the earth. I know that when young men are working around here, going to the canyon, working on the farm, going to the theatre, and so on, their minds are not much occupied with these things. But when they are called upon to take a part in the drama themselves, many of them will wish they had paid more attention to the instructions they have received, and had made themselves more familiar with the Bible, Book of Mormon, and the Doctrine and Covenants.

TEACH WITH POWER.—These missionaries are now going to school to teach others, and in teaching others they themselves will be instructed, and when they rise to speak in the name of Israel's God, if they live in purity and holiness before him, he will give them words and ideas of which they never dreamed before.    I have traveled hundreds and thousands of miles to preach this gospel among all grades and conditions of men, and there is one thing that always gave me satisfaction—I never yet found a man in any part of the world who could overturn one principle that has been communicated to us; they will attempt it, but error is a very singular weapon with which to combat truth; it never can vanquish it.

When men go forth in the name of Israel's God, there is no power on earth that can overturn the truths they advocate.    Men may misrepresent and calumniate them; they may circulate false reports, for as a general thing men love lies better than truth; but when men go forth possessing the truths of the everlasting gospel which God has revealed, they have a treasure within them that the world knows nothing about.    They have the light of revelation, the fire of the Holy Ghost, and the power of the priesthood within them—a power that they know very little about even themselves, which, like a well-spring of life, is rising, bursting, bubbling, and spreading its exhilarating streams around.    Why, says the Lord, with you I will confound the nations of the earth, with you I will overturn their kingdoms.— *JD*, 12:395-397, April 14, 1867.

USE OF THE BIBLE.—The Bible is believed by all! Suppose we transplant them to Hindustan or China.    What evidence would they have to present before the people?    They present the scriptures, and tell the people that they are true.    But how are we to know it, say the people.    We tell you so.    That is all very well; but we want some proof.    Well, say you, they speak of Jesus' coming to atone for the sins of the world.    Yes; but the Jews tell us he was an impostor and a wicked man.    But we believe him to be a good man, and the Son of God.    Did you ever see him?    No.    How do you know anything about him then?    We believe him to be good.    Who wrote this book?    His apostles.    Oh, *his particular friends!*    Yes.    Did you ever see them?    No.    Did you ever see anybody that had?    No.    Well, we do not put much confidence in your remarks; but we will read your book.

Having read it, they say, oh, I perceive that certain signs are to follow them that believe—the sick are to be healed, devils cast out; they are to speak in other tongues, have the gift of prophecy, etc. Do these signs follow you? Oh, no! But you say you are believers, and your Bible says these signs shall follow them that believe. Oh, they are done away and not necessary. But one of your apostles (Paul) says, "Follow after charity, and desire spiritual gifts." (I Corinthians 14:1.) But they are not needed. Strange! Your apostle, Paul, says, "the eye cannot say to the hand, I have no need of thee: nor again the head to the feet, I have no need of you." (I Corinthians 12:21.) But shall we not receive these gifts if we believe in Jesus, repent, and are baptized? No. Oh, you have a friend here, I see, who is also a Christian minister. Do you believe in the same book, sir? Yes. Do you believe in the same doctrine? No. But do you get yours from the same book? Yes! And does it teach you differently? We believe differently.

But you have, we perceive, another friend here; is he also a minister? Yes. Which of your doctrines does he believe? Neither. Do you all believe the Bible? Yes. Do you believe it to be true or false? True. Does a true book teach three different ways? Those are our opinions. Oh, I thought you had come to teach truth; if opinions are all, we have plenty of them already, and can dispense with your services. Your Bible says that the gospel was to be preached to all the world, and these signs would follow the belief and obedience to it. Do you live in the world? Yes. Then it must apply to you. I can have no confidence, gentlemen, in men who present me with a book, and call it the word of God, and then deny that word.—*PD*, 16, 1850.

THE "GRIND."—Those who have to go out have to put their noses to the grindstone, and keep them there, and let them grind at it, and not murmur a word. . . . You need not attempt to without faith in God; and you will have need of all the wisdom and intelligence you can command. You cannot go and convert the world all at once, for it is too far sunken in folly and vice.—*JD*, 6:259, August 28, 1852.

## THE WARNING TO THE NATIONS

THE MESSAGES BEING FULFILLED.—Years and years ago, I preached abroad among the nations of the earth, and I see around me here many of my brethren, the elders, whose heads are now as gray as mine, who did the same. We preached to many of you who are here, and told you that the world would wax worse and worse, deceiving and being deceived. Did we not preach this doctrine? I think we did, ten, twenty, thirty, and forty years ago. We told you then that in consequence of the wickedness that would exist upon the earth, thrones would be

cast down, empires demoralized, and that wars and bloodshed
would exist upon the face of the earth, and that God would
arise and vex the nations and bring them to judgment, because
of their iniquities. Is it anything astonishing that these words
should be fulfilled? Why, they are the words of truth! They
were spoken by the spirit of revelation, and were in accordance
with the revelations given to ancient men of God, who spoke as
they were moved upon by the Holy Ghost, and who, while rapt
in prophetic vision, saw and foretold what should transpire on
the earth. God revealed the same things to us that he did to them.
—*JD*, 14:247-248, October 8, 1871.

Quite a favorite theme has been with many of our elders,
that the "little stone" spoken of in the scriptures has been cut
out of the mountain without hands, and it is destined to strike the
image whose head was of gold, breast and arms of silver, belly
and thighs of brass, legs of iron, and feet part of iron and part of
clay, upon its feet, breaking it to pieces; and that the materials,
which represent the various nations of the earth, composing the
image, should become like the chaff of a summer's threshing-floor,
carried away by the wind until there was no place found for it.
This is exactly as it has been foretold many thousands of years
ago. . . . When this little stone, then, as it rolls forth, strikes
the toes of the great image, are you surprised that there should
be a little kicking? You don't like to have your toes trodden upon
any more than anybody else. The fact is, the same great conflict
is going on between the two great powers; the only difference is
that we are in much better circumstances than many who lived in
earlier days who had to wander about in sheep and goat skins,
seeking the dens and caves of rocks as places of retreat and safety.—
*JD*, 21:5-6, August 31, 1879.

ATTITUDE TOWARD THE WORLD.—In relation to the inhabitants of the world generally, I sometimes think that we entertain very erroneous notions concerning them—that our ideas are
too narrow and too contracted, that we do not comprehend the
relationship in which they stand to God our Heavenly Father—
and we are apt to fall into an error which was indulged in by
the Jews in former ages, and to cry out, "The temple of the
Lord, the temple of the Lord, the temple of the Lord are we."
Because God has conferred upon us light and intelligence, and
revealed his will unto us, we are too apt to look down upon the
rest of mankind as aliens and undeserving of divine regard; but
we are told that God has made of one blood all the families of the
earth, and that he has given unto them a portion of his spirit to
profit withal. We are also informed, that God is the God and
Father of the spirits of all flesh. We are given to understand
that he feels interested in the welfare of all the human family, for

it is written that they are all his offspring. Therefore, we as Latter-day Saints, ought to feel towards the world and the inhabitants thereof as God our Heavenly Father feels towards them; for we are told that God so loved the world, that he gave his Only Begotten Son to atone for their sins, that whosoever believeth on him might not perish, but have everlasting life, and if this is the feeling of our Heavenly Father towards the inhabitants of the earth, we ought to entertain the same sentiment.— *JD*, 24:287-288, October 7, 1883.

WHAT MORMONISM IS DOING.—The world want to know what Mormonism is doing. Some of us hardly know. But it is known that we are building temples, but the Christian world do not know what temples are for. If temples were built for them, they would not know how to administer in them. And we did not know until God revealed it. And unless Elijah had come and conferred the keys, it would not have been revealed. Hence I was showing you who and what Joseph Smith was. He has introduced the gospel together with the dispensation of the fulness of times, which embraces all other things.

Then again, did Enoch build up a Zion? So we are doing. What is it? The Zion of God. What does it mean? The pure in heart in the first place. In the second place those who are governed by the law of God—the pure in heart who are governed by the law of God. Shall we build up a Zion? We shall; but we shall not, every one of us, have our own way about it. We shall feel that we need the will of God; and we shall feel that we require the priesthood, under his direction, to guide and direct us. Not men who are seeking to aggrandize themselves; but men who are seeking to build up the church and kingdom of God upon the earth; men of clean hands and pure hearts, every one honoring his priesthood and magnifying it. . . . Now, this is what we are building up, and they built up a similar thing before the flood; and the elders went forth in those days as they now go forth; and they baptized people and laid hands upon them, and gathered them to Zion; and after a while that Zion was caught up from the earth. And we will build up a Zion: that is what we are aiming at. And that Zion also, when the time comes, will ascend to meet the Zion from above, which will descend, and both, we are told, will fall on each other's necks and kiss each other.— *JD*, 26:109-110, October 20, 1881.

THE METHOD.—At the commencement of the dispensations God sends out his elders generally to all the world to preach the gospel to every creature. In this dispensation he not only does this; but, as we live in a gathering dispensation, he also gathers in the people. When they learn a little of his law, there are many ordained to the priesthood and sent out as messengers, and we keep sending them out to preach the gospel and to gather in the elect; and we send them to their own people to tell them what God has done and is doing. And they keep coming and going.

And whom do we send? If we send to England, we send Englishmen, or men who can speak the English language; if to Scandinavia, we send Scandinavians. We send generally their own people, accompanied with men of experience, after the gospel has been introduced to them. Why? That they may go and teach their own people the way of life and salvation. What then? They come back again and build temples. And what then? They and their people from the various nations of the earth go into these temples and administer for their fathers, and grandfathers, their uncles and aunts, their friends and relatives, and thus reach back, back into distant times to redeem and save others.

And who are these men? Just such as the ancient prophets talked about. They are saviors upon Mount Zion, are they not, saving and redeeming their people—and those men who are quarrying and hauling the rock, and those who are engaged in laying up these terrace and temple walls, and those who are otherwise engaged in making the necessary preparation for the building of the temple are all laboring in the same direction. The Lord requires this work at our hands in order to test us, to see whether we will carry out his laws or not. And when we build our temples and he accepts of them, we will then enter into them and administer in the name of God; and administering in them we become saviors upon Mount Zion, as it is written.—*JD*, 21: 96-97. April 13, 1879.

MEN OF THE WORLD.—If the men of the world, if the princes and potentates of the earth, if the statesmen and great men among the nations could . . . understand the gospel as it has been revealed to us—if they could know anything of our high calling's glorious hope, and of the principles that animate our bosoms, they would, many of them, lay down their honors and their thrones, and come down and ask for admission into this kingdom. But they have got to receive the kingdom of God like a little child, just the same as you and I, or they cannot enter it. They have to enter by the door into the sheepfold; and hence there is a test for every man to try him by; and hence the difference between our views and position which necessarily produces a difference in our feelings. They think differently; they speak differently; they look upon things in a different point of view to what we do. They look upon us as being enthusiastic, foolish, wild, and visionary, and among the rest as being polluted; and they would, forsooth, sympathize with us, some of them, and think we are in the most dreadful position of any people under the face of the heavens—that we are degraded and fallen. But they know not the spirit that animates our bosoms; they know not the hope that God has inspired in our hearts; they know not the things pertaining to the kingdom of God. . . .—*JD*, 5:145, August 23, 1857.

UNITY OF PEOPLE IN THE GOSPEL.—We have been in the world and we have preached the gospel to the world and are doing it, and that is part of our duty, and we are fulfilling it as fast as the Lord opens the way. We have done a great deal. I think that at an assembly some little time ago there were twenty-five nationalities represented. Is there any difference of sentiment among these diverse people? No. In speaking with a gentleman recently on some of the difficulties between the English and the Irish people, I told him that it was lamentable that such a feeling should exist. Well, said he, they are two different races and they cannot affiliate, one being Celtic and the other Anglo-Saxon, and their sympathies and feelings are dissimilar. Their ideas and feelings differ; their education and their instincts differ. That is very true so far as it goes. But what of us? We are gathered here under the inspiration of the Holy Ghost, and that as I before said, produces a unity of feeling and spirit, a oneness and sympathy that does not exist in the world and Jesus has said, "By this shall all men know that ye are my disciples, if ye have love one to another." (John 13:35.) . . . And how is it, brethren? Are we Scandinavians; are we English; are we Scotch, Swiss or Dutch, as the case may be? No; the Spirit of God, which we obtained through obedience to the requirements of the gospel, having been born again, of the water and of the Spirit, has made us of one heart, one faith, one baptism; we have no national or class divisions of that kind among us.—*JD*, 24:2, February 11, 1883.

THE LAMANITES.—The work of the Lord among the Lamanites must not be postponed, if we desire to retain the approval of God. Thus far we have been content simply to baptize them and let them run wild again, but this must continue no longer; the same devoted effort, the same care in instructing, the same organization of priesthood must be introduced and maintained among the house of Lehi as amongst those of Israel gathered from gentile nations. As yet, God has been doing all, and we comparatively nothing. He has led many of them to us, and they have been baptized, and now we must instruct them further, and organize them into churches with proper presidencies, attach them to our stakes, organizations, etc. In one word, treat them exactly, in these respects, as we would and do treat our white brethren.— *MS*, 44:733; a letter from Salt Lake City dated October 18, 1882.

# CHAPTER XXIII

# THE ECONOMY OF THE KINGDOM: THE UNITED ORDER AND COOPERATION

## THE BASIC PRINCIPLES

THE ABUNDANT EARTH.—The gold and the silver are God's, and the cattle upon a thousand hills. All that we possess is the gift of God. We should acknowledge him in all things. We sometimes talk about men having this right and the other right. We have no rights, only such as God gives us. And I will tell you what he will show to the Latter-day Saints. He will yet prove to them that the gold and the silver are his, and the cattle upon a thousand hills, and that he gives to whom he will, and withholds from whom he pleases. He will yet show you this is a matter of fact. Our safety and happiness and our wealth depend upon our obedience to God and his laws, and our exaltation in time and eternity depends upon the same thing.—*JD*, 24:267, June 24, 1883.

ACKNOWLEDGEMENT OF GOD.—We are told that with none is the Lord angry, except those who do not acknowledge his hand in all things. Seek for his blessing upon everything you engage in. If you have a farm, dedicate it to God, and pray that his blessing may be upon it. If you build a house, dedicate it to God; also your garden, your cattle and sheep, and all that you possess, and pray that his blessing may rest upon you and upon everything that pertains to you.—*JD*, 22:313, October 19, 1881.

TEMPORAL WELFARE.—I will tell you a secret. If we could only prepare ourselves to do the will of God and keep his commandments and live our religion so that God could trust us with more means than we have, he would so order things, and that too by natural ways, that our desires in that direction would be fully gratified. But we are not prepared for it. It would only destroy us and lead us to the devil and the Lord knows it. At the same time, we cannot complain in this regard; the Lord has treated us very well. I do not know of a people anywhere that are better off as a whole than we are. It is true we do not have the amount of wealth among us that may be found in older countries; but then we do not have the poverty, the suffering, and distress that may be found elsewhere. It is for us to introduce principles that will obviate all these difficulties, and that will prepare us to receive blessings from God, and to administer the same wisely.—*JD*, 21:217, March 1, 1880.

AN EXAMPLE OF COOPERATION.—Some time before we left the city of Nauvoo, a conference was called and a unanimous vote was taken in the temple of the Lord that we would assist all the Saints in Nauvoo who wished to remove, to the extent of our property, until there should not be one worthy Saint left. This resolution so far has been faithfully carried out, and every exertion has been made by the council of the twelve for the accomplishment of this object, and by trustees appointed for that purpose. Men have scoured the country for one hundred miles round, to purchase cattle, mules, etc., for the removal of the saints; and we have drained the surrounding country for that distance, and for several hundred miles on the route we have traveled, of all the cattle they could spare, and we have, in fact, the best cattle and horses in the country.—*MS*, 8:116, November 15, 1846.

CONSECRATION THE TEST OF FAITH.—I will tell you how I feel about the principle of consecration, that has been presented by the president before the conference; but there is one thing that will perhaps make a difference with me, I have not much to consecrate or sacrifice, consequently I cannot boast much in these matters. No matter about that, let it come; for I feel I am enlisted for the war, and it is going to last for time, and throughout all eternity; and if I am a servant of God, I am under the direction of those servants of God, whom he has appointed to guide and counsel me by revelation from him. . . .

The principle that was laid before us has been published years ago in the revelations of God, and the saints have anxiously looked forward to the time when it would be fully entered into by them. But there is one thing you may set down for a certainty: . . . if a man feels right in one, he will in all the revelations from that source. I would hate, after struggling, and trying to master the evil around me, and to conquer the evil disposition that besets me, to let some little thing upset me, and root me up, and cause me to lose my high calling's glorious hope, and make a shipwreck of my faith, and send me down to perdition; and I know you would hate it also. We have got to follow the oracles of heaven in all things; there is no other way but to follow him God has appointed to lead us and guide us into eternal salvation. He is either delegated from heaven to do this, or he is not; if he is, we will follow his counsel; if he is not, then we may kick up our heels, and every man help himself the best way he can.—*JD*, 1:375, April 19, 1854.

NEW STEPS IN THE WORK.—We are called upon once in a while to take a new step in this great work. At one time it was polygamy, at another it was baptism for the dead, then it was building temples, then certain endowments, then the sealing of our children to us, then certain promises made to ourselves, such as God made to Abraham in former days, and now it is that we must get a little closer together, and be more united in regard to our temporal affairs, that we may be prepared to act and to operate in all things according to the mind and will of God.—*JD,* 17:177, October 9, 1874.

A FUNDAMENTAL LAW.—Referring to the United Order, the Lord has given us to understand that whosoever refuses to comply with the requirements of that law, his name shall not be known in the records of the church, but shall be blotted out; neither shall his children have an inheritance in Zion. Are these the words of the Lord to us? I suppose there are none here today but would say, Yes. How, then can I or you treat lightly that which God has given us? It is the word of God to me; it is the word of God to you. And if we do not fulfil this requirement, what is the result? We are told what the result will be.

These things have not taken place now; but we have been wandering about from place to place, and the Lord has blessed us in a remarkable degree. And we are gathered together, as I have said, for the purpose of building up Zion, and we are supposed to be the servants of God having engaged to perform this work; and individually, I would say, I do not want to profess to be a Saint if I am not one, nor if the work we are engaged in is not of the Lord. If the principles we believe in are false, I do not want anything to do with them; on the other hand, if they are true then I want to be governed by them, and so do you. We must carry out the word and will of God, for we cannot afford to ignore it nor any part of it. If faith, repentance, and baptism, and laying on of hands are right and true and demand our obedience, so do cooperation and the United Order.

Some may say, here such and such a man has been connected with the United Order, and how foolishly he has acted, and others have gone into cooperation and made a failure of it. Yes, that may be all very true, but who is to blame? Shall we stop baptizing people and make no further efforts to establish the kingdom of God upon the earth, because certain ones have acted foolishly and perhaps wickedly? Do the actions of such people render the principles of the gospel without effect or the doctrines we teach untrue? I think you would not say so. What do we do with such cases? We purge them out; we cut them off according to the laws God has laid down; but we do not stop the operations of the gospel. Such a thought never enters our minds, for we know the work already commenced is onward and upward. Shall we then think of putting an end to these other principles because men have acted foolishly and selfishly and done wrong? No, I think not; I do not think we can choose one principle and reject another to suit ourselves. I think that all of these things, as we have received them, one after another, are equally binding upon us.— *JD*, 21:58-59, September 21, 1878.

INFORMATION ABOUT THE UNITED ORDER.—We have heard a good deal . . . in relation to what is called the Order of Enoch, the New Order, the United Order, or whatever name we may give to it. It is new and then it is old, for it is everlasting as I understand it. I am asked sometimes—"Do you understand it?" . . . We know that such an order must be introduced, but are not informed in relation to the details, and I guess it is about the same with most of you. We have been talking about an order that is to be introduced and established among the saints of God for the last forty-two years, but we have very little information given us concerning it, either in the [biblical] scriptures or in the Book of Mormon. The fullest detail that we have of it is in the Doctrine and Covenants, and that is the case with almost everything pertaining to the kingdom of God on the earth. . . .

A REALISTIC OUTLOOK.—When the president communicated with us a little before starting from the south, about this new order, I really did not know what shape it would assume or how it would be introduced, but it has got to come.

And then on the other hand, I do not know that we need have very much anxiety in relation to the matter, for if it be of God, it must be right, and its introduction is only a question of time. As to the *modus operandi,* that is another question. . . .— *JD*, 17:47, April 19, 1874.

COOPERATION AND SELF-SUFFICIENCY.—We have been praying a long while that we might go back to Jackson County, and build up the center stake of Zion; that we might enter into the United Order of God, and be one in both temporal and spiritual things, in fact, in everything; yet when it comes along, it startles us, we are confused and hardly know what to think of it.

This reminds me of an anecdote, which I will relate to you. Among the passengers on a steamer crossing the Atlantic, was a very zealous minister who was all the time preaching to those on board about the glory and happiness of heaven, and how happy they would all be when they got there. During the voyage a very heavy storm arose, and the vessel was drifted from her course and was in great danger of striking on a reef of rocks. The captain went to examine his chart, and after a while returned with a very sorrowful face, and said—"Ladies and gentlemen, in twenty minutes from this time we shall all be in heaven." "God forbid!" said the minister.

Many of us are a good deal like this minister; for years we have been talking about a new order of things, about union and happiness, and about going back to Jackson County, but the moment it is presented to us we say—"God forbid." But then, on sober, second thought, another feeling seems to inspire us, and wherever we go a spirit seems to rest upon the people which leads them almost unanimously to embark in these things; and when we reflect, saying nothing about our religion, an extended system of cooperation seems to agree with every principle of good, common sense. Is there anything extraordinary or new in the doctrine that it is well for a community to be self-sustaining?

HUMAN NEEDS.—Now, for instance, we require a great many things in connection with human existence. We need boots and shoes, stockings, pants, vests, coats, hats, handkerchiefs, and shirts. We need cloth of various kinds, and dresses, shawls, bonnets, etc. And in every reflecting mind the question naturally arises, is it better for us to make these things ourselves at home, or to have somebody abroad make them for us? Is it better for each man to labor separately, as we do now, or to be organized so as to make the most of our labor? We have a large number of hides here in this territory, what do we do with them generally? Send them to the states. We raise a large amount of wool here, what do we do with it? We export a great deal of it to the states. We have got a large amount of excellent timber here; what do we do for our furniture? We send to the states for a great deal of it. Where do we get our pails and our washtubs, and all our cooperware from? We send to the states for it. Where do we get our brooms from? From the states; and so on all the way through the catalogue, and millions on millions of dollars are sent out of the territory every year for the purchase of articles, most of which we could manufacture and raise at home. This is certainly very poor economy, for we have thousands and thousands of men who are desirous to get some kind of employment, and they cannot get it. Why? Because other people are making our shoes, hats, clothing, bonnets, silks, artificial flowers, and many other things that we need. This may do very well for a while in an artificial state of society. But the moment any reverse comes, that kind of thing is upset, and all our calculations are destroyed.

ORGANIZING FOR NEED AND EMERGENCY STRESS.—I believe in organizing the tanners and having the hides tanned at home. When the hides are tanned, I believe in organizing the shoemakers, and manufacturing our own shoes and boots. I believe in keeping our wool at home, and in having it manufactured in our own factories, and we have as good factories here as anywhere. They should work up all the wool in the country, and if there is not enough raised to keep them running, import more. Then I believe in organizing men to take care of our stock—our cattle and sheep, and increasing the clip of wool, that we may have enough to meet the demands of the whole community. Then, when our cloth is made, I believe in organizing tailors' companies to manufacture that cloth into clothing—pants, coats, vests, and everything of the kind that we need. Then for our furniture, I believe in going into the mountains and cutting down the timber, framing it into proper shape, and then manufacturing the various articles of furniture that we need. If we require another kind of timber, import that. But make the furniture here.

PRODUCTION, THE KEYNOTE.—When we talk about cooperation, we have entered but very little into it, and it has been almost exclusively confined to the purchase of goods. There is not much in that. I wish we would learn how to produce them instead of purchasing them. I wish we could concentrate our energies, and organize all hands, old, middle-aged, and young, male and female, and put them under proper direction, with proper materials to manufacture everything we need to wear and use. We have forgotten even how to make sorghum molasses, and our memories are getting short on other points. We can hardly make a hat or coat, or a pair of boots or shoes, but we have to send to the states and import these paper ones, which last a very short time and then drop to pieces, and you have your hands continually in your pockets to supply these wants, and by and by your pockets are empty. It is therefore necessary that we right-about face, and begin to turn the other end to, and be self-sustaining.

UNITY.—The president said he would like the elders to give both sides of the question; but there is only one side to this question, and that is union in all our operations, in everything we engage in. They started a little thing like this in Box Elder County some time ago, and I was very much pleased to see the way things went there. I have spoken about it once or twice in public. They have got their cooperative store, it is true; but that is only a small part of it. Sometime ago I asked them—"You have a factory here, haven't you?" "Yes." "Well, do you sell your wool, send it to the states to mix up with shoddy and get an inferior article, or do you make it up yourselves?" "We make it up ourselves." "Then you don't sell your wool, and keep your factory standing idle?" "No, we don't; our factory has never

stood idle a day for want of wool since it was organized." Said
I—"That looks right. What do you do with your hides? Do
you send them off?" "No, we have a very good tannery and we
tan them, and make them into leather for shoes, and for harness
and for other purposes." "Oh, indeed!" "Yes, that is the way
it is." "Well, then, what next?" "Why, when we get our shoes
made, we have a saddlers' organization, and they make all the
saddlery and harness we want." "And what do you do with
your cows? Do you let them run on the plains, and live or die,
just as it happens, without making any cheese or butter?" "No,
we have a cooperative dairy, and we have our cows in that, and
we receive so much from them all the time regularly." "Well,"
said I, "that looks right. And are you all interested in this?"
"Well, about two-thirds or three-fourths of us are all engaged
in these matters." "How about your store, does it run away with
the best part of it?" "No." "Does the factory get the cream of
it?" "No." "Does some keen financial man get his fingers in
and grab it?" "No, we are all mutually interested in everything,
the profits as well as the losses." I have learned, since I was there,
that they have made it a great success.

Now, then, if you can organize one little thing in that way,
everything can be done in the same way. I was talking with
President Lorenzo Snow, and he told me that they pay their men
every Saturday night. They have a money of their own, and they
pay their hands with it, and that is good for everything they
require. And they make their arrangements unitedly, and they
operate together for the general good. Said I, "How do they feel
about this United Order?" "Oh," I was told, "They are ready
for anything that God may send along." That is the feeling
among the saints, I believe, generally.—JD, 17:66-68, May 7,
1874.

## PRINCIPLES OF THE UNITED ORDER

A REVELATION FROM THE MOST HIGH.—We have had a
great deal said about the United Order, and about our becoming
one. And some people would wish—oh, how they do wish, they
could get around that principle, if they could! But you Latter-
day Saints, you cannot get around it; you cannot dig around it;
it will rise before you every step you take, for God is determined
to carry out his purposes, and to build up his Zion; and those
who will not walk into line he will move out of the way and no
place will be found for them in Israel. Hear it, you Latter-day
Saints, for I say to you in the name of Israel's God that it is a
revelation from the Most High, and you cannot get around it.
There seem to be difficulties in the way at present; but we shall

surmount these. The only way for us to do now, in consideration of the weaknesses and infirmities with which we are surrounded, is to do the very best we can, and advance those interests
as near as we can, practically and in their spirit and essence, until
we can bring about the thing that God designs, for men are not
prepared for these things yet in full. But we are in part, as they
of old prophesied in part, and understood in part; and by and
by that which is perfect in relation to these matters will be
introduced.

PREVIOUS EFFORTS.—Joseph Smith tried to introduce this
order, but such was the corruption, covetousness, fraud, and injustice of men that he found it almost impossible to do it. This
was the idea he conveyed, if not the precise words that he used
in speaking upon this subject. We have made various attempts
to do what the Prophet Joseph tried to do. In some places they
are doing very well, and in other places very poorly. I can tell
you this much about it, it is pretty hard work to make sheep
out of goats. Did any of you ever try it? . . .

There are some things that Brother Lorenzo Snow is doing
that are very creditable; but it is not the United Order. He is
working with the people something after the same principle that
our sisters teach the little ones how to walk. They stand them in
a sort of chair which rolls along, and the babies appear delighted;
they think they are walking. But we have not learned how to
walk yet. And then there are other institutions scattered throughout the territory, having the same laudable object in view. Many
of them have most excellent principles among them, and they
manifest a most admirable spirit; but they only see in part, and
know and comprehend in part. . . .

THE ORDER MUST LIVE IN THE HEARTS OF THE PEOPLE.
—I suppose these things could go on and increase, and everything
in regard to your commercial relations could be operated with one
common consent, under the proper authority and administration
of the priesthood, and you all labor unitedly, with singleness of
heart before God. And what would be the result? You could
not be preyed upon by outsiders; you would have no middlemen
living off you, and what speculations might be entered into would
be in the interest of the community. And then you could operate
in regard to your farming interests, and the disposing of your
grain, and cooperating together, you will be able to form a
phalanx in this valley that will become a power in this part of
the land. And then if you could go to work and manufacture
your own boots and shoes and harness, and your own wearing
apparel, men's and women's wear, as they are doing in Brigham
City, a great deal of remunerative employment could be furnished

your own people, and it would be the means of putting trades in the hands of many of your boys; and by and by you could become a self-sustaining people. . . .

We have had enough talk about these things; the only thing left is to contrive in all our various settlements, to introduce such things, gradually and according to circumstances, as will subserve the interests of the people and make them self-sustaining. And then let the people throughout the territory do the same thing, and we shall be progressing in the march of improvement, and get, by and by, to what is called the United Order. But I will tell you one thing you can never do—unless you can get the United Order in the hearts of the people, you can never plant it anywhere else. Articles and constitutions amount to very little. We must have this law, which is the law of God, written in our hearts. Many men associated with these institutions do not act in good faith. I have seen men unite with them, thinking that they could get a very easy living by preying upon the people who were more confiding and honorable than themselves. Will such men be blessed? No, they will not, but the curse of God will rest upon them for trying to pervert his purposes; and it would have been better for them never to have entered into such connections. These have been some of my reflections in relation to these matters.—JD, 20:43-44-45, August 4, 1878.

MATTERS OF FACT.—In the first place, it has been a matter of facts with me, for years and years, that such a state of things has to be introduced amongst us. I think that is an opinion that prevails very generally among the Latter-day Saints, and I do not think there is much difference of opinion in relation to it. We have read about it in the Doctrine and Covenants. I think there are as many as a dozen revelations in that book in reference to this subject, and perhaps more than that. I do not propose to quote them, however, at the present time. . . .

CONFORMITY WITH THE LAW OF THE LAND.—Well, we have to go with the general stream; or at least it is necessary that we protect ourselves from legal cormorants, and from every man who would devour, tear in pieces, and destroy, who is after our property and our lives. This class of persons would be very glad to take not only the property but the lives of some of the leaders of God's people here on the earth. Nothing would suit them better; they are so holy, pure, and law-abiding. These are the circumstances that we are placed in. Now what shall be done? There are certain principles that emanate from God; but we have to protect ourselves in carrying them out, and make them conform, as near as we can, to the laws of the land.

STEWARDSHIPS.—In the Doctrine and Covenants it is said, in the first place, that a man shall place his property at the feet of the bishop. That is what that lays down, and you say that is what you would like to do. Some would, very many would not. The bishop, after examining into the position and circumstances of the man, and finding out what his wants are, and what his capabilities and talents, what the size of his family, etc., appoints to him a certain amount of means, which he receives as a stewardship.

THE PROBLEM OF FREEDOM.—"Well," say some, "how does this order you are talking about introducing agree with that? Where does the stewardship come in?" I will tell you. We have organized this as near as may be on the principles of cooperation, and the voice you have in selecting your officers, and in voting for them and the stock you hold in these institutions is your stewardship. You may say—"Is not that taking away our freedom?" I do not think it is. I am not prepared to enter into details, but I should say that one-third, perhaps one-half, of the wealth of the world is manipulated just in the same way. How so? Why, there are among the nations national securities of various kinds issued, which are taken by the people; we have United States bonds, state bonds, county and city bonds in this country as well as in Europe, to which the people subscribe and in which they have an interest, all of which is voluntary, and the free act of the people. Then we have railroad bonds, steamship bonds, and we have telegraph, mercantile, manufacturing, and cooperative associations, which are represented by those who hold stock therein, and there are hundreds and thousands of millions of dollars throughout the world that are operated in this way by financiers, statesmen, men of intelligence—merchants, capitalists, and others, in every grade and condition in life; none of whom consider that there is any coercion associated with it. These men all have their free agency.

What is the *modus operandi?* For illustration,—a company is organized, men subscribe stock into that company, or they purchase bonds perhaps from a government, for which that government pays interest; or, if it is in a company, that company manipulates and arranges matters, not the stockholders individually, they never think of it; they select the officers to do these things for them, and all they have to do with it is to vote in these officers, each person voting according to the amount of stock he holds in the institution. And then they draw their dividends at certain specified times. This is the way, I presume, that one-half or perhaps three-quarters of the wealth of the civilized world is manipulated today.

Well, is freedom taken from these men? Are the men engaged in these operations thieves and robbers? Some of them act very fraudulently it is true, and the amount of defalcation and fraud in our country, of late, is painful to reflect upon. But then, they consider they have a perfect right to buy or to sell any of this stock, and if parties enter into institutions of any kind, mercantile or manufacturing, they must be subject to the rules or laws thereof. But the stockholders do not individually operate these institutions, and what I wanted to say is, that herein we, as they, have our stewardship and freedom of action. . . .

THE IDEAL OF UNITED BROTHERHOOD.—I cannot conceive of anything more beautiful and heavenly than a united brotherhood, organized after the pattern laid down in the Doctrine and Covenants; when all act for the benefit of all—when while we love God with all our hearts we love our neighbor as ourselves; where our time, our property, our talents, our mental and bodily powers are all exerted for the good of all; where no man grabs or takes advantage of another; where there is a common interest, a common purse, a common stock; where, as they did on this continent, it is said of them that "they all dealt justly to each other," and all acted for the general weal, "when every man in every place could meet a brother and a friend," when all the generous and benevolent influences and sympathies of our nature are carried out, and covetousness, arrogance, hatred, and pride, and every evil are subdued and brought into subjection to the will and Spirit of God. These principles are very beautiful and would be very happifying for a community, a territory, a state, nation, or the world.

A CELESTIAL LAW.—Now, then, these things are presented before us, and I suppose we shall have to come into them as best we can, and if we ever get into the celestial kingdom of God we shall find that they are just such a set of people. If ever we build up a Zion here on this continent, and in case Zion ever comes down to us, and we expect it will, or that ours will go up to meet it, we have got to be governed by the same principles that they are governed by, or we can not be one. And if we ever get into the eternal worlds, we shall have to be heirs of God and joint heirs with Jesus Christ.—*JD*, 17:177-181, October 9, 1874.

THE PRIESTHOOD MUST LEAD THE WAY.—We read of the Zion that was built up by Enoch, and that this Zion and the people that were united with Enoch, who were subject to the same laws which God is seeking to introduce among us, were caught up into the heavens. We have been expecting all along to build up a similar Zion upon these mountains, and we have talked a great deal about going back to Jackson County. We can not build up a Zion unless we are in possession of the spirit of Zion, and of the light and intelligence that flow from God, and under the direction of the priesthood, the living oracles of God, to lead us in the paths of life.—*JD*, 18:78-79, August 31, 1875.

THE COOPERATIVE MOVEMENT.—I will tell you, Latter-day Saints, that unless we can enter into our cooperative institutions and the United Order with singleness of heart and pure motives, as the elders do when they go forth to preach the gospel, because it is God's command, your efforts will be of small avail. We do not want to stop and ask, is there money in it?

Is it his will, his law and principle? When we combine our interests on this principle, and work to it, we will succeed and prosper. But in too many instances our cooperative institutions have jumped the track. What, the big co-op? Yes, and little co-ops too. Have you got a co-op here? No, you have not. Do you know of any? We find little institutions they call co-ops in most of our settlements, but when you come to inquire into affairs connected with them we generally find, that, instead of their being run in the interest of the community, and with a view to build up the kingdom of God, a few individuals represent the co-op, who are the ones who are benefited by it. That is the trouble. But is the principle right? Yes, if you can live it, dealing honestly one with another; but if you cannot, you need not try it, for instead of giving satisfaction, it will only be a disappointment. But I will promise the Latter-day Saints that if they will go into these things allowing God to dictate in the interests of Israel and the building up of his Zion on the earth, and take themselves and their individual interests out of the question, feeling they are acting for him and his kingdom, they will become the wealthiest of all people, and God will bless them and pour out wealth and intelligence and all the blessings that earth can afford. But if you will not, you will go downward, and keep going the downward road to disappointment and poverty in things spiritual as well as temporal. I dare prophesy that in the name of the Lord.

That is the way that I look at these things, and that is the way I figure them up, and not in the light of every man looking for gain from his own quarter. These things are stumbling-blocks in the way of the people, and have been for some time. Well, what shall we do? Why, do the best we can, and keep on trying to improve upon our present condition, always keeping in view the object to be gained, dealing honestly upon a fair basis and correct principles, then we will succeed and things will move on pleasantly, and we shall be a united people, owned and blessed of the Lord. It was on this principle that the Nephites became a prosperous, a blessed and happy people; it was not because one was a little smarter than another, or through his smartness taking advantage of his neighbor; it was not that a man was a good financier, that he should "financier" other peoples' property into his own pockets and leave them without.—*JD*, 20:163-164, March 2, 1879.

TO SUSTAIN COOPERATION.—We took a vote at the priesthood meeting . . . and so far as I could discern, the brethren all voted to sustain cooperation, and that those in the merchandise business will purchase of the co-op.

But some may say, have not the cooperative organizations made many blunders? Yes, they have, and in many instances acted very foolishly. But shall we give up the principle of cooperation because of the unwise acts of a few individuals? We do not act thus in regard to other matters. We baptize men into the church, and lay our hands upon them that they may receive the Holy Ghost, and after they have thus been blessed with the light, spirit, and power of God, many of them act very foolishly, violate their covenants, and transgress the laws of God. Shall we, therefore, repudiate baptism and the laying on of hands because of their folly and wickedness? Certainly not. The Lord has provided a way to purge the church, and those men are dealt with according to the laws of the church, and are rooted out. This is the way that we ought to manage in our temporal affairs. If the people do wrong, deal with them according to the laws of the church, and if the cooperatives do wrong, professing to be governed by correct principle, deal with them in the same way, and let those wrongs be righted and evil eradicated.—*JD*, 20:59, September 22, 1878.

COOPERATION: AN ANECDOTE ABOUT SOME FINANCIERS. —A smart young man had just returned from college, and at the table he wished to show his parents what extraordinary advancements he had made. "Why, father," says he, "you can hardly conceive of the advance I have made."

"Well, my son," says the father, "I am sure I am glad to hear you say so, and I trust you will make a great man." There happened to be two ducks on the table for dinner, and this young man proposed to give his father a specimen of his smartness.

"Now," he says, "you see there are only two ducks, don't you?"

"Yes," answered the father.

"Well, I can prove to you that there are three ducks."

"Can you," says the father, "that's quite extraordinary really; how can you do it?"

"Well," says the son, "I will show you. That's one?"

"Yes."

"And that's two?"

"Yes."

"Well, two and one make three, don't they?"

"Quite so," says the father, "it is very extraordinary, and to show how much I appreciate it, I will eat one of these ducks, and your mother will eat the other, and we will leave the third for you."

Some of our "financiers" have made this kind of discovery, but when it comes to the practical thing they, like the boy, have got to fall back on father's duck or mother's duck. This kind of proficiency may be all very well in its place, but then we have no place for it; we want to act honestly and begin right, and then carry it out right. Let the big co-op straighten itself out, and then the little co-ops do the same, and let us stick to one another and all act one with another, and lay aside our scheming; and let us have honest, honorable men, elders of Israel who have at heart the building up of God's kingdom, to do our business, who will act for the welfare of all. That is my doctrine on that point.— *JD*, 20:164-165, March 2, 1879.

BABYLON AND BUSINESS.—Now then, in regard to our temporal affairs, these are the things which seem to perplex us more or less. We have been brought up in Babylon, and have inherited Babylonish ideas and systems of business. We have introduced, too, among us, all kinds of chicanery, deception, and fraud. It is time that these things were stopped, and that matters assumed another shape. It is time that we commenced to place ourselves under the guidance and direction of the Almighty. You can not talk in any places about temporal matters, but everybody is on the alert at once, and the idea is—Do you want my property? No. Do you want my possessions? No, no; there is no such feeling, but we do want men and women to give God their hearts; we do want people, while they profess to fear God, not to be canting hypocrites and to depart from every principle of right.

We remember the time very well, or most of us, when we first entered into this Church, if a man was found lying he would be brought before the Church and dealt with. If a man was found stealing he would be brought up before the Church and dealt with. If a man defrauded his neighbor, and it could be proved, he was brought up and dealt with; and so if a man got drunk and for all these delinquencies, if parties did not repent of them they were immediately cut off the Church as unworthy of fellowship. And now, after so many years' travail, are we to continue and fellowship all these evils? No, no, we can not do it, and God will not do it; and if we carry them along with us, we shall not enter into the celestial kingdom of God.—*JD*, 18:79-80, August 31, 1875.

# CHAPTER XXIV

# THE ECONOMY OF THE KINGDOM: TITHING, REVENUES, AND SOME ECONOMIC PROBLEMS

## TITHING

BACKGROUND OF THE REVELATION.—The people were anxious at the time the revelation was given in Far West, to know what the Lord required as a tithing from his saints. I was there at the time. It was in 1838—quite a little time to look back to. Some time, however, before this revelation was given, God had revealed the principle of the United Order, which, as you know, the people could not abide; and when we come to think about it, it could hardly be expected that they could do so, they having been in the Church but a short time, taken out of the world, with all the prejudices and weaknesses that you and I have. But the time will come when we will obey these things as they are given by the revelations of God, and it will not be a hardship either; it will be a pleasure to those who are under the influence of the Lord. But, like all other things, it will be "free will and free grace."

THE COMMAND TO THE SAINTS.—Now, then, we come to this. Here is a command given; whom to? Not to outsiders, not to men of the world, not to people who do not believe in God nor in his laws. But it is given directly to us who profess to have faith in him, in his laws, and in his priesthood. The question then is, what is our duty, as we have not obeyed the other law? I will remark here, incidentally, that when this law of tithing was given, a great many people were gathering up to Far West and to that district of country, as we are to this country; but it would apply more to our early settlements than at the present time. This people thus gathering to Far West, were told that it was required of them to give their surplus property—I will read it:

Verily, thus saith the Lord, I require all their surplus property to be put into the hands of the bishop of my church in Zion,

For the building of mine house, and for the laying the foundation of Zion and for the priesthood, and for the debts of the Presidency of my Church.

And this shall be the beginning of the tithing of my people. (D. & C. 119:1-3.)

What then?

And after that, those who have thus been tithed shall pay one-tenth of all their interest annually; and this shall be a standing law unto them forever, for my holy priesthood, saith the Lord. (D. & C. 119:4.)

Now, here is a people, of whom we form a part, who met together to ask the prophet of the Lord to inquire for them the will of the Lord concerning this matter of tithing; and he gives it in these words:

> And this shall be a standing law unto them forever. (D. & C. 119:4.)

I will ask, has the Lord ever annulled this? No. Then it stands in full force today to this people. Then again:

> Verily I say unto you, it shall come to pass that all those who gather unto the land of Zion shall be tithed of their surplus properties, and shall observe this law, or they shall not be found worthy to abide among you. (D. & C. 119:5.)

THE LAW CAME BY REQUEST OF THE PEOPLE.—That is very plain talk. Is there any compulsion about it? No; but if they do not do it, they shall not be considered worthy to abide among you. What are we to make of it? . . . I did not make it. President Young did not make it. Neither did Joseph Smith make it, but by the request of the people he asked the Lord what his will was, and this was the answer; and this was given in 1838. And does it not seem strange that we do not comprehend it? I think it does sometimes. Here we have had the Doctrine and Covenants in our hands, which contains this revelation, since the year 1838; that is nearly forty-three years ago. We have had forty-two years to study this doctrine, and it is as plain as you can make it, and yet it would seem that we cannot understand it. Do we want to understand the laws of God? If we do and will read these things under the influence of that spirit which I have referred to, I think that we will understand our duties without much trouble. . . .

TITHING AND THE BUILDING OF ZION.—Now, if we abide this, all well and good. If not, it is written, "They shall not be found worthy to abide among you." What will you do with them? I often think that there are a great many people who are not worthy to abide among us; don't you? And then if God were to put judgment to the line, and righteousness to the plummet, most of us would be in a very poor fix. I will tell you what I think should be done. . . .I think the people ought to be instructed in these things, and then if they do not live up to them, you will not then be held responsible to the authorities that preside over you. The Lord tells us that they shall not be worthy of a place among us. Do we want to alter that? Not one iota. Would I wish to be harsh to men that are ignorant? No, I would not; I would bear with them, and teach them, and instruct them. And if I were a bishop I should instruct my teachers to do it; and then by and by, after they were fully informed, and had every opportunity to become acquainted with things, we might take final action in relation to their standing. I would not wish to enforce that law at present, until men were thoroughly informed. For instance, the case I referred to yesterday.

There were two men; one paid one hundred dollars in tithing, the other paid twenty-five dollars in tithing. Both of them owned about the same amount of property; but the first paid his tithing, the other did not. The second, however, paid some seventy-five dollars in donations; but he did not pay his tithing; he only paid a quarter of it. That now may have arisen from ignorance with regard to the law. The last paid out as much money as the first; and he may have been wrongly taught. Some of the bishops do not understand these things, and yet we have had this doctrine given unto us for forty-two years. Has a man a right to turn and change things as he pleases? I have not, and I do not believe any other man has. And if any bishop or a president of a stake or anybody else tells you that you can do as you please about the disposition you make of the means you pay, as long as you pay a certain amount, or you may pay it on tithing or not, as you please, I tell you that he teaches false doctrine. But should we be hard with such people? No. If they have been under influences of this nature and been wrongly taught, I will say, as a certain party said to me who had been doing these things, "I will switch off and pay my tithing according to the law." You, bishops and presidents of stakes, switch off and get the people to do things right. There is no commandment about donations, but there is about tithing; and I am not at liberty to change this, neither any other man.—*JD*, 22:11-13, January 9, 1881.

TITHING: THE TESTING OF FAITH.—Speaking of tithing, we as a people acknowledge that the law of tithing emanates from the Lord; then how is it that we need talking to so much in relation to it. If we are not honest with ourselves, and honest with our God, of what good to us are all our professions of being representatives of God, of being elders in Israel, of being clothed with the holy priesthood, of being teachers of the ways of life. The ancient Jews, the old Pharisees with all their wickedness and corruption, could boast of paying tithes of all they possessed. We profess to be better than the old Pharisees, and yet it seems that it is very difficult for men among us to be honest with themselves and with their God in relation to so simple a principle as this is.

What is the matter? We have been dug out of the mire, been born in sin, and shapen in iniquity, as it were. We have been clothed in corruption and mixed up in the abominations of the world; we have come out from a people that did not acknowledge God, and are dishonest in their acts, and it seems almost impossible for us to lay aside our dishonesty and wickedness. If we cannot attend to these little things, how is it possible that we can rise in the political horizon and be as a beacon for all nations to gaze upon. The Lord does not care a straw whether we pay our tithing or not, it does not make him one particle richer or poorer. The gold and silver are his and the cattle upon a thousand hills. The world and all its fulness belong to him, for he organized and framed it. But as it is, of what benefit is it to him? He wants in the first place to get men to acknowledge God, I was going to say in one little carnal principle, one little earthly principle, he wants to get them to acknowledge him, by giving him a certain little part, or one-tenth of what he gives to them to see whether they will be honest in this trifle, to see whether they will act as honorable high-minded men or not, or whether they will try to cheat him out of it. If we do this honestly and conscientiously until we have fulfilled our duty, we are then prepared for anything else. It is the principle and not the tithing we pay that is esteemed of the Lord; he cares not for our tithing, but he cares about our doing right. If we cannot be faithful in a few things, we cannot expect to be made rulers over many things.—*JD,* 10:280-281, October 25, 1863.

We have been taught to pay our tithing, that we might acknowledge to God that we are his people, and that if he gave us all we ask, we might give one-tenth back to him, and by that act acknowledge his hand. Does the Lord care about these things? . . . No. He does not care about them, so far as they benefit him, but he does, so far as they develop perfection in the saints of God, and show that they acknowledge his hand as the author and the giver of every blessing they enjoy.—*JD,* 11:164-165, Salt Lake City, October 7, 1865.

THEN WHY RESORT TO VOLUNTARY DONATIONS?—We are engaged in this place in building a tabernacle [the Assembly Hall], in which we can meet during the winter season. We do not call upon you outside brethren to assist us in this undertaking, because it is local and belongs to this stake. This is a matter that was designed by President Young before his death; and we have been desirous, as Brother Cannon said this morning, to carry out the views of our venerated president as far as we can. We have commenced to build this house; we want to put it up without delay. In this, as in every other matter, we do not wish anybody to contribute his means or labor toward it, unless he feels free to do it; for there are plenty that will do it willingly, and it will be built; and we shall have a nice, comfortable place to worship in through the winter, and it will serve the priesthood for all necessary purposes, as well as the public. . . . It will be done by voluntary donations and by utilizing labor tithing. Some people may say, why do it by voluntary donations? Why not use the tithing for all such purposes? Is not that sufficient? Yes, if all of you strictly paid it, but then you do not all do this, and consequently we have to resort to other means. But, as I have before said, in this and everything else, we do not wish to press the people, nor place any in unpleasant positions.—*JD*, 19:128-129, October 7, 1877.

## SOME ECONOMIC PROBLEMS

AN EDITORIAL ON LABOR, CITY OF NAUVOO, OCTOBER 15, 1844.—Labor is the manufacturer of wealth. It was ordained of God as the medium to be used by man to obtain his living: hence it is the universal condition of this great bond *to live.* . . .

God never meant to bemean his creation, especially his own *image*, because they had to labor:—no; never; God himself according to the good old book labored on this world, six days; and when Adam was animated from clay to life, by his spirit's making use of him for a dwelling, we read that God put him into the garden *to dress it:*—Therefore, in connection with the samples of all holy men, we are bound to honor the laboring man: and despise the idler. . . .

Let them labor like men, prepare for that august hour, when Babylon and all her worldly wisdom, her various delicacies, and delusive fashions, shall fall with her to rise and trouble the earth no more! What a glorious prospect, to think that drunken Babylon, the great city of sin, will soon cease, and the kingdom of God rise in holy splendor, upon her ashes, and the people serve God in a perpetual union! . . . God will soon make a man more precious than fine gold. *Do you know it?* Let the world traffic, we must make men better by wisdom, virtue, and industry.—*TS*, 5:679-680, October 15, 1844.

A MISTAKEN NOTION.—It is a mistaken notion that wealth makes people happy. Cattle, sheep, houses, possessions would not bring you happiness. The scriptures tell us that he that hath eternal life is rich: and the Lord has told us to seek after the riches of eternal life.—*JD*, 22:314, October 19, 1881.

THE ECONOMIC PROBLEM AND THE PROBLEMS OF LIFE.— God has given unto us a land. But there are houses to build, farms to open, fences to make, our wants to be provided for, our animals to be taken care of, etc. All these are necessaries that seem to crowd themselves upon us. Bishop Hunter says, children never come into the world with shoes and stockings on.

No, nor clothes either, and if they did, their clothes would soon be too small for them. We have to try to make provision for the wants of our families, and to make them comfortable. The difficulties that you have to contend with, we have experienced; and as far as difficulties are concerned, none of us is free from them. Men of wealth among us, as elsewhere, who command their tens and hundreds of thousands, who have their every want supplied, have more anxiety, care, and perplexity than many of you, who have to struggle for a comfortable living. And if you were placed in their position you would be a great deal more uneasy than you are now. We do not realize these things, but they are given unto us for our experience, and we should learn to understand and appreciate the position we occupy here upon the earth. . . . If . . . I were living here and was rearing a family, the first thing which I should do would be to dedicate myself and my family, my house and garden, my land, my cattle, and everything I possessed to God, and should ask his blessing upon them. Then every morning when I arose, I should kneel down to supplicate his blessing upon me and mine during the day, to preserve us from evil influences, accidents, and dangers, and to otherwise bless our labors in obtaining a livelihood. And then I would pray for those who presided over me in the priesthood.—*JD*, 22:313-314, October 19, 1881.

PROBLEMS AND POSSIBILITIES.[1]—I will tell you a feeling I had some years ago. I was over at Fillmore. From there you can see right on to this desert. And I thought—as I looked across this immense valley—if there was only water there, what a magnificent country that would make! I remember I thought thousands and tens of thousands could inhabit that land if it only had water. I did not then know the position of things. I have now had an opportunity of visiting Deseret and looking at the river, and am pleased to find you have such an abundant supply of water. An immense population could be sustained with the amount you have. I suppose the river shows its best now; the water is high; but if that water could be properly manipulated, it does seem to me—provided you can conquer the mineral in the soil—that a vast amount of land can be put under cultivation and an immense population sustained. . . . You certainly have a fair opportunity for development; having a large area of land, which I am told is productive, and with the proper application of the water, and a concentration of effort I can see no reason why this can not be made a very flourishing,

---

[1]The reference is to the areas within Millard County, Utah. Brigham Young once thought the Pauvan Valley alone could, if water were available, support 100,000 people. See M. R. Hunter, *Brigham Young The Colonizer* (1940), p. 268.

beautiful and populous place.—*JD*, 24:201-202, June 18, 1883.

LATTER-DAY SAINT COMMUNITY BUILDING: MALAD, OC-
TOBER 20, 1881.—Now, you who live in this little place, look
to it that you are found in the line of your duty. You have a
beautiful location, and I would like to see you make the most of
it. I would like to see at least a hundred times more apple, pear,
and cherry trees planted out; and all of your streets lined with
shade trees. And improve your dwelling houses. If you cannot
find the style of house to suit you, go off to other places until
you do find one, and then come back and build a better one.
Beautify this place, and make your homes pleasant and agreeable,
that you may have nice places for your wives and children, and
thus help to fulfil that scripture which says, that Zion shall become the praise of the whole earth; and that kings will come to
gaze upon her glory. . . .
    Then you have a public square, make some nice grounds
in and about it. And then beautify your private squares at your
own homes. Let every man make his own grounds pleasant and
agreeable. And let every woman make her husband as happy
as she can. The sisters ought to be like angels, ought they not?
Be full of good, kind, pleasant, and agreeable feelings. And we
men who profess to be saints of God—saints of God! What
an expression! Do we understand it? There is a peculiar form
of expression in the German language. The term Latter-day Saint
in the German is: *Der Heiligen der Letzten Tage*, which being
interpreted is, the holy of the last days. There is something very
expressive about that. We should be the holy of the last days,
under the influence and guidance of the Lord.—*JD*, 26:111,
October 20, 1881.

    CITY BEAUTIFICATION.—We want to see beautiful cities,
beautiful houses, and pleasant homes, and everything around you
calculated to promote your happiness and well being.—*JD*,
25:267, August 17, 1884.

CHAPTER XXV

# SOME PRINCIPLES OF EDUCATION

## THE MEANING OF EDUCATION

THE NEED FOR DISCRIMINATE THOUGHT.—We heard some remarks made this morning upon education—about words and language, and so forth. In relation to the education of the world generally, a great amount of it is of very little value, consisting more of words than ideas; and whilst men are verbose in their speaking or writing, you have to hunt for ideas or truth like hunting for a grain of wheat among piles of chaff or rubbish. It is true that a great amount of it is really valuable, and it is for us to select the good from the bad.

The education of men ought to be adapted to their positions, both as temporal and eternal beings. It is well to understand the arts and sciences; it is well to understand language and history; it is well to understand agriculture, to be acquainted with mechanics, and to be instructed in everything that is calculated to promote the happiness, the well being, and the comfort of the human family.

TRUE EDUCATION MUST BE PUT TO USE FOR HUMAN BENEFIT.—That education which but amounts to a little outward appearance and applies only to a few conveniences of this life is very far short of that education and intelligence which immortal beings ought to be in possession of. The education of the present day is generally misapplied. Indeed, men have misapplied the education which they have received for generations and generations.

The priests in Egypt had mysteries immediately associated with themselves, and the calculation was to keep their people ignorant of those things which they knew, that they might govern them the more readily and that they might reign and tyrannize over them. Among the various nations in different ages, their sages and wise men held their intelligence as a secret mystery to be divulged almost or altogether to their disciples, who generally conveyed it in unknown character symbols, or hieroglyphics. The Egyptians had their priests; the Assyrians, their magi and astrologers; the Greeks, their philosophers; and the Jews, their wise men; and all more or less mysterious or cabalistic.

This was a misapplication of information, or that which they might possess, although, in many instances, the information amounted to nothing in reality.

The same is applicable, in a great measure, to our lawyers, doctors, and priests. They make use of terms that nobody can understand but the initiated. If you study medicine, law, or botany, and many of the sciences, you must study Latin first, because the doctors and professors make use of that language to convey their ideas in; and the calculation is for all except men of science or linguists to be befogged and bewildered—yes, all except the initiated few who have been able to bestow the same amount of time as they have in learning some of the dead languages.

Whom does their learning benefit? Certainly not the multitude. I will tell you my idea of true intelligence and true eloquence. It is not as some people do—to take a very small idea and use a great many grandiloquent words without meaning— something to befog and mystify it with—something to tickle the ear and please the imagination only. That is not true intelligence. But it is true intelligence for a man to take a subject that is mysterious and great in itself, and to unfold and simplify it so that a child can understand it. I do not care what words you make use of, if you have the principles and are enabled to convey those principles to the understandings of men.

It is true, at the same time, that a man who has a good use of language can present his ideas to better advantage than one who has not in some instances, and in some he cannot; for the Lord gives some men a natural talent and powers of description that others do not possess and cannot acquire. But the great principle that we have to come to is the knowledge of God, of the relation- ship that we sustain to each other, and of the various duties we have to attend to in the various spheres of life in which we are called to act as mortal and immortal, intelligent, eternal beings, in order that we may magnify our calling and approve ourselves before God and the holy angels. And if we obtain knowledge of this kind, we shall do well; for this is the greatest good of the whole. It embraces everything that we want.

In relation to the principles of eternal life, we are told that these treasures we have in earthen vessels were given of the Lord and retained in those vessels through our faithfulness.

A CRITIQUE OF KNOWLEDGE.—Now, then, if men, without much of the advantage of what is termed education in this world, are filled with the Spirit of God, the revelations of the Holy Ghost, and can comprehend the relationship of man to God, can know their duties, and can teach a people, a nation, or a world how they may be saved and obtain thrones, principalities, powers, and dominions in the eternal worlds—if men can understand these principles by the gift of the Holy Ghost and the revelations of the Most High, and are enabled to place them before the people so that they can comprehend them, then, I say, these are the men of education—the men of intellect—the men who are calculated to bless and ennoble the human family. This is the kind of education that we want and the more simple those principles can be conveyed the better. They are more adapted to the wants and intelligence of the human family. . . . Do you repudiate education, then? No—not at all. I appreciate all true intelligence, whether moral, social, scientific, political, or philosophical. But I despise the folly that they hang on to it, and the folly that they call education.—*JD*, 5:259-261, September 20, 1857.

GOD AND KNOWLEDGE.—It is good for men to be taught in the history and laws of nations, to become acquainted with the principles of justice and equity, with the nature of disease and the medicinal properties of plants, etc. But there is no need of their being without the knowledge of God, for in fact every branch of true knowledge known to man has originated in God, and men have come in possession of it from his word or from his works. O, the folly of men in not acknowledging God in all things, in laying aside God and his religion, and trusting in their own judgment and intelligence. All the intelligence which men possess on the earth, whether religious, scientific, or political —proceeds from God. Every good and perfect gift proceeds from him, the fountain of light and truth, wherein there is no variableness nor shadow of turning. The knowledge of the human system has proceeded from the human system itself, which God has organized.

Again, if you trace the old English laws and the laws of ancient nations, it will be seen that the principles of justice, which are the foundation of them, are gathered from the Bible, the revealed will of God to the children of Israel for their government and guidance, to a certain extent, in some of the principles of law, justice, and equity. Did knowledge of any kind that is in the world originate in man? No. Franklin possessed great information relating to natural laws. He drew the lightning from the clouds but he could not have done that if there had not been lightning in the clouds. He merely discovered a certain principle, and developed the action of a certain law that existed co-equal with the earth. Then how foolish it is for men under these circumstances, to lay aside God, and think that they can progress, and be smart and intelligent without him.—*JD*, 10:275, October 25, 1863.

EDUCATION FOR HEALTH.—We should seek to know more about ourselves and our bodies, about what is most conducive to health and how to preserve health and how to avoid disease; and to know what to eat and what to drink, and what to abstain from taking into our systems. We should become acquainted with the physiology of the human system and live in accordance with the laws that govern our bodies, that our days may be long in the land which the Lord our God has given us. And in order to comprehend ourselves fully we must study from the best books, and also by faith. And then let education be fostered and encouraged in our midst. Train your children to be intelligent and industrious. First teach them the value of healthful bodies, and how to preserve them in soundness and vigor; teach them to entertain the highest regard for virtue and chastity, and likewise encourage them to develop the intellectual faculties with which they are endowed.

GEOGRAPHY AND AGRICULTURE.—They should also be taught regarding the earth on which they live, its properties, and the laws that govern it; and they ought to be instructed concerning God, who made the earth, and his designs and purposes in its creation, and the placing of man upon it. They should know how to cultivate the soil in the best possible manner; they should know how to raise the best kind of fruits adapted to the soil and climate; they should be induced to raise the best kinds of stock, and to care for them properly when they come into their possession. And whatever labor they pursue, they should be taught to do so intelligently; and every incentive, at the command of parents to induce children to labor intelligently and understandingly, should be held out to them.

ARCHITECTURE.—Again, the subject of architecture should receive attention from you. Your children should be encouraged to improve in the building of houses, and not be satisfied merely to copy after what their fathers did in the days of their poverty. The building rock at your command is of the very best, and it is easily procured; what remains for you to do is to put the material together in such a shape as shall reflect your best judgment and intelligence consistent with due regard to health and convenience. The building of the temple here will no doubt have a tendency to awaken the desire on your part to improve in this direction. I have noticed that the building of our temples affords a great many young men the opportunity of learning trades which, perhaps, otherwise would not be the case; and by the time such a building is erected, they become competent tradesmen, prepared to work in the various branches of mechanism that they learn on these buildings.

"IMPROVEMENT IN ALL THINGS."—Improvement in all things relating to our spiritual and temporal welfare should be our aim in life, and we should encourage in our children this desire to improve, and not feel all the time, "Come day, go day, God send Sunday."

It is highly necessary that we should learn to read and write and speak our own language correctly; and where people are deficient themselves in education, they should strive all the more to see that the deficiency be not perpetuated in their offspring. We ought to take more pains than we do in the training and education of our youth. All that we can possibly do by way of placing them in a position to become the equals, at least, of their race, we ought to take pleasure in doing; for in elevating them we bring honor to our own name, and glory to God the Father. To do this requires labor and means, and it also requires perseverance and determination on the part of all concerned. . . .

THE SELECTION AND PAYMENT OF TEACHERS.—Whatever you do, be choice in your selection of teachers. We do not want infidels to mold the minds of our children. They are a precious charge bestowed upon us by the Lord, and we cannot be too careful in rearing and training them. I would rather have my children taught the simple rudiments of a common education by men of God, and have them under their influence, than have them taught in the most abstruse sciences by men who have not the fear of God in their hearts. . . . The acme of scientific development in the world is predicated upon a knowledge of the laws of nature in its multifarious forms.

We need to pay more attention to educational matters, and do all we can to procure the services of competent teachers. Some people say, we cannot afford to pay them. You cannot afford not to employ them. We want our children to grow up intelligently, and to walk abreast with the peoples of any nation. God expects us to do it; and therefore I call attention to this matter. I have heard intelligent practical men say, it is quite as cheap to keep a good horse as a poor one, or to raise good stock as inferior animals. Is it not quite as cheap to raise good intelligent children as to rear children in ignorance?—*JD*, 24:167-169, May 19, 1883.

PROFANITY AND OATHS.—It is a disgrace for men of education and intelligence to be unable to utter five words without an oath. Every child ought to point the finger of scorn at any man that will come down to such a mean standard.—*JD*, 7:201, November 13, 1859.

TRUTH AND INTELLIGENCE.—Truth and intelligence have a tendency to enlarge the capacity, to expand the soul, and to show man his real position—his relationship to himself and to his God, both in relation to the present and the future, that he may know how to live on the earth and be prepared to mingle with the Gods in the eternal worlds.

Now, if men will teach me these principles, I do not care what words they use. If truth comes, tail or head foremost, I am not very particular.—*JD*, 5:262, September 20, 1857.

Those men who profess so much intelligence that they cannot listen to the word of the Lord, and have so much egotism and philosophy that they cannot listen to sound reason and common sense, cannot be edified by these things, while we, who have not such lofty pretensions, enjoy them.—*JD*, 5:241, September 13, 1857.

There is not a particle of the human system but what is full of intelligence and displays forethought, prescience, design, skill, and creative power; and everything bespeaks the handiwork of a wise, intelligent, omnipotent Creator, or God.—*JD*, 20:220, December 15, 1878.

## EDUCATION IN THE CHURCH

We want . . . to be alive in the cause of education. We are commanded of the Lord to obtain knowledge, both by study and by faith, seeking it out of the best books. And it becomes us to teach our children, and afford them instructions in every branch of education calculated to promote their welfare, leaving those false acquirements which tend to infidelity, and to lead away the mind and affection from the things of God. We want to compile the intelligence and literacy of this people in book form, as well as in teaching, preaching; adopting all the good and useful books we can obtain; make them. And instead of doing as many of the world do, take the works of God to try to prove that there is no God, we want to prove by God's works that he does exist, that he lives and rules and holds us, as it were, in the hollow of his hand.—*JD*, 19:310, April 8, 1878.

EDUCATION CANNOT BE NEGLECTED.—And then we want to study also the principles of education, and to get the very best teachers we can to teach our children; see that they are men and women who fear God and keep his commandments. . . . Let others who fear not God take their course; but it is for us to train our children up in the fear of God. God will hold us responsible for this trust. Hear it, you elders of Israel and you fathers and you mothers! . . . We want to get together to train our children up in the fear of God, to teach them correct principles ourselves, and place them in possession of such things as will lead them in the paths of life.—*JD*, 20:179, April 8, 1879.

"MONEY IS NOT TO BE COMPARED WITH INTELLIGENCE."
—And then with regard to our educational pursuits, let us do
all we can in that direction. Some people talk about the means
it takes. Why, money is not to be compared with intelligence.
—*JD*, 20:169, March 2, 1879.

THE EDUCATION OF LATTER-DAY SAINTS.—You will see
the day that Zion will be as far ahead of the outside world in
everything pertaining to learning of every kind as we are today
in regard to religious matters. You mark my words, and write
them down, and see if they do not come to pass. We are not
dependent upon them, but we are upon the Lord. We did not
get our priesthood nor our information in regard to his law from
them. It came from God. . . .

I remember talking with some celebrated scientists from
Europe some time ago, and I explained to them some of the
principles relative to the heavenly bodies that were revealed
through the Prophet Joseph Smith. They were astonished to
know that ideas so grand could be developed through one that
was comparatively unlearned. One of them remarked that
they were the most magnificent principles he had ever heard of.
Another one said that he had read and studied a great deal, but
he had a good deal more yet to learn. We are, as the French would
say, *en rapport*, with God; that is in communication with God.
Let us live so that we can keep that up, so that angels can
minister to us and the Holy Spirit dwell with us.—*JD*, 21:100,
April 13, 1879.

TEACHING THE THINGS OF GOD.—There is no man living,
and there never was a man living, who was capable of teaching
the things of God only as he was taught, instructed and directed
by the spirit of revelation proceeding from the Almighty. And
then there are no people competent to receive true intelligence and
to form a correct judgment in relation to the sacred principles of
eternal life, unless they are under the influence of the same
spirit, and hence speakers and hearers are all in the hands of the
Almighty.—*JD*, 17:369, April 8, 1875.

SCHOOLS, TEACHERS AND AUXILIARIES.—Our young
people's Improvement Associations are very creditable institutions,
and the fruits of the labors of those engaged in this work are
already manifesting themselves. I feel in my heart to say, God
bless the young men and young women of Israel. Let it be the
desire of your hearts to imitate the virtues of your parents and
of all good men and women, keeping your bodies and spirits pure
before God and man.

Then, we have our Sunday Schools, and many of our brethren and sisters in this direction are doing a good work. I would advise the superintendents of Sunday Schools to endeavor to collect the best talent they can to teach and instruct our children. What greater or more honorable work can we be engaged in than in teaching the children the principles of salvation? You that are diligent and that give your hearts to these things, God will bless, and the day will come when the youth of Israel will rise up and call you blessed.

Then with regard to our common schools, let us try to instruct our youth as best we can, and get the best of teachers, men and women of intelligence and education who are not only moral, but good Latter-day Saints; men and women who are not only capable of imparting to our children the rudiments of education, but who are also capable of teaching them the laws of God as he has revealed them for our guidance. And when you get good teachers you should appreciate them, and you should cooperate with them in their endeavors to teach our youth; and then see that they are properly remunerated for their services.—*JD*, 21: 368-369, August 8, 1880.

SUNDAY SCHOOL INSTRUCTION.—Our brethren and sisters should always remember that the work of teaching in our Sunday Schools impose upon them a moral obligation to make their daily walk and conversation accord with their teachings. Of all lessons, the living lesson is the best. Children are surprisingly shrewd in detecting inconsistencies between the instructions and habits of their instructors. Besides, the teacher who seeks to live up to his own advice, not only benefits his scholars, but his teachings exert a salutary influence upon himself, and he profits by his own lessons.—Epistle of the First Presidency, April 8, 1887, *JH*, April 8, 1887, p. 2.

"TRAIN UP OUR CHILDREN IN THE FEAR OF GOD AND I WILL RISK THE BALANCE."—Let us continue to go in every good word and work. Let our young people's Improvement Associations, and our Sunday and day schools receive our encouragement and aid; and let our children be taught by our friends and not our enemies.

It is for us to keep the commandments, to train up our children in the fear of God, to live unto God, and I will risk the balance.—*JD*, 26:97, February 12, 1882.

"WE SEEK AFTER THESE THINGS."—God expects Zion to become the praise and glory of the whole earth so that kings, hearing of her fame, will come and gaze upon her glory. God is not niggardly in his feelings towards us. He would as soon we all lived in palaces as not. But he wants us to observe his laws and fear him, and standing as messengers to go forth to the nations clothed upon with the power of the priesthood which has been conferred upon us; seeking "first the kingdom of God, and his righteousness;" seeking first the welfare and happiness of our fellow men, and God will add unto us all the gold and silver and possessions and everything that may be good for us to receive. I was going to say, perhaps more than would be good for us. But all these things shall be added, for no man that forsakes father and mother, houses and lands, wives and children for God and his kingdom, but what shall receive in this world a hundred-fold, and in the world to come life everlasting. This was true anciently, it is true today. This being the case, we ought to foster education and intelligence of every kind; cultivate literary tastes, and men of literary and scientific talent should improve that talent; and all should magnify the gifts which God has given unto them. Educate your children, and seek for those to teach them who have faith in God and in his promises, as well as intelligence. . . . If there is anything good and praiseworthy in morals, religion, science, or anything calculated to exalt and ennoble man, we are after it. But with all our getting, we want to get understanding, and that understanding which flows from God.—*JD*, 20:47-48, August 4, 1878.

CHAPTER XXVI

# THE LAW OF MARRIAGE

## ON MARRIAGE

A NATURAL PRINCIPLE.—Marriage is the legitimate union of the sexes. God made male and female, not only of man, but of all animals, fowls, fishes, and, as stated, everything that creepeth upon the earth; and endued them with organs and power to propagate their own species. He also endued the herbs, plants, flowers, trees, grasses, and all the vegetable kingdom with fecundity, whose seed (as expressed in the scriptures) should be in itself. Thus everything in the animal and vegetable kingdoms was prepared to propagate, increase, and perpetuate its own species. That principle, and the organs and media necessary for its development, have continued intact from the commencement up to the present time and it is a fact that all life in this creation, animal or vegetable, possesses the inherent power within itself fully to maintain and perpetuate its own species. This principle applies to the lower as well as to the higher grades of creation. The most repulsive animal and venomous reptile possess this power, as well as those that are the most refined, symmetrical, beautiful, or intellectual; and the most noxious and poisonous weeds or plants possess this fecundity, in common with the most lovely, sweet, nutritive, aromatic, or life-sustaining species. So that this grand, life-giving, preserving, and perpetuating power exists among all life, whether vegetable or animal.—M, 1-2.

MARRIAGE AND THE LAW OF THE GOSPEL.—The gospel, when introduced and preached to Adam after the fall, through the atonement of Jesus Christ, placed him in a position not only to have victory over death, but to have within his reach and to possess the perpetuity, not only of earthly, but of heavenly life; not only of earthly, but also of heavenly dominion; and through the law of that gospel enabled him (and not him alone, but all his posterity) to obtain, not only his first estate, but a higher exaltation on earth and in the heavens, than he could have enjoyed if he had not fallen; the powers and blessings associated with the atonement being altogether in advance of and superior to any enjoyment or privileges that he could have had in his first estate. Hence, he and his partner became the father and mother of lives—lives temporal, lives spiritual, and lives eternal, and were placed in the position to become Gods, yea, the sons and daughters of God, and to the increase and extent of their dominion there was to be no limit; worlds without end.

But it became necessary that Adam should obey, observe, and keep the law of the gospel, and it also became necessary that his posterity, who would possess the same exaltation and blessings, should also keep and observe the same law; and if they did not, they could not obtain the blessings of celestial lives and exaltations in the eternal worlds. But, while this was the law pertaining to celestial affairs, man was not deprived of the power, the right, and the privilege, the faculties and instincts of the association of the sexes, nor of the propagation of his own species; and hence, when man had transgressed the law of God and had corrupted himself to such a degree that it is said of him that his thoughts were only evil, and that continually; and when it had become an act of justice with the Almighty, in reference to the unborn spirits, in consequence of the extreme degradation of the human family, to introduce a better race, man possessing the power, while living, to propagate his own species, he could only accomplish and bring about this design by destroying that corrupt race, and appointing a selected and chosen race for the above named purpose.

The law before referred to was the law of the gospel. When the gospel is lived up to and enjoyed, its powers and blessings are also enjoyed, pertaining both to time and eternity; but when the law of the gospel is not lived up to, yet the principle of procreation and the association of the sexes still continues as a principle separate and distinct from that of the gospel [law]; and the nearer we can approach pure and correct principles, whereby the chastity of the race may be preserved, in our marital relations, the more will our actions be acceptable to our Heavenly Father. Hence, it has always been considered, among all intelligent and right thinking people in the nations, both in a social and political capacity, that it is in the interests of humanity that the marital relations should be sustained, that virtue and chastity should be preserved, and that in proportion as these principles are disregarded has the elevation or degradation of the race been manifested.—*M*, 3-4.

THE LAW OF CELESTIAL MARRIAGE.—The Lord has revealed unto us the ancient law, which was revealed to Adam through the gospel, and which is called the law of celestial marriage. This, as before stated, applies only to certain conditions of men, and can only be enjoyed by parties who have obeyed the everlasting gospel. It is one of the eternal principles associated therewith, uniting mortal and immortal beings by eternal covenants that will live and endure forever. . . . But with regard to the law of celestial marriage, there are certain safeguards thrown around it, as there always were, and those safeguards are, and

always were, in the hands of the proper authorities and priesthood, delegated by God to man for the protection and preservation
and right use of this most important, sacred, exalting, and eternal
ceremony or covenant. These things are clearly defined in the
revelation on celestial marriage, and can rightly only be enjoyed
and participated in by such as are considered worthy, according
to the laws, rites, privileges, and immunities connected therewith. . . . Are the barriers placed around this sacred institution
to be broken down and trampled underfoot? And are unworthy
characters who do not fulfil the requirements of the gospel to have
conferred upon them the blessings of eternal lives, of thrones, and
powers, and principalities in the celestial kingdom of God? We
emphatically answer, No!

FREEDOM TO ACCEPT OR REJECT THE LAW.—On the other
hand, are men and women, who, while nothing immoral can be
laid to their charge, and who are considered worthy of a standing
in the church, but who may be thoughtless, careless, and in-
different in regard to many religious matters, and who either do
not comprehend the gospel, or who do not appreciate the privileges
conferred by the celestial law of marriage connected therewith
—are they, while they cannot enjoy the greater privileges of the
gospel, to be deprived of the privileges and blessings arising from
the marital relations, and of the proper exercise of the impulses and
instincts of nature? We as emphatically answer, No! There ought
to be placed within the reach of the young of both sexes a full
and fair opportunity of correctly fulfilling the perpetuation of their
species, free and untrammelled, leaving it for themselves to embrace or reject the higher or more exalted law, as all men are left
free to receive or reject the gospel; thus preserving the free agency of
man in this as in all other things. While the parties themselves
do not take a course to embrace and enjoy the higher privileges
of the gospel, it is not for us to throw barriers in their way, but
to encourage, by all possible means, our youth to enter into
such marital relations as they are capable or worthy of enjoying,
leaving it for them in the future to receive or reject the fulness
of the gospel; and thus preserve the virtue, chastity and purity of
our youth. . . .—M, 5-7.

CIVIL MARRIAGE.—The question arises, what shall be done
in regard to those persons, who, being members of the church,
are not worthy to enter into those sacred and eternal relations
of which we have been speaking? This is probably a question that
concerns our civil polity rather than our religion, but we have
deemed it worthy of our consideration, and after due deliberation
have determined that in cases where recommends cannot be justifi-
ably given for the blessings of the house of the Lord, the parties

desiring marriage be united by the bishop, inasmuch as they are worthy of the recognition of their brethren and sisters and have not forfeited their right to be esteemed members of the church, though not sufficiently valiant in the cause of righteousness to be deemed altogether worthy of those weightier blessings that belong to the new and everlasting covenant. But that holier order to which we have referred is the law of marriage as it exists in its fulness, in its completeness, in the strength and beauty of its purity, without end or change, but eternal as the existence of the soul, abiding forever.

This recommendation, with regard to those who cannot live the higher law, who do not possess much faith, but possess a little faith, is given as a means of purification among some of our youth and others, who, while they are desirous to marry and fulfil the great law of nature and be fruitful and multiply, are not justly and consistently entitled to those blessings which the fulness of the gospel covenant provides. It has therefore been deemed best by myself and council, as well as by the council of the apostles, under our present circumstances, to place them in the hands of the bishops, rather than to have them go for the performance of the marriage ceremony to justices of the peace and others, who, in their operations, do not carry the weight of blessing and responsibility which belongs of right to the priesthood in all its ministrations and labors.

The foregoing ideas and considerations were submitted by me to the council of the apostles, and were approved by that body, and have already been read from the manuscript to assemblies of the priesthood or saints in Salt Lake City and other places. They are now presented to the presiding authorities in the various stakes and wards, and unity of action and concord of feeling may exist on this as on all other subjects in which we, as the servants of the Lord, and all the saints, are directly concerned.[1]—*M, 7-8.*

## ETERNITY OF THE MARRIAGE COVENANT

THE ORDER OF GOD'S KINGDOM.—God has shown us, in regard to our marital relations, that our wives are to be sealed to us for time and eternity. By what authority? By the authority of that holy priesthood that administers on the earth and in heaven, and of which Jesus said that whatever they should bind on earth should be bound in heaven, and whatsoever they should loose on earth should be loosed in heaven; and these relationships that exist among us here are calculated to be consummated there,

---

[1]This document was published over the official signature, "JOHN TAYLOR, *President of the Church of Jesus Christ of Latter-day Saints.*"

and men and women who understand their true position expect to enjoy each other's society and association there, as much as they do in their own homes here, just the same. And though they may sleep in the dust, yet, by the power of the resurrection . . . when the trump shall sound and the dead in Christ shall rise, they will burst the barriers of the tomb and come forth, each and all claiming their proper mates—those with whom they were associated on the earth—through eternity. . . .—*JD*, 18:141, October 10, 1875.

LEGITIMACY[1] OF ETERNAL MARRIAGE.—Why is a woman sealed to a man for time and all eternity? Because there is legitimate power on earth to do it. This power will bind on earth and in heaven. It can loose on earth, and it is loosed in heaven. It can seal on earth, and it is sealed in heaven. There is a legitimate, authorized agent of God upon earth. This sealing power is regulated by him. Hence what is done by that, is done right, and is recorded. When the books are opened, every one will find his proper mate, and have those that belong to him, and every one will be deprived of that which is surreptitiously obtained.—*JD*, 1:232, April 8, 1853.

ETERNITY OF THE MARRIAGE COVENANT REVEALED TO JOSEPH SMITH.—The Lord, however, has revealed many other great and important principles to us, and among these the eternal covenant between man and woman. Did Joseph reveal that principle? Yes, he did. Do you know it? Yes, I do know it. If nobody else knows it, I do. Did he tell you of it? Yes, he did. But I have had other manifestations besides that, and therefore I know of what I speak, and I know the principle is of God. —*JD*, 21:166, December 7, 1879.

## SOME FAMILY LIFE PROBLEMS

CHARGE TO PARENTS.—We have been commanded of the Lord to set our households in order. Apostles, Presidents of Stakes and Bishops, have you done this with your own households? Have you also seen that the Saints have done the same? Have you impressed upon the people under your charge the absolute necessity of purity if they desire the blessing and protection of the Most High? Wolves never watched with greater cunning and more ravenous hunger a flock of sheep and lambs than the people of your wards and stakes are now being watched by those who are ready to devour them. Are you awake to this danger, and do you take every precaution against it?

Parents, are you full of fidelity yourselves to every principle

---

[1]For use of the word "legitimacy" see the material in Chapter 30.

of godliness, and do you surround your sons and daughters with every safeguard to shield them from the arts of the vile? Do you teach them that chastity in both man and woman should be more highly esteemed than life itself? Or do you leave them in their ignorance and inexperience to mix with any society they may choose, at any hour that may be convenient to them, and to be exposed to the wiles of the seducer and the corrupt? These are questions you will all have to answer either to your shame and condemnation or to your joy and eternal happiness. Know this, that God, in giving us the precious blessings we possess, demands from us a suitable return. By receiving them we are placed under obligations. If these are not discharged, condemnation inevitably follows.

ROLE OF THE CHURCH AUXILIARIES IN MEETING FAMILY LIFE PROBLEMS.—We hear favorable accounts of the action of Primary Associations, Sunday Schools, Young Men's and Young Women's Mutual Improvement Associations, and Relief Societies. These organizations have unlimited opportunities of doing good. If those who have them in charge are faithful in attending to their duties, great will be their reward. If we desire the prosperity of Zion, we will carefully guard and train our young. They come to us pure from the Lord. By proper training we can make them mighty instruments for good. But, Superintendents and teachers of Primary Associations and Sunday Schools, and Presidents of Young Men's and Young Women's Associations and Relief Societies, remember this, *that God will never bless an unvirtuous people, and while a flood of corruption, destructive of all true morality and virtue, is sweeping over the land, we must erect barriers to stop its contaminating influence.* You have the young in your charge. Teach and impress them by every means in your power how dreadful a sin is unchastity. They are taught to shrink in horror from murder; and they should be taught to shrink with abhorrence from the next great sin to shedding blood, and that is *unchastity.—Epistle of the First Presidency,* October 6, 1885; *MS,* 47:715-716 (1885).

THE HOME ENVIRONMENT.—We should live together in love. There should be union in every family circle and harmony in every neighborhood and city. We should be cleanly in our persons, in our dress, and in our habitations and surroundings. Industry should be habitual with the adults of our community, and the rising generation should be taught its lessons and be impressed with its value as a means of happiness. God has given us the earth as a dwelling place, and when mankind live as they should do, it is a delightful residence. It is our duty to adorn and beautify it—to make it so lovely and attractive that angels may condescend to visit it. We should, therefore, have fruitful farms, choice orchards, well arranged gardens, and if every dwelling is surrounded by flowers it will neither detract from its beauty in the eye of visitors, nor make it less attractive as their home to the children of the household.

In some quarters there has been ruinous neglect on the part of parents in making their homes attractive to their children. A well-ordered, lovely home, in which peace and good-will prevail is a place of perpetual delight to those who reside there, whether old or young. Where such homes exist the young who live there are not found loafing at street corners or stores, nor spending their time in gadding about from house to house and in improper company at late hours. Books and musical instruments are now so cheap as to be within the reach of the most humble. By furnishing means of instruction, amusement, and enjoyment at home, parents can . . . tie their children to them by bonds of affection that can never be broken. In after years those children will think of that home as the brightest and dearest spot in their memories; in their minds it will always be surrounded by a heavenly halo.— *Epistle of the First Presidency,* March, 1886; *MS,* 48:321-322 (1886).

FAMILY RELATIONS.—Husbands, do you love your wives and treat them right, or do you think that you yourselves are some great moguls who have a right to crowd upon them? They are given to you as a part of yourself, and you ought to treat them with all kindness, with mercy and long suffering, and not be harsh and bitter, or in any way desirous to display your authority. Then, you wives, treat your husbands right, and try to make them happy and comfortable. Endeavor to make your homes a little heaven, and try to cherish the good Spirit of God. Then let us as parents train up our children in the fear of God and teach them the laws of life. If you do, we will have peace in our bosoms, peace in our families, and peace in our surroundings.—*JD,* 21:118-119, November 28, 1879.

FAMILY PRAYERS.—Do you have prayers in your family? . . . And when you do, do you go through the operation like the grinding of a piece of machinery, or do you bow in meekness and with a sincere desire to seek the blessing of God upon you and your household? That is the way that we ought to do, and cultivate a spirit of devotion and trust in God, dedicating ourselves to him, and seeking his blessings.—*JD,* 21:118, November 28, 1879.

UNCHASTITY.—There is another thing which is most grievous, afflicting, and distressing to contemplate. When a man takes to himself a woman that properly belongs to another, and defiles her, it interferes with the fountain of life and corrupts the very source of existence. There is an offspring comes forth as the fruit of that union, and that offspring is an eternal being—how can it be looked upon? To reflect upon it wounds the finest feelings of human nature in time, and will in eternity. For who can gaze upon the degradation of his wife and the corruption of his seed without peculiar sensations? How much more is this feeling enhanced when the wronged man considers that he has been robbed by one who professed to be his friend? This thing is not to be trifled with, but is of the greatest importance; hence the necessity of the sealing powers, that all things may be pure, chastity maintained, and lasciviousness be rooted out from among the saints. Why so? That we may have a holy offspring that shall be great and clothed with the mighty power of God, to rule in his kingdom, and accomplish the work we propose they shall fulfil; and that when we go to sleep, we may sleep in peace, knowing that justice will be administered in righteousness. . . .—*JD*, 1:232, April 8, 1853.

THE RESPONSIBILITY OF HUSBANDS.—God expects you to be true to your vows, to be true to yourselves, and to be true to your wives and children. If you become covenant breakers, you will be dealt with according to the laws of God. And the men presiding over you have no other alternative than to bring the covenant breaker to judgment. If they fail to do their duty, we shall be under the necessity of looking after them, for righteousness and purity must be maintained in our midst.—*JD*, 24:171-172, May 18, 1883.

CHAPTER XXVII

# THE TEMPLES AND THEIR WORK

## UNIVERSAL SALVATION

REDEMPTION FOR ALL.—There was a great and comprehensive plan designed by the Almighty in his economy connected with the salvation of the human family who are his children, for he is the God and the Father of the spirits of all flesh. It means that he is interested in their welfare, in their prosperity, in their happiness, and in all that pertains to their exaltation in time and throughout the eternities that are to come. Being thus interested, and so little of the gospel having been revealed in the different ages, and so much of the power of darkness and iniquity having prevailed among men, it was necessary that something should be done for the dead as well as the living. God is interested in the dead as well as the living.—*JD*, 25:181-182, May 18, 1884.

We are here to cooperate with God in the salvation of the living, in the redemption of the dead, in the blessings of our ancestors, in the pouring out of blessings upon our children; we are here for the purpose of redeeming and regenerating the earth on which we live, and God has placed his authority and his counsels here upon the earth for that purpose, that men may learn to do the will of God on the earth as it is done in heaven. This is the object of our existence; and it is for us to comprehend the position. —*JD*, 21:94, April 13, 1879.

WORK FOR THOSE WHO HAVE PASSED AWAY.—It is reserved for us to do a work for those who have passed away, who have not obeyed or had the gospel in their lifetime. We are here to do a work connected with the redemption of the dead. When the temple was commanded to be built in Nauvoo, after the temple had been built in Kirtland, and after so many keys had been turned, and after so many manifestations, visions, and ministrations had been had, yet it was said then that there was not a place upon the earth in which to perform the ordinance of baptism for the dead and Joseph was commanded to build a house for that purpose. . . . We are all of us indebted to the revelations of God, through the medium of the holy priesthood, for these things.

JOSEPH SMITH AND THE NAUVOO TEMPLE.—Joseph Smith before his death, was much exercised about the completion of the temple in Nauvoo, and the administering of ordinances therein. In his anxiety and for fear he should not live to see the temple completed, he prepared a place over what was known as the brick-store—which many of you who lived in Nauvoo will recollect—where to a chosen few he administered those ordinances that we now have today associated with endowments, so that if anything should happen to him—which he evidently contemplated—he would feel that he had then fulfilled his mission, that he had conferred upon others all the keys given to him by the manifestations of the power of God.

At first these things were only partially made known to him, and as they were partially developed he called upon the twelve that were then living—many of you gray-headed people will remember it—to commence and be baptized for the dead, and they were baptized in the Mississippi River. Immediately after these baptisms, the prophet had a revelation which more clearly developed the order in relation to such baptisms. According to that revelation it appeared that, notwithstanding all the visions, revelations, keys, etc., that had heretofore been given, there was not a place, not even in the Kirtland Temple, wherein those things could be carried out, and hence a font, such as we have in this temple, was built in the temple at Nauvoo, and it was there, under proper circumstances and proper administration, and according to the principles that he had laid down, that those ordinances were administered then, and are administered now.—*JD, 25:182-183,* May 18, 1884.

THE MILLENNIUM.—We read sometimes about the millennium. But what do we know about it? It is a time when this work will be going on, and temples, thousands of them, will be reared for the accomplishment of the objects designed, in which communications from the heavens will be received in regard to our labors, how we may perform them, and for whom. This is the work devolving upon us.—*JD, 25:185,* May 18, 1884.

SAVIORS ON MOUNT ZION.—God is looking upon us, and has called us to be saviors upon Mount Zion. And what does a savior mean? It means a person who saves somebody. Jesus went and preached to the spirits in prison; and he was a savior to that people. When he came to atone for the sins of the world, he was a savior, was he not? Yes. And we are told in the revelations that saviors should stand upon Mount Zion; and the kingdom shall be the Lord's. Would we be saviors if we did not save somebody? I think not. Could we save anyone if we did not build temples? No, we could not; for God would not accept our offerings and sacrifices. Then we came here to be saviors on Mount Zion, and the kingdom is to be the Lord's.

Then what shall we do? We will build temples. And what then? Administer in them, when we get them done. Do we know how? Yes, we do, for God has told us how. And whom shall we save? Our fathers and mothers, our uncles and our aunts, our grandfathers and our grandmothers, and we will look after the interest of all we can trace; we will still go to work, after we have settled individual matters and attended to our family affairs and a few little things among us—for we are a small people comparatively, notwithstanding that we talk about extending our power; we are a few people comparatively, but God has chosen us and selected us and planted us here, and told us what to do. Then after we get through with our own affairs, what next? There are myriads who have died without a knowledge of the gospel, that God and Jesus and the ancient patriarchs and prophets and men of God were interested in as they are in us, and whom we are informed shall have the opportunity of receiving the gospel if they had it not on this earth.—*JD*, 22:308, August 28, 1881.

## WHY BUILD TEMPLES

REVELATION.—Why do we build temples? Because Elijah conferred certain keys which he held upon Joseph Smith. And when he laid his hands upon elders conferring on them the holy priesthood, they carried the principles imparted by Elijah to Joseph to you and to others, and you received it without knowing it. And by and by as the church began to gather together, we began to talk about building temples in which to receive and to administer ordinances which had been revealed unto Joseph Smith, pertaining to the interest of the living and the dead and necessary to our salvation and exaltation in the kingdom of our God, as well as for those for whom we administer. And we have not only talked about it but have done considerable in that direction.—*JD*, 22:306, August 28, 1881.

Now, I will ask, whoever thought of building temples until God revealed it? Did you? If you did, I wish you would tell us of it. And did you know how to build them? No. And did you know how to administer in them after they were built? No, you did not. We are indebted to the Lord for these things. —*JD*, 21:95, April 13, 1879.

TEMPLES AND THE MISSION OF ELIJAH.—After you received the gospel and the spirit of the same, the great desire of your hearts was to go to Zion. And in order to accomplish this you put away your little savings, and you began to contrive how to dispose of your little properties, and many of you were almost ready to sell yourselves to get to Zion. You could not tell why you had such feelings, but you did have them, and you could not get rid of them until you were brought here. You would not have come here had it not been for that, would you? I have no idea that you would. When you were told to build temples, what made you build them? Because you had received the gospel in your hearts, associated with which was the mission of Elijah which was to turn the hearts of the children to the fathers, and the hearts of the fathers to the children.—*JD*, 21:95-96, April 13, 1879.

TEMPLES COMMANDED.—Now the command is to build temples. For what purpose? That they over whom Satan has had power may be administered for, reaching back, back to the beginning of time, that they may be brought forth and inherit the blessings and privileges of the kingdom of God, and that we, ourselves, may be prepared to live and reign with him for ever. Let us continue to live in humility and meekness before God, seeking in faith and good works to get an increased portion of his Holy Spirit, that we may comprehend the laws of God and live according to the principles of eternal truth. . . . —*JD*, 18:334-335, December 31, 1876.

BUILDING THE SALT LAKE TEMPLE.—The temple we are now building, in comparison, is no more than a little plaything, but in doing it we shall learn better how to perform temporal things and spiritual things.—*JD*, 10:149-150, April 6, 1863.

COMMENT AT COMPLETION OF LOGAN TEMPLE.—We have finished our temple. What is it for? Not a building to look at; not a house to brag about; for before we get through we shall have built some temples so much better, that you will not feel to boast about this temple. The temple that the people built in Kirtland was only a small building compared with this one, and they were a very small and poor people who built it, yet it was built in accordance with the commands of God. In Nauvoo, also, the people were very poor. They had just been driven from the land of Missouri, yet they were commanded of God to build it. What was obtained in these temples? In the Kirtland Temple Jesus appeared, and Moses, Elias, and Elijah appeared also, and all these things that I have read to you and spoken about, transpired on that occasion. Communication was opened between the heavens and the earth, between the priesthood in the heavens and the priesthood on the earth, and the keys of that priesthood imparted to Joseph and others on the earth. It was left to those in this world to keep open those communications, to see that the road was clear, and that there was no barrier interposed between earth and the heavens, and to lead forward and progress in other principles yet to be developed.—*JD*, 25:184-185, May 18, 1884.

WHAT ARE TEMPLES FOR?—We have now finished this temple, and some people inquire, what is it for? For many things: that our sealings and ordinances may be performed in a manner that will be acceptable before God and the holy angels; that whatsoever is bound on the earth according to the laws of the eternal priesthood shall be bound in the heavens; that there may be a connecting link between the living and the dead, between those who have lived, all those ancient fathers of which I have spoken who are interested in the welfare of their posterity; that there may be a royal priesthood, a holy people, a pure people, a virtuous people on the earth to officiate and operate in the interests of the living and the dead; not looking so much after themselves, but after God, after the work of God, and after the accomplishment of those things which God has designed to be carried out in the dispensation of the fulness of times when all things are to be united in one, and that they may be prepared to operate with the priesthood in the heavens in the redemption of the inhabitants of this world from the days of Adam unto the present time.

TEMPLES INTRODUCE HIGHER BRANCHES OF EDUCATION. —It is also intended to introduce the higher branches of education—literary, scientific, linguistic, philosophical and theological; for we are told to obtain a knowledge of laws, languages, governments, justice, equity, rule, authority, dominion, and all those great cosmopolitan principles exhibited in the laws of nature and among the peoples, by the wisdom, prescience, power and intelligence of "nature's God." That we may thus be acquainted with earthly and heavenly things, in accordance with everlasting laws that have existed in the heavens and on the earth from the beginning; and that all those great and eternal principles by which the worlds are governed may be comprehended by us.—*JD*, 25: 185, May 18, 1884.

## SERVICE IN THE TEMPLES

THE REQUIREMENTS OF ENTRANCE.—In the first place people desirous to go and attend to ordinances in these houses, must have a recommendation from their bishop. That is one of those—I was going to say—ugly facts. That is, ugly to those who are not prepared to pass through that ordeal, whose lives have been careless, whose actions have been improper, and whose standing perhaps is precarious—that is one of those facts that must be faced. Then when they have obtained this recommendation from the bishop, it must be endorsed by the president of the stake, and after that have the sanction of the president of the church. This is quite an ordeal for many men to go through. For men and women who are upright, virtuous, and honorable, it is very simple matter; there is no difficulty in their way at any time. But to those who have been careless of their duties, who have departed from the laws of God, and who have tampered with, or violated the ordinances of the gospel—to such people it is a critical time.

However, there is something far more difficult than that yet to come. That is only a starting point in these matters. The things that are ahead are a great deal more difficult to accomplish. What are they? The time will come when we shall not only have to pass by those officers whom I have referred to—say, to have the sanction and approval of our bishop, of the president of the stake, and of the president of the church—but we are told in this book (The Doctrine and Covenants) that we shall have to pass by the angels and the Gods. We may have squeezed through the other; we may have got along tolerably well, and been passed and acted upon, and sometimes a "tight squeeze" at that. But how will it be when we get on the other side, and we have the angels and the Gods to pass by before we can enter into our exaltation? If we cannot pass, what then? Well, we cannot, that is all. And if we cannot, shall we be able to enter into our exaltation? I think not. What do you think about it?—*JD*, 25:161-162, June 15, 1884.

UNNATURAL INFAMIES.—No woman murderer, no man murderer can have a place among the Latter-day Saints, and I speak of it that the presidents of stakes and the bishops may be apprised of these things. And some of these people would try to pass by the bishops, and then by the presidents of stakes, and then by the president of the church, and crawl with all their slime and damnable hypocrisy into the temples of the living God. They may pass by these, but they will have to pass by the angels and the Gods, before they get through, and they will never inherit the kingdom of God. Hear it, you sisters! Hear it, you brethren! Hear it, you bishops, and you presidents of stakes! Watch well and know well what you are doing, when you sign recommends for doubtful characters to go into these holy places. We do not want them there. It is not their place, and you will have to account for your acts if you permit these things knowingly. It is necessary that you should be particular about these matters, for you will have to answer for your doings as I have for mine. We cannot, because of relationship, because somebody is a cousin, or an uncle, or an aunt, or a brother, or a sister, or a son or a daughter, or a father or a mother—we cannot admit and will not admit them to any of these holy places unless they are worthy. I call upon you if you know of adulterers or adulteresses, or people that practice these unnatural infamies, to sever them from the church; they shall not have a place in the church and kingdom of God.—JD, 25:316-317, October 6 and 7, 1884.¯

TEMPLE WORKERS.—We will have to fix upon a number of men and women—for the sisters will be required as well as the brethren—that will be needed. These can go along, leaving their farms and their merchandizing, or whatever they may have in hand, and go into the temple of the Lord, on a mission for six months, or twelve months, or two or three years as the case may be, the same as others who go out into the world. If I today were not engaged as I am I should say, "Won't you be kind enough to give me . . . an opportunity to officiate in the temple?" and I should feel it an honor to be privileged to work in the house of God.—JD, 25:186-187, May 18, 1884.

TEMPLE ORDINANCES ARE ETERNAL.—When Elijah the prophet appeared to Joseph Smith, he committed to him the keys of this dispensation; and hence we are at work building temples; but some of us hardly know why. We go at it the same as we follow plowing, sowing, planting, reaping, and such kinds of pursuits. There are other things behind that. There are ordinances associated behind these things that go back into eternity; and forward unto eternity; that are the offspring of God, that are intended for the welfare, the happiness, and exaltation of mankind; for those who are living and those that are dead and for those that will live hereafter, pertaining both to our progenitors and our posterity. And that is one of those keys that have been turned. —JD, 21:95, April 13, 1879.

## A FORWARD LOOK

In looking still forward we find that there are other things ahead of us. One thing is the building of temples, and that is a very important item, and ought to rest with force upon the minds of all good saints.

CONVERSATION WITH ROTHSCHILD.—I remember, some time ago, having a conversation with Baron Rothschild, a Jew. I was showing him the temple here, and said he—"Elder Taylor, what do you mean by this temple? What is the object of it? Why are you building it?"

Said I, "Your fathers had among them prophets, who revealed to them the mind and will of God; we have among us prophets who reveal to us the mind and will of God, as they did. One of your prophets said—The Lord whom ye seek shall suddenly come to his temple, but who may abide the day of his coming? For he shall sit as a refiner's fire and a purifier of silver!" "Now," said I, "sir, will you point me out a place on the face of the earth where God has a temple?"

Said he, "I do not know of any."

"You remember the words of your prophet that I have quoted?"

Said he—"Yes, I know the prophet said that, but I do not know of any temple anywhere. Do you consider that this is that temple?"

"No, sir, it is not."

"Well, what is this temple for?"

Said I, "The Lord has told us to build this temple so that we may administer therein baptisms for our dead (which I explained to him) and also to perform some of the sacred matrimonial alliances and covenants that we believe in, that are rejected by the world generally, but which are among the purest, most exalting and ennobling principles that God ever revealed to man."

"Well, then, this is not our temple?"

"No, but," said I, "you will build a temple, for the Lord has shown us, among other things, that you Jews have quite a role to perform in the latter days, and that all the things spoken by your old prophets will be fulfilled, that you will be gathered to old Jerusalem, and that you will build a temple there; and when you build that temple, and the time has arrived, 'the Lord whom you seek will suddenly come to his temple.' Do you believe in the Messiah?"

"Yes."

"Do you remember reading in your old prophets something like this—'They shall look upon him whom they have pierced, and mourn, and be in bitterness for him, as one that is in bitterness for his firstborn. And one shall say, what are these wounds in thine hands and in thy side? And he will say—These with which I was wounded in the house of my friends?' "

"Ah! Is that in our Bible?"

"Yes, sir, that is in your Bible."

I spoke to him then about the Nephites having left Jerusalem and told him that the Book of Mormon represents them as descendants of their people, and that Jesus came among them, and that they, because of their iniquity and departure from the word and law of God, were stricken with blackness.

Said he—"What, as Cain was?"

"Yes, sir, as Cain was." Said I—"These people, the Lamanites, according to this record," a French copy of which I gave him, he being a Frenchman; "this people are beginning to feel after these things, and they are coming by hundreds and by thousands and demanding baptism at our hands, just as you find recorded in that book that they would do, and that is given there as a sign that God's work had commenced among all nations. Said he—"What evidence have you of this?"

This conversation took place in the Townsend House, and when the baron asked me for evidence, said I—"Sir, if you will excuse me a few minutes I will give you some evidence;" and I went to Savage's book stand, in the Townsend House, and obtained a photographic copy of David Cannon baptizing Indians, standing in the midst of a great crowd of them. Said I—"Here is the evidence."

"Well, what shall we do?"

Said I—"You can do nothing unless God directs. You as a people are tied hand and foot, and have been for generations, and you can't move a peg unless God strikes off your fetters. When he says the word the things spoken of by the prophets will be fulfilled. Then, the measuring line will go forth again in Jerusalem, then your Messiah will come, and all those things spoken of by the prophets will be fulfilled."

I mentioned these matters to Baron Rothschild merely to exhibit some ideas pertaining to the work in which we are engaged; and in speaking of the temple—"Well, this is not the temple?" "No, not that you are going to build; this is ours, and we expect to build hundreds of them yet, and to administer in them in carrying out the work of God." I speak of this, that you may reflect a little, you Latter-day Saints.—*JD*, 18:199-200, April 6, 1876.

# BOOK FIVE

## THE KINGDOM OF GOD AND THE KINGDOMS OF MEN

*"The worst wish we have for the human family is that the principles enunciated in our Constitution may reverberate over the wide earth, and spread from shore to shore until all mankind shall be free."*
—JOHN TAYLOR,
*JD,* 14:267
*Dec.* 17, 1871,

# CHAPTER XXVIII

# WORLD PROBLEMS

## THE NEED FOR THE STUDY OF POLITICAL PRINCIPLES

THE PROBLEM STATED.—Notwithstanding the opposition we have had to combat, the people not only look upon us as a religious community, but as a great people politically, occupying a desirable position upon this continent. It is true when we have the Spirit upon us we look forward to the time when we shall have the literal kingdom of God established, and when we shall exercise rule and dominion, and when we shall increase, and so continue until the kingdoms of this world shall become the kingdoms of our God and of Christ. These feelings occupied our breasts in our infancy, in the church, but some ideas of the reality of the vast unborn future were more or less confused; it was very difficult for us to have just conceptions of God's dealings with us and with the nations of the earth. It was thought by many that when Joseph Smith offered himself as a candidate for president of the United States that it was a dangerous and foolish policy, and, in fact, it was quite difficult for many to bring their feelings up to that point.

We have been struggling against the powers of darkness, so far as religion is concerned, from the year 1830; as we have increased in numbers we have naturally assumed a social and political status, and have been obliged to organize a government, and make laws in accordance with those of that nation with which we are associated. We are now struggling and expect to have to struggle for our religious, social, and political rights. . . .

THE DUTY TO STUDY CORRECT POLITICAL PRINCIPLES.—In a political point of view we have had doubts whether some systems were not as good as ours, and whether we had not better be governed by the powers of the world than ·listen to the teachings of God. However, as we have progressed the mist has been removed, and in relation to these matters, the elders of Israel begin to understand that they have something to do with the world politically as well as religiously; that it is as much their duty to study correct political principles as well as religious, and to seek to know and comprehend the social and political interests of man, and to learn and be able to teach that which would be best calculated to promote the interests of the world.—*JD*, 9:339-340, April 13, 1862.

DESTRUCTION OF THE NATIONS.[1]—This nation and other nations will be overthrown, not because of their virtue, but because of their corruption and iniquity. The time will come, for the prophecies will be fulfilled, when kingdoms will be destroyed, thrones cast down, and the powers of the earth shaken, and God's wrath will be kindled against the nations of the earth, and it is for us to maintain correct principles, political, religious, and social, and to feel towards all men as God feels.—*JD*, 17:4, February 1, 1874.

I tell you, my brethren, in the name of God, that right among the nations of Europe, where many of you have come from, there will be some of the bloodiest scenes that you ever read of; and God expects you to assist in warning the nations, and in gathering out the honest in heart. Then when you come back, having accomplished a good mission, you can say, "My garments are clean from the blood of this generation." Many of you cannot say that now, therefore I wish to remind you of these things, that you may reflect upon them, and prepare yourselves for the work that is before you.—*JD*, 20:47, August 4, 1878.

UNREST IN THE WORLD: THE SAINTS TO SUSTAIN LIBERTY. —We see many signs of weakness which we lament, and we would to God that our rulers would be men of righteousness, and that those who aspire to position would be guided by honorable feelings—to maintain inviolate the Constitution and operate in the interest, happiness, well-being, and protection of the whole community. But we see signs of weakness and vacillation. We see a policy being introduced to listen to the clamor of mobs and of unprincipled men who know not of what they speak, nor whereof they affirm, and when men begin to tear away with impunity one plank after another from our Constitution, by and by we shall find that we are struggling with the wreck and ruin of the system which the forefathers of this nation sought to establish in the interests of humanity.

But it is for us still to sustain these glorious principles of liberty bequeathed by the founders of this nation, still to rally round the flag of the Union, still to maintain all correct principles, granting the utmost extent of liberty to all people of all grades and of all nations. If other people see fit to violate these sacred principles, we must uphold them in their entirety, in their

---

[1]See Doctrine and Covenants, Section 87.

purity, and be patriotic and law-abiding and act honorably toward our nation and to its rulers.—*JD*, 22:143-144, July 3, 1881.

## THE NATION-STATE SYSTEM

WORLD DISUNITY.—We find the world split up and divided into different nations, having different interests, and different objects, with their religious and political views as dissimilar as light and darkness, all the time jealous of each other, and watching each other as so many thieves. That man at the present day (and it has been the case for ages) is considered the greatest statesman, who, with legislation or diplomacy, can make the most advantageous arrangement with, or coerce by circumstances, other nations into measures that would be for the benefit of the nation with which he is associated, no matter how injurious it might be to the nation or nations concerned. The measure that would yield his nation an advantage might plunge another in irremediable misery, while there is no one to act as father and parent of the whole, and God is lost sight of. What is it that the private ambition of man has not done to satisfy his craving desires for the acquisition of territory and wealth, and what is falsely called "honor" and "fame"?

Those private, jarring interests have kept the world in one continual ferment and commotion from the commencement until the present time; and the history of the world is a history of the rise and fall of nations—of wars, commotions, and bloodshed —of nations depopulated and cities laid waste. Carnage, destruction, and death have stalked through the earth, exhibiting their horrible forms in all their cadaverous shapes, as though they were the only rightful possessors. Deadly jealousy, fiendish hate, mortal combat, and dying groans have filled the earth, and our bulwarks, our chronicles, our histories, all bear testimony to this; and even our most splendid paintings, engravings, and statuary are living memorials of bloodshed, carnage, and destruction. Instead of men being honored who have sought to promote the happiness, peace, and well-being of the human family, and greatness concentrating in that, those have been generally esteemed the most who produced the most misery and distress, and were wholesale robbers, ravagers, and murderers. . . .

Here is evidently a lack of that consummate wisdom, that moral and physical control, that parental power which balances the universe, and directs the various planets. For let the same recklessness, selfishness, individuality, and nationality there be manifested, and we should see the wildest confusion.—*GG*, 8-9, 1852.

THE PATTERN OF WORLD POLITICS.—When nations and
rulers set the pattern, they generally find plenty to follow their
example; hence, covetousness, fraud, rapine, bloodshed, and
murder prevail to an alarming extent. If a nation is covetous,
an individual thinks he may be also; if a nation commits a fraud,
it sanctions his acts in a small way; and if a nation engages in
wholesale robbery, an individual does not see the impropriety of
doing it in retail; if a strong nation oppresses a weak one, he does
not see why he may not have the same privilege. Corruption
follows corruption, fraud treads on the heels of fraud, and all
those noble, honorable, virtuous principles that ought to govern
men are lost sight of and chicanery and deception ride rampant
through the world. The welfare, happiness, exaltation, and glory
of man are sacrificed at the shrine of ambition, pride, covetousness, and lasciviousness. By these means nations are overthrown,
kingdoms destroyed, communities broken up, families rendered
miserable, and individuals ruined.—GG, 13-14, 1852.

Those great national evils of which I have spoken are things
which at present seem to be out of the reach of human agency,
legislation, or control. They are diseases that have been generat-
ing for centuries; that have entered into the vitals of all institutions, religious and political; that have prostrated the powers and
energies of all bodies politic, and left the world to groan under
them, for they are evils that exist in church and state, at home
and abroad; among Jew and gentile, Christian, pagan, and
Mohammedan; king, prince, courtier, and peasant; like the deadly
simoon, they have paralyzed the energies, broken the spirits,
damped the enterprise, corrupted the morals, and crushed the
hopes of the world.

Thousands of men would desire to do good if they only
knew how; but they see not the foundation and extent of the
evil, and long-established opinions, customs, and doctrines blind
their eyes and damp their energies. And if a few should see the
evil and try a remedy, what are a few in opposition to the views,
power, influence, and corruption of the world?

No power on this side of heaven can correct the evil. It is
a world that is degenerated, and it requires a God to put it right.
—GG, 14-15, 1852.

WARS AND COMMOTIONS.—Why is it that thrones will be
cast down, empires dissolved, nations destroyed, and confusion and
distress cover all people, as the prophets have spoken? Because
the Spirit of the Lord will be withdrawn from the nations in
consequence of their wickedness, and they will be left to their own
folly.—JD, 6:24, November 1, 1857.

When the potsherds of the earth strive with the potsherds

of the earth, and God does not interfere, they will be more likely
to accomplish the destruction of each other.—*JD*, 9:234, April
28, 1861.

They are all very loyal; they profess to be very patriotic,
and they all believe they are fighting for their own, and they
pray to the god of battles to give them success; and it is quite
common to hear them boast, "We will regulate matters in a short
time." But who is this god of battles? Why, the devil, the prince
and power of the air, who rules in the hearts of the children of
disobedience. He is the god they risk their cause with, and it is
for him to handle them as he sees fit.—*JD*, 9:236, April 28, 1861.

A PROPHECY DURING THE AMERICAN CIVIL WAR.—The
world has been full of darkness and wickedness, and has not
understood the things of God; but many of the past as well as
the present generations have been full of blood-thirstiness, fraud,
and oppression, without any correct principles, without the
Spirit of the Lord to direct them. It is so now, and hence the
wars and turmoils that at present exist in these United States—
a war of brother against brother to destroy each other and to
bring each other into bondage. This is the condition of things as
they exist in this country at the present time, and this state of
things will increase throughout the whole world, and all the
inhabitants thereof will participate in the very things that are
now transpiring in this nation.—*JD*, 9:341-342, April 13, 1862.

THE NEED FOR CONSTRUCTIVE IDEALISM.—If men and
nations, instead of being governed by their unruly passions,
covetous desires, and ambitious motives, were governed by the
pure principles of philanthropy, virtue, purity, justice, and honor,
and were under the guidance of a fatherly and intelligent head,
directed by that wisdom which governs the universe and regulates
the motions of the planetary systems, there would be no need
of so many armies, navies, and police regulations which are now
necessary for the protection of those several nations from the
aggressions of each other, and internal factions. Let any one
examine the position of Europe alone, and he will find this statement abundantly verified.—*GG*, 11, 1852.

EUROPEAN NATIONALISM.—The continental nations of
Europe are very differently constituted to what we are; they are
generally a distinct people, but they have more or less become
amalgamated years ago, and at present have assumed a degree
of nationality, having their own peculiar theories, customs, and
ideas of religion and politics, and their own notions and standards
of a social system. Their systems have been codified to a certain
extent—have been taught in their schools, their lyceums, and their

churches, and been discussed in their legislative assemblies, and form what is generally termed *idées nationale*—they have been written about, thought about, lectured about, and preached about.

There are certain mediums through which the ideas of those nations flow generally, which differ according to the position they occupy politically and religiously, and the kind of government which they are under. These theories and systems are peculiarly influenced and modified by the peculiar languages through which their ideas are conveyed. Those nations are organized under strictly political principles or systems—their organizations are almost exclusively of a political nature, although they have arrangements pertaining to church government which regulate and control in many instances the consciences of their subjects. They have a certain kind of religion in which they generally are, no doubt, conscientious, and which is sustained by law.

THE UNITED STATES AND THE LATTER-DAY SAINTS.— The United States differ from them; for, although organized on political principles, yet, they have no religion which they acknowledge as such nationally, leaving the people free to worship as they please.—*JD*, 11:51-52, January 18, 1865.

# WILL IT EVER BE THE UNITED STATES OF THE WORLD?

THE FACTOR OF THE PRESS AND PUBLIC OPINION.— Through the press we are made aware of the affairs of distant nations, and through the facilities of rapid communication they are brought into our immediate neighborhood. The result is an increased individual interest of all in the affairs of the most distant nations and tribes. We look over the periodicals of the day, as we would go into a museum to look upon the past, present, and future. . . .

AN ENLIGHTENED PUBLIC OPINION SEEKS FOR IMPROVEMENT.—Will the concentrated intelligence of past ages, with the improvements of the present, advance man in the scale of being, and lead him to seek for improvement in the science of life? We think it will, for man is a progressive being. It is an era of transition, an age of active, busy preparation. Is it to the establishment of some vast permanent moral, political, or religious government, or is it to eventuate in a combination, of all in one magnificent structure, under which all the nations of the earth may gather? The idea of a government, extending over the diversified tribes and nations of the earth, classifying, organizing, and controlling the whole, has been considered chimerical, a sort of monomania raving of some besotted Alexander, hair-brained

Peter of Russia, or unprincipled fatalism of a Napoleon—some bigoted believer in the Revelation of Patmos—Daniel, or some other old prophet of the dark ages. Changes of circumstances always require change in the administration; this would apply to individual states—why not to the world?

THE DREAM OF WORLD GOVERNMENT.—Although the present distracted state of the world might seem to forbid the expectation of an immediate amalgamation, yet the rapid increase of means of communication, the sure and decided commingling of interests, a universal interchange of sentiment, an increasing desire among mankind to shake off the shackles of despotism and enjoy the liberty of speech and conscience all conspire to show that such a combination of circumstances must eventually result in some kind of universal government—moral, religious, and political. . . .

SOME SOCIOLOGICAL CONSIDERATIONS.—The direction taken by inquiring minds is not only to the outward forms of government, but the public eye is turned to its interior arrangements and upon all that has a bearing upon the future prospects of community life. In this connection has public attention been drawn to the subject of family organization, in consideration of its forming the basis of all governments. There are comparatively few who are bold enough at present to risk their reputation in an attack upon the old and long cherished order of family government, although men are convinced there are vast moral, political, and religious evils arising directly or indirectly from the present . . . order; yet the few, who at this early day venture upon this subject before the public, denote an agitation and a spirit of investigation among the people, that will ultimately result in the only true basis of good domestic and popular government—the ancient and honored patriarchal order, the only one ever sanctioned by heaven. . . .

The intelligence of the people will soon see the necessity of adopting rules and regulations, which will bring them to a closer acquaintance with long-disused and forgotten laws of God of former days, which, when compared with human laws, will be seen to be so far superior, that the universal *vox populi* will be for its establishment, as the only permanent and true basis of good and wholesome government, notwithstanding the objections of learned casuists or would-be moralists of the present-day.—*The Mormon*, November 24, 1855, Vol. 1, No. 40.

NATIONAL OBSTACLES TO WORLD UNITY.—Professedly every good man thinks that it is good to be united in anything that is good. But the great difficulty with the world is to bring this about. The nations of the world are not united, and each

nation is divided and split up, and confusion and the spirit of
war and animosity and evil abound everywhere. They are not
united, but they are full of jealousy, hatred, strife, envy, and
malice.

Witness the late European wars. What did they fight for?
Who can tell? They fought for nothing, and they made peace
for nothing. I have searched the papers diligently, but I must
confess that I have been unable to discover what they fought for;
and I question very much if . . . the opposing powers could tell
you. Yet one hundred thousand men have been sent into eternity
to satisfy the caprice of a few individuals, and for what purpose?
I cannot tell, and I do not know anybody else that can. I have
not met with a man or with a writer yet that knew what they
fought for, or what they made peace for. What are they now
doing? France is building extra ships, and England is building
extra ships. What for? They do· not know.

A nation is afraid its neighboring nations are going to possess
a little more power than it possesses, and it must create more
power to cope with them. That is all the union I know anything
about in the world.—JD, 7:319, October 7, 1859.

HUMAN MEANS AT UNION WILL FAIL.—The great evils
that now exist in the world are the consequences of man's departure from God. This has introduced this degeneracy and imbecility,
and nothing but a retracing of his steps, and a return to God can
bring about a restitution. . . .

And all human means made use of at the present time to
ameliorate the condition of the world must fail, as all human
means have always done. There are some who suppose that the
influence of Christianity, as it is now preached and administered,
will bring about a millennial reign of peace. . . .

Christianity has prevailed more or less for eighteen hundred
years. If it should still continue and overspread the world in its
present form, what would it accomplish? The world's redemption
and regeneration? No, verily. Its most staunch supporters and
most strenuous advocates would say, No. For like causes always
produce like effects: and if it has failed to regenerate the nations
where it has had full sway for generations, it must necessarily
fail to regenerate the world. If it has failed in a small thing, how
can it accomplish a large one?[1]—GG, 15-16, 18, 1852.

If you examine the philosophy of France and Germany, and
other parts of the earth, you will find them to be on a par with
the religious world: they are going to ameliorate the condition
of mankind and to perform wonders, according to their professions. If you attempt to reason with them about their philosophy,

---

[1] It should be observed that John Taylor refers, of course, to apostate Christianity.

like the paddy's flea, when you attempt to put your finger on them, they are not there.—*JD*, 5:261-262, September 20, 1857.

THE WORLD'S PROBLEM.—The world, at the present time, is all confused, and it seems to me, sometimes, that even we have made very little improvement indeed, according to the light and intelligence God has communicated to us. But what has the world done? Whether you look at it morally, religiously, philosophically, or politically, or in what way you please, you will find it is all a chaotic mass.—*JD*, 1:149, 150, June 12, 1853.

THE METHOD OF WORLD PEACE.—The religion of Jesus Christ will develop the plan of putting down the high-handed power of tyranny and oppression which now pervades the earth, and how to establish the principles of peace, righteousness, and virtue upon the earth, and how to place the world of mankind in that position which God has destined they should occupy when his kingdom shall rule upon the earth, and when "every creature in heaven, on earth, and under the earth shall be heard to say, Blessing, honour, and glory, and power be unto him that sitteth upon the throne, and unto the Lamb for ever and ever."[1]

The germs of this peace are with us; the intelligence concerning these matters has begun to be developed. . . .—*JD*, 6:164, January 17, 1858.

---

[1]Compare Rev. 5:13.

# CHAPTER XXIX

# MORMONISM AND THE AMERICAN SYSTEM

## THE MORMON POSITION WITH REGARD TO THE AMERICAN NATION

### (A Doctrine of Inherent Rights)

INHERENT RIGHTS.—There are certain principles that are inherent in man, that belong to man, and that were enunciated in an early day, before the United States government was formed, and they are principles that rightfully belong to all men everywhere. They are described in the Declaration of Independence as unalienable rights, one of which is that men have a right to live; another is that they have a right to pursue happiness; and another is that they have a right to be free and no man has authority to deprive them of those God-given rights, and none but tyrants would do it.[1] These principles, I say, are unalienable in man; they belong to him; they existed before any constitutions were framed or any laws made. Men have in various ages striven to strip their fellow men of these rights, and dispossess them of them. And hence the wars, the bloodshed, and carnage that have spread over the earth. We therefore are not indebted to the United States for these rights. We were free as men born into the world, having the right to do as we please, to act as we please, as long as we do not transgress constitutional law nor violate the rights of others.

SOME LEGAL RIGHTS.—Being organized, then, into a government such as it is—that is, the name of a government, the name of a legislature, the name of a free people—being organized as we are, what next? We are necessarily obliged to look after our affairs as men, our political affairs. Our mission to the world is a mission of peace. The gospel proclaims peace on earth and good will to man. . . .

THE POLITICAL MISSION OF THE SAINTS.—Our mission is to call upon this nation and all nations to repent of their sins, of their lasciviousness, adulteries, fornications, murders, blas-

---

[1] "We hold these truths to be self-evident, that all men are created equal, that they are endowed by their Creator with certain unalienable rights, that among these are life, liberty, and the pursuit of happiness."—From the Unanimous Declaration of the Thirteen United States of America, 1776.

phemies, and of all dishonest and corrupt practices. But in this we use no force. Having laid these matters before them, they have their free will to receive or reject. . . . As politicians or statesmen they must at least give us the benefit of the Constitution and laws. These, as a portion of the body politic, we contend for as part of our political rights. We do not claim, nor profess, nor desire to interfere with any man's religion or conscience. We have nothing to do with their religion, nor they with ours. Religious faith or belief is not a political factor. The Constitution has debarred its introduction into the arena of politics;[1] and every officer of the United States has pledged himself under a solemn oath to abide by and sustain that instrument, and not one of them can interfere with it [religion] without a violation of his oath. . . .

TO MAINTAIN HUMAN RIGHTS.—Another thing God expects us to do, and that is to maintain the principle of human rights. . . . We owe it to ourselves as men, we owe it to our families, our children, and to posterity. We owe it to the lovers of freedom in this land, of which there are thousands, yea, millions, who despise acts of oppression and tyranny. We owe it to all liberty-loving men to stand up for human rights and protect human freedom, and in the name of God we will do it. . . .
Joseph, the despised of his father's house, became their deliverer. Moses, the foundling and outcast of Egypt, became the deliverer and law-giver of Israel. Jesus, the despised Nazarene, introduced principles that revolutionized the moral ideas and ethics of the world. And it may not be among the improbabilities, that the prophecies of Joseph Smith may be fulfilled and that the calumniated and despised Mormons may yet become the protectors of the Constitution and the guardians of religious liberty and human freedom in these United States—*JD*, 23:262-266, October 8, 1882.

THE CONSTITUTION OF THE UNITED STATES.—I will tell you what I think about the Constitution. I have just the same opinion of it that Joseph Smith had, and he said it was given by inspiration of God. The men did not know this who wrote it. The men did not know it who adopted it. Nevertheless it is true. There is an embodiment of principles contained therein calculated to bless and benefit mankind.
"What do you think about the government of the United States as a government?" I think it is a good deal ahead of most

---

[1]The compiler entertains the belief that President Taylor's meaning here was that the Constitution *debars political influence in the field of religion*, and not vice-versa, as the words appear. This belief conforms to constitutional practice and to President Taylor's essential meaning elsewhere.

governments, but I think the administrators are apostatizing very fast from the principles that the fathers of this nation instituted.[1] It has become quite a question nowadays, whether men can be preserved in their rights or not, whether men can worship God according to the dictates of their conscience or not, or whether we are living in a land of freedom or not. What is the matter? Why, they are like the religionists. How is it with them? They profess to believe in the Bible. They do believe it shut, but when you open it, they deny it. The people of this nation profess to believe in the Constitution. They do until it comes to be applied to the people, and then they do not. That is perhaps too broad a saying, but I will say there are many who feel like this—not all by a long way. There are thousands and tens of thousands who are imbued with the same principles as were the framers of the Constitution and who desire to see human freedom perpetuated. . . .

We would say then in regard to religionists—if you profess a religion be true to it. If you profess to believe in the Bible when shut, believe it when open, and practice its principles. We would say to men who profess so much loyalty and patriotism to the government, be true to your institutions, be true to the Constitution of the United States, as we say to all our people to be true to the same. We expect the Latter-day Saints to be so, and to be subject to law, to avoid lawlessness of every kind and interference with men's rights in any shape.—*JD*, 22:295-296, October 9, 1881.

THE FUNDAMENTAL LAW AND INHERENT RIGHTS.—There is an inherent principle of right planted in the human bosom, which God has placed there and which man never could, can not now, nor ever will uproot—principles of inherent right which all intelligent men, when they have sought for the truth with unbiased mind and desired sincerely to know, have invariably found. Governed by the principles of right, and uninfluenced by party, power, or wealth, there have always been men inspired by an infallible divine afflatus, who have recognized an innate, inalienable principle of justice and equity, in every age and among all nations, and the records of the Babylonians, the Medo-Persians, the Greeks, Romans, and more modern nations bear ample testimony to this fact. The principle of right is implanted in the human bosom and inherent in the human family, among all governments that have ever existed, and men of virtue, honor, and truth have always arrived at the same conclusions that we have.

The founders of our government, under the inspiration of

---

[1]This was spoken on the eve of the establishment by Congress of the Utah Commission (1882).

the Almighty, and goaded by an oppressive power, discovered the same elements, the same principles, the same ideas that we have, and enunciated those eternal principles and made them known to the world,—"that all men are born free and equal and have a right to life, liberty, and the pursuit of happiness." The founders of the French Republic, about the same time, made a declaration almost verbatim. It is the violation of the natural rights of man that has deluged the earth with blood in all ages. These principles were enunciated by Joseph Smith; he believed in them, so do we, in the right to think, in the right to speak, in the right to act, in the right to do all things that are right and good and proper, but not in the right to interfere with any other man's rights, any other man's religion, any other man's principles. These are our views. . . . The worst wish we have for the human family is that the principles enunciated in our Constitution may reverberate over the wide earth, and spread from shore to shore, until all mankind shall be free.—*JD*, 14:267, December 17, 1871.

THE CONSTITUTION: AN ENTERING WEDGE FOR A NEW ERA.—It is true that the founders of this nation, as a preliminary step for the introduction of more correct principles and that liberty and the rights of man might be recognized, and that all men might become equal before the law of the land, had that great palladium of liberty, the Constitution of the United States, framed. This was the entering wedge for the introduction of a new era, and in it were introduced principles for the birth and organization of a new world.

The Prophet Joseph Smith said that the Constitution of the United States was given by the inspiration of God. But good, virtuous, and holy principles may be perverted by corrupt and wicked men. The Lord was opposed by Satan; Jesus had his Judas; and this nation abounds with traitors who ignore that sacred palladium of liberty and seek to trample it under foot. Joseph Smith said they would do so, and that when deserted by all, the elders of Israel would rally around its shattered fragments and save and preserve it inviolate. But even this, good as it was, was not a perfect instrument. It was one of those steppingstones to a future development in the progress of man to the intelligence and light, the power and union that God alone can impart to the human family.—*JD*, 21:31, April 9, 1879.

THE CONSTITUTION.—We believe that our fathers were inspired to write the Constitution of the United States, and that it is an instrument, full, lucid, and comprehensive; that it was dictated by a wise and foreseeing policy, and does honor to the heads and hearts of its framers; that it is the great bulwark of American liberty; and that the strict and implicit observance of which is the only safeguard of this mighty nation. We therefore rest ourselves under its ample folds.

LEGISLATURES.—We believe that all legislative assemblies should confine themselves to constitutional principles; and that all such laws should be implicitly obeyed by every American.

THE RIGHTS OF MAN.—We believe that all men should have a right to do good; a perfect freedom of action; and be protected in that right; "free trade and sailors' rights"; but that no man is free, or at liberty to do wrong, or transgress law.

We believe that all men are responsible to God for their religious acts, and therefore ought to have perfect freedom of conscience.

POLICY AND ADMINISTRATION.—We believe that the president, governors, judges, and governmental officers ought to be respected, honored, and sustained in their stations; but that they ought to use their positions and power, not for political emolument, or party purposes; but for the administration of justice, and equity, and for the well being and happiness of the people.

PARTIES AND POLITICS.—We believe that legislators ought to be chosen on account of their intelligence, honor, integrity, and virtue; and not because they belong to some particular party clique.

We believe that the high party strife, logrolling, wirepulling, and political juggling, and spoliation, are a disgrace to any politician; that they are beneath the dignity of an American, and disgraceful and humiliating, alike to the people and statesmen of this great republic.

We believe that legislative enactments ought to be for the good of the whole, and not for any particular location or district; and that anything else is at variance with the spirit and genius of our institutions.

We believe that although there is much to lament, and room for very great improvement, both in our executive, judiciary, and legislative departments, that we have the most liberal, free, and enlightened government in the world. . . .—*The Mormon,* February 17, 1855.

CALLING OF THE LATTER-DAY SAINTS.—We are called of God to be an upright people, a virtuous people, an honorable people. We are called upon to maintain correct principles, and to introduce them among the peoples of the earth, and especially among the people of this nation.—*JD,* 25:93, February 10, 1884.

By and by, you will find they will tear the Constitution to shreds, as they have begun now. They have started long ago to rend the Constitution of our country in pieces; and in doing so they are letting loose and encouraging a principle which will react upon themselves with terrible consequences. For if law-makers and administrators can afford to trample upon justice, equity, and the Constitution of this country, they will find thou-sands and tens of thousands who are willing to follow in their wake in the demolition of the rights of man, and the destruction of all principles of justice, and the safeguards of the nation. But we will stand by and maintain its principles and the rights of all men of every color, and every clime. We will cleave to the truth, live our religion, and keep the commandments of God, and God will bless us in time and throughout the eternities that are to come.—*JD*, 26:38-39, December 14, 1884.

APPEAL FOR AN ENLIGHTENED PUBLIC OPINION.—We have no fault to find with our government. We deem it the best in the world. But we have reason to deplore its maladministra-tion, and I call upon our legislators, our governors and president to pause in their careers and not to tamper with the rights and liberties of American citizens, nor wantonly tear down the bul-warks of American and human liberty. God has given to us glorious institutions. Let us preserve them intact and not pander to the vices, passions, and fanaticism of a depraved public opinion. —*JD*, 23:65-66, April 9, 1882.

THE BLESSINGS OF AMERICANS.—When I was in Hamburg, there were 30,000 soldiers quartered in the city, and that is called a free city. If you ask any of the inhabitants what they are doing there, they will answer—*Ich weiss nicht*, (I don't know,) but we have to keep them. They are there because the emperor of Austria placed them there, and he had power to have them there.

In Paris, you would suppose you were in an armed city, for you could not step anywhere without meeting soldiers at every step.

When I was in Hamburg, I had to go and get a permit to authorize me to stay one month, and when that was done, I had to get another to authorize me to stay another month. The only thing we can do in that country at present is to baptize some of the citizens, and set them to preaching, as they have more rights and privileges than a stranger. No man has a right to receive his own son into his own house, if not a citizen, without a card, or a permit from the government; and that is a free city, so called. We cannot know anything about the blessings and privileges we have as Americans, without becoming acquainted with the condi-tion of other nations. This is one of the greatest countries in the world, but they (the Americans) do not appreciate their privileges.—*JD*, 1:27-28, August 22, 1852.

## AMERICA AND ITS DESTINY

THE AMERICAN DESTINY: ARE WE COMPETENT?—A great destiny lies before the United States. The question is, is she competent for the task? She has outridden the fiery test of revolution, hurled defiance at a despot's power, and grasped the sceptre of liberty with a nervous, powerful grip. She has, out of the chaotic, confused mass of material associated with corrupt governments, organized a system of government and framed a constitution that while it is honorable to its founders, guarantees to all, to the fullest extent, *"Liberte, Egalite, Fraternite."* . . . Liberty here is more than a name. Here man is free to speak, free to think, free to write, free to act, free to do good. The very genius of our Constitution and institutions is freedom. If there is a fault, it is the fault of party, sectional strife, or narrow bigotry; it is not in our institutions. . . .

WHO CAN TAKE THE HELM?—Such is America at present. What is her future? Her destiny is evidently onward; for although yet in her youth, she has grown to be a giant among the nations. Again we ask, who can take the helm of state? Whilst new political elements are rising, and our healthy institutions grow, spread, and increase; whilst wave after wave of population strikes our shore and penetrates our territories; whilst demagogues at home, or cabals and intrigants abroad, worry and fret us, who can say to the troubled elements, *"peace be still?"* With the improvements that are daily progressing, what are her capabilities for using them, for preserving and maintaining them? Is she competent for the task? Is she equal to the emergency? . . .

What might we not do with a firm, pure, stable, reliable government? Our national sins have been small in comparison with other nations. We are at the present time, comparatively, in our infancy. By pursuing a just and honorable course we should soon become the arbiter of nations and the wonder and admiration of the world. . . .

HEMISPHERE SOLIDARITY.—When our government shall be sufficiently strong, pure, and honorable, islands, states, and dynasties will seek shelter under its wings; the Canadas, the Central American States, Mexico, . . . Bolivia, Peru, Chili, Brazil, and all of South America will naturally follow. They will need no coercion. They will seek to be one with us.—*The Mormon,* October 6, 1855, Vol. 1, No. 33.

# CHAPTER XXX

# THE MORMON THEORY OF LEGITIMACY

## THE POLITICAL THEORY OF LEGITIMACY[1]

THE POLITICAL POSITION OF THE CHURCH.—Let us now notice our political position in the world. What are we going to do? We are going to possess the earth. Why? Because it belongs to Jesus Christ, and he belongs to us, and we to him. We are all one, and will take the kingdom and possess it under the whole heavens, and reign over it for ever and ever. Now, ye kings and emperors, help yourselves, if you can. This is the truth, and it may as well be told at this time as at any other.[2]—*JD*, 1:230, April 8, 1853.

We began with the power of God, with the government of heaven, and with acknowledging his hand in all things; and God has sustained us, blessed and upheld us to the present time; and it is the only government, rule, and dominion under the heavens that will acknowledge his authority.

Brethren, if any of you doubt it, go into some of those nations, and get yourselves introduced into the presence of their kings and rulers, and say, "Thus saith the Lord God." They would at once denounce you as a madman, and straightway order you into prison. What is the matter? They do not acknowledge the legitimacy, the rule, and government of God, nor will they inquire into them. They receive not their authority from him. Nations honor their kings, but they do not honor the authority of their God in any instance; neither have they from the first man-made government to the present time. If there has been such a nation, or if there is at this time such a government, it is a thing of which I am ignorant.—*JD*, 1:225, April 8, 1853.

THE NECESSITY AND REALITY OF THE PRINCIPLE OF LEGITIMACY.—To do right in our present state, then, we must carry out the principles of legitimacy according to a correct rule, and if we profess to be subjects of the kingdom of God, we must be subject to the dominion, rule, legitimacy, and authority of God. No person can escape from this unless he apostatizes and

---

[1]This idea, seemingly arrogant on its face (today as well as in 1853), must be associated with the Christian hope of a Millennium and the ideal of a free, pluralistic, world-society as developed elsewhere by John Taylor and included in this work.
[2]See above.

goes to the devil like a fool. He must be a fool who would barter away eternal life, thrones, principalities, and powers in the eternal world for the paltry trash which exists in the shape of wealth and worldly honor; to let go his chance of heaven and of God, of being a king and priest unto him, of living and reigning forever, and of standing among the chiefs of Israel. I cannot help calling such men fools, for they are damned now in making such a choice, and will be hereafter.—*JD*, 1:231, April 8, 1853.

THE LEGITIMACY OF THE GOVERNMENT OF GOD: AN INTERPRETATION OF HISTORY.—We will now come to the principle of *legitimacy.* . . . Paul, when speaking of Jesus Christ, gives us to understand that he is the firstborn of every creature, for by him were all things made that were made, and to him pertains all things; he is the head of all things, he created all things, whether visible or invisible, whether they be principalities, powers, thrones, or dominions. All things were created by him and for him, and without him was not anything made that was made. If all things were created by him and for him, this world on which we stand must have been created by him and for him. If so, he is its legitimate, its rightful owner and proprietor, its lawful sovereign and ruler. We will begin with him, then, in the first place, in treating on the subject of legitimacy.

But has he had the dominion over all nations, kindreds, peoples, and tongues? Have they bowed to his sceptre and acknowledged his sway? Have all people rendered obedience to his laws and submitted to his guidance? Echo answers, no! Has there ever been a kingdom, a government, a nation, a power, or a dominion in this world that has yielded obedience to him in all things? Can you point out one? . . .

What then has been the position of the world for generations past? They have been governed by rulers not appointed of God. If they were appointed by him it was merely as a scourge to the people for their wickedness, or for temporary rulers in the absence of those whose right it was to govern. They had not the legitimate rule, priesthood, and authority of God on the earth, to act as his representatives in regulating and presiding over the affairs of his kingdom. . . .

THE MEANING OF PRIESTHOOD.—The question, "What is priesthood?" has often been asked me. I answer, it is the rule and government of God, whether on earth, or in the heavens; and it is the only legitimate power, the only authority that is acknowledged by him to rule and regulate the affairs of his kingdom. When every wrong thing shall be put right, and all usurpers shall be put down, when he whose right it is to reign shall take the dominion, then nothing but the priesthood will bear rule; it alone will sway the sceptre of authority in heaven and on earth, for this is the legitimacy of God.

THE RULE OF FORCE.—In the absence of this, what has been the position of the nations? You who have made yourselves acquainted with the political structure and the political intrigues of earthly kingdoms, I ask, whence did they obtain their power? Did they get it from God? Go to the history of Europe, if you please, and examine how the rulers of those nations obtained their authority. Depending upon history for our information, we say those nations have been founded by the sword. If we trace the pages of history still further back to the first nation that existed, still we find that it was founded upon the same principles. Then follow the various revolutions and changes that took place among subsequent nations and power, from the Babylonians through the Medo-Persians, Grecians, Romans, and from that power to all the other powers of Europe, Asia, and Africa of which we have any knowledge. And if we look to America from the first discoveries by Columbus to the present time, where are now the original proprietors of the soil? Go to any power that has existed upon this earth, and you will find that earthly government, earthly rule and dominion, have been obtained by the sword. It was the sword of men that first put them in possession of this power. They have walked up to their thrones through rivers of blood, through the clotted gore and the groans of the dying, and through the tears and lamentations of bereaved widows and helpless orphans; and hence the common saying is, "Thrones won by blood, by blood must be maintained." By the same principle that they have been put in possession of territory, have they sought to sustain themselves—the same violence, the same fraud, and the same oppression have been made use of to sustain their illegitimacy.

FRAUD AND FORCE INCOMPATIBLE WITH LEGITIMACY.—Some of these powers, dominions, governments, and rulers had in their possession the laws of God, and the admonitions of Jesus Christ. And what have they done to his servants in different ages of the world, when he has sent them unto them? This question I need not stop to answer, for you are already too familiar with it. This, then, is the position of the world. Authority, dominion, rule, government has been obtained by fraud, and consequently is not legitimate. . . .

It is impossible that there can be any legitimate rule, government, power, or authority, under the face of the heavens, except that which is connected with the kingdom of God, which is established by new revelation from heaven.—*JD*, 1:223-225, **April 8, 1853.**

LEGITIMACY AND RIGHT.—I have, with my own eyes, seen holy prophets expire who were killed by the hands of a murderous gang of bloodthirsty assassins, because they bore the same testimony that the holy prophets did in the days of old.[1] How many more of their brethren who dared acknowledge the truth have fallen beneath the same influences—have been shot, whipped, imprisoned, and put to death in a variety of ways, while hundreds of others, driven from their homes in the winter, have found their last bed. They were worn out with suffering and fatigue; the weary wheels of life stood still; they were obliged to forsake the world, in which they could no longer remain because of the persecution heaped upon them by the enemies of the truth.

The reason of all this vile outrage upon innocent men, women, and children is because there is no legitimate rule upon the earth. God's laws and government are not known, and his servants are despised and cast out.

Legitimacy and right, whether in heaven or on earth, cannot mix with anything that is not true, just, and equitable; and truth is free from oppression and injustice, as is the bosom of Jehovah. Nothing but that will ultimately stand.—*JD*, 1:227-228, April 8, 1853.

## THE SOVEREIGNTY OF GOD

THE NEED FOR THE GOVERNMENT OF GOD.—Everything is disordered and in confusion in the world. The reason is because no legitimate authority has been known or acknowledged on the earth. Others have been trying to build up and establish what they supposed to be the kingdom of God. . . . A change of government changes not the condition of the people, for all are wrong and acting without God.

Our ideas are that the time has come to favor God's people; a time about which prophets spoke in pathetic strains, and poets sang. These men of God looked through the dark vista of future ages, and being wrapped in prophetic vision, beheld the· latter-day glory—the time of the dispensation of the fulness of times, spoken of by all the holy prophets since the world began. For they all looked forward with joyful anticipations to the things which have commenced with us. They all had their eyes upon the time when legitimacy would obtain its proper place upon the earth, in the shape of the kingdom of God established in the world, when all false rule and dominion would be put down, and the kingdoms of this world would become subject to God and his Christ. These

---

[1]John Taylor was in Carthage Jail, Illinois, June 27, 1844, when Joseph and Hyrum Smith were murdered. See Chapter 35.

are the ideas that they had, and these are the things we are seeking to carry out.—*JD*, 1:228-229, April 8, 1853.

THE BASES OF AUTHORITY IN THE KINGDOM OF GOD.— Who have we for our ruling power? Where and how did he obtain his authority? Or how did any in this church and kingdom obtain it? It was first obtained by a revelation from the Lord of the universe, by the opening of the heavens, by the voice of God, and by the ministering of holy angels. It is by the voice of God and the voice of the people that our present president[1] obtained his authority. . . . He obtains his authority first from God, and secondly from the people; and if a man possesses five grains of common sense, when he has a privilege of voting for or against a man, he will not vote for a man that oppresses the people. He will vote according to the dictates of his conscience for this is the right and duty of this people in the choice of their president and other leading officers of the kingdom of God. While this is being done here, it is being done in every part of the world, wherever the Church of Jesus Christ of Latter-day Saints has a footing. Is there a monarch, potentate, or power under the heavens that undergoes a scrutiny as fine as this? No, there is not; and yet this is done twice a year, before all the Saints in the world. Here are legitimacy and rule. You place the power in their hands to govern, dictate, regulate, and put in order the affairs of the kingdom of God. This is, *Vox Dei, vox populi*. God appoints, the people sustain. You do this by your own act. Very well then, it is legitimate, and must stand, and every man is bound to abide it if it takes the hair off his head. I know there are things sometimes that are hard, tough, and pinching. But if a man is a man of God, he has his eyes upon eternal things and is aiming to accomplish the purposes of God, and all will be well with him in the end.

What advantage is there, then, between this government and others? Why, we have peace, and as eternal beings we have a knowledge of eternal things. While listening to the remarks made on this stand, what have we not heard—what have we not known? The curtains of heaven have been withdrawn, and we have gazed as by vision upon eternal realities, while, in the professing world, doubt and uncertainty throw their dark mantle over every mind. —*JD*, 1:229-230, April 8, 1853.

## SUMMARY: "LEGITIMACY AND ILLEGITIMACY"

Nothing contrary to the authority, rule, and government of

---

[1]Brigham Young. Authority in the Church rests on common consent as well as calling and ordination.

heaven will stand in time or in eternity; and if any man wants to be blessed and honored, and to obtain a high place in the eternal world, let him pursue a course of honor, righteousness, and virtue before his God; and if he wants to find himself among usurpers, defrauders, oppressors, and those in possession of illegitimate claims, let him take an opposite course.—*JD*, 1:233, April 8, 1853.

THE PRINCIPLE OF "LEGITIMACY."—We hear a good deal about one-man power. I want to examine that power a little, and see how it exists, and how far it extends. We believe in two principles—one is the voice of God, the other is the voice of the people. . . . How does this priesthood stand in relation to the people? It is not thrust upon them as the queens of England, the kings of France, the emperor of Austria, or as the former king, but now emperor of Prussia, are. No, it is not thrust upon the people in any such way. It is precisely in the same way that the Israelites were organized in former times—God gave them certain laws, and the people said "Amen"; then the laws became binding upon Israel.

The position we occupy is this: the Holy Ghost, which has been given to all who have obeyed the gospel, and have lived faithful to its precepts, takes of the things of God and shows them forth through a living priesthood to a people enlightened and instructed by the spirit of revelation from God. And the people thus enlightened, instructed and blessed by the spirit of light, voluntarily and gladly sustain the priesthood who minister unto them. When Joseph Smith was upon the earth, he did not force himself upon the people as these kings and emperors do, but he presented himself before them every six months, at the annual or semi-annual conference, and the people had a chance to lift up their hands to receive or reject him. That was the position occupied by Joseph Smith, and those associated with him, in guiding the affairs of the church and kingdom of God upon the earth, and it is precisely so with President Young. He stands here as the representative of God to the people, as the president of the Church of Jesus Christ of Latter-day Saints. He is, or ought to be, full of light, life, revelation, and the power of God, and he is, and bears testimony to it. He ought to be able to lead the people in the paths of life, and he is. He is the choice of God, and what more? He is the choice of the people of God. Has he a right to say, "I am chosen, I am elected, I am president, and I will do as I please, and help yourselves?" No, he presents himself before you, and if there is any man who has aught against him, he has the privilege of holding up his hand to signify the same. That is the position of our president. He is brought to a test every six months, as it rolls around, before the assembled conference of the Church of Jesus Christ of Latter-day Saints. It is the same with the twelve, the president of the stake, the high council, the presidents of seventies, and with all the leading officers of the Church. They are all put to this test twice a year, and the people have the privilege of voting for or against them, just as they please.

Here then, on one hand, there is the voice of God. . . . What next? Then comes the freedom of man. On the one hand the guidance of God, on the other the freedom of man. We ask God to dictate us and he does. He has given us a president, apostles, prophets, bishops. He has organized his Church in the most perfect and harmonious manner.

DESPOTISM: ONLY IF THE PEOPLE WILL IT.—What next? God having given us a president inspired by his holy Spirit, we are required to vote for him—will we have him or will we reject him? We lift up our hands and say, "Yes, we will receive him." The world say this is despotism, being governed by one man. Is it despotism for every man and every woman to have a voice in the selection of those who rule over them? Is that despotism, tyranny, or oppression? If it is, I do not know what the terms mean. There are no people on the face of the earth today who have to undergo so severe a criticism as the president and priesthood of this Church before the people, and why is it that the people vote unanimously for them? "Well," say the world, "there is a kind of influence, we hardly know what, we wish it did not exist, for we do not like this one-man power." I know you do not, for it is one thousand men, ten thousand men power; it is the power of the kingdom of God on the earth, and the power of God united with it, that is what it is. As I have already said, it is not only the president of the Church who has to undergo this test, but the twelve, the seventies, and all the presiding officers of the Church have to go through the same ordeal.—*JD*, 15:215-218, October 7, 1872.

THE PEACE OF CHRIST.—Jesus Christ says, "my peace I give unto you: not as the world giveth, give I unto you." (John 14:27.) Wherever this peace exists, it leaves an influence that is comforting and refreshing to the souls of those who partake of it. It is like the morning dew to the thirsty plant. This peace is the gift of God alone, and it can be received only from him through obedience to his laws. If any man wishes to introduce peace into his family or among his friends, let him cultivate it in his own bosom; for sterling peace can only be had according to the legitimate rule and authority of heaven, and obedience to its laws.—*JD*, 1:228, April 8, 1853.

# Chapter XXXI

# FRAGMENTS ON POLITICAL AND SOCIAL PHILOSOPHY

## RELIGION AND POLITICS[1]

FREEDOM MUST BE PRESERVED.—There are peculiar notions extant in relation to the propriety or impropriety of mixing religion with politics, many of which we consider to be wild and visionary. Having witnessed in the proceedings of some of our old European nations a policy that was dangerous, hurtful, and oppressive in the union of church and state, and seen in them an overgrown oligarchy, proud and arrogant, with a disposition to crush everything that opposed its mandate, we have looked with abhorrence upon the monster, and shrink from the idea of introducing anything that would in the least deprive us of our freedom, or reduce us to a state of religious vassalage. Living under a free republican form of government, sheltered by the rich foliage of the tree of liberty, breathing a pure atmosphere of religious toleration, and basking in the sunbeams of prosperity, we have felt jealous of our rights, and have been always fearful lest some of those eastern blasts should cross the great Atlantic, wither our brightest hopes, nip the tree of liberty in the bud, and that our youthful republic should be prostrated and the funeral dirge be chanted in the "land of the free, and the home of the brave," in consequence of a union between church and state. . . .

FITNESS FOR POLITICAL LIFE A DETERMINANT OF RELIGION.—Certainly if any person ought to interfere in political matters, it should be those whose minds and judgments are influenced by correct principles—religious as well as political. Otherwise those persons professing religion would have to be governed by those who make no professions; be subject to their rule; have the law and word of God trampled under foot, and become as wicked as Sodom and as corrupt as Gomorrah, and be prepared for final destruction. We are told "when the wicked rule the people mourn." (D. &. C. 98:9.) This we have abundantly proved in the state of Missouri, and having had our fingers once burned, we dread the fire. The cause of humanity, the cause of justice, the cause of freedom, the cause of patriotism, and the cause of God requires us to use our endeavors to put in righteous rulers. Our

---

[1] An editorial in the *Times and Seasons*, March 15, 1844.

revelations tell us to *seek diligently* for good and for wise men. (D. & C. 85:2.)

Let every man then that hates oppression, and loves the cause of right, not only vote himself but use his influence to obtain the votes of others, that we may by every legal means support that man whose election will secure the greatest amount of good to the nation at large.—*TS,* 5:470-471, March 15, 1844.

## THE DIFFERENCE BETWEEN MORMON PRINCIPLES OF GOVERNMENT AND DEMOCRACY[1]

THE NEED FOR THE ALMIGHTY.—There is a little difference between our principles, or, I should say, the principles of the Church of Jesus Christ of Latter-day Saints, and what are called democratic principles. Democracy governs by the people alone; and . . . where the people are pure and living under the influence of correct principles, and are seeking to do right, it is one of the best governments on the earth. But where the people are wicked and corrupt, that alters the case very materially. . . .

There have been a variety of governments on the earth, and very powerful ones too have existed in different ages of the world. Those governments have generally been established and maintained by force of arms—by power. Thus many submit to the few, and the majority have had very little to say in the matter. We have generally been in the habit of supposing that our republican institutions are the most perfect of anything that can exist among men—the *ne plus ultra* of human government; and hence we have had a very favorite motto ready always upon our tongue's end—*Vox populi, vox Dei.* I do not believe that the voice of the people is the voice of God, but would ask, is it the northern or southern states that are governed by the Almighty? We have one of the best human governments upon the earth governed by the voice of the people, and yet we are divided, torn asunder, and confused, and appear to be on the eve of having two governments, and both republican in their form. But which of them is governed by God? . . . The proper mode of government is this—God first speaks, and then the people have their action. It is for them to say whether they will have his dictation or not. They are free; they are independent under God. The government of God is not a species of priestcraft . . . where one man dictates and everybody obeys without having a voice in it. We have our voice and agency, and act with the most perfect freedom. Still we believe

---

[1]President Taylor appears to accept Aristotle's usage of the term "democracy" (or rule by the *demos*) on its face, then interprets it for himself in drawing the distinctions made.

there is a correct order—some wisdom and knowledge somewhere that is superior to ours; that wisdom and knowledge proceeds from God through the medium of the holy priesthood. We believe that no man or set of men, of their own wisdom and by their own talents, are capable of governing the human family aright.—*JD*, 9:9, April 6, 1861.

A THEORY OF THE ORIGIN OF THE SECULAR STATE.—If we look at the very foundation of government, we may inquire, how were governments formed? Who organized them, and whence did they obtain their power? It is a subject for deep thought and reflection, and one that very few have understood; nor is it very easy to define, definitely, the rights of man politically, socially, and nationally.

Now, I will suppose there was no government in the world, but that we were thrown right back into the primitive state, and that we had to form a government to regulate ourselves; what would be the position? Why, the strong man would intrude upon the weak, even as a strong animal intrudes upon a weaker, taking from it its rights; for that is a natural animal propensity that exists in all the creatures, as well as in man.

How was society organized? Upon natural principles. I am not now speaking about God and his government, but upon the rights of man. If there were a few bullies in the land, and we had to organize the government anew, the people would combine to protect themselves against them—to protect themselves against those who had injured them, that would rob them of their labor, of their cattle, of their grain, or of anything they might have.

What would be the result of this course? It would be that a combination would exist that would organize to protect themselves, that the weak might be protected in his rights, that the feeble might not be trampled underfoot. This would be the natural construction and organization of society.

Very well; when society became large and extensive, and could not convene in a general assembly to represent themselves, they would send their representatives, who would combine to represent their interests by delegation, or proxy.

Who would those individuals represent? They would represent the parties of that neighborhood, of that state, of that country, or district of country that sent them, would they not? And what would you think of those men that were sent if they attempted to rule over those who sent them? Why, you would say; "Come back here, you rascals, and we will send others; we sent you to represent us, and now you are combining to put your feet upon our necks."

This has been the case ever since governments were organized; and hence have arisen governors, kings, and emperors. They have generally contrived to get the reins of power into their own hands; and, through the cunning of priestcraft and kingcraft, they have generally managed to bring the people under their feet and to trample upon their rights. Such has been the case in the nations of Europe and Asia. It is, in fact, the history of the world.—*JD,* 5:182-183, August 30, 1857.

THE METHOD OF GOVERNMENT.—What is it that will enable one man to govern his fellows aright? It is just as Joseph Smith said to a certain man who asked him, "How do you govern such a vast people as this?" "Oh," says Joseph, "it is very easy." "Why," says the man, "but we find it very difficult." "But," said Joseph, "it is very easy, for I teach the people correct principles, and they govern themselves." And if correct principles will do this in one family, they will in ten, in a hundred, and in ten hundred thousand. How easy it is to govern the people in this way! It is just like the streams from City Creek; they spread through the valleys and through every lot and piece of lot. So it is with the government of God; the streams of life flow from the Great Fountain through the various channels which the Almighty has opened up, and they spread not only throughout this city but throughout the world, wherever there are any Saints that have yielded obedience to the commandments of God. The fountain is inexhaustible, and the rivers of life flow from the fountain unto the people.—*JD,* 10:57-58, May 18, 1862.

THE PRINCIPLE OF FREEDOM.—There are two things I have always said I would do, and I mean to carry them out, living or dying. One is to vote for whom I please and the other to worship God as I please. There is a principle of freedom planted in the human mind that has always existed there, and no man nor any power has yet been able to obliterate it.—*JD,* 14:338, March 3, 1872.

And if we have presidents or apostles or anybody that we don't like, let us vote them out, and be free men, and cultivate and cherish in our bosoms the principles of liberty. But let us be careful that we do not grieve the Spirit of the Lord, and while we are looking at these things let us look at our own eternal interests and lean upon God for wisdom and instruction.—*JD,* 15:219, October 7, 1872.

EQUAL RIGHTS.—Pursue your own course, worship as you please, do as you please, follow your own inclinations in any other way, only do not interfere with the rights of men nor violate the laws of the land. That is all we ask, and you have full liberty to carry out any views and feelings you please. I remember reading a few lines of some very zealous Protestant who wrote over some public building: "In this place may enter Greek, Jew, or atheist, anything but a papist." Now I say let the papist come in too, the Moslem, the Greek, the Jew, the pagan—believer and unbeliever—the whole world.—*JD, 14:341, March 3, 1872.*

THE ECONOMIC MOTIVE.—The earth was made for our possession. The lands, water, mountains, valleys, the trees, the minerals, vegetation of all kinds, plants, shrubs, and flowers— all these things were made for the use of man, and it is for us to appropriate them to their proper use, to estimate them to their proper value, and as rational, intelligent, immortal beings, to comprehend the object of the creation of these things, as well as the object of our creation, and why and how, and under what circumstances we can enjoy them, and how long we can retain possession of them. In examining the human mind you will find many correct feelings and instincts planted there, if men would be governed by them. I do not know but it is this the Prophet Job has reference to when he says, "there is a spirit in man: and the inspiration of the Almighty giveth them understanding." (Job 32:8.) Another scripture says, "But the manifestation of the Spirit is given to every man to profit withal." (I Cor. 12:7.) But then, many men do not profit by it; and although they have this light or intuition within themselves, they are not governed by it. There is a party of religionists called Quakers, so strongly impregnated with this idea, that they think this inward monitor is sufficient to guide men in all their acts in life. . . .

Who is it that will possess the earth? Is it those ancient monarchs who fought, conquered, subdued, and slew their thousands, waded through seas of blood to gain empire? No, not at all. Is it the man, who, by fraud, deception, trickery, dishonesty, and chicanery, took advantage of those around him, and so amassed large wealth and possessions? Verily no. Who will, then? Let Jesus speak. Says he, "Blessed are the meek: for they shall inherit the earth." (Matthew 5:5.) They are the ones who will rejoice before God in the possession of the blessings of earth, and not the kings and other characters to whom I have referred.— *JD, 15:267-270, January 5, 1873.*

## A COMPARATIVE APPROACH:
## MORMONISM AND THE UTOPIAN SOCIALISTS[1]

It is rather a strange anomaly, particularly in the estimation of the world, that a people so numerous as the Latter-day Saints should be gathered together in one place, having the one faith, and believing in the same doctrines. It is the more strange because there have been various social and political movements, aided by philosophy, established among men in various ages of the world; and almost, if not all of these, have signally failed.

ROBERT D. OWEN.—Among the number of social movements in our day, there is that of Robert Dale Owen, who thought he could ameliorate the condition of mankind by a sort of communism, having a fellowship of goods among them—a sort of common stock principle. Everything pertaining to this speculation, however, has flattened out; and in all his schemes and movements, whether in England or in this country, they have signally failed.

CHARLES FOURIER.—It is so also with Fourierism—a species of French philosophy, established by one Fourier, a Frenchman, and advocated by Greeley of the New York *Tribune*. They had tried it in France, and then came over to this country; and not far from New York a society of this kind was established. They had a good deal of property, and I am informed they established something of the nature of what is called the free love principle. But within twelve months back, while I was residing in New York, everything they had was sold under the hammer.

ETTIENE CABET.—Mr. Cabet commenced lecturing in France, and had very extensive societies there. About the time we left Nauvoo to come to this land, Mr. Cabet, with a company of his men (the Icarians) came there. This is a species of communism. They are called "communists," believing, with Mr. Owen, in a community of goods.[2] They published a newspaper in Nauvoo, and one or more in France. I baptized one of their editors while in Paris on my mission—a man who is now in this valley, by the name of Bertrand.

A CONVERSATION WITH AN ICARIAN.—Mr. Krolokoski, who

---

[1]Many have compared Mormon political theory with the movement called Utopian Socialism, often identifying both as parts of a whole upsurge in recent thought. President Taylor distinguishes them, *q. v.*

[2]The reader should note that the word, "communism," underwent much popular change after the Marxist manifesto of 1848, and more especially since the Russian Revolution of 1917.

was also an editor of the same paper with Mr. Bertrand, came to me to have a conversation about the first principles of the gospel. After a long conversation, he said, "Mr. Taylor, do you propose no other plan to ameliorate the condition of mankind than that of baptism for the remission of sins?"

I replied—"This is all I propose about the matter."

"Well," he said, "I wish you every success; but I am afraid you will not succeed."

Said I, "Mr. Krolokoski, you sent, some time ago, Mr. Cabet to Nauvoo. He was considered your leader—the most talented man you had. He went to Nauvoo when it was deserted —when houses and lands were at a mere nominal value. He went there with his community at the time we left. Rich farms were deserted, and thousands of us had left our houses and furniture in them, and there was everything that was calculated to promote the happiness of human beings there. Never could a person go to a place under more happy circumstances. Mr. Cabet, to try his experiment, had also the selection in France of whom he pleased. He and his company went to Nauvoo, and what is the result? You have seen the published account in the papers. We were banished from civilized society into the valleys of the Rocky Mountains to seek for that protection among savages which Christian civilization denied us—among the *peau rouges,* or red skins, as they call them. There our people have built houses, enclosed lands, cultivated gardens, built schoolhouses, opened farms, and have organized a government, and are prospering in all the blessings and immunities of civilized life. Not only this, but they have sent thousands and thousands of dollars over to Europe to assist the suffering poor to go to America, where they might find an asylum. You, on the other hand, that went to our empty houses and farms—you, I say, went there under most favorable circumstances. Now, what is the result? I read in all of your reports from there, published in your own paper in Paris, a continued cry for help. The cry is to you for money, money: 'We want money to help us to carry out our designs.' The society that I represent comes with the fear of God—the worship of the great Elohim. They offer the simple plan ordained of God—viz., repentance, baptism for the remission of sins, and the laying on of hands for the gift of the Holy Ghost. Our people have not been seeking the influence of the world, nor the power of government, but they have obtained both; whilst you, with your philosophy independent of God, have been seeking to build up a system of communism and a government which is, according to your own accounts, the way to introduce the millennial reign. Now, which is the best—our religion, or your philosophy?"

"Well," said he, "I cannot say anything."

He could not, because these were facts that he was familiar with. What has become of that society? There are very few of them left.[1] They have had dissensions, bickerings, trouble, and desertions, until they are nearly dwindled to nothing. I might enumerate many societies of a similar nature, commenced in different parts of the world and at various times. The results, however, would be proved to be the same: they commenced in the wisdom of man, and ended as speculative bubbles. Truth, based on eternal principles, alone can stand the test.

If Owen, Fourier, Cabet, and other philosophers have failed, —if all the varied schemes of communism have failed—if human philosophy is found to be at fault, and all its plans incompetent, and we have not failed, it shows there is something associated with this people and with Mormonism that there is not with them.—*JD*, 5:237-238, September 13, 1857.

## SOME SOCIAL ETHICS

A PLEA FOR LIBERTY.—We cannot afford to follow after the ways of the gentiles, nor to copy after their illiberality. We want the principles of liberty to extend and to expand so that all men can worship God as they please, without any one to interrupt them.—*JD*, 26:113, October 20, 1881.

MORALS AND ETHICAL STANDARDS.—We talk sometimes about the world, we Latter-day Saints, and we are very flippant in referring to their follies and foibles. We have enough follies of our own; and I often very much question whether they do not live as near to their religion as we do to ours. "How is that," says one. "We are a much more moral people than they are." We ought to be. We make greater professions than they do. They do not talk about having revelation. They do not talk about having any special mission to the nations of the earth, and we do. They do not talk about any celestial glory, and know nothing about it. We profess to know a little about it. They do not aim at a celestial glory, for they do not know what it is; and we understand a very little about it.

THE MORMON STANDARD.—One thing we do know; one thing is clearly told us, and that is if we are not governed by the celestial law and cannot abide a celestial law, we cannot inherit a celestial kingdom. What is it to obey a celestial law? Where

---

[1]The last Icarian community expired in Iowa in 1895. See C. C. Maxey, *Political Philosophies*, (N. Y., MacMillan Co., 1938) p. 528. See his Chapter 28 for an account of the Utopian Socialists.

does the celestial law come from to begin with? From the heavens. Very well. What have the people here to do with it generally— that is, outsiders? Nothing. They do not say they have had any revelation. They have had no principle of that kind unfolded to them. They are living under what might be termed a terrestrial law; and many of them, I think, under the circumstances, do quite as well as we do under our circumstances. We profess to be moving on a more elevated plane than they are. We profess to have come out from the world; to have separated from the ungodly. We profess to be under the guidance of apostles and prophets, pastors and teachers, etc., and to be living under the inspiration of the Most High. They do not profess anything of the kind.

TOLERANCE.—These are some of the things we profess to believe in, and some of the things that the world do not believe in. We have, however, enough to do in attending to the duties of our priesthood and calling without troubling ourselves with the follies and foibles of those who are not of us. As I have already said they do not profess what we do. We profess to be governed by high principles and nobler motives, and by more exalted ideas. Let us try and live up to our profession.—*JD*, 26: 324-325, July 20, 1884.

LIBERTY: THE SOCIAL IDEAL.—I say unto you, continue to cherish those principles [of liberty]. Let them expand. And if the tree of liberty has been blasted in this nation—if it has been gnawed by worms, and already blight has overspread it, we will stand up in defense of our liberties, and proclaim ourselves free in time and in eternity.—*DHC*, 6:296, Nauvoo, April Conference, 1844.

THE MORMON DOCTRINE OF GROUP RIGHTS OR POLITICAL —RELIGIOUS PLURALISM.[1]—I want to talk about a principle here. We get up sometimes a very rash feeling against people who do not think as we do. They have a right to think as they please; and so have we. Therefore, if a man does not believe as I do, that is none of my business. And if I do not believe as he does, that is none of his business. Would you protect a man that did not believe as you do? Yes, to the last bat's end. He should

---

[1]Political philosophers could call this a doctrine of "pluarlism," hence the heading above. Pluralism is the peculiar development and inheritance of the American political tradition. President Taylor expressed and developed this theory, throughout his entire life. He deserves a permanent place among American political theorists. The entire defense of the Mormon position resolves itself into the advocacy of a liberal doctrine of pluralism. Otherwise it becomes a stilted separatism.

have equal justice with me; and then I would expect to be protected in my rights. We have in Salt Lake City, Methodists, Presbyterians, Baptists, Roman Catholics, and all kinds. Do we interfere with them? No, not at all. . . . I would not wish to interfere with their political rights, nor have them interfere with mine. I think that is correct doctrine. It is good democracy and good republicanism which we can all subscribe to.—*JD*, 26:111, October 20, 1881.

THE RIGHT TO PROSELYTE.[1]—But what have we to do with the people of the world? We complain sometimes that they do not treat us exactly right. Well, they do not in all respects, and I do not think this is very difficult to understand. But there is nothing new about that; God has revealed unto us his law, and they do not comprehend it, neither do they want to; nor did the antediluvians. They were very wicked, very corrupt, and very depraved, very immoral, and very dishonest. But that was a matter between them and the Lord, and he dealt with them. And it is his business to deal with the nations of the earth at the present time and not ours, further than we are directed by him. What is the mission that we have to perform to this nation? It is to preach the gospel.—*JD*, 23:260, October 8, 1882.

I repeat, our mission is to preach the gospel, and then to gather the people who embrace it. And why? That there might be a nucleus formed, a people gathered who would be under the inspiration of the Almighty, and who would be willing to listen to the voice of God, a people who would receive and obey his word when it was made known to them. And this people in their gathered condition are called Zion, or the pure in heart.—*JD*, 23:260-262, October 8, 1882.

WHO ARE THE WORLD?—Who are the world, as we sometimes denominate those that are not of our Church? The children of our Heavenly Father, for God, we are told, "has made of one blood all nations of men for to dwell on all the face of the earth, and hath determined the times before appointed, and the bounds of their habitation;

"That they should seek the Lord, if haply they might feel after him, and find him, though he be not far from every one of us." (Acts 17:26, 27.)—*JD*, 23:369-370, February 11, 1883.

---

[1]In the development of American pluralism, the freedom for groups to organize developed first, its history commencing roughly with Roger Williams' exile from Massachusetts. The continuing process was to see the slow recognition accorded organized groups, to proselyte their views freely and attract membership. Like the former, this right, as witnessed by the experience of Mormons, Quakers, Catholics, Jehovah's Witnesses, women, labor, negroes—is still in process of development.

"A MAN'S HOUSE IS HIS CASTLE."—"But do you not allow liberty of conscience?" Yes. You can worship what you please—a donkey or a red dog—but you must not bring that worship into my house. I do not believe in your gods; I believe in the God of Israel, in the Holy Ghost, in the spirit of truth and intelligence, and all good principles and if you want to worship your gods, worship them somewhere else. And if anybody else wants to worship them, he can do so. You can go on to one of those mountains and worship your gods, or if you are living in a house here, you can be a worshipper of Buddha if you please; but I do not want it in my house, and I do not want the spirit that you have—the spirit of those gods, visible or invisible. I do not want their teachings, spirit, nor influences. . . . I want to know who dances with my . . . daughters, and whether they have a reputation or not, and if they have reputation, what kind of people they are. This I have a right to do in a social capacity, independent of all religion, and I mean to do it.

SOME PRACTICAL ETHICS.—I will now turn the tables another way round. Did you ever see any of the elders of this church out abroad among the nations try to crowd themselves upon any people, and seek to go into their balls and assemblies, or families, contrary to rule and to the principles laid down? No, never. Did you ever hear of them wanting to take their daughters to balls and parties, etc. No, never. We claim the same kind of treatment. . . .—JD, 11:58-59, January 18, 1865.

RELIGION AND INDIVIDUAL TESTIMONY.—If it was not for the religion I profess, which gives me to know something about the matter, by revelation, for myself, I would not have anything to do with religion at all. I would worship God the best way I knew how, and act justly and honorably with my neighbor; which I believe thousands of that class of men called infidels do at the present day. But I never would submit to be gulled with the nonsense that exists in the world, under the name of religion.—JD, 1:150, 151, June 12, 1853.

CHAPTER XXXII

# FAITH, TRIALS, AND PERSECUTION

## THE POWER OF FAITH

THE HOPE BUOYANT.—Good men have had to endure affliction, privations, trials, and sorrow, it is true. Abraham had to pass through afflictions that were harrowing to his feelings. Men of God have had to wander about in sheep skins and goat-skins, and been considered the scum and offscourings of society by men who understood not their relationship to God. They appeared destitute, but were, in reality, not. They had a hope that was buoyant, and looked for a city that had foundations, whose builder and maker is God. Events of a similar kind have transpired among us.—*JD*, 8:97, June 17, 1860.

IF MEN WOULD BE VALIANT.—Don't you know how men will twist and pick and cringe to get hold of a dollar or two? If men would be as valiant in trying to pray to God to give them wisdom and power to control themselves and their thoughts and passions, then in all their business transactions, they would feel that they know themselves to be accepted of the Almighty. They would feel and know that they had ears to hear and hearts to understand and comprehend the mind and will of God. They would then feel ten thousand times more interest in the kingdom and to work for the spread of true and holy principles, and in all things pertaining to the great work in which they are engaged, than in those little temporal matters.—*JD*, 10:55, May 18, 1862.

FAITH, THE GIFT AND FIRST PRINCIPLE OF GOD.—We are informed in scripture that faith is the gift of God, and we have endeavored to show . . . that all and every species of the animal creation share in this inestimable gift or blessing. Well, says one, we have always been taught by our fathers and ministers to have faith, and we should be saved; but according to your reasoning, not only mankind, whether good or bad, but all the animal creation, will be saved.

Yes, this would be true, if faith alone was required, and that, too, unqualified. But if we examine the scriptures with reference to this, we will find that neither is the case. If we examine the plan of salvation, taught by Jesus and his apostles, as recorded in the New Testament, we shall find that faith is the first principle in that plan instituted by the Almighty for all who should come up to its requirements. And if we examine still further, we find that faith essentially qualified. Instead of faith to accomplish any of those objects we have named, unqualifiedly, we are pointed directly to Jesus Christ as the only object through which our faith will avail us in the least towards being saved in the celestial kingdom of God. . . . Here, then, is the line of distinction drawn between those who have faith in the Lord Jesus Christ, on the one hand, and the unbelieving among mankind, and the inferior brute creation which are not capable of receiving the gospel, on the other. This faith, then, is a different kind, if you please, a qualified faith, while the other is unqualified. Of the latter there is an abundance, and of the former there is very little lack, if we judge by the professions of men, but judging by their fruits, which is the scripture rule, there is much room for improvement.

HOW FAITH COMES.—The Savior told his apostles on one occasion, when they had not faith sufficient to cast out devils, that that kind by which he accomplished it came only by fasting and prayer. How does the faith required as the first principle in the plan of salvation or gospel come? Let Paul answer: "So then faith cometh by hearing, and hearing by the word of God." (Romans 10:17.) It is not the letter then that bringeth faith, but hearing the word of God dispensed by a living oracle or minister of God, clothed upon with power from on high. It is not a recorded gospel, but the preached word which emanates with power from a man of God inspired by the Holy Ghost. . . .

Faith without works being dead, it is evident that living faith and that which is acceptable to God, is that which not only believes in God, but acts upon that belief. It is not only the cause of action, but includes both cause and action. Or in other words it is belief or faith made perfect by works. . . .—*The Mormon*, New York, August 25, 1855, Vol. 1, No. 27.

## TRIALS AND PERSECUTIONS

BETTER TO SUFFER WRONG THAN TO DO WRONG.—Remember that it is a great deal better to suffer wrong than to do wrong. We have enlisted in this kingdom for the purpose of working righteousness, growing up in righteousness and in purity that we might have a heaven in our families, in our city and neighborhoods, a Zion right in our midst, live in it ourselves, and persuade everybody else to abide its holy laws.—*JD*, 10:56, May 18, 1862.

A PHILOSOPHY FOR TRIALS.—So far as I am concerned, I say, let everything come as God has ordained it. I do not desire trials. I do not desire affliction. I would pray to God to "lead me not in temptation, and deliver me from evil; for thine is the kingdom, the power, and the glory." But if the earthquake bellows, the lightnings flash, the thunders roll, and the powers of darkness are let loose, and the spirit of evil is permitted to rage, and an evil influence is brought to bear on the Saints, and my life with theirs is put to the test, let it come, for we are the Saints of the most High God, and all is well, all is peace, all is right, and will be, both in time and in eternity.

But I do not want trials. I do not want to put a straw in anybody's way; and, if I know my own feelings, I do not want to hurt any man under the heavens, nor injure the hair of any person's head. I would like to do every man good. These are the feelings, the spirit which the gospel has implanted in my bosom, and that the Spirit of God implants in the bosoms of my brethren. And if men will pursue an improper course, the evil of course, must be on their own heads.

I used to think, if I were the Lord, I would not suffer people to be tried as they are. But I have changed my mind on that subject. Now I think I would, if I were the Lord, because it purges out the meanness and corruption that stick around the Saints, like flies around molasses.—*JD*, 5:114-115, August 9, 1857.

THE SPIRIT OF JOB.—I remember hearing a woman say in Missouri, "I'll be damned if I will stand it any longer; for this is the fifth house the mob have burned down for me in less than two years." Job did not feel so. He was indeed severely tried, but when he came down to sober reflection, he said in his heart: the Sabeans may take my asses, and the Chaldeans may fall upon my servants and kill them and steal my sheep, and my house be thrown down with the storm, and I may lie in the ashes, and men that I would not associate with the dogs of my flocks may wear away my life, and my body may go to dust; yet, though worms prey upon it, in my flesh shall I see God. Naked I came into the world, and naked I shall go out: blessed be the name of the Lord.

Was not this a good feeling to manifest? Let us try to imitate it and acknowledge the chastening rod of the Almighty. —*JD*, 7:198, November 13, 1859.

I have seen men tempted so sorely that finally they would say, "I'll be damned if I'll stand it any longer." Well, you will be damned if you do not. So you had better bear it and go to the Lord and say, O God, I am sorely tempted; Satan is trying to destroy me, and things seem to be combined against me. O Lord, help me! Deliver me from the power and grasp of the devil. Let thy Spirit descend upon me that I may be enabled to surmount this temptation and to ride above the vanities of this world. This would be far better than giving way to sin, and proving yourself unworthy of the association of the good and pure.—*JD*, 22:318, October 19, 1881.

PURPOSE OF ORDEAL.—There are many of our good Latter-day Saints who are grasping and covetous and who take advantage of one another, and who frequently act dishonorably and who say things that are improper and wrong, and that are contrary to the principles of justice and equity; and sometimes it is necessary that men should be shaken up a little. God in his wisdom has handled us from time to time. I can see men around me tonight whom I have seen and known for forty years—do you remember, brethren, when we had to leave the state of Missouri, "all hands and the cook?" And did we cry about it? I think not. I felt as happy then as I do now, and I feel quite comfortable tonight. . . .

We have learned many things through suffering. We call it suffering. I call it a school of experience. I never did bother my head much about these things. I do not today. What are these things for? Why is it that good men should be tried? Why is it, in fact, that we should have a devil? Why did not the Lord kill him long ago? Because he could not do without him. He needed the devil and a great many of those who do his bidding just to keep men straight, that we may learn to place our dependence upon God, and trust in him, and to observe his laws, and keep his commandments. When he destroyed the inhabitants of the antediluvian world, he suffered a descendant of Cain to come through the flood in order that he might be properly represented upon the earth. And Satan keeps busy all the time, and he will until he is bound; and I expect they will then have good times until he is loose again. The time will be when he will be cast into the bottomless pit, and he will not be able to deceive the nations any more until the thousand years have expired. I have never looked at these things in any other light than trials for the purpose of purifying the Saints of God, that they may be, as the scriptures say, as gold that has been seven times purified by the fire.—*JD*, 23:336, October 29, 1882.

APOSTASY.—We have met on the road a great many apostates. I do not want to say much about them. If they can be happy, all right. But they do not exhibit it. When a man deserts from the gospel, from the ordinances, from the priesthood and its authority, from the revelations of the Spirit of God, from the spirit of prophecy, from that sweet, calm influence that broods over the upright man in all his acts, he loses the blessing of God and falls back into error; and, as the scripture says, the last state of that man is worse than the first. (Compare Matthew 12:45.)

It has become proverbial, where apostate Mormons live, to say, "Oh, he is only an apostate Mormon." They look upon them as ten times meaner than a Mormon.

I happened to go into a barber's shop, one day, to get shaved. A man came in, and when he went out again the inquiry was made, "Who is that man?" "Oh, he is only an apostate Mormon." Their mouths are full of cursing; and you will find them chewing tobacco and getting drunk, thinking that, by so doing, they will recommend themselves to the people. But they have not learned the art very well. They can't swear and degrade themselves so naturally as others, and the people find them out and repudiate them. . . . Where is their hope of salvation?—*JD, 5:115, August 9, 1857.*

GOD WILL HAVE A CONTROVERSY WITH THE NATIONS.— We complain sometimes about our trials. We need not do that. These are things that are necessary for our perfection. We think sometimes that we are not rightly treated, and I think we think correctly about some of these things. We think there are plots set on foot to entrap us; and I think we think so very correctly. At the same time we need not be astonished at these things. We need not be amazed at a feeling of hatred and animosity. Why? Because we are living in a peculiar day and age of the world, which is distinctively called the latter days, wherein it is said that God will have a controversy with the nations of the earth.—*JD, 25:344, October 19, 1884.*

"LET THE CONSEQUENCE FOLLOW."—If you have got a religion that is different from that of other people, won't they persecute you? Yes, but what of that? We dare to have a religion of our own. Years ago we dared to have faith for ourselves, and to come forth amongst the contumely of the world and to say we were Saints, and that we had taken upon us the name of Jesus Christ, and were resolved to fulfil the obligations which the Church of Christ had imposed upon us. This we felt years and years ago. Did we experience it? Certainly. Men would persecute us, laugh at us, and deprive us of our happiness if they could. A great many influences were brought to bear against us. Well, now, is it consistent that all the churches that are spoken of in the Book of Mormon as well as in the Bible, that have been and still are being built up to get gain, and for the purpose of keeping hordes of men living upon the people in comparative idleness—I ask is it reasonable that all these systems and organizations of men will give up without a struggle? I tell you, nay. If such be the position of the religious world, I would further ask, is it reasonable that the political powers of the earth will give up without a struggle? It would be at variance with history, with scripture and prophecy, and human nature, and contrary to anything we ever heard of. The question may be asked, then, what shall we do; yield to the prejudices and diction of men or to the laws of God? The poet says:—"Do what is right, let the consequence follow." This is the duty of the Latter-day Saints in their attempts and endeavors to build up Zion, and not to ask any questions as to what men may think of us or our acts, that we, as a people, this nation and the world, are in the hands of God.—*JD*, 9:340-341, April 13, 1862.

# Chapter XXXIII

# SOME PRACTICAL ADVICE

## SOME ETHICS OF "THE KINGDOM"

"THE MYSTERIES."—I have never said much about the beasts, etc., in my preaching. When I have done it, it has been to attract attention and keep the people from running after a greater fool than myself.—*DHC*, 5:345, April 8, 1843.

"THE ELEVENTH COMMANDMENT."—There are more people attending to the eleventh commandment in the city of Nauvoo than in any other place of the same size on the globe—that is *they mind their own business in Nauvoo*, without interfering with others.—*Nauvoo Neighbor*, April 7, 1845.

FREE AGENCY.—Would you allow everybody to worship as he pleases? Certainly. What? If you knew he was in error? Certainly. I would not wish to control the human mind. I would not control the actions of men. God does not do it, he leaves them to their own agency to combat with the trials, temptations, adversities, and evils of every kind that are in the world, to which humanity is, or can be incident. He puts within their reach, however, certain principles and would like to lead them to himself if they would be led. If not, he then does the very best with them that he can.—*JD*, 21:16, February 8, 1880.

SUPREMACY OF GOD'S LAWS.—We have been brought up in the world, and have imbibed many ideas in common with mankind generally pertaining to commerce, trade, and manufactures. But we need the inspiration of the Almighty in all of the affairs of life, for we profess emphatically to be the people of God, and as it is with us in our religion so it·ought to be with our politics, our trade, and manufactures. They ought, in all things, to be subservient to one grand principle, and that is the acknowledgment of God and his laws.—*JD*, 21:30, April 9, 1879.

DEPENDENCE ON THE LORD.—I desire your faith and prayers, for we are all dependent upon the Lord; none of us can do or say anything that is good or useful or beneficial to society unless we are under the aid, guidance, and control of the Lord. A man cannot speak aright unless he speaks under the inspiration of the Almighty; and then the people cannot hear aright, nor

understand aright unless they have a portion of the same Spirit.—
*JD*, 21:91-92, April 13, 1879.

THE USES OF CRITICISM.—Suppose there are some who do
not do exactly right in some places, what of that? There are
many things that are not right. Never mind. Everything that is
wrong will in due time be righted. Permit me to bring a figure
before you. A year ago last winter there was a very severe frost,
and it injured the fruit trees. Some who professed to be judges
thought it best to cut down the peach trees. Some thought that
if left alone they would still grow, and therefore they left them
alone to see how many would live. There was quite a difference
of opinion upon the subject, and some adopted one plan, and
some another. The general impression was, I believe, that it
would be best to cut off those limbs that were frost-bitten and
that did not appear to have much sap in them.

Now, my doctrine is, prune the trees, or, in other words, the
branches of the great tree to which we are connected, just at the
time when it will do the least injury. It requires great wisdom,
however, to prune and regulate the Church of Christ. There were
a great many of our people got frost-bitten—a kind of dead in
their spirits, and some were for going right to work and pruning.
But hold on. Said Jesus, the wheat and tares must grow together
until harvest. Perhaps you would pull up the wheat with the
tares, if you were to do it when you think best. If there is nothing
good in a man, he will by and by develop the evil that is in him,
and then everybody will agree that the pruning ought to be done,
and the branch ought to be cut off. But if the good preponderates,
it would be wrong, because of prejudice or ignorance, to destroy
the good. It is best to leave it to the husbandman, and then all
the congregation will say Amen.—*JD*, 9:13-14, April 6, 1861.

FELLOWSHIP AND FORGIVENESS.—Talking about people
giving away to passion and giving expression to hard words. Such
things do not belong to the gospel, to no part of it. They come
from beneath. This has been pointed out and made very plain
to us. Every spirit, says one, that tends to good is of God; and
every spirit that tends to evil is of the wicked one and comes
from beneath. I hear a man say sometimes, "I hate such a man."
Why, I do not know of a person that I hate in the world. The
command is to love one another. When Jesus was about to leave
his disciples, the burden of his prayer was, "Father, I pray for
these whom thou hast given me; thine they were, and thou gavest
them me. I pray for them, Father, that they may be one, even
as I and thou art one, that they may be one in us." (Compare
John 17:20-23.) What, a sister or brother, a citizen of the kingdom of God, a member of the Church of Jesus Christ of Latter-

day Saints, one who has received peradventure of the ordinances of the house of God, and who expects to associate with the Saints of God, quarrels with his brother about peanuts and baby toys and then talk about your honor being infringed upon! I tell you if you take care of yourselves, your honor will take care of itself and you need not be concerned about it.

Treat one another aright. Have you sinned one against another? Then go and make restitution. Have you defrauded one another? Go and make it right. Have you spoken unkindly to your brother or sister? Then go and acknowledge your wrong and ask to be forgiven, promising to do better in the future. And then he or she might say, on the other hand, "Yes, and I said so and so the other day, won't you please forgive me?" How much better and how much more in keeping with the calling of a saint of God such a course would be than to harbor hard feelings in the heart.—*JD*, 21:98-99, April 13, 1879.

SOME ADVICE IN 1871.—I will tell you what we have to do as Latter-day Saints—live our religion, keep the commandments of God, and be virtuous. . . . Remember your prayers, be true and faithful to each other and to your covenants, keep the commandments of the Almighty, and the blessings of Israel's God will rest upon you, and no power this side of hell or the other side either shall harm you.—*JD*, 14:269, December 17, 1871.

A LESSON IN TOLERANCE.—We talk sometimes about Babylon—"Come out of her, my people, that ye be not partakers of her sins, and that ye receive not of her plagues." (Revelation 18:4.) We need not say too much about those people, for we came out from them ourselves and it would not be becoming on our part to speak badly about our former status.—*JD*, 23:262, October 8, 1882.

SABBATH OBSERVANCE.—I call upon you, ye Latter-day Saints, to repent of your iniquities, and keep the Sabbath day holy, set it aside as a day of rest, a day of meeting together to perform your sacraments and listen to the words of life, and thus be found keeping the commandments, and setting a good example before your children.—*JD*, 20:23-24, July 7, 1878.

AMUSEMENTS.—We have given the religious world a lesson upon this point. We have shown that social enjoyment and amusements are not incompatible with correct conduct and true religion. Instead of forbidding the theatre and placing it under ban, it has been the aim of the Latter-day Saints to control it and keep it free from impure influences, and to preserve it as a place where all could meet for the purpose of healthful enjoyment.— *Epistle of the First Presidency*, April 8, 1887.

CIGARETS.—There is a tendency, almost amounting to an epidemic in some places, among the young people to indulge in cigaret smoking. The habit is filthy, and pernicious generally. God has spoken so plainly on this subject that there is no room to question the impropriety of this practice. The teachers should make it their especial business in all kindness and in a mild instructive spirit to reason and remonstrate with young people upon this habit. Every effort should be made to check its growth among us.—*Epistle of the First Presidency, April 8, 1887.*

## WHAT SHOULD MEN SEEK?

SEEK YE FIRST THE KINGDOM OF GOD.—I think it foolishness in men to seek after the things of this world and place their affections on them. I see men, and I have seen a great many men in my time, grasping after the world, and they sometimes will succeed in gathering considerable together; and when they have gathered it, they would fold their arms and say, Soul, take thine ease; eat, drink and be merry, for I have much good laid up in store; I am not dependent on any man, soul, take thine ease. That man hears a little whisper; the finger of God is laid upon him, and this whisper says, Thou fool, this night shall thy soul be required of thee; and then, whose shall these things be that thou possessest? Who shall have them then? O, I will leave them to my children! But somebody may cheat them out of it.

It is a very difficult thing for people to leave things for their children, and have things done just as they wish, there being so many people to interrupt and grasp after this world's goods, righteously or unrighteously. What a fool to gather large posses-sions, and now only to occupy a few feet of mother earth. . . . While it is proper for us to seek after everything that is right and honorable, on the other hand it is quite as right and very proper that we should set God before us all the time and render obedience to his law, so that we may acquire an eternal inheritance in the kingdom of God. God is now establishing his kingdom upon the earth. If it is the kingdom of God, and he is establishing it, he expects us to be subject to his law, and to be governed by it, and to keep his commandments.—*JD, 5:112, August 9, 1857.*

PEACE.—Peace is the gift of God. Do you want peace? Go to God. Do you want peace in your families? . . . If you do, live your religion, and the very peace of God will dwell and abide with you, for that is where peace comes from and it doesn't dwell anywhere else. We had peace societies in the world, it is true, for many years, but what have they done? Simply nothing. But peace is good, and I say seek for it, cherish it in your bosoms, in your neighborhoods, and wherever you go among your friends and associates, for they are good principles and dwell in the bosom of God, and if we only get that peace that dwells in the bosom of God all will be right.—*JD*, 10:56, May 18, 1862.

Union, virtue, and perseverance, will prepare the way for the millennium.—*TS*, 6:840, March 15, 1845.

PROMOTE HAPPINESS.—Then, lay aside your covetousness. That is idolatry. And while laboring to be industrious, do not covet any man's house, nor his farm, nor anything that is his; nor defraud one another, nor bite nor devour one another. But love one another, and work the works of righteousness, and look after the welfare of all, and seek to promote the happiness of all. That is what God is doing. That is why he has told us to go to the nations of the earth—and many of us have been hundreds and thousands of miles without purse or scrip.—*JD*, 26:113, October 20, 1881.

DESTINY AND WILL.—Are we not the framers of our own destiny? Are we not the arbitrators of our fate? This is another part of my text, and I argue from it that it is our privilege to determine our own exaltation or degradation. It is our privilege to determine our own happiness or misery in the world to come. What is it that brings happiness now—that makes us so joyous in our assembling together? It is not wealth; for you may pour wealth, honor, influence, and all the luxuries of this world into the lap of man; and, destitute of the Spirit of God, he will not be happy, for that is the only source from which true happiness and comfort can come.

If I am doing right, I am preparing for thrones, principalities, and dominions, resolved by the help of God that no man shall rob me of my crown. With this view of the subject, all the outward circumstances of this life do not trouble me.

I know it is the case that many men would like to have everything they can desire or think of. And I used to think, if I were the Lord, I would give the people everything they wanted— all the money, all the honor, all the riches, and all the splendor their hearts could desire. But experience and observation have caused me to change my mind, for I know that such policy would not be good for the human family.—*JD*, 8:100, June 17, 1860.

RIGHTS.—There was a time when I thought I had a great many rights of my own, but now I have got to understand that I have all the rights that God will give me, and I don't want to have any more. I want to live in the light of his countenance, to ask him to give me his Spirit, and then I know I shall prosper. When you feel like talking about your rights, let me advise you to go into your closet, forget your imaginary rights, and ask the Lord to give you wisdom to guide you aright, that you may act before him as children of the light, and not be the means of throwing a stumbling block in the way of others. By pursuing this course, you will get along much easier, and there will not be nearly so much of that spirit of grumbling and complaining.—*JD*, 9:13, April 6, 1861.

VIRTUE.—Virtue does not consist simply in being prevented from committing evils, but in having temptations presented before us and then governing our passions and appetites.—*JD*, 22:339, January 1, 1882.

He that makes a pin, does more than he who commands armies; and he that invents a new thing for the benefit of man, should be honored more than a king. Wisdom is better than wealth. To be great, be good; to be rich, be contented; and to be respected, respect yourself.—*Nauvoo Neighbor*, August 21, 1844.

A PHILOSOPHY OF HAPPINESS.—As we travel along through what is sometimes called this "vale of tears," there are many thoughts that occupy our minds and many subjects for reflection present themselves, sometimes concerning the living and sometimes concerning the dead. However, it is with the living that we have to do at the present time, and it is "life and the pursuit of happiness" that ought to occupy the attention of all intellectual beings. Mankind have various views and ideas in relation to the attainment of happiness upon the earth, and also after we leave the earth, and those views and ideas that are entertained by us in relation to these matters influence, to a greater or less extent, our actions and proceedings in life.

We look at things through another medium, and judge of them from another standpoint, than which they are generally viewed by the inhabitants of the earth. We look upon it that the greatest happiness that we can attain to is in securing the approbation of our Heavenly Father, in fearing God, in being made acquainted with his laws—with the principles of eternal truth, and with those things that we consider will best promote not only our temporal, but our eternal happiness.—*JD*, 11:87, March 5, 1865.

## SOME FAVORITE SAYINGS[1]

Money is of little importance where truth is concerned.

---

[1]The following sayings were selected as favorites of President Taylor, by his family, November 1, 1921, upon the 113th anniversary of his birth. They are all reproduced from Volume 25 of the *Improvement Era*, p. 79, *q. v.*

If a thing is done well, no one will ask how long it took to do it, but, who did it?

I would rather have God for my friend than all other influences and powers outside.

Never do an act that you would be ashamed of man knowing, for God sees us always, both day and night, and if we expect to live and reign with him in eternity, we ought to do nothing that will disgrace us in time.

It is the crowns, the principalities, the powers, the thrones, the dominions, and the associations with the Gods that we are after, and we are here to prepare ourselves for these things—this is the main object of existence.

I would rather trust in the living God than in any other power on earth.

We should be strictly honest, one with another, and with all men; let our word always be as good as our bond; avoid all ostentation of pride and vanity; and be meek, lowly, and humble; be full of integrity and honor; and deal justly and righteously with all men; and have the fear and love of God continually before us, and seek for the comforting influence of the Holy Ghost to dwell with us.

I pray God the Eternal Father that when we have all finished our probation here, we may be presented to the Lord without spot or blemish, as pure and honorable representatives of the church and kingdom of God on the earth, and then inherit a celestial glory in the kingdom of our God, and enjoy everlasting felicity with the pure and just in the realms of eternal day, through the merits and atonement of the Lord Jesus Christ, our Savior and Redeemer, in worlds without end.

# Chapter XXXIV

# THE PROSPECT AND THE FUTURE

## THE CONTEMPORARY SCENE

HISTORY REPEATS ITSELF.—We have noticed some things
. . . wherein the world are at fault, because of their lack of experience. Take, for instance, one half of the world, I mean China, and the great majority in Europe. Notice their position at the present time, and can any of you point out a remedy that will restore amity and peace among them? Is there a master mind, or spirit—a man possessed of sufficient intelligence to walk forth among the nations of Europe and say to the hydra-headed monster, "War, lie still and be thou quiet?" Is there a man who can go into China and do the same thing, and straighten out the snarled condition of the world?

Let us come nearer home. Can any of you regulate the affairs of this nation and put them right? I do not believe you can; and if you cannot do such small things that are associated with time, things that we can see, know, and understand, how are you going to put in order the things of God? How are you going to order ends that are to come? To know what will be the best course to pursue when the nations shall be convulsed, thrones cast down, and empires destroyed; when nation shall rush madly upon nation, and human blood shall flow as rivers of water? What would we do in such circumstances? Some people have thought we were in a dreadful condition when the Indian difficulties were among us in these mountains, and our distant neighbors have been surprised how we have existed; but what would you think if you were in some of the European nations at the present time? Suppose you were one of the kings of those nations, or one of the counselors, and some of the largest nations should undertake to command you to supply a number of men to help fight their battles, and you would say, "We wish to remain neutral." The reply would be, "But we will make you fight, and if you do not do it we will exterminate you to begin with." Suppose you were in a position like that.

I think we are no worse off in these mountains, than the world are. We may be in some circumstances, but in many other respects we are much better off than they. I think our young men, for instance, would think it very hard if they were obliged to spend from three to five years in soldiering in times of peace, which they have to do in many nations of Europe, or bring a substitute to go in their place. I think sometimes we might be a great deal worse off than we are, and I think it is necessary men should be tried in order that they may be proved, and that they may know themselves; and that some should be destroyed, as they have been on this continent, or on the other. It is all in the wise providence of God; life and death are of little moment to him. It is a matter of great importance to know the truth, and obey it, to have the privilege of learning his will, at the mouths of the servants of God, and then to have the privilege of doing it unmolested, no matter what it is, whether to live or die, or whatever course we may have to pursue. I think it is a great privilege for us to be associated with the kingdom of God.—*JD*, 1:373-374, April 19, 1854.

A SURVEY, FORECAST, AND PROPHECY OF 1882.—We have peacefully, legally, and honorably possessed our lands in these valleys of the mountains, and we have purchased and paid for them. We do not revel in any ill-gotten gain. These lands are ours. We have complied with all the requisitions of law pertaining thereto, and we expect to possess and inhabit them. We covet no man's silver or gold, or apparel, or wife, or servants, or flocks, or herds, or horses, or carriages, or lands, or possessions. But we expect to maintain our own rights. If we are crowded upon by unprincipled men or inimical legislation, we shall not take the course pursued by the lawless, the dissolute, and the unprincipled. We shall not have recourse to the dynamite of the Russian nihilists, the secret plans and machinations of the communists, the boycotting and threats of the Fenians, the force and disorder of the Jayhawkeers, the regulators or the Molly Maguires,[1] nor any other secret or illegal combination; but we still expect to possess and maintain our rights, but to obtain them in a legal, peaceful, and constitutional manner. . . .

A terrible day of reckoning is approaching the nations of the earth; the Lord is coming out of his hiding place to vex the inhabitants thereof; and the destroyer of the gentiles, as prophesied of, is already on his way. Already the monarchs of the earth are trembling from conspiracies among their own people. . . . Already have two of the presidents of this republic been laid low by the hands of the assassin; and the spirit of insubordination, misrule, lynching, and mobocracy of every kind is beginning to ride rampant through the land. Already combinations are being entered into which are very ominous for the future prosperity, welfare, and happiness of this great republic. The volcanic fires of disordered and anarchical elements are beginning to manifest themselves and

---

[1]These were all contemporary groups, associated in the public mind with violent methods.

exhibit the internal forces that are at work among the turbulent and unthinking masses of the people.—*JD*, 23:61-63, April 9, 1882.

THE ORDER OF GOD.—There may be circumstances arise in this world to pervert for a season the order of God, to change the designs of the Most High, apparently, for the time being. Yet they will ultimately roll back into their proper place—justice will have its place, and so will mercy, and every man and woman will yet stand in their true position before God. . . .—*JD*, 1:222-223, April 8, 1853.

THE JUDGMENTS BEGIN AT THE HOUSE OF GOD.—We have received his guidance and instruction. It is for us now to go on from truth to truth, from intelligence to intelligence, and from wisdom to wisdom. And while nations shall crumble and thrones be cast down, and the God of heaven arise and shake terribly the earth, while the elements melt with fervent heat in fulfilment of ancient as well as modern prophecy; while these things are going on he will whisper, peace to Zion. But the judgments will begin at the house of God. We have to pass through some of these things, but it will only be a very little compared with the terrible destruction, the misery, and suffering that will overtake the world who are doomed to suffer the wrath of God. It behooves us, as the saints of God, to stand firm and faithful in the observance of his laws, that we may be worthy of his preserving care and blessing.—*JD*, 21:100, April 13, 1879.

THE KINGDOM IS ONWARD.—God is with us and will be with us, and will sustain us, and no power on earth or in hell can stop the progress of this work; for it is onward according to the decree of Almighty God, and will be from this time henceforth and forever. And as the prophets have said, so say I, woe to those men and woe to that nation or to those nations that lift up their hands against Zion, for God will destroy them. I prophesy that in the name of the Lord God of hosts. And he will be with his Israel, and will sustain his people and bring them off victorious; and if faithful. to the end, we shall obtain thrones, principalities, powers, dominions, exaltations, and eternal lives in the kingdom of our God.—*JD*, 23:179-180, July 24, 1882.

FUTURE EVENTS

THE COMING SCENE.—In relation to the events to come, they will be developed just as fast as we are prepared for them, and I fear faster. Will God operate upon the Lamanites, and fulfil his word to the Jews? Yes. Will he gather the ten tribes? Yes.

Will he establish his name and kingdom in the earth? Yes. Will he overthrow the wicked nations that fight against him? Yes, and he will continue to extend his principles and power until "the kingdoms of this world are become the kingdoms of our Lord, and of his Christ." (Revelation 11:15.) God will have his laws honored, and in his time his decrees must be consummated, until every tongue confess and every knee bow to him who is the Lord of all. These are things which will most assuredly be accomplished. —*JD*, 18:286, November 5, 1876.

THE LORD'S WORK.—Do you think we are going to fail? Do you think the' Lord is going to back down? I think not. Men may combine against us ignorantly, for many of them are very ignorant. I do not cherish the least feeling of wrath in my heart when I see the courts, legislators, or Congress take steps inimical to us. They do not know what they do, hence we should feel charitably disposed to those who seek our injury.—*JD*, 21:98, April 13, 1879.

Men will not always entertain towards us the feelings they do today. When they find that we are not the people the world has held us up to be, when we shall have proven to the world that we are not what they have believed us to be, but that we are a virtuous and law-abiding people, the honorable among men will acknowledge our worth. And the day will come when it will be said of our children as the old prophets have prophesied, that such and such a one was born in Zion. It will be considered a great blessing and one of the greatest honors that could have been inherited by our children to have been born in Zion among the people of God.—*JD*, 22:317, October 19, 1881.

A PROPHECY.—We have got to put our trust in God, let the consequences be as they may. And as long as we do this, and as long as we keep the holy covenants we have entered into with him and with one another, Zion will triumph; and the wicked will waste away until there will be no place found for them; and the man or the nation that lifts up his hand against Zion will wither before Almighty God. I will prophesy that in the name of Jesus Christ, and I will meet the consequences of what I say.

But I will tell you what we have to do, my brethren and sisters, we must fear God in our hearts; we must lay aside our covetousness and our waywardness, our self-will and foolishness of every kind. As brethren, we must humble ourselves before the Lord, repenting of our sins, and henceforth preserve our bodies and spirits pure, that we may be fit receptacles for the Spirit of the living God, and be guided by him in all our labors both for the living and the dead. Our desires must be for God and his righteousness, until we shall exclaim with one of old: O God, search me, and try me, and if there be any way of wickedness in me, bid it depart. It is for us, as fathers and mothers, to go before the Lord in all humility and call upon him that his peace may be in our hearts; and wherein we may have done wrong, confess that wrong and repair it as far as we possibly can; and in this way let every man and woman in Israel begin to set their houses in order, and forever cultivate the spirit of peace, the spirit of union and love.

And if the families of Israel do this throughout all the land of Zion, all fearing God and working righteousness, cherishing the spirit of humility and meekness, and putting our trust in him, there is no power in existence that can injure us.—*JD*, 23:337, October 29, 1882.

THE PLATFORM OF PROPHECY.—Nothing but the Spirit of God can enlighten men's minds. Standing on this platform, we view all things of a political and religious nature associated with the earth we are living on as being very uncertain, intangible, and unphilosophical. We expect to see the nations waste, crumble, and decay. We expect to see a universal chaos of religious and political sentiment, and an uncertainty much more serious than anything that exists at the present time. We look forward to the time, and try to help it on, when God will assert his own right with regard to the government of the earth; when, as in religious matters so in political matters, he will enlighten the minds of those that bear rule, he will teach the kings wisdom and instruct the senators by the Spirit of eternal truth; when to him "every knee shall bow and every tongue confess that Jesus is the Christ." Then "the earth shall be full of the knowledge of the Lord, as the waters cover the sea." (Isaiah 11:9.) Then shall the mists of darkness be swept away by the light of eternal truth. Then will the intelligence of heaven beam forth on the human mind, and by it they will comprehend everything that is great, and good, and glorious.—*JD*, 11:94, March 5, 1865.

LEAVE THE WICKED TO GOD.—We will leave the wicked in the hands of God. He will deal with them in his own way. We are told that the wicked shall slay the wicked; and one thing that I am sorry over in this nation is this: that they are striking at the tree of liberty and trying to fetter humanity and bring men into bondage; they are laying the axe at the root of this government, and unless they speedily turn round and repent and follow the principles they have sworn to sustain—the principles contained in the Constitution of the United States—they will be overthrown, they will be split up and divided, be disintegrated, and become weak as water; for the Lord will handle them in his own way. I say these things in sorrow. But as sure as God lives, unless there is a change of policy these things will most assuredly take place.[1]—*JD*, 23:270, October 8, 1882.

There seem to be some hard-hearted people in the world trying to fire the indignation of ungodly men against the Latter-day Saints. But he that sits in the heavens puts hooks in their noses and leads them into the pit they had dug for their neighbor. So, knowing that there are other judgments in store for the whole earth, we will venture a prediction, and that shall be *storm and hail* enough to cause a famine, and show the whole of the earth that Jesus Christ, and not the Mormons, vexes the nation. Enough of the present generation shall see, hear, and feel it, to be witnesses that the servants of God tell the truth.

Watch, for you know not the hour, nor the day; and you cannot accuse the Mormons of making hail, so, watch! for the hail, the earthquakes, and war shall come and vex all nations.— *Nauvoo Neighbor*, August 6, 1845.

ROLE OF THE JEWS.—Nor are we alone in the dealings of God with the people in this dispensation. The Jews will have to perform quite a role in these last times. They also will have to endure a large amount of trials, persecutions, and difficulties which have yet to come upon them. They will in due time be gathered together to their own lands as we are gathered here; and nations will go up against them, and then too will certain nations come against us. But we have not yet got through with the United States. In relation to events that will yet take place, and the kind of trials, troubles, and sufferings which we shall have to cope with, it is to me a matter of very little moment. These things are in the hands of God. He dictates the affairs of the human family, and directs and controls our affairs; and the great thing that we, as a people, have to do is to seek after and cleave unto our God, to be in close affinity with him, and to seek for his guidance, and his blessing and Holy Spirit to lead and guide us in the right path. Then it matters not what it is nor who it is that we have to contend with, God will give us strength according to our day. —*JD*, 18:281, November 5, 1876.

---

[1]Mention here and frequently in this work of the threat to liberty, usually refers to the special legislation leveled against "The Mormon Menace" by Congress, 1862-1887.

# BOOK SIX

## SOME PERSONAL REFLECTIONS AND FOOTNOTES TO HISTORY

*"I do not care anything about shooting: I have been shot. Neither do I care anything about dying: for I could have died many a time if I had desired to; but I had not got ready. But I do care about those principles of truth which I have received; and I would not exchange my position for that of any emperor, king, or potentate in any nation under heaven."*
—JOHN TAYLOR,
*JD,* 5:248,
*Sept.* 13, 1857.

# CHAPTER XXXV

# JOSEPH SMITH THE PROPHET

## THE CHARACTER OF JOSEPH SMITH

HIS INTELLIGENCE.—Who was Joseph Smith? The Book of Mormon tells us he was of the seed of Joseph that was sold into Egypt, and hence he was selected as Abraham was to fulfil a work upon the earth. God chose this young man. He was ignorant of letters as the world has it, but the most profoundly learned and intelligent man that I ever met in my life, and I have traveled hundreds of thousands of miles, been on different continents and mingled among all classes and creeds of people, yet I have never met a man so intelligent as he was. And where did he get his intelligence from? Not from books, not from the logic or science or philosophy of the day, but he obtained it through the revelation of God made known to him through the medium of the everlasting gospel.—*JD*, 21:163, December 7, 1879.

THE DIVINE CALLING OF JOSEPH SMITH.—Joseph Smith in the first place was set apart by the Almighty according to the councils of the Gods in the eternal worlds, to introduce the principles of life among the people, of which the gospel is the grand power and influence, and through which salvation can extend to all peoples, all nations, all kindreds, all tongues, and all worlds. It is the principle that brings life and immortality to light, and places us in communication with God. God selected him for that purpose, and he fulfilled his mission and lived honorably and died honorably. I know of what I speak, for I was very well acquainted with him and was with him a great deal during his life, and was with him when he died. The principles which he had placed him in communication with the Lord, and not only with the Lord, but with the ancient apostles and prophets; such men, for instance, as Abraham, Isaac, Jacob, Noah, Adam, Seth, Enoch, and Jesus, and the Father, and the apostles that lived on this continent, as well as those who lived on the Asiatic continent. He seemed to be as familiar with these people as we are with one another. Why? Because he had to introduce a dispensation which was called the dispensation of the fulness of times, and it was known as such by the ancient servants of God.—*JD*, 21:94, April 13, 1879.

THE COURAGE OF JOSEPH SMITH.—One of the first things I ever heard preached by the elders of this church was that the world would grow worse and worse, deceiving and being deceived. Should we be surprised at its coming to pass? Another thing that I have heard from the beginning is, that people would persecute us, commencing with neighborhoods and villages, and then it would extend to cities and counties, and then to states, and then to the United States, and afterwards to the world. We have got about fifty millions of people on our backs now—and it is a pretty heavy load to carry, too. But the Lord will see us through.

We are acting in the interests of humanity. We are proclaiming salvation to a fallen world, and in this we are carrying out the word and will of God made known and manifested directly to us. We are warning the people of their position, and we will continue to send forth our missionaries for this purpose until God says, it is enough. And if they persecute us in one city, we will do as Jesus told his disciples—we will flee to another, searching out the honest in heart. Persecution has been our lot from the beginning, and it has followed us to this day.

I am reminded of a circumstance that occurred in Missouri, which I will mention to show the kind of feeling that Joseph Smith was possessed of. Some . . . years ago, in Far West, a mob—one of those semi-occasional occurrences—had come against us with evil intent, placing themselves in position to give us battle; and there were not more than about two hundred of us in the place. We had one fellow who was taken with a fit of trembling in the knees, and he ordered our people to retreat. As soon as Joseph heard this sound, he exclaimed, "Retreat! where in the name of God shall we retreat to?" He then led us out to the prairie, facing the mob, and placed us in position. And the first thing we knew a flag of truce was seen coming towards us. The person bearing it said that some of their friends were among our people for whose safety they felt anxious. I rather think it was a case in which the wife was in the Church but not the husband, and the mob wished these parties to come out as they, he said, were going to destroy every man, woman and child in the place.

But these folks had a little "sand" in them, as the boys say. They sent word back that if that was the case they would die with their friends. Joseph Smith, our leader, then sent word back by this messenger. Said he, "Tell your general to withdraw his troops or I will send them to hell." I thought that was a pretty bold stand to take, as we only numbered about two hundred to their thirty-five hundred. But they thought we were more numerous than we really were. It may be that our numbers were magnified in their eyes. But they took the hint and left, and we were not sorry. The Lord, through simple means, is able to take care of and deliver his people, but they must put implicit faith and confidence in him; and when they are crowded into a tight place they must not be afraid to make sacrifice for the sake of maintaining the truth, and all will be well with us whether living or dying, in time or in eternity.—*JD*, 23:36-37, March 5, 1882.

JOHN TAYLOR'S "AFFIDAVIT."—I testify that I was acquainted with Joseph Smith for years. I have traveled with him; I have been with him in private and in public; I have associated with him in councils of all kinds; I have listened hundreds of times to his public teachings, and his advice to his friends and associates of a more private nature. I have been at his house and seen his deportment in his family. I have seen him arraigned before the tribunals of his country, and have seen him honorably acquitted, and delivered from the pernicious breath of slander, and the machinations and falsehoods of wicked and corrupt men. I was with him living, and with him when he died, when he was murdered in Carthage jail by a ruthless mob . . . with their faces painted. I was there and was myself wounded; I at that time received four balls in my body. I have seen him, then, under these various circumstances, and I testify before God, angels, and men, that he was a good, honorable, virtuous man—that his doctrines were good, scriptural, and wholesome—that his precepts were such as became a man of God—that his private and public character was unimpeachable—and that he lived and died as a man of God and a gentleman. This is my testimony. If it is disputed, bring me a person authorized to receive an affidavit, and I will make one to this effect. I therefore testify of things which I know and of things which I have seen.—*PD*, 23-24, 1850.

JOSEPH SMITH AND THE COURTS.—We hear about Joseph Smith's crimes. He was tried thirty-nine times before the tribunals of his country, and nothing proved against him. Why do not these gentlemen bring some legal, authenticated testimony from those courts? Why did not the authors of these books do this? Because they could not.—*PD*, 10, 1850.

JOSEPH SMITH AS A PROPHET.—If I did not believe that Joseph Smith was a true prophet, I should not have been here. If he was a true prophet, and spake the word of the Lord, that is just as binding on the human family as any other word spoken by any other prophet. The scriptures tell us that "Man shall not live by bread alone, but by every word that proceedeth out of the mouth of God." (Matthew 4:4.) . . . Gentlemen, I again say that Joseph Smith was a virtuous, high-minded, honorable man, a gentleman and a Christian. But he introduced principles which strike at the root of the corrupt systems of men. This necessarily comes in contact with their prepossessions, prejudices, and interests; and as they cannot overturn his principles, they attack his character. And that is one reason why we have so many books written against his character, without touching his principles, and also why we meet with so much opposition. But truth, eternal truth, is invulnerable. It cannot be destroyed, but like the throne of Jehovah, it will outride all the storms of men, and live for ever. —*PD*, 13, 1850.

JOSEPH SMITH AND THE TRUTH.—Suppose Joseph Smith was all you represent him to be—your systems are still as unscriptural. And the next thing you will have to do will be to prove the scriptures false, if you would sustain them. The eternal truths of God are still the same, and whether Joseph Smith was a good or a bad man, the truths we preach are scriptural, and you cannot gainsay them; and if they are, what avails your attack upon character? Your soporiferous draughts may lull the people to sleep for a while, but truth will roll forth. The honest in heart will be aroused from their slumber. The purposes of God will roll forth. The kingdom of God will be established, and in spite of your puny efforts, truth will stand proud and erect, unsullied and uncontaminated by the pestiferous breath of calumniating mortals, and no power can stay its progress.—*PD*, 7, 1850.

THE VOICE OF THE PROPHET IN COUNCIL.—Many a time have I listened to the voice of our beloved prophet, while in council . . . his eyes sparkling with animation, and his soul fired with the inspiration of the Spirit of the living God. It was a theme that caused the bosoms of all who were privileged to listen, to thrill with delight. Intimately connected with this were themes upon which prophets, patriarchs, priests, and kings dwelt with pleasure and delight; of them they prophesied, sang, wrote, spoke, and desired to see, but died without the sight. My spirit glows with sacred fire while I reflect upon these scenes, and I say, O Lord, hasten the day! Let Zion be established! Let the mountain of the Lord's house be established in the tops of the mountains! Let deliverance be proclaimed unto Zion! Let redemption echo from mountain to mountain, from hill to hill, from nation to nation! Let the world hear! Let the law go forth from Zion, and the word of the Lord from Jerusalem! Let the dead hear a voice and live! Let the captives be set free! Let the saints possess the kingdom, and the kingdoms of this world become the kingdoms of our God and his Christ!—*MS*, 8:97-98, November 1, 1846.

## SOME TEACHINGS OF THE PROPHET

THE BOOK OF MORMON RECORD.—Stephens and Catherwood, after examining the ruins that were found at Guatemala, in Central America, and gazing upon magnificent ruins, mouldering temples, stately edifices, rich sculpture, elegant statuary, and all the traces of a highly cultivated and civilized people, said— "Here are the works of a great and mighty people that have inhabited these ruins; but now they are no more. History is silent on the subject, and no man can unravel this profound mystery. Nations have planted, and reaped, and built, and lived, and died, that are now no more; and no one can tell anything about them or reveal their history."

Why, there was a young man in Ontario county, New York, to whom the angel of God appeared and gave an account of the whole. These majestic ruins bespeak the existence of a mighty people. The Book of Mormon unfolds their history. O yes; but his was of too humble an origin, like Jesus of Nazareth. It was not some great professor, who had got an education in a European or an American college, but one who professed to have a revelation from God—and the world doesn't believe in revelation. But nevertheless it is true, and we know it.—*JD*, 5:240-241, September 13, 1857.

THE LAST DAYS.—In speaking with the Prophet Joseph once on this subject, he traced it from the first down to the last, until he got to the Ancient of Days. He wished me to write something for him on this subject, but I found it a very difficult thing to do. He had to correct me several times. We are told that the "judgment shall sit and the books be opened." He spoke of the various dispensations and of those holding the keys thereof, and said there would then be a general giving up or "accounting for." I wrote that each one holding the keys of the several dispensations would deliver them up to his predecessor, from one to another, until the whole kingdom should be delivered up to the Father and then God would be "all in all." Said he, "That is not right." I wrote it again, and again he said it was not right. It is very difficult to find language suitable to convey the meaning of spiritual things. The idea was that they should deliver up or give an account of their administrations, in their several dispensations, but that they would all retain their several positions and priesthood. The Bible and Doctrine and Covenants speak about certain books which should be opened; and another book would be opened, called the Book of Life, and out of the things written in these books would men be judged at the last day.—*JD*, 18: 329-330, December 31, 1876.

## THE MARTYRDOM

THE AFTERNOON OF JUNE 27, 1844.—I do not remember the names of all who were with us that night and the next morning in jail, for several went and came; among those that we considered stationary were Stephen Markham, John S. Fullmer, Captain Dan Jones, Dr. Willard Richards, and myself. Dr. Bernhisel says that he was there from Wednesday in the afternoon until eleven o'clock next day. We were, however, visited by numerous friends, among whom were Uncle John Smith, Hiram Kimball, Cyrus H. Wheelock, besides lawyers, as counsel. There was also a great variety of conversation, which was rather desultory than otherwise, and referred to circumstances that had transpired, our former and present grievances, the spirit of the troops around us, and the disposition of the governor; the devising for legal and other plans for deliverance, the nature of testimony required; the gathering of proper witnesses, and a variety of other topics, including our religious hopes, etc.

During one of these conversations Dr. Richards remarked: "Brother Joseph, if it is necessary that you die in this matter, and if they will take me in your stead, I will suffer for you." At another time, when conversing about deliverance, I said, "Brother Joseph, if you will permit it, and say the word, I will have you out of this prison in five hours, if the jail has to come down to do it." My idea was to go to Nauvoo, and collect a force sufficient, as I considered the whole affair a legal farce, and a flagrant outrage upon our liberty and rights. Brother Joseph refused.

Elder Cyrus H. Wheelock came in to see us, and when he was about leaving, drew a small pistol, a six-shooter, from his pocket, remarking at the same time, "Would any of you like to have this?" Brother Joseph immediately replied, "Yes, give it to me," whereupon he took the pistol, and put it in his pantaloons pocket. The pistol was a six-shooting revolver, of Allen's patent; it belonged to me, and was one that I furnished to Brother Wheelock when he talked of going with me to the east, previous to our coming to Carthage. I have it now in my possession. Brother Wheelock went out on some errand, and was not suffered to return. The report of the governor having gone to Nauvoo without taking the prisoners along with him caused very unpleasant feelings, as we were apprised that we were left to the tender mercies of the Carthage Greys, a company strictly mobocratic, and whom we knew to be our most deadly enemies; and their captain, Esquire (Robert F.) Smith, was a most unprincipled villain. Besides this, all the mob forces, comprising the governor's troops, were dismissed, with the exception of one or two companies, which the governor took with him to Nauvoo. The great part of the mob was liberated, the remainder was our guard.

We looked upon it not only as a breach of faith on the part of the governor, but also as an indication of a desire to insult us, if nothing more, by leaving us in the proximity of such men. The prevention of Wheelock's return was among the first of their hostile movements.

Colonel Markham went out, and he was also prevented from returning. He was very angry at this, but the mob paid no attention to him. They drove him out of town at the point of the bayonet, and threatened to shoot him if he returned. He went, I am informed, to Nauvoo for the purpose of raising a company of men for our protection. Brother Fullmer went to Nauvoo after witnesses. It is my opinion that Brother Wheelock did also. . . . We all of us felt unusually dull and languid, with a remarkable depression of spirits. In consonance with those feelings, I sang a song, that had lately been introduced into Nauvoo, entitled, "A Poor Wayfaring Man of Grief," etc.

The song is pathetic, and the tune quite plaintive, and was very much in accordance with our feelings at the time, for our spirits were all depressed, dull, and gloomy, and surcharged with indefinite ominous forebodings. After a lapse of some time, Brother Hyrum requested me again to sing that song. I replied, "Brother Hyrum, I do not feel like singing;" when he remarked, "Oh, never mind; commence singing, and you will get the spirit of it." At his request I did so. Soon afterwards I was sitting at one of the front windows of the jail, when I saw a number of men, with painted faces, coming around the corner of the jail, and aiming towards the stairs. The other brethren had seen the same, for, as I went to the door, I found Brother Hyrum Smith and Dr. Richards already leaning against it. They both pressed against the door with their shoulders to prevent its being opened, as the lock and latch were comparatively useless. While in this position, the mob, who had come upstairs and tried to open the door, probably thought it was locked and fired a ball through the keyhole. At this Dr. Richards and Brother Hyrum leaped back from the door, with their faces towards it. Almost instantly another ball passed through the panel of the door, and struck Brother Hyrum on the left side of the nose, entering his face and head. At the same instant, another ball from outside entered his back, passing through his body and striking his watch. The ball came from the back, through the jail window, opposite the door, and must, from its range, have been fired from the Carthage Greys, who were placed there ostensibly for our protection, as the balls from the firearms, shot close by the jail, would have entered the ceiling, we being in the second story, and there never was a time after that when Hyrum could have received the latter wound. Immedi-

ately, when the ball struck him, he fell flat on his back, crying
as he fell, "I am a dead man!" He never moved afterwards.

I shall never forget the deep feeling of sympathy and regard
manifested in the countenance of Brother Joseph as he drew nigh
to Hyrum, and, leaning over him, exclaimed, "Oh! my poor, dear
brother Hyrum!" He, however, instantly arose, and with a firm,
quick step, and a determined expression of countenance, approached
the door, and pulling the six-shooter left by Brother Wheelock
from his pocket, opened the door slightly, and snapped the pistol
six successive times. Only three of the barrels, however, were
discharged. I afterwards understood that two or three were
wounded by these discharges, two of whom, I am informed, died.
I had in my hands a large, strong hickory stick, brought there by
Brother Markham and left by him, which I had siezed as soon
as I saw the mob approach; and while Brother Joseph was firing
the pistol, I stood close behind him. As soon as he had discharged
it he stepped back, and I immediately took his place next to the
door, while he occupied the one I had done while he was shooting.
Brother Richards, at this time, had a knotty walking-stick in his
hands belonging to me, and stood next to Brother Joseph a little
farther from the door, in an oblique direction, apparently to avoid
the rake of the fire from the door. The firing of Brother Joseph
made our assailants pause for a moment. Very soon after, however, they pushed the door some distance open, and protruded and
discharged their guns into the room, when I parried them off with
my stick, giving another direction to the balls.

It certainly was a terrible scene. Streams of fire as thick as
my arm passed by me as these men fired, and, unarmed as we were,
it looked like certain death. I remember feeling as though my
time had come, but I do not know when, in any critical position,
I was more calm, unruffled, energetic, and acted with more prompt-
ness and decision. It certainly was far from pleasant to be so
near the muzzles of those firearms as they belched forth their
liquid flames and deadly balls. While I was engaged in parrying
the guns, Brother Joseph said, "That's right, Brother Taylor,
parry them off as well as you can." These were the last words
I ever heard him speak on earth.

Every moment the crowd at the door became more dense,
as they were unquestionably pressed on by those in the rear ascending the stairs, until the whole entrance at the door was literally
crowded with muskets and rifles, which, with the swearing, shout-
ing, and demoniacal expressions of those outside the door and
on the stairs, and the firing of the guns, mingled with their horrid
oaths and execrations, made it look like pandemonium let loose,
and was, indeed, a fit representation of the horrid deed in which
they were engaged.

After parrying the guns for some time, which now protruded farther and farther into the room, and seeing no hope of escape or protection there, as we were now unarmed, it occurred to me that we might have some friends outside, and that there might be some chance of escape in that direction, but here there seemed to be none. As I expected them every moment to rush into the room—nothing but extreme cowardice having thus far kept them out—as the tumult and pressure increased, without any other hope, I made a spring for the window which was right in front of the jail door, where the mob was standing, and also exposed to the fire of the Carthage Greys, who were stationed some ten or twelve rods off. The weather was hot; we all of us had our coats off, and the window was raised to admit air. As I reached the window, and was on the point of leaping out, I was struck by a ball from the door about midway of my thigh, which struck the bone and flattened out almost to the size of a quarter of a dollar, and then passed on through the fleshy part to within about half an inch of the outside. I think some prominent nerve must have been severed or injured, for as soon as the ball struck me, I fell like a bird when shot, or an ox when struck by a butcher, and lost entirely and instantaneously all power of action or locomotion. I fell upon the window sill, and cried out, "I am shot!" Not possessing any power to move, I felt myself falling outside of the window, but immediately I fell inside, from some, at that time, unknown cause. When I struck the floor, my animation seemed restored, as I have seen it sometimes in squirrels and birds after being shot. As soon as I felt the power of motion I crawled under the bed, which was in a corner of the room, not far from the window where I received my wound. While on my way and under the bed, I was wounded in three other places; one ball entered a little below the left knee, and never was extracted; another entered the forepart of my left arm, a little above the wrist, and, passing down by the joint, lodged in the fleshy part of my hand, about midway, a little above the upper joint of my little finger. Another struck me on the fleshy part of my left hip and tore away the flesh as large as my hand, dashing the mangled fragments of flesh and blood against the wall.

My wounds were painful, and the sensation produced was as though a ball had passed through and down the whole length of my leg. I very well remember my reflections at the time. I had a very painful idea of becoming lame and decrepit, and being an object of pity, and I felt as though I would rather die than be placed in such circumstances.

It would seem that immediately after my attempt to leap out of the window, Joseph also did the same thing, of which circumstance I have no knowledge only from information. The first thing that I noticed was a cry that he had leaped out of the window. A cessation of firing followed, the mob rushed downstairs, and Dr. Richards went to the window. Immediately afterward I saw the doctor going towards the jail door, and as there was an iron door at the head of the stairs adjoining our door which led into the cells for criminals, it struck me that the doctor was going in there, and I said to him, "Stop, Doctor, and take me along." He proceeded to the door and opened it, and then returned and dragged me along to a small cell prepared for criminals.

Brother Richards was very much troubled, and exclaimed, "Oh! Brother Taylor, is it possible that they have killed both Brother Hyrum and Joseph? It cannot surely be, and yet I saw them shoot them;" and elevating his hands two or three times, he exclaimed, "Oh Lord, my God, spare Thy servants!" He then said, "Brother Taylor, this is a terrible event;" and he dragged me farther into the cell, saying, "I am sorry I can not do better for you;" and, taking an old, filthy mattress, he covered me with it, and said, "That may hide you, and you may yet live to tell the tale, but I expect they will kill me in a few moments!" While lying in this position, I suffered the most excruciating pain.

Soon afterwards Dr. Richards came to me, informed me that the mob had precipitately fled, and at the same time confirmed the worst fears that Joseph was assuredly dead. I felt a dull, lonely, sickening sensation at the news. When I reflected that our noble chieftain, the Prophet of the living God, had fallen, and that I had seen his brother in the cold embrace of death, it seemed as though there was a void or vacuum in the great field of human existence to me, and a dark gloomy chasm in the kingdom, and that we were left alone. Oh, how lonely was that feeling! How cold, barren, and desolate! In the midst of difficulties he was always the first in motion; in critical positions his counsel was always sought. As our prophet he approached our God, and obtained for us his will; but now our prophet, our counselor, our general, our leader, was gone, and amid the fiery ordeal that we then had to pass through, we were left alone without his aid, and as our future guide for things spiritual or temporal, and for all things pertaining to this world, or the next, he had spoken for the last time on earth.

These reflections and a thousand others flashed upon my mind. I thought, why must God's nobility, the salt of the earth, the most exalted of the human family, and the most perfect types of all excellence, fall victims to the cruel, fiendish hate of incarnate devils?

The poignancy of my grief, I presume, however, was somewhat allayed by the extreme suffering that I endured from my wounds.

Soon afterwards I was taken to the head of the stairs and laid there, where I had a full view of our beloved and now murdered brother, Hyrum. There he lay as I had left him; he had not moved a limb; he lay placid and calm, a monument of greatness even in death; but his noble spirit had left its tenement, and was gone to dwell in regions more congenial to his exalted nature. Poor Hyrum! He was a great and good man, and my soul was cemented to his. If ever there was an exemplary, honest, and virtuous man, an embodiment of all that is noble in the human form, Hyrum Smith was its representative.

While I lay there, a number of persons came around, among whom was a physician. The doctor, on seeing a ball lodged in my left hand, took a penknife from his pocket and made an incision in it for the purpose of extracting the ball therefrom, and having obtained a pair of carpenter's compasses, made use of them to draw or pry out the ball, alternately using the penknife and compasses. After sawing for some time with a dull penknife, and prying and pulling with the compasses, he ultimately succeeded in extracting the ball, which weighed about half an ounce. Some time afterwards he remarked to a friend of mine that I had "nerves like the devil" to stand what I did in its extraction. I really thought I had need of nerves to stand such surgical butchery, and that, whatever my nerves may be, his practice was devilish.

This company wished to remove me to Mr. Hamilton's hotel, the place where we had stayed previous to our incarceration in jail. I told them, however, that I did not wish to go. I did not consider it safe. They protested that it was, and that I was safe with them; that it was a perfect outrage for men to be used as we had been; that they were my friends; that I could be better taken care of there than here.

I replied, "I don't know you. Whom am I among? I am surrounded by assassins and murderers; witness your deeds. Don't talk to me of kindness or comfort; look at your murdered victims. Look at me! I want none of your counsel nor comfort. There may be some safety here; I can be assured of none anywhere, etc."

They G——d—— their souls to hell, made the most solemn asseverations, and swore by God and the devil, and everything else that they could think of, that they would stand by me to death and protect me. In half an hour every one of them fled from the town.

Soon after a coroner's jury were assembled in the room over the body of Hyrum. Among the jurors was Captain Smith of

the "Carthage Greys" who had assisted in the murder, and the
same justice before whom we had been tried. I learned of Francis
Higbee as being in the neighborhood. On hearing his name
mentioned, I immediately arose and said, "Captain Smith, you are
a justice of the peace; I have heard his name mentioned; I want
to swear my life against him." I was informed that word was
immediately sent to him to leave the place, which he did.

Brother Richards was busy during this time attending to
the coroner's inquest, and to the removal of the bodies, and
making arrangements for their removal from Carthage to Nauvoo.

When he had a little leisure, he again came to me, and at
his suggestion I was removed to Hamilton's tavern. I felt that
he was the only friend, the only person, that I could rely upon
in that town. It was with difficulty that sufficient persons could
be found to carry me to the tavern, for immediately after the
murder a great fear fell upon all the people, and men, women, and
children fled with great precipitation, leaving nothing nor anybody in the town but two or three women and children and one
or two sick persons.—*DHC, 7:99-108.*

EDITORIAL ON THE SUCCESSION OF THE TWELVE, CITY
OF NAUVOO, SEPTEMBER 2, 1844.—Great excitement prevails
throughout the world to know "who shall be the successor of
Joseph Smith!"

In reply, we say, be patient, *be patient* a little, till the proper
time comes, and we will tell you all. "Great wheels move slow."
At present, we can say that a special conference of the Church
was held in Nauvoo on the 8th ult., and it was carried *without
a dissenting voice,* that the "twelve" should preside over the
whole church, and when any alteration in the presidency shall
be required, seasonable notice will be given; and the elders abroad
will best exhibit their wisdom to all men by remaining silent
on those things they are ignorant of.[1] Bishops Whitney and
Miller have been appointed trustees, to manage the financial concerns of the Church, and will soon enter on the duties of their
calling.—*TS, 5:632, September 2, 1844.*

ON THE POSITION OF THE CHURCH IN 1844.—The idea
of the Church being disorganized and broken up because of the
Prophet and the patriarch being slain is preposterous. This
Church has the seeds of immortality in its midst. It is not of
man, nor by man—it is the offspring of Deity. It is organized
after the pattern of heavenly things, through the principles of

---

[1]Reference is to the significant conference of August 8, 1844, when, by the
law of common consent and popular vote, as explained above, the próper basis of
authority was reestablished in harmony with the revelations.

revelation; by the opening of the heavens; by the ministering of angels, and the revelations of Jehovah. It is not affected by the death of one or two, or fifty individuals. It possesses a priesthood after the order of Melchizedek, having the power of an endless life, "without beginning of days, or end of years." It is organized for the purpose of saving this generation, and generations that are past. It exists in time and will exist in eternity. This church fail? No! Times and seasons may change, revolution may succeed revolution; thrones may be cast down; and empires be dissolved; earthquakes may rend the earth from center to circumference; the mountains may be hurled out of their places, and the mighty ocean be moved from its bed, but amidst the crash of worlds and the crack of matter, truth, eternal truth, must remain unchanged, and those principles which God has revealed to his saints be unscathed amidst the warring elements, and remain as firm as the throne of Jehovah.—*TS*, 5:744, December 15, 1844.

CHAPTER XXXVI

# SOME PERSONAL REFLECTIONS

## JOHN TAYLOR'S CONVERSION TO MORMONISM

THE STATE OF MIND.—I . . . allude to an incident in my personal experience to show the state of the world religiously some forty or fifty years ago. Not being then acquainted with this church, a number of us met together for the purpose of searching the scriptures and we found that certain doctrines were taught by Jesus and the apostles, which neither the Methodists, Baptists, Presbyterians, Episcopalians, nor any of the religious sects taught. We concluded that if the Bible was true, the doctrines of modern Christendom were not true; or if they were true, the Bible was false. Our investigations were impartially made, and our search for truth was extended. We examined every religious principle that came under our notice, and probed the various systems as taught by the sects, to ascertain if there were any that were in accordance with the word of God. But we failed to find any.

In addition to our researches and investigations, we prayed and fasted before God, and the substance of our prayers was that if he had a people upon the earth anywhere, and ministers who were authorized to preach the gospel, that he would send us one. This was the condition we were in. . . .

THE ANSWER TO THE QUEST.—We prayed earnestly, and in answer to our prayers the Lord sent us Elder Parley P. Pratt. . . . Brother Pratt, in relating the circumstances, says that Brother Heber C. Kimball came to his house one night after he had retired; that Brother Kimball requested him to get up, which he did, and then began to prophesy to him. He told him there was a people in Canada who were seeking for a knowledge of the gospel, and they were praying to God to send them a minister who should reveal to them the truth. Brother Kimball then commissioned him to repair to Canada, telling him that the Lord would bless him and open up his way.

Just previous to that time the saints had been engaged in building the temple in Kirtland, Ohio, and were all very much embarrassed as to means, Brother Pratt with the balance, having devoted everything he had to spare for that purpose. Among other things that Brother Kimball told him was, that where he was going he would find means to relieve himself, and that many of the people would embrace the gospel, and that it would be the means of introducing the gospel to England. And furthermore, said he, your wife who is now childless shall have a son. In the course of time she did have a son, and they named him Parley. I do not know but that he may be present; but I was going to say, I knew him before he was born. (Laughter.)

I speak of this to show that there was at that time nobody, of whom we had any knowledge, from whom we could obtain any information with regard to the gospel of the Son of God, or that could teach us the doctrines Jesus and his apostles taught, as contained in the scriptures. Brother Pratt came and found us, and he came in answer to our prayer; at least, that is my faith in regard to the matter.

MEANS OF INTRODUCING MORMONISM TO GREAT BRITAIN. —And were all these things accomplished? Yes. I was baptized, myself and others. And I baptized many others in that country; and it was the means also of sending the gospel to England. John Goodson, who apostatized long ago, John Snyder, a good faithful man who was one of the committee of the Nauvoo House, and who died in the Seventeenth Ward of this city, Isaac Russell, and Joseph Fielding, uncle to Brother Joseph F. Smith, were of our number, embraced the gospel, and were afterwards called to accompany Brother Heber C. Kimball and Orson Hyde to England for the purpose of opening up the work in that land; and I was the first person that wrote a letter to England on the subject of the gospel. I did it at the request of Brother Fielding, who got me to write for him to a brother and brother-in-law of his who were ministers in England. These were the men that helped to introduce the gospel into England in the early day. I speak of this for the information of many of you.—*JD,* 23:30-31, March 5, 1882.

THE DETAIL OF P. P. PRATT'S VISIT.—I was living in the city of Toronto, Upper Canada. I was associated with a number of gentlemen in searching the scriptures. Many of us were connected with the Methodist Society; we did not believe their doctrines because they did not accord with scripture. Nevertheless we did not interfere with them; we considered them as near correct as others. We rejected every man's word or writing, and took the Word of God alone. We had continued diligently at this for two years. We made it a rule to receive no doctrine until we could bring no scriptural testimony against it. The gentlemen with whom I associated were, many of them, learned and intelligent.

We gathered from the scriptures many important truths. We believed in the gathering of Israel, and in the restoration of the ten tribes. We believed that Jesus would come to reign personally on the earth. We gathered from the scriptures that just judgment would overtake the churches of the world, because of their iniquity. We believed that the gospel which was preached by the apostles was true, and that any departure from that was a departure from the order of God, and that churches having thus departed were consequently corrupt and fallen. We believed that there ought to be apostles, prophets, evangelists, pastors, and teachers as in former days, and that the gifts of healing and the power of God ought to be associated with the church. We, of course, believed that where these things did not exist there could not be a true church. But we believed that we had no authority ourselves to teach these principles. We were praying men, and asked our Heavenly Father to show us the truth, and we fasted and prayed that if God had a true church on the earth he would send us a messenger.

About this time Parley P. Pratt called on me with a letter of introduction from a merchant of my acquaintance. I had peculiar feelings on seeing him. I had heard a great many stories of a similar kind to those that you have heard, and I must say that I thought my friend had imposed upon me a little in sending a man of this persuasion to me. I, however, received him courteously as I was bound to do. I told him, however, plainly, my feelings, and that in our researches I wanted no fables. I wished him to confine himself to the scriptures. We talked for three hours or upwards, and he bound me as close to the scriptures as I desired, proving everything he said therefrom. I afterwards wrote down eight sermons that he preached, in order that I might compare them with the work of God. I found nothing contrary.

I then examined the Book of Mormon, and the prophecies concerning that. That was also correct. I then read the Doctrine and Covenants; found nothing unscriptural there. He called upon us to repent and be baptized for the remission of sins, and we should receive the Holy Ghost. But what is that, we inquired. The same, he answered, as it was in the apostles' days, or nothing. A number of others and myself were baptized, and we realized those blessings according to his word. The gifts and power of God were in the church, the gift of tongues and prophecy; the sick were healed, and we rejoiced in the blessings and gifts of the Holy Ghost.—*PD*, 17-20, 1850.

THE BASIS OF SCRIPTURE.—The first thing that I heard from a priest, after hearing this gospel preached by Parley P. Pratt, some twenty years ago, was the cry, "Delusion!" I was immediately informed that "Joe Smith was a money-digger," that he tried to deceive people by walking on planks laid under the water, and that he was a wicked and corrupt man, a deceiver, and one of the biggest fools in creation, and so forth. I heard every kind of story; and the priests have kept up the same things, pretty much, to the present day.

I remember, when I first had an elder introduced to me, I said to him, "I do not know what to think about you Mormons. I do not believe any kind of fanaticism. I profess to be acquainted with the Bible; and, 'Sir,'" said I, "in any conversation we may have, I wish you to confine yourself to the Bible, for I tell you I shall not listen to anything in opposition to that word."

From the report which I had heard of Mormonism, I thought it was anything but a religious system. I was told about the French prophets. I was told about Mattias, Johanna Southcote, and of all the follies that had existed for centuries; and then they put Mormonism at the end of them all.

In my researches, I examined things very carefully and critically . . . in order that I might compare them with the Bible, and I could not find any difference. I could easily controvert any other doctrine, but I could not overturn one principle of Mormonism.—*JD*, 5:239, September 13, 1857.

MY FEELINGS UPON ENTERING THE CHURCH.—I will now tell you about some of my feelings when I first came into this church. It is a long while ago. When I first heard the gospel, I was compelled to admit there was something reasonable about it. I almost hoped it was not true. "If it is true," said I, "as an honest man I shall be obliged to obey it, or else I cannot have any confidence in myself." When I had investigated the subject, and became convinced that it was true, I said, "I am in for it; I must embrace it; I cannot reject the principles of eternal truth." And I will say, moreover, I don't know of a time in my life when, if anybody presented a truth that could not be controverted, but I was ready to obey it and I am today. If any person in the religious world, or the political world, or the scientific world, will present to me a principle that is true, I am prepared to receive it, no matter where it comes from. Well, says one, you believe the Bible? Yes. You believe in the Book of Mormon? Yes. You believe the Book of Doctrine and Covenants? Yes. I believe all that God has ever written or spoken, everything that we have on record, and I am prepared to believe everything that he will communicate to the human family. We profess to believe in all truth, and to be governed by all truth.—*JD*, 25:90, February 10, 1884.

I expected when I came into this church, that I should be persecuted and proscribed. I expected that the people would be persecuted. But I believed that God had spoken, that the eternal principles of truth had been revealed, and that God had a work to accomplish which was in opposition to the ideas, views, and notions of men, and I did not know but it would cost me my life before I got through. It came pretty near it at one time; yes, at many times. I have had to "stand the racket" in a way that many of you folks don't know much about. More than once I have had to face large crowds of people in the shape of armies, expecting to come into contact every moment—no farther off, perhaps, than the length of this hall. That is not a very pleasant position to be in.

But I was in a worse scrape in Carthage jail, when Joseph and Hyrum were killed—penned up in a room and attacked by a blackened mob. I had to stand at the door and ward off the guns while they were trying to shoot us, and we without arms, and under the protection of the governor of the state. Dr. Bernhisel and myself were sent by Joseph Smith to wait upon the governor, and lay before him the facts of the case. We told him we were competent to take care of ourselves, and did not require any of his aid, for we had an organized body of militia that were quite competent to protect us from their mobs, and asked his advice. He thereupon stated it would be better for us not to bring an armed force, and pledged his faith and the faith of the state, as governor, for our protection. We consented. This he said to Dr. Bernhisel and myself; and that pledge was violated by the murder of Joseph and Hyrum Smith in Carthage jail, and I myself received four balls in my person; but then I am here yet.

Was there anything surprising in all this? No. If they killed Jesus in former times, would not the same feeling and influence bring about the same results in these times? I had counted the cost when I first started out, and stood prepared to meet it.—*JD*, 25:91-92, February 10, 1884.

WHAT MY RELIGION MEANT.—Now, if I understand my religion aright, if I understand the scriptures and the operations of the Spirit of God, we have got, as a people, to come to this—let us know the will of God, and we will do it, no matter where it strikes, what interest it may come in contact with, or whose views it may overturn. That is my idea of Mormonism, as I have learned it. I consider that God is at the helm. We have not dictated or found out anything belonging to the problem we are working, not a man among us. All we have received comes from God. If I understand anything concerning these things, it is that the word of God is *law* and must be obeyed.—*JD*, 18:282-283, November 5, 1876.

## THE GOSPEL TO THE NATIONS

SIDELIGHT ON THE 1840 MISSION OF THE TWELVE TO ENGLAND.—I told you about our coming to Liverpool. The first time I preached ten came forward (for baptism). We have been baptizing since; last week we baptized nine; we are to baptize tomorrow, but how many I know not. The little stone is rolling forth. One of the brethren dreamed he saw two men come to Liverpool. They cast a net into the sea and pulled it out full of fishes. He was surprised to see them pick the small fish out first and then the large. Well, if we get all the fish I shall be satisfied.

Brother Woodruff has lately left the Potteries and has gone to another neighborhood, and is making Methodist preachers scarce. He baptized thirty-two persons in one week—thirteen of them were Methodist preachers. Elder Clark is preaching and baptizing in and about Manchester. The latest account from Elder Turley, he was well, preaching and baptizing in the Potteries. Elder Willard Richards is very busy at this period, in visiting and setting in order the branches of the church in Preston, Clithero, and all the regions round about, and holding correspondence with the elders abroad.—*DHC*, 4:96, March 16, 1840.

INTRODUCTION OF THE GOSPEL TO FRANCE.—I will here give a short history of some of my proceedings. I was appointed to go to France some years ago, in company with some of the twelve, who were appointed to go to other places. The First Presidency asked us if we would go. Yes, was the reply; we can go anywhere, for if we cannot do little things like these, I don't know what else we can do. Some people talk about doing great things; but it is not a great thing to travel a little, or to preach a little. I hear some of our elders saying, sometimes, that they are going to do great things—to be rulers in the kingdom of God, kings and priests to the Most High, and are again to exalt thousands of others to thrones, principalities, and powers, in the eternal worlds. But we cannot get them out of their nests to travel a few miles here. If they cannot do this, how will they ever learn to go from world to world?

We went, and were blessed in our journeying. We had a pretty hard time in crossing the plains, and I should not recommend people to go so late in the season as we did. We should have lost all our horses, but the hand of God was over us for our good. He delivered us out of all our dangers, and took us through safely. When we got to the Missouri River, the ice was running very strong, so that it was impossible to ferry; but in one night the river froze over, and we passed over as on a bridge, in perfect safety. But as soon as the last team was over, the ice again removed. Thus the Lord favored us in our extremities.

You may inquire, how did you get along preaching? The best way that we could, the same as we always do. We went to work (at least I did). I went into the city of Boulogne, and I obtained permission there from the mayor to preach. This I was under the necessity of doing. . . .

I went from there right into the city of Paris, and commenced translating the Book of Mormon, with Brother Bolton to assist me. We baptized a few, some of them men of intelligence and education, and capable of assisting us in the work. Brother Pack went to Calais, and raised a small church there. We afterwards united some English branches, Boulogne *en* France, to it, called the Jersey Islands. There the people speak half English, half French; and Brother Pack went to preside over them. Brother Bolton and I remained principally in Paris, and in that neighborhood, we there organized a church. Before I came away, we held a conference, at which four hundred members were represented, including those branches that were added to the branch in Calais. . . .

We found many difficulties to combat, for it is not an easy thing to go into France and learn to talk French well. But at the same time, if a man sets to work in good earnest, he can do it. I have scratched the word "can't" out of my vocabulary long since, and I have not got it in my French one. . . .

When you get into France, Germany, or any of the foreign nations, where the language is different from ours, the spirit of the people is different, and it appears to me that a different spirit is carried along with these languages, which is peculiar to them. . . .

I had thought, after having completed the translation of the Book of Mormon into the French language, in which I was assisted by Brother Bolton, of returning home last year, but I met with the epistle of the First Presidency, from which I could learn their desire that we should stay another year. I, therefore, thought I would alter my course immediately, and follow the directions of the Spirit of God—for I wished all the time, as Paul says, to be obedient to the heavenly calling. I wished at all times to pursue the course the Spirit of the Lord should dictate. . . .

To GERMANY.—As it stated in the epistle that it was better for the brethren to extend their labors to other nations, it immediately occurred to my mind to go to Germany. So I made a plan before I got up in the morning, for thought flows quickly, you know. The plan was—to publish the Book of Mormon there. I wrote to Brother Hyde to send me out some brother that was acquainted with the German language, and my letter got there about the time he left for the Valley, and he did not get it. I said to Brother Bolton, and Brother De La Mere, who was from the island of Jersey, that there was one man in the Valley I wished was here, and that was Brother Carn. There was one brother in France, who was a German, and was well acquainted with the languages, both German and French. I engaged him to go with me to Germany, that is, to translate. However, I went over to England, and thought we would hunt in England to find some person qualified to go and preach in Germany. I found many Germans, but none with sufficient experience in the Church. Finally, I thought I would start by myself. When I got to London, I met with Brother Dykes. He had said something about going to Germany, but he concluded he had better be with Brother Snow, as he was acquainted with the Danish language. He had got his discharge from that engagement, and was on his way home when I met him. This placed things in another position. He said he would like to go if his family could be provided for, but I could not say anything particular about his family.

I finally had him go for a month or two, for I did not wish to put a thing upon him I would not do myself. He felt a desire to go, and said he would do as I said, so I told him to go for two months. I made an appointment to meet him in Germany, as I had to go through France.

When we arrived there, we started the translation of the Book of Mormon, and it was half completed before I came away. We also started to publish a paper in Germany, called *Zions Panier*, (Zion's Banner.) I wished to be perfectly satisfied that the translation was right. Brother Richards and I heard some of it read in Boulogne, and we thought it was very good, but still it had to be altered. I, therefore, got some of the best professors in the city of Hamburg to look over it. Some few alterations were necessary, but not many. Also, with regard to the paper, one of the professors said he would not have known it was written in English and translated; he should, if not told to the contrary, have supposed it written originally in German.—*JD*, 1:19-24, August 22, 1852.

## TRIBUTE TO BRIGHAM YOUNG

Brigham Young needs no fictitious aid to perpetuate his memory. His labors have been exhibited during the last forty-five years in his preaching, in his writing, in his counsels, in the wisdom and intelligence he has displayed, in our exodus from Nauvoo; in the building of cities throughout the length and breadth of this territory, in his opposition to vice and his protection of virtue, purity, and right. These things are well known and understood by the Latter-day Saints, and also by thousands and millions of others. But, as with his predecessor, Joseph Smith, who had to leave, while we are called upon to mourn a president dead, angels announce a president born in the eternal worlds. He has only gone to move in another state of existence. But then in speaking of these things we would not eulogize only the man, for Brigham Young, although so great a man, could have done nothing towards developing the purposes of God unless aided and sustained by him. Joseph Smith could have done nothing. Neither, as I have already said, can the twelve apostles accomplish anything unless they receive the same divine support.—*JD*, 19:123, October 7, 1877.

## THE EXODUS FROM NAUVOO

"FEBRUARY, 1846."—All things are in preparation for a commencement of the great move of the Saints out of the United States. (We had like to have said, beyond the power of Christianity.) But we will soften the expression, by merely saying, *and back to their "primitive possessions,"* as in the enjoyment of Israel. It is reduced to a solemn reality, that the rights and property, as well as the lives and common religious belief of the Church of Jesus Christ of Latter-day Saints, *cannot be protected* in the realms of the United States, and, of course, from one to two hundred thousand souls must quit their freedom among freemen and go where the land, the elements, and the worship of God *are free.*

About two thousand are ready and crossing the Mississippi to pioneer the way, and make arrangements for summer crops at some point between this and the Pacific, where the biggest crowd of good people, will be the old settlers.

To see such a large body of men, women, and children, compelled by the inefficiency of the law, and potency of mobocracy, to leave a great city in the month of February, for the sake of the enjoyment of *pure religion,* fills the soul with astonishment, and gives the world a sample of fidelity and faith, brilliant as the sun, and forcible as a tempest, and as enduring as eternity.

May God continue the spirit of fleeing from false freedom, and false dignity, till every saint is removed to where "he can sit under his own vine and fig tree" without having any to molest or make afraid. *Let us go—let us go.—TS,* 6:1114, Nauvoo, February 1, 1846.

NAUVOO: "ONE GREAT WAGON SHOP."—The twelve, the high council, and about four hundred families left the city of Nauvoo in the month of February (1846) last, and launched forth, in an American winter, braving the frost, the snow, and the chilling winds, and commenced their journey to the far distant West. We left at that time for the purpose of assuaging the anger of an infuriated mob, and to preserve the peace, lives, and property of our brethren whom we left behind; and as most of their indignation was kindled against the leaders of the Church, this step had a tendency to cool their wrath and give the brethren whom we left behind a better opportunity to dispose of their property, settle up their business, and prepare their wagons and teams for a removal in the spring. To this all their energies were directed, all other business subsided, and Nauvoo was converted into one great wagon shop. In fact, nothing else seemed to be spoken or thought of but making wagons, purchasing teams, and preparing for a removal. Those who had left the city were very much exposed, living in tents and wagons. But as there is an abundance of timber in that country, we made large fires in the woods, and thus were enabled to preserve ourselves from the cold. As there was no grass, we were necessitated to purchase corn and hay to feed our horses and cattle, although we had left an immense amount behind. This, however, was mostly obtained for labor, which in that country is high, while produce is very low. *MS*, 8:113, November 15, 1846.

NAUVOO IN RETROSPECT.—It is a number of years now since we left the city of Nauvoo; it was a large city then, and surrounded by a rich country that we cultivated. In consequence of our religious views we could not stay there. We were persecuted and driven, and had to go into the wilderness, had to carry with us our husbandry utensils, seed, grain, tools of every kind, and provisions a distance of over thirteen hundred miles by land, with ox-teams, into an unknown and unexplored country, among the savages of the desert. . . .

We expect still to continue to progress and to advance in religious intelligence, in political intelligence, in religious power, and in political power. We are still expecting to carry out our social principles, which differ very materially from others.—*JD*, 11:53-54, January 18, 1865.

## SOME WESTERN HISTORY

SCENE: CROSSING THE PLAINS (1852).—It gave me great joy, on my way home, to find the Saints leaving Kanesville. It seemed as though they were swept out with a besom almost.[1] When I was there, I rode out in my carriage one day to a place called Council Point. I thought I would go and visit some of the folks there. But, when I got there, behold, there were no folks to see. I hunted round, and finally found a place with something like "grocery" written upon it. I alighted, and went into the house, and asked a person who presented himself at the door if

---

[1] A "besom" is a broom of twigs or heather.

he was a stranger there. Yes, says he, I have only just come. And the people have all left, have they? Yes, was the answer. I next saw a few goods standing at the side of a house, but the house was empty; these were waiting to be taken away. I went into another house, and there were two or three waiting for a boat to take them down the river, and these were all the inhabitants I saw there.

When I first reflected upon this removal, my heart felt pained. I well knew the disposition of many of the men in those frontier countries, and I thought that some miserable wretches might come upon them after the main body of the saints had removed, and abuse, rob, and plunder the widow, the orphan, the lame, halt, blind, and destitute, who might be left as they did in Nauvoo; and thus the old, decrepit, and infirm would be abused, insulted, and preyed upon by wretches in human shape, who never have courage to meet men, but are cruel and relentless with the old, infirm, the widow, orphan, and destitute. But, thank God, they are coming, nearly all, old and young, rich and poor.—*JD*, 1:18, August 22, 1852.

## THE FOUNDING OF UTAH AND MORMON COLONIZATION

We are quite a long distance from the outside world. It is true there are railroads, and more are being made; and it is right there should be. That is their part of the business. In this way, and in many instances, they are assisting us to build up the kingdom of God, but they don't know it. If they did, they would not like to do it.

WHY SALT LAKE CITY?—The position that we occupy in these valleys of the mountains is a very peculiar one. When we came up here, the first place that was designated was Salt Lake City. President Young said that he had a manifestation that that was the place. There was a valley, a very good valley, a comparatively rich valley, a valley that was well watered, a valley that could be irrigated without much labor, where the streams were quite easy of access and where a small community could easily raise their sustenance. And this we did. Now, had we landed in a place like this [St. George] at first, it would have been more difficult. People would have become more discouraged and some of them felt very much discouraged as it was—some going to California because everything looked so forbidding. Yet others thought it would be a pleasant place to reside in, a place where a living could be as easily obtained as in most other places, except we go to some of the rich lands of Missouri, Illinois, Iowa, etc.

But there were other circumstances associated with these things that would have made it difficult for us to sustain ourselves even in those places.

THE MISSOURI PERIOD.—For instance, we lived in a rich land back in Missouri. Everything there seemed to grow at a very rapid rate; everything increased very fast. I have heard some people tell such big stories about the productiveness of that country that I have sometimes been afraid to tell what I myself knew of it, for fear that people would not believe me; for instance, I have seen fields of corn that a regiment of soldiers could ride into and they would be out of sight; and I have seen beans grow where corn has been planted, where the cornstalks have served as bean poles; and I have seen pumpkins and squash grow among them, three crops growing the same year and at the same time. That country, nevertheless, has many drawbacks. In that country we were very unhealthy. We were subject to what is called fever and ague every year. In fact, in the spring we used to think we did well if we didn't happen to die off in the fall.

Why could we not stop there? Because the land was too good, and we were easy of access to men desirous to possess our property, and they told us to move on, and we had to go. We had to leave Missouri, and I suppose God intended to try the saints, to let them pass through certain kinds of experience and place them in a position that they would have to lean on him. Some of the people rebelled against these things in their feelings. Among the rest, I remember being much shocked at the remarks of Sidney Rigdon after he had been imprisoned with the Prophet Joseph in Richmond jail, as well as many others. I visited them in jail, and Sidney Rigdon made a remark soon after he got out, to the effect that if God did not care anything more about us than he seemed to do, that if he allowed us to be hauled around as we had been, he did not care about serving such a God. That is, he found the trials were heavier for him than he was capable of bearing, notwithstanding that he had seen the Lord and had had visions pertaining to the celestial, terrestrial, and telestial kingdoms, in which he had seen the position of men in the future, and the purposes of God regarding the nations of the earth, and had borne testimony of it in connection with Joseph Smith, as we find recorded in the Book of Doctrine and Covenants. Yet when trials came, his knees faltered, and the knees of many others have faltered in the same way.

Now, we talk about lands, good rich land. Why did we not stay in Missouri? Because people would not let us. It was just so in Illinois. Why did we leave there? Because, as I have heard Brother George A. Smith say, we left because we could not help ourselves; at least, that was the purport of his saying.

SALT LAKE VALLEY THE RIGHT PLACE.—I think the Lord was very merciful to us in Salt Lake Valley. I believe we landed just in the right place. The people commenced to establish themselves. They began to find that they could raise crops there, and that the land was very productive. We stayed there for a while and began to make little settlements and little excursions out into the surrounding country. The people had all kinds of difficulties. I remember once, in Bountiful, there were three or four families went up to settle there, and they felt that there was not enough water, and that they could hardly get along. They got to quarreling about water rights, as we do sometimes. I do not know of much quarreling down here. I do not think you have as much water to quarrel over as they had.

THE SETTLEMENTS EXPAND.—Afterwards President Young was moved upon to begin to make settlements in other places. We had now obtained a foothold. We had a place where we could raise all the grain necessary for our sustenance, where we could raise sheep, cattle, etc. We pushed out to Ogden on the one hand and to Provo on the other, and then occupied some of the best places in Salt Lake Valley, in Utah Valley, and on the Weber. We began to increase. More immigrants came in, and others began to come from above.

SALT LAKE TEMPLE.—Things went on. A temple was started [in Salt Lake City] but it seemed to progress very slowly; as well it might when we consider the substantial nature of the building. When we started, we had nothing but wagons to haul the rock on, and they were very big rock, if you remember. Those rocks had to be hauled about seventeen miles in those wagons, and owing to the liability of the wagons to break down, this work gave us a great deal of trouble. Today, and right along for a number of years past, since the railroad has been built, it is not uncommon to bring in some three or four carloads at a time, delivering the rock in the temple yard.

THE SOUTHERN SETTLEMENTS.—Then it was thought best to commence down here. [St. George.] Why? Let me tell you some other things, and show you about the settlements north and south, and especially south. If you remember, Brother George A. Smith, as much as twenty-five years ago—I don't remember exactly how long—came down and made a settlement at Parowan in 1851, and another at Cedar—and here is Brother Henry Lunt present, who was one of that number. He came to Cedar at that time, and they tried to start iron works at that place. And then Brother Joseph Horne and some others were sent down to see if cotton could not be raised in this district of country in the hope that something could be done whereby we might produce the raw material for the manufacture of our clothes. And they stayed a little while somewhere not far from here, some five miles south on the Santa Clara, I am told. There was a rich little settlement up there. Some time after, a great deal of it was washed away.

I remember the struggles Brother George A. used to have. He labored under difficulties, being so very heavy, and not as active as most men. But he was a man of great energy. He would come down here and bring a few men, and would settle them down and go back again. By and by he would bring some more down, all that he could pick up that would volunteer. By the time he came down again, he would find half of the others had gone. They did not want to stop. They thought the land was set up on edge and had never been finished, and they had all kinds of notions. Then he would return to the city, and drum up a few more recruits, and take them down; and by the time he got here, he would find that a good many of those he left had also gone. Finally, they became weeded out and left, until he got many folks who, if they had considered it a duty to go on to a barren rock and stay there until they should be instructed to leave, would have done it. It needed just such an element to come to this country. What Brother Snow said here, referring to the sad fact of there being such a number of widows in this place whose husbands had gone to their graves through having worked themselves to death, was perfectly true. But then, we don't want to cry about it. We may as well laugh as cry about the past. You have done a great deal of hard work. In coming down from Pine Valley we found immense dugways in the most forbidding places, and it has required all the perseverance, energy, intelligence, and faith of even those men who were capable of living on a dry rock—it required the combined energy of the whole to accomplish these things, and a good deal of faith too.

BUILDING OF THE ST. GEORGE TEMPLE.—Still President Young urged forward the people. Brother George A. Smith and Brother Erastus Snow urged them forward, and others urged them forward, and there was a general feeling to build up this southern country. Finally it was found that our temple in Salt Lake City would take such a long time to build, it was thought best to erect one down here. Why? Because there was a people living here who were more worthy than any others. Who were more worthy of the blessings of a temple than those who had displayed the self-abnegation exhibited by the pioneers of the south? God inspired President Young to build a temple here because of the fidelity and self-abnegation of the people; and, furthermore, that there might be an asylum here for those living further south to be administered to in the holy ordinances of God. I speak this for your credit—not that all of you are of that class, but let those that are worthy take the credit, and those that are not need not take it. . . .

THE STRATEGY OF MORMON COLONIZATION.—But we will look at this matter again. Could we be in a better place? I think not. Let me show you the reason for that. We are a very small people, and we are in the midst of a very large people. We occupy these valleys among these rugged mountains, and we dwell in deserts, and in many of the most forbidding places. We see people living in little places, on little streams of water trickling along, and perhaps all of it would go through an inch pipe without much pressure, and they are professing to farm and raise fruits, vegetables, and vines in such places, wrenching their living from the barren desert soil. And they do live, but it is hard sledding, and there is a great deal of it here. . . . But wherever there is a habitable place, Latter-day Saints are living on it, and consequently living in these little places they control the mountains and the country. Is not that a fact?

And suppose we did not have these little, forbidding, barren places, the little springs and little rivulets that come along, reminding one of oases in the deserts—if we did not have them we could not have the country. But we have them and God has given us possession of them. If we had not possessed these narrow valleys and defiles, they would have been in the possession of bands of Gadianton robbers, who would have preyed upon the people and their property, as "cowboys" and guerillas are now doing in Arizona. But our possessing them gave strength and protection to our more important settlements.—*JD*, 23:11-18, November 9, 1881.

DEALING WITH JOHNSTON'S ARMY.—I do not remember having read in any history, or had related to me any circumstance, where an army has been subjugated so easily, and their power wasted away so effectually without bloodshed, as this in our borders. If this is not the manifestation of the power of God to us, I do not know what is. Has any man's life been lost in it? No—not one. It is true our brethren have been fired upon; but the balls failed of doing the injury that was expected. Our brethren were told not to retaliate, and they did not do it. Where is there such a manifestation of the power of God?

Suppose you or I had had the dictation of this matter; we should have been firing clear away on the Sweetwater, and killed a lot of them before they got here. It was not we, then, that directed this matter. No. Who was it? Why, it was those who are placed over us; and those very things that seemed hard for us to do at that time have really accomplished one of the greatest things that history has yet developed. The power of God never was made more manifest. . . . But God does not see as man; he reasons not as man. Although we may partially comprehend our individual duties, we do not understand how to regulate the church of God. It needs the regular organization and the Spirit to direct through the proper channels; and hence the result of these events that are manifest now before our eyes.

Would you like the soldiers away? I do not know that I would; I do not care anything about it. Perhaps the Lord may have hung them up there, like the mother hangs up the rod and points to it. . . .

Suppose Uncle Sam should rise up in his red-hot wrath, and send fifty thousand men here . . . who of us can tell the result? I speak of these things that we may reflect. Who can tell what will come next? . . .

What if we should be driven to the mountains? Let us be driven. What if we have to burn our houses? Why, set fire to them with a good grace, and dance a jig round them while they are burning. What do I care about these things? We are in the hands of God, and all is right, Brother Brigham says we are used to it, and we shall not feel it hard.—*JD*, 6:112-114, December 6, 1857.

HORACE GREELEY ON GOVERNING UTAH (1859).—Horace Greeley says it is nonsense for the United States to send any public officers here, and advises the government to appoint President Young governor of the Territory of Utah; for he says he carries the "keys of the territory in his breeches pocket" anyway.—*JD*, 7:320, Salt Lake City, October 7, 1859.

A MISSION OF PEACE AND SALVATION.—I have traveled abroad myself quite extensively among the nations of the earth. Did I ever interfere with them? No, not in the least particular. Did I see things that were wrong? Yes, but it was not for me to right them. That was not my mission. I had no command of the kind. My mission was to preach the gospel of salvation to the nations of the earth, and I have traveled hundreds of thousands of miles to do this, without purse or scrip, trusting in God.—*JD*, 22:142-143, July 3, 1881.

# APPENDIX

## POEMS BY JOHN TAYLOR

### GO, YE MESSENGERS OF HEAVEN

Go, ye messengers of heaven,
Chosen by divine command;
Go and publish free salvation
To a dark, benighted land.

Go to island, vale, and mountain,
To fulfil the great command;
Gather out the sons of Jacob;
To possess the promised land.

When your thousands all are gathered,
And their pray'rs for you ascend,
And the Lord has crown'd with blessings
All the labors on your hand,

Then the song of joy and transport
Will from ev'ry land resound;
Then the heathen, long in darkness,
By the Savior will be crown'd.


### THE GLORIOUS PLAN

The glorious plan which God has given
To bring a ruined world to heaven,
Was framed in Christ ere time had birth.
Was sealed in heaven ere known on earth.

As in the heavens they all agree,
The records given there by Three,
On earth three witnesses are given,
To lead the sons of men to heaven.

Our God, the Father, is the one,
Another, His Eternal Son,
The Spirit does with them agree,
The witnesses in heaven are three.

Nor are we in the second birth
Left without witnesses on earth,
To grope, as in eternal night.
About the way to endless light.

But buried 'neath the liquid wave
To know the Spirit's power to save,
To feel the virtue of His blood,
Are witnesses ordained of God.

In heaven they all agree in One,
The Father, Spirit, and the Son,
On earth these witnesses agree:
The water, blood, and Spirit three.

One great connecting link is given
Between the sons of earth and heaven:
The Spirit seals us here on earth,
In heaven records our second birth.

If we on earth possess these three,
Mysterious, saving unity,
The Book of Life will record bear,
Our names are surely written there.


## THE VALLEY

Let me go to the Valley far off in the west
To my kindred and brethren whom I love best;
Where love and affection our hearts will o'erflow,
To my home in the mountains—oh! there let me go.

Let me go to the Valley, and find me a rest,
And live with the righteous and dwell with the best,
Where contentment and peace, like the rivers do flow;
To the beautiful Valley—oh! there let me go.

Let me go, for my friends and my brethren are there,
With whom I'm united in praise and in prayer,
Who like gold have been tried and are pure as the snow;
To the faithful in Zion—oh! there let me go.

Let me go to my lov'd ones, who've long been oppress'd
Who have fled to the Valley far off in the west,
Where no feuds can assail nor foul mobs overthrow;
To the lovely and virtuous—oh! there let me go.

Let me go to the saints that in Zion do dwell,
Let me roam in the valley and rest in the dell;
Let me share in their joys, or partake in their woe,
To the home of the righteous—oh! there let me go.

Let me go to the Zion, which God hath prepared
As the hope of the saints—as rest and reward,
Where the fountains and rivers in purity flow,
And the earth teems with plenty—oh! there let me go.

Let me go, for the light of eternity's there,
And join with the faithful in praise and in prayer;
Where celestial streams from Jehovah do flow,
To the pure and the just ones—oh! there let me go.

Let me go where the banner of freedom's unfurled
To all creeds and professions throughout the wide world;
Where all tribes, hues, and nations in safety may flow,
And be free from oppression—oh! there let me go.
*Millennial Star* 12:208.

### SONG

O! this is the land of the free!
  And this is the home of the brave,
Where rulers and mobbers agree
  'Tis the home of the tyrant and slave.

Chorus:
  For this is the land of the free!
    And this is the home of the brave,
  Where rulers and mobbers agree,
    'Tis the home of the tyrant and slave.

Here liberty's poles pierce the sky
  With her cup gaily hung on the vane;
The gods may its glories espy,
  But, poor mortals, it's out of your ken.

The eagle soars proudly aloft,
  And covers the land with her wings,
But oppression and bloodshed abound,
  She can't deign to look down on such things.

Here the stars and the stripes proudly float,
  And glitter in every breeze,
But the patriot who reared it's forgot,
  And is robbed of his freedom and peace.

No monarch or autocrat reigns,—
  No kingly dominion is here,
But the modest *vox populi* deigns
  To take what he wants without fear.

Composed by Elder John Taylor, while reflecting on American freedom
and liberty, on his way from England to the camp.
*Millennial Star,* Vol. 9, p. 351.


### O, GIVE ME BACK MY PROPHET DEAR

O, give me back my Prophet dear,
And Patriarch, O give them back,
The saints of Latter-days to cheer,
And lead them in the gospel track!
But, O, they're gone from my embrace,
From earthly scenes their spirits fled,
Two of the best of Adam's race,
Now lie entombed among the dead.

Ye men of wisdom, tell me why—
No guilt, no crime in them were found—
Their blood doth now so loudly cry,
From prison walls and Carthage ground?
Your tongues are mute, but pray attend,
The secret I will now relate,
Why those whom God to earth did lead,
Have met the suffering martyrs' fate.

It is because they strove to gain,
Beyond the grave a heav'n of bliss,
Because they made the gospel plain,
And led the saints to righteousness;
It is because God called them forth,
And led them by his own right hand,
Christ's coming to proclaim on earth,
And gather Israel to their land.

It is because the priests of Baal
Were desperate their craft to save,
And when they saw it doomed to fall,
They sent the prophets to their grave.
Like scenes the ancient prophets saw,
Like these the ancient prophets fell,
And, till the resurrection dawn,
Prophet and Patriarch farewell.

### THE SEER

The Seer, the Seer, Joseph the Seer!
I'll sing of the Prophet ever dear;
His equal now cannot be found,
By searching the wide world around.
With Gods he soared in the realms of day,
And men he taught the heavenly way.
The earthly Seer! the heavenly Seer! .
I love to dwell on his memory dear;
The chosen of God and the friend of man,
He brought the priesthood back again;
He gazed on the past, and the future too,
And opened the heavenly world to view.

Of noble seed, of heavenly birth,
He came to bless the sons of earth;
With keys by the Almighty given,

He opened the full rich stores of heaven;
O'er the world that was wrapped in sable night,
Like the sun, he spread his golden light;
He strove, O, how he strove to stay
The stream of crime in its reckless way!
With a mighty mind and a noble aim,
He urged the wayward to reclaim;
'Mid foaming billows of angry strife
He stood at the helm of the ship of life.


The saints, the saints, his only pride!
For them he lived, for them he died!
Their joys were his, their sorrows too,
He loved the saints, he loved Nauvoo.
Unchanged in death, with a Savior's love,
He pleads their cause in the courts above,
The Seer, the Seer! Joseph the Seer!
O, how I love his memory dear!
The just and wise, the pure and free,
A father he was and is to me.
Let fiends now rage in their dark hour—
No matter, he is beyond their power.


He's free! he's free! the Prophet's free!
He is where he will ever be,
Beyond the reach of mobs and strife,
He rests unharmed in endless life.
His home's in the sky, he dwells with the Gods.
Far from the furious rage of mobs.
He died! he died for those he loved,
He reigns, he reigns in the realms above.
He waits with the just who have gone before,
To welcome the saints to Zion's shore.
Shout, shout, ye saints, this boon is given:
We'll meet our martyred Seer in heaven.


## GO, YE MESSENGERS OF GLORY


Go, ye messengers of glory;
    Run, ye legates of the skies;
Go and tell the pleasing story,
    That a glorious angel flies,
       Great and mighty.
With a message from the skies.


Go to every tribe and nation;
    Visit every land and clime;
Sound to all the proclamation
    Tell to all the truth sublime:
       That the gospel
Does in ancient glory shine.

Go! to all the gospel carry,
  Let the joyful news abound;
Go till every nation hear you,
  Jew and gentile greet the sound;
  Let the gospel,
Echo all the earth around.
Bearing seed of heavenly virtue,
  Scatter it o'er all the earth;
Go! Jehovah will support you,
  Gather all the sheaves of worth,
  Then, with Jesus,
Reign in glory on the earth.


LINES


*Written in the Album of Miss Abby Jane Hart, of New York City*


Abby: Knowest thou whence thou camest? Thine
Origin? Who thou art? What? and whither
Thou art bound? A chrysalis of yesterday:
Today a gaudy fluttering butterfly—
A moth; tomorrow crushed, and then an end
Of thee. Is this so? And must thou perish
Thus, and die ingloriously without a
Hope?

      Ah, no; thou'rt no such thing. Thou in the
Bosom of thy Father bask'd, and liv'd, and
Mov'd thousands of years ago. Yes, e'er this
Mundane sphere from chaos sprung, or sun, or
Moon, or stars, or world was fram'd: before the
Sons of God for joy did shout, or e'er the
Morning stars together sung—thou liv'dst.
      Thou liv'dst to live again. Ah, no! thou liv'd
But to *continue* life eternal—to
Live, and move, and act eternally. Yes;
Long as a spirit, God, or world exists;
From everlasting, eternal, without end.
And whilst thou dwelt in thy paternal home,
And with thy brethren shar'd ecstatic bliss,
All that a spirit could not cloth'd in flesh,
Thou through the vista of unnumbered years
Saw'st through the glimmering veil that thou would'st
Dwell in flesh—just as the Gods.
                                Tread in the
Footsteps of thine elder brother, Jesus—
The "Prince of Peace," for whom a body was
Prepared.
Thou hop'd for this. At length it came; and thou
Appear'd on this terraqueous ball,
Body and spirit; a living soul, forth
From the hands of Elohim—eternal
As himself—part of thy God. A small spark

Of Deity struck from the fire of his
Eternal blaze.
          Thou came! thou came to live! Of life thou art
A living monument; to it thou still


Dost cling eternal life. To thee all else
Are straw and chaff and bubbles, light as air;
And will be all, until thou gain once more
Thy Father's breast; rais'd, quicken'd, immortal;
Body, spirit, all: a God among the
Gods forever bles't.

        Abby: and hast thou dared to launch thy
Fragile barque on truth's tempestuous sea;
To meet the pelting storm, and proudly brave
The dangers of the raging main; and through
The rocks, and shoals, and yawning gulfs, pursue
The *nearest* way to life, in hopes that thou
Would'st speedy gain a seat among the Gods?
A living monument; to it thou still

        Seest thou the multitudes who sail in
Gilded barques, and gently float along the
Silvery stream? Downward they go with sweet
Luxurious ease, and scarce a zephyr moves
The tranquil bosom of the placid stream.
Unconscious of the greatness of the prize
They might obtain, they glide along in peace;
And as they never soar aloft, nor mount
On eagle's wings, nor draw aside the veil
Of other worlds, they know none else than this—
No other joys. They dream away their life,
And die forgot. Just as the butterfly
They gaily flutter on: today they live—
Tomorrow are no more.

                    And though, like thee,
In them is the eternal spark, thousands
Of weary years must roll along e'er they
Regain the prize they might with thee have shar'd.
Regain it? Never! No! They may come where
Thou wert, but never can they with thee share
Ecstatic bliss.

                    For whilst in heaven's progressive
Science skill'd, thou soared'st from world to world, clad
In the robes of bright seraphic light; and
With thy God, eternal—onward gcest, a
Priestess and a queen—reigning and ruling in
The realms of light—unlike the imbeciles
Who dared not brook the scorn of men, and knew not
How to prize eternal life.
        Abby: the cup's within thy reach; drink thou
The vital balm and live.

                    *New York, September 5th, 1846.*
                    *—Millennial Star* 8:178-179.

*Revelation Given Through President John Taylor*
*At Salt Lake City, Utah Territory,*
*October 13, 1882*

Thus saith the Lord to the Twelve, and to the priesthood and people of my Church: Let my servants George Teasdale and Heber J. Grant be appointed to fill the vacancies in the Twelve, that you may be fully organized and prepared for the labors devolving upon you, for you have a great work to perform; and then proceed to fill up the presiding quorum of Seventies, and assist in organizing that body of my priesthood who are your co-laborers in the ministry. You may appoint Seymour B. Young to fill up the vacancy in the presiding quorum of Seventies, if he will conform to my law; for it is not meet that men who will not abide my law shall preside over my priesthood; and then proceed forthwith and call to your aid any assistance that you may require from among the Seventies to assist you in your labors in introducing and maintaining the gospel among the Lamanites throughout the land. And then let High Priests be selected, under the direction of the First Presidency, to preside over the various organizations that shall exist among this people; that those who receive the gospel may be taught in the doctrines of my church and in the ordinances and laws thereof, and also in the things pertaining to my Zion and my kingdom, saith the Lord, that they may be one with you in my Church and my kingdom.

Let the Presidency of my Church be one in all things; and let the Twelve also be one in all things; and let them all be one with me as I am one with the Father.

And let the High Priests organize themselves, and purify themselves, and prepare themselves for this labor, and for all other labors that they may be called upon to fulfill.

And let the Presidents of Stakes also purify themselves, and the priesthood and people of the Stakes over which they preside, and organize the priesthood in their various Stakes according to my law, in all the various departments thereof, in the High Councils, in the Elders' quorums, and in the Bishops and their councils, and in the quorums of Priests, Teachers and Deacons, that every quorum may be fully organized according to the order of my Church; and, then, let them inquire into the standing and fellowship of all that hold my holy priesthood in their several Stakes; and if they find those that are unworthy let them remove them, except they repent; for my priesthood, whom I have called and whom I have sustained and honored, shall honor me and obey my laws, and the laws of my holy priesthood, or they shall not be considered worthy to hold my priesthood, saith the Lord. And let my priesthood humble themselves before me, and seek not their own will but my will; for if my priesthood, whom I have chosen, and called, and endowed with the spirit and gifts of their several callings, and with the powers thereof, do not acknowledge me I will not acknowledge them, saith the Lord; for I will be honored and obeyed by my priesthood.

And, then, I call upon my priesthood, and upon all of my people, to repent of all their sins and short-comings, of their covetousness and pride and self-will, and of all their iniquities wherein they sin against me; and to seek with all humility to fulfill my law, as my priesthood, my saints and my people; and I call upon the heads of families to put their houses in order according to the law of God, and attend to the various duties and responsibilities associated therewith, and to purify themselves before me, and to purge out iniquity from their households. And I will bless and be with you, saith the Lord, and ye shall gather together in your holy places wherein ye assemble to call upon me, and ye shall ask for such things as are right, and I will hear your prayers, and my Spirit and power shall be with you, and my blessing shall rest upon you, upon your families, your dwellings and your households, upon your flocks and herds and fields, your orchards and vineyards, and upon all that pertains to you; and you shall be my people and I will be your God; and your enemies shall not have dominion over you, for I will preserve you and confound them, saith the Lord, and they shall not have power nor dominion over you; for my word shall go forth, and my work shall be accomplished, and my Zion shall be established, and my rule and my power and my dominion shall prevail among my people, and all nations shall yet acknowledge me. Even so, Amen. (B. H. Roberts, *The Life of John Taylor*, pp. 349-351).

# INDEX

*John Taylor*

AS PRESIDENT OF THE CHURCH